LEAVE NO MAN BEHIND

LEAVE NO MAN BEHIND

Liberation and Capture Missions

David C. Isby

WEIDENFELD & NICOLSON

In remembrance of six truly special American warriors,
US Army Airborne and Special Forces:

Larry Dring, USA, 1988

Lance Motley, Burma, 1989

Louis Dupree, USA, 1989

Al Mar, USA, 1992

Robert C. MacKenzie, Sierra Leone, 1995

Alexander M. S. McColl, USA, 2002

'Let me not mourn for the men who have died fighting,
but rather let me be glad that such heroes have lived.'

GEN George S. Patton, 7 June 1945

Weidenfeld & Nicolson

The Orion Publishing Group Ltd
Orion House, 5 Upper Saint Martin's Lane, London WC2H 9EA

ISBN 0-297-84674-4

Designed by Gwyn Lewis
Cartography by Peter Harper

Printed and bound in the USA

TABLE OF CONTENTS

LIST OF MAPS

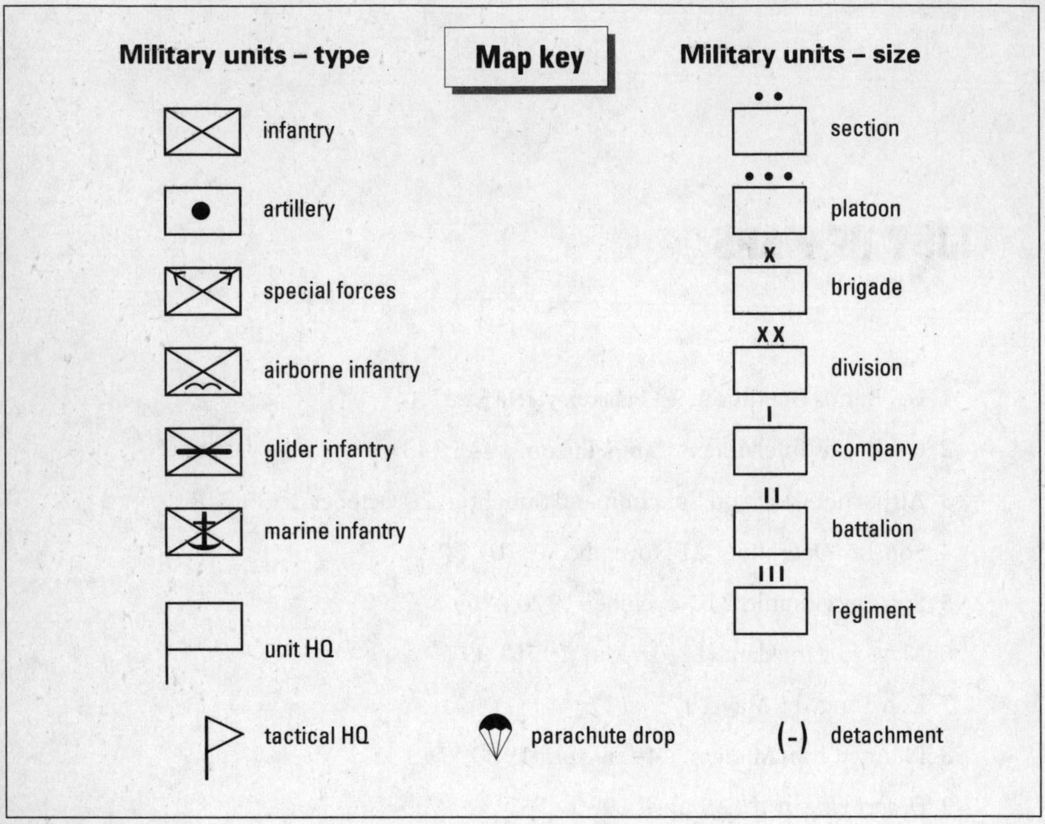

Map key

Military units – type

- infantry
- artillery
- special forces
- airborne infantry
- glider infantry
- marine infantry
- unit HQ
- tactical HQ

Military units – size

- section
- platoon
- brigade
- division
- company
- battalion
- regiment

parachute drop

(-) detachment

ACKNOWLEDGEMENTS

I would like to thank Ian Drury, noted *pistolero* and my editor, for his hands-on support throughout this project. Many thanks also to Caroline Cambridge for her help with editing, to the copy editor, Lisa Rogers, and to Anne Marie Shackleton for reviewing the proofs.

Research was helped by: Timothy Nenninger and Ken Schlesinger at the National Archives, College Park, Maryland; Conrad Crane and Richard Baker at the US Army Military History Institute, Carlisle Barracks, Pennsylvania; Jim Ginther at the Marine Corps archives at the Grey Research Center, Quantico, Virginia; Sue Bechtel at the National Security Archives at George Washington University, Washington DC.

I would also like to apologize to those who actually participated in each of the actions studied in the following pages. Each chapter represents an action on which entire books have been written. There was so much more of each story that could have been told that simply would not fit into a single volume. My objective has been to look at the history, development and changing role of special operations from 1945 to the present, and this has meant that much of value simply could not be included. The bravery of the fighting forces involved in each action could indeed fill a book by itself.

CHAPTER 1 INTRODUCTION

And this I write that young men may learn, if they should meet with such trials as we met with there . . . to preserve themselves from danger, for policy is needful in wars as well as strength.

Lion Gardiner, from the conclusion of *The Pequot War* (1660), the first work of American military history and analysis.

There have been decisive battles that have saved countries. A few – Marathon, Tours, the Battle of Britain – may have saved civilizations. The battles described in the following chapters were of a much smaller and more immediate scope: they were concerned with individuals or small groups of people, with either setting them free or taking them prisoner.[1]

Historically, when the US armed forces have set people free or taken them prisoner, it has usually been in the context of larger, decisive operations carried out with the aid of allies or coalition partners. Images of these large-scale liberations – and indeed of crowds of prisoners being led away – are familiar from film footage of Europe in 1944–5, and were reprised in television images of Afghanistan in 2001–2 and Baghdad in 2003. This book, however, deals with US special operations forces carrying out liberation or seizure missions either independently of other forces or as part of a larger operation, rather than during the overall tide of victory.[2]

The liberation missions included freeing US prisoners or internees in wartime (Los Banos, Korea, Son Tay, Nasiriya) and US civilian hostages being held in conditions short of all-out war (the *Mayaguez* incident, Iran, two prisons in Panama). Liberation missions have also had the objective of preventing the capture or execution of those perceived to be in danger of being taken hostage or killed by hostile political leaders (Grenada, Panama). On Grenada, the objective of one of several special operations missions was to ensure the safety of the chief of state of that island country, who was thought to be in danger.[3] The seizure missions aimed to put into US custody *de facto* or would-be heads of state or officials from North Korea, Grenada, Panama, Somalia, Afghanistan, Iraq and the international Al Qaida terrorist network.

The significance of these missions has often exceeded that of more decisive – certainly larger – operations. In the Second World War, Korea and Vietnam, consciousness of the inhumane treatment of US PoWs provided an impetus for liberation missions. The national humiliation and political cost of having US citizens held hostage – exemplified in Iran – also helped to motivate the *Mayaguez*, Grenada and Panama operations. The rescue of a single US Army PoW during a liberation raid in Iraq in 2003 made her a national figure and overshadowed the more substantive war news for days, providing a much-needed boost to US morale.[4] The political significance of such operations dictates that each must be considered in terms both of the larger overall situation that led to it taking place, and of the changed situation that resulted from it.

Such political significance also applies to seizure missions. The capture of heads of state was seen as a political necessity in situations where the US applied its power to invade and change the government in small countries. In the US military actions in Grenada, Panama and Afghanistan, the enemy was not the population or even the government, but rather the individuals who had hijacked the state. Noriega, Aideed, bin Laden and Saddam Hussein have all attracted the attention – and deep enmity – of American presidents. They were seen as being 'the centre of gravity' of US opponents. These individuals acquired the political significance of a capital city in a more conventional conflict.

Prisoners, hostages and heads of state share a number of characteristics. They are normally not to be found near the front lines, but rather deep inside enemy territory. They are all soft targets, vulnerable to being killed by the enemy or misapplied US fire power. They are more valuable alive than dead. Success in liberation and capture missions cannot be assured – and will usually be prevented by the massive application of enemy fire power. Nor can any of these types of mission be accomplished from a distance. Carrier task forces and bombers – though they may form an integral part of these missions – cannot actually carry them out.

Liberation and seizure missions both require the presence of troops on the ground. The forces described in the following examples were deployed to liberate or capture either as part of a larger action or as specific special missions (though in several cases there were larger operations in progress at the same time as these special missions were carried out). Most of these raids required action independent of contact with other friendly forces, although assistance from such forces, in the form of diversions, support and logistics, was vital. In some cases, the independence of the action by the SOF – the SEALs at Government House on Grenada, TF Ranger in Mogadishu – was greater than intended because back-up forces failed to appear. Sometimes, as in Grenada and Panama, the liberation and seizure operations can only be disaggregated from those of larger forces in retrospect, in ways that would not have made sense to those who had to plan or execute them at the time.

Liberation and seizure missions fall into the second definition of 'raid' outlined in the US Army's capstone manual FM100-5 *Operations* as 'a limited objective attack into enemy territory for a specific purpose other than gaining or holding ground'. These missions are for the purpose of freeing people who need to be freed or capturing people who are a danger walking around loose.

Raids are usually small in size (to preserve the element of surprise and to ensure a speed of manoeuvre that would be less achievable with a larger force), limited in duration and are not intended to gain or hold terrain, but rather to end in a planned withdrawal or via relief by other forces. Swift movement (especially rapid penetration to the target) and, above all, the element of surprise are intended to keep the 'objective' alive and to compensate for the lack of weight of numbers and fire power that could both ruin surprise and result in the death of the objectives. While surprise is considered critical, if it is lacking, it can be compensated for by using speed, shock, fire power or superior fighting capability. The key is for the raiders to retain a 'relative advantage' great enough to accomplish their mission and to keep alive the people to be liberated or seized.[5]

For the purpose of targeting raids, air strikes or other military operations, the US military teaches the acronym CARVER: criticality, accessibility, recouperability, vulnerability, effect on population and recognizability are the rough-cut criteria by which targets are compared. In liberation or seizure missions, these criteria tend to be extreme. Criticality is invariably high: the objectives of liberation missions are those, usually Americans, being held against their will or in imminent danger of being so; the objectives of seizure missions are key enemy personnel, usually leaders. Accessibility is usually low in both scenarios – neither hostages nor enemy leaders are likely to be found near the front lines. This makes penetration – and egress – critical. Recouperability is likely to be low – once prisoners or hostages are liberated or enemy leaders are US prisoners, the situation is unlikely to be changed. Vulnerability of the objectives – people – is high. The use of fire power has to be moderated to avoid killing those to be liberated or seized. Effect on population is potentially high – such actions can bring down governments or end resistance. Recognizability is usually low – prisoners or hostages can be held just about anywhere, and the objectives of seizure missions will do everything possible to reduce their recognizability. The CARVER process of tactical mission analysis provides some indicators as to why, historically, these actions have proven both critical to attempt and difficult to execute.

Most raids are tactical, ordered by divisional or unit commanders to strike objectives on or near the battlefield, often within range of artillery and supporting forces. Some – such as Los Banos in 1945 or Nasiriya in 2003 – are operational, ordered by the theatre commander and employing a range of in-theatre forces to achieve objectives as part of a larger operation. Other examples included here are effectively strategic operations because they were aimed directly at the enemy's centre of gravity (such as capturing General Aideed in Somalia or strongman Manuel Noriega in Panama) or the root cause of the international dispute (the US hostages in Iran). The order to carry out these actions usually came from the US national command authorities. In some of these instances – Son Tay, the *Mayaguez*, Iran – the diplomatic and political impact of the raids turned out to be more significant than the liberation of Americans that was their original motivation. Nor were those executing some of the raids ignorant of the importance of such impact – reporters or camera teams were present in Korea, Afghanistan and Nasiriya. Improving morale was an objective in a number of these raids.

The larger context of these missions – the forces available to carry them out, the political leadership that must order the raids and accept their consequences – remains uniquely American. There have been many similar missions carried out by foreign special operations forces. The gold standard remains the successful Israeli raid on Entebbe airport on 1 July 1976 to recover passengers from a hijacked airliner. The British SAS has demonstrated its expertise in saving hostages' lives at Mogadishu airport in 1977 (along with Germany's GSG-9), at the Iranian embassy in London in 1980 and in Sierra Leone in 2000. The tactics, planning and execution demonstrated in these actions remain of great value to special operations forces worldwide, including those of the US. However, future US liberation and capture missions and those involved in planning and executing them will be best guided by the analysis of prior US examples. The political significance of such missions in the US is likely to be greater than in some countries that have a similar capability.

Success in liberation and seizure missions has always required careful and meticulous planning, and planning in particular often determines the success or failure of these operations. Because there may be little ability to change tactics or improvise while an operation is in progress, planning is even more important in liberation and seizure situations than in conventional military operations. Effective planning, however, requires intelligence to guide it, and intelligence has often been lacking. The complexity of such operations puts a premium on training and rehearsal, especially in operations involving many different elements or participants. Yet the time required for such detailed preparation has the potential to undercut the overall effectiveness of the mission.

The story of liberation and seizure operations is, in many ways, a story about intelligence. When intelligence has been lacking, US forces have been sent in blind to locate prisoners or enemy leaders in the teeth of enemy fire power, as happened to the 3-187th Airborne Infantry in Korea in 1950 and the 2-9th Marines on Koh Tang in 1975. Some of the successes – Los Banos in 1945, the liberation of American civilian prisoners in Panama in 1989, the liberation of PFC Lynch in Iraq in 2003 – reflected effective use of intelligence, especially human intelligence (HUMINT). Without such intelligence, the extensive training and rehearsals associated with operations such as the Son Tay raid and Operation Acid Gambit in Panama would not have been possible.

The complex nature of liberation or seizure operations and their reliance on speed and surprise for success usually requires that they are carried out by specially trained and equipped units: true special operations forces. However, such operations have also been carried out – in some cases with great success – by units that do not have the 'special' designator but which are well trained in what they are doing. 'Line' infantry, airborne or Marine units have found themselves carrying out liberation or capture missions with little training or rehearsal in some of these situations (such as Los Banos, Korea, the *Mayaguez* and, most recently, in Iraq in 2003). In almost all cases, these special forces, dedicated or otherwise, have been co-ordinated with other military resources necessary for supplying supporting tasks for the particular operation.

Due to the need for speed and surprise or the distance to the objective, these forces normally arrive by air – by parachute or by helicopter. In a few situations, they have come in an amphibious assault. But since 1945, liberation and capture missions have largely been air–ground operations, requiring effective planning and co-ordination. Command, control and communications are essential for tying the different elements together and linking them, in turn, to higher direction.

No liberation or capture operation can hope to prevail by weight of numbers or through superior fire power without risking killing their objective. Intelligence, therefore, is critical. Because the objectives in these raids are people rather than a static physical location, knowing exactly where they are is usually the single most critical element in determining success or failure. Knowing where the enemy is allows a US force to plan around them, to attempt to avoid pitched battles or to integrate the liberation or capture missions with the operations of larger forces.

In addition to these liberation and capture missions, similar operations have been carried out for other purposes by US forces over the years since 1945. Combat search and rescue (CSAR) is also about rescuing people – normally shot-down aircrew. CSAR takes place on the battlefield, in contested waters or, more often, in the heart of enemy territory. CSAR is also often an air–ground operation, relying post-1945 on helicopters. There have been many important CSAR operations, although none have shared the strategic goals of some of the liberation and capture operations. In recent years, the US Marine Corps has had success with their version of

CSAR – designated tactical recovery of aircraft and personnel (TRAP), with their big CH-53 helicopters allowing the downed aircraft as well as the aircrew to be lifted out of danger in some situations.

Noncombatant evacuation operations (NEOs) are, by definition, normally missions to save people from situations where it would be unhealthy for them to remain. In recent years, there has usually been at least one failed or failing state or boiling civil war annually that has required an NEO. Fortunately, they have mostly been carried out without the need for fighting, but US armed forces have been on hand to deny anyone interested in causing trouble the opportunity of profiting by it.

Since 1997, the US has defined liberation missions, CSAR/TRAP and NEO, as part of the joint 'personnel recovery' (PR) mission. In an increasingly turbulent world, it is likely that US troops will be called on to carry out these missions in a wide range of conditions and situations. The ability of future forces, institutions and organizations to apply the lessons of the past will help to determine their success or failure. Thus, it is critical to identify the elements of previous liberation and capture missions that can provide guidance for future decision makers, planners and special forces who may have to consider or carry out such missions. This is the justification for the exercise of going over the decisions made in past missions by political leaders, planners or raiders who had limited or inaccurate information and little time to think over the range of options available to them. It is only through an examination of these past decisions that those in the future – when the intelligence is likely to be just as incomplete or misleading and the need for action just as urgent – will be able to benefit from the dear-bought wisdom of previous liberation and seizure missions.

In addition to the missions themselves, the forces that have carried them out over the years have also evolved. This is the story of forces as well as missions. As mentioned earlier, the forces that have carried out liberation and seizure missions were not always officially defined as 'special operations forces', but the results of the missions have had to meet the same highly exacting requirements. The outcomes of these missions have necessarily had an effect on the forces carrying them out. The failure of the Iran Raid in 1980 was seminal, compounded by problems encountered on Grenada in 1983. Responses to these problems were reflected in changes in how US SOF were organized and used later in the 1980s.

The missions were challenging even for the most capable forces. Over the whole period of 1945–2003, the number of US PoWs liberated and the number of high-ranking enemy leaders seized were low. The risks of such operations remain high despite increased investment in this mission area. Yet the capability to order US SOF to carry out liberation or seizure missions is likely to be one that US leaders – both the national command authority in Washington and the combatant commanders/CINCs fighting a theatre conflict – will want in the future.

CHAPTER 2 LOS BANOS,
THE PHILIPPINES · 23 February 1945

*A rescue operation involved considerable risk. But
intelligence reports indicated that the plight of the
internees was desperate and that the risk was justified.
The whole operation was a complete success because of
the careful planning and brilliant execution. It reflected
great credit upon all concerned.*

    GEN Walter A. Krueger, *From Down Under to Nippon.*

Hell was in session at Los Banos camp, on the largest Philippine island of
Luzon, on the morning of 23 February 1945. The Japanese were withholding rations from their 2,100 US and Allied civilian internees and a few prisoners of war, and conditions were rapidly deteriorating beyond even the
pain that had prevailed in the camp for almost three years, since the surrender in 1942 of US forces and their Filipino allies to the invading Japanese.
Internees were dying of starvation. Particularly devoted to his vocation of
creating hell on earth was Warrant Officer Sadaaki Konishi, the sadistic
deputy camp commandant who ran the camp largely to the exclusion of his
aged boss, Major T. Iwanaka. Konishi was reportedly looking to bring his
current assignment to a spectacular close by slaughtering every last one of
his prisoners any day now.

    But on that day, the sun would not go down on that situation in Los
Banos camp, for by its close a surprise US raid had defeated the Japanese
garrison and set the prisoners free. One of the most successful raids carried
out by the US Army in the Second World War, the events of 23 February
1945 were to have effects that lasted long after the thrill of liberation passed.

ADVANCE TO LIBERATION

On 9 January 1945, the US Army returned to Luzon. The liberation of the Philippines was entering its decisive phase. It soon became clear that the fighting on Luzon was different from anything the US had experienced in the long advance across the Pacific. While the terrain was still often difficult and mountainous, the size of Luzon meant that multiple US armies could advance side by side. The US also had to take Manila, a large, densely populated city fanatically defended by the Japanese.

The population of Luzon, especially around Manila, was subject to increasing Japanese repression and brutality, and consequently the Filipinos were, by and large, pro-Allied. While the Philippines was a US possession at the time of the Japanese invasion in 1941, it had been scheduled for independence. This factor, coupled with the brutality of the Japanese occupation, had led to the emergence of a Filipino resistance movement throughout the country. While often politically divided, the Filipino resistance was able to carry out effective guerrilla operations in much of Luzon.

The US forces arriving on Luzon were an army of liberation, and part of their mission was to liberate prisoners of war and civilian internees. On 28 January, as US forces advanced on the town of Cabanatuan, a reinforced company of the US Army's 6th Ranger Battalion liberated some 500 US prisoners being held at a camp east of town. Reaching Manila on 3 February, the 8th Cavalry Regiment of the 1st Cavalry Division freed 3,500 civilian internees being held in a camp at Santo Tomas University. A further 275 prisoners were held hostage by the Japanese commandant and his guards until they were granted safe passage from the camp. The next day, the 8th Cavalry freed over 1,200 military and civilian prisoners from Old Bilibad prison. As was usually the case in 1944–5, the advance of US forces brought liberation.

LOS BANOS PREPARATIONS

The weakened condition of the liberated prisoners suggested that others still being held elsewhere in the Philippines might not be able to survive until the advancing US Army, now concentrating to liberate Manila, finally liberated their camps. At the same time, information was arriving detailing Japanese atrocities: 140 prisoners had been massacred on the island of Palawan in December. If any more prisoners were to be liberated, the action would have to be swift. On 4 February, therefore, the US commander-in-chief GEN Douglas

MacArthur, at the South West Pacific Area General Headquarters (SWPA/ GHQ), gave the order to the 11th Airborne Division for a raid to liberate the camp at Los Banos.[1]

The 11th Airborne Division was not considered a special operations force by the dictionary definition, but it was highly capable and, perhaps more importantly, was under the command of generals who knew how to use it. MacArthur and his subordinate 6th Army Commander, GEN Walter Krueger, had both used SOF effectively in New Guinea and the Philippines, as demonstrated by the actions of units such as the 6th Ranger Battalion and the Alamo Scouts. MacArthur appears to have assigned the mission to the 11th Airborne because many of these assets were already committed to missions in and around the Manila area. The 11th was on the scene and, most importantly, MacArthur had confidence that the unit and its commanding general would be able to carry out the mission without top-down micro-management by his headquarters.

On 4 February, the 11th Airborne was south of Manila, driving towards the city from the beachhead at Nasugu where most of the division had landed in an amphibious operation the week before. Japanese resistance had been expected along the heights of Tagaytay Ridge, but when the 511th Parachute Infantry Regiment jumped in on 3–4 February, this position was found to be abandoned, its enemy defenders pulled back to Manila. The airdrop itself had not gone well, with transport aircraft and paratroopers alike getting lost in the air and on the ground. However, the 4 February operation did produce fresh intelligence about Los Banos, provided by a Filipino guerrilla leader who contacted the 511th. He had with him an American civilian escapee from Los Banos.

Los Banos was on the large inland lake of Laguna de Bay, some 32 km behind Japanese lines from the 11th Airborne's forward positions. While an advance engaging Japanese resistance through rough terrain could be slow and costly, US control of the air and the potential for use of the lake for movement made a raid possible.

ACTIONABLE INTELLIGENCE: EYES ON LOS BANOS

Co-ordination between the Filipino guerrillas and the 11th Airborne staff was routed through MAJ Jay Vanderpool, MacArthur's GHQ representative located with the guerrillas in Batangas Province. Three intelligence officers were parachuted into the Los Banos area to link up with Filipino guerrillas. Others were infiltrated through the Japanese lines. Army Air Force photo reconnaissance of the area provided images of the Los Banos camp. This was supplemented by further vital HUMINT provided by two additional escapees from Los Banos.

The Filipino guerrillas in the Los Banos area were among the strongest and best organized of the groups in southern Luzon. Designated the 45th Hunters–ROTC Regiment (many of its leaders had, pre-war, been ROTC members at Los Banos Agricultural College), its members would provide eyes-on surveillance of the camp, the routes leading to it and the planned US advance routes. LTC Gustavo Ingles was the guerrilla leader most responsible for the Los Banos liberation mission. Members of the Hunters guerrilla staff infiltrated through Japanese lines to work with the 11th Airborne's staff at their CP in planning the raid. Complicating factors were that in addition to the Hunters, there were competing Communist and Chinese guerrilla organizations active in the Los Banos area. These would also have to be brought into the plan.

The guerrillas also had the advantage of fresh HUMINT not only from their own patrols and observation posts, but also via reports from the many Filipinos employed by the Japanese. These reports provided valuable inside information about the camp and its garrison, including the news that the Japanese were preparing to massacre the prisoners, and that this plan would be accelerated if it appeared that liberation was imminent. The guerrillas had been planning their own raid to liberate the Los Banos prisoners when they were brought into the 11th Airborne's operation via the insertion of the intelligence officers. Signal Corps personnel from the 11th Airborne, inserted by canoe among the guerrillas, transmitted the guerrillas' intelligence back to divisional headquarters.

The eyes-on HUMINT provided critical information on the location of Japanese personnel and their routine: for example, all except sentries would be doing callisthenics at 0700 and would be vulnerable to a surprise attack. Included in the information reaching the 11th Airborne was the strength of the camp's garrison and its ability to be reinforced. In addition to eighty guards at the camp itself, there was an infantry company with four machine guns and two 105 mm guns at a gravel quarry 3 km west of the camp. Another company was split between Mayondon Point and the San Juan

River crossing, with two 75 mm guns and two three-inch coast-defence guns. These were members of the Fuji Heidan, a group made up of garrison troops and remnants of destroyed units. Their Los Banos sector unit was estimated at 400 men. Overall Japanese strength in Los Banos Province was about 6,000 men.

The Japanese 8th Infantry Division was also in the area, with its main positions in the hills along Highway 1 from Santo Tomas through Alaminos to San Pablo, about 11 km south of Los Banos. Its commander, MG Masatoshi Fujishige, also commanded the Fuji Heidan. Some 9–10,000 strong, this pre-war infantry division was assessed a significant threat that would require a major operation to defeat. A truck-mobile battalion from the area around Alaminos – identified as the divisional reserve – could reinforce the Los Banos town area itself in about ninety minutes. Against the guerrillas, the Japanese had also deployed detachments of the Makapili, the Filipino collaborationist militia feared for their brutality.

PLANNING THE RAID

The 11th Airborne's commanding general, MG Joseph Swing, received this fresh HUMINT at the same time as MacArthur's order to free the prisoners arrived at headquarters, east of Swing's division's position on Tagaytay Ridge. Both division and commander were well suited to carry out Mac-Arthur's order: Swing was a highly effective combat commander; the 11th Airborne was already proving to be highly capable of both airborne and conventional operations. Frontline troops and division staff alike had been honed by months of fighting in the Philippines.

The 11th Airborne Division's headquarters staff began planning for the raid immediately, under the direction of the division's assistant chief of staff for operations (G-3), COL Douglass Quandt, assisted by the assistant chief of staff for intelligence (G-2), LTC Frank 'Butch' Mueller. However, Swing had to report back to MacArthur that he was not ready to carry out his orders immediately. The division was engaged in heavy fighting near Manila, some 80 km from the objective, with five blown bridges separating them from their new target. This gained time for 11th Airborne Division staff to plan the operation.

The divisional staff prepared a detailed plan for the raid. It would begin with the infiltration of a small team to act as pathfinders, who would observe the camp and prepare to kill the camp sentries before they could massacre the prisoners in the event of liberation. One airborne company would make a direct parachute assault on the prison camp, linking up with guerrillas and 11th Airborne reconnaissance troopers, liberating the prisoners and neutralizing the garrison, also with the aim of preventing a massacre. The main force of the raiders – a parachute infantry battalion (minus the parachuting company and without most of its combat-support assets) – would arrive in amphibious tractors (amtracs) in an over-the-beach assault timed to arrive simultaneously with the airdrop. The prisoners would then be withdrawn in the amtracs to a secure area and the raiders would withdraw overland, linking up with the diversionary force launched to draw away Japanese reinforcements. This would also provide a cross-country withdrawal route for the liberated prisoners in case anything went wrong with the amphibious operation.

Complicating the plans was the information, provided by the escaped internees, that of the reported 2,300 prisoners, some 600 would be unable to walk to the beach and that many were likely to bring along baggage and belongings in any evacuation.

MG Swing approved the plan and put COL Robert Soule in overall command of the Los Banos Force. On 17 February, they received the preparatory order setting D-Day for 23 February.

MOVING UP TO THE LINE OF DEPARTURE

The different elements of the Los Banos Force started to move to their jumping-off positions on 18 February. 1LT George Skau's pathfinder platoon from the 11th Airborne Reconnaissance Company prepared to infiltrate across Laguna de Bay. Placed under the command of the 11th Airborne Division for this operation, LTC Joseph Gibbs' 672nd Amphibious Tractor Battalion's 59 LVT-4A amtracs had to make an arduous 16 km road journey over difficult terrain before they all finally made it to a concealed assembly area near Muntilupa. There they married up with the 11th Airborne units that would make up the amphibious-assault component of the raid: MAJ Henry Burgess' 1st Battalion of the 511th (1-511th) Parachute Infantry (minus the one company to be dropped in the assault), plus Company C of the 127th Airborne Engineer Battalion and two 75 mm pack howitzers from Battery D, 457th Parachute Field Artillery. On 22

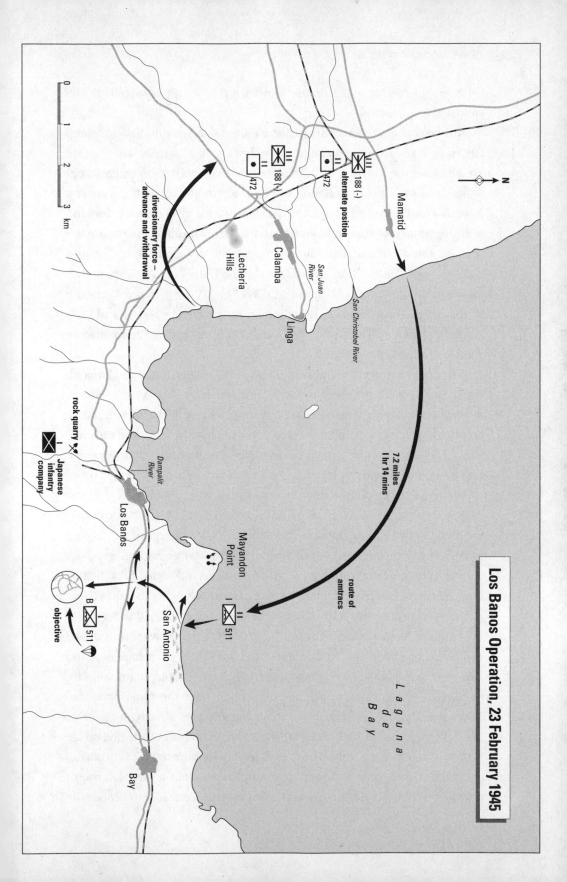

Los Banos Operation, 23 February 1945

0
1
2
3
km

N

diversionary force –
advance and withdrawal

472

188 (-)

472

188 (-)
alternate position

Mamatid

Lecheria
Hills

Calamba

San Juan
River

Linga

San Christobel River

7.2 miles
1 hr 14 mins

route of
amtracs

rock quarry

Japanese
infantry
company

Dampalit
River

Los Banos

Mayandon
Point

San Antonio

B
511
objective

*Laguna
de
Bay*

Bay

February, the force moved to the jumping-off point at Mamatid on the shores of Laguna de Bay.

The ground diversionary attack force moved south simultaneously along Highway 1 towards the Japanese front lines near Calamba. They would attack across the San Juan River to block any Japanese reinforcements from Santo Tomas reaching Los Banos and be ready to link up with the raiding force as it fell back after the operation. COL Soule, while in overall command of the operation, positioned himself with this force and did not try to run the fighting at Los Banos. This diversionary force consisted of LTC Ernest LaFlamme's 1-188th Glider Infantry and the 637th Glider Artillery Battalion from the 11th Airborne Division reinforced by XIV Corps troops: Company B, the 637th Tank Destroyer Battalion and supported by the 472nd Field Artillery Battalion. The rest of the 11th Airborne was still committed to combat in the Manila area.

XIV Corps sent trucks, ambulances and medical personnel to Mamatid, where the liberated prisoners would be brought before being evacuated to medical facilities or a transit camp. There was a great deal of concern over security, and journalists and war correspondents were banned from the area. While US air superiority limited Japanese air reconnaissance, the Japanese had many other means of detecting the raid as its components formed up.

The 1-511th Parachute Infantry was tasked with the mission because, with 412 men out of a TO&E of 650, it was the strongest parachute battalion in the 11th Airborne Division. Its commander, MAJ Burgess, was trusted by MG Swing to carry out an independent mission; he had an excellent combat command and training record and had demonstrated his initiative on an earlier occasion by stealing the refrigerator belonging to one of MacArthur's more pompous staff officers and presenting it as a gift to Swing.

1LT John Ringler, commander of Company B, 1-511th, was only notified about the operation on 20 February and told that his company – the strongest in the battalion, with ninety-three men – would be jumping in, reinforced with an extra machine-gun section from the same battalion. There was no time for rehearsal – his company was already engaged in heavy fighting east of Nichols Field. They were pulled out of the line on 21 February and moved to the airfield, and drew parachutes on 22 February.

Ringler carried out the detailed planning for the airdrop. 'My plan was to drop at low altitude and as close as possible outside the camp to surprise the

Japanese garrison and to avoid a concentration of enemy ground fire. The three rifle platoons would assemble around their own leaders and move directly to their objective areas to engage the enemy.'[2] Ringler ordered 2LT Roger Miller and two enlisted men from the company to make a reconnaissance of the DZ along with the division reconnaissance platoon, in time to return to the company to provide fresh reconnaissance and then jump in with them.

Nine C-47s were required for the airdrop. C-47s were a scarce and valuable commodity on Luzon, needed for missions ranging from casualty evacuation to resupply. Notified of the mission on 20 February, nine C-47 troop-carrier aircraft were ready the next day. This included pressing a specialized search and rescue aircraft into service to carry paratroops. The raid was made a major priority for fighter sorties, charged with both hitting pre-planned targets in the camp area and providing a combat air patrol that would block enemy air or ground reaction.

The C-47 pilots met with 11th Airborne planners at Nichols Field on 21 February. All had the recent experience of the Tagaytay Ridge drop to work out procedures. The planning went well. CPT Herbert Parker of the 65th Troop Carrier Squadron, 433rd Troop Carrier Group, was to fly as co-pilot to the troop carriers' commander, MAJ Don Anderson: 'Don was quite concerned that as the 65th approached the drop zone at low altitude with paratroopers we might be sitting ducks for an enemy machine gun that might be located on a hill over which we would have to fly. We were subsequently assured that 11th Airborne personnel had recently reconnoitred that particular hill and that no enemy forces were present.'[3] Anderson asked for and received permission to do a one-pass reconnaissance mission over Los Banos so he could personally look at conditions and the potential DZ. It was the afternoon of 22 February before the C-47s and the paratroopers were finally concentrated at Nichols Field.

Working in close co-operation with the guerrillas raised operational security (OPSEC) concerns. While the guerrillas had unmatched intelligence sources, it was also known that their ranks had been infiltrated by pro-Japanese collaborators and that Filipino politics could outweigh military requirements in their decision-making. Despite this, Swing and the divisional staff realized that there could be no raid without the guerrillas; they would be fully integrated in the plan despite the OPSEC concerns.

RECON MOVES OUT

Skau's reconnaissance platoon, reinforced by Miller and his team, set sail from Muntilupa on 21 February, paddled across Laguna de Bay by Filipino guerrillas in three native *banca* fishing boats to a rendezvous point east of Los Banos. There, linking up with some 300 Filipinos, the platoon was split into three teams: drop zone marking and security, amphibious landing area marking and security, and camp surveillance. While the platoon took up concealed positions – the arrival of twelve of the twenty-four men was delayed for several hours aboard a slow-moving *banca* – Skau met with the guerrilla leadership and two escaped internees. Together, they planned for an initial ground assault, timed for the instant of the first parachute drop, which would prevent any Japanese massacre of the internees.

SGT Terry Santos was part of the reconnaissance platoon. 'Were it not for the Filipino guides, with their intrinsic knowledge of the terrain, the Recon Platoon would never have found their objectives: the drop zone and the beach landing zone.'[4]

During the night, the guerrillas and the reconnaissance platoon, including SGT Martin Squires, moved into position. 'We stopped a couple of times to listen in silence while a Japanese patrol passed. Why they made so much noise, I'll never know, but it certainly worked in our favour. Our orders were not to return fire if fired upon. We could not alert them to the fact that troops were in the area.'[5] Some 326 Filipino guerrillas moved into position on all sides of the camp.

Near midnight on 22 February, a final night reconnaissance mission by a USAAF P-61 night fighter brought back an alarming report: large numbers of Japanese vehicles had been seen moving in the Los Banos area. The information was quickly reported to Swing. While concerned that this might indicate that Japanese intelligence had compromised the operation, he decided that the information did not justify calling off the raid. However, Swing quickly acted to provide reinforcements to the diversionary force so that they could fight their way through to support the raiders, if required. The 2-511th Parachute Infantry was alerted to serve as a reserve to the diversionary force. Swing moved an advance divisional command post to Calamba, co-located with Soule's CP to co-ordinate the ground battle if necessary. He decided to go there in person during the operation, abandoning his personal plan to jump on the camp with the raiders.

It was later determined that Japanese listening posts had heard the movement of the amphibious tractors and thought they were tanks. The Japanese moved in reinforcements from elsewhere in Los Banos Province to guard against an armour-supported thrust up the shores of Laguna de Bay.

THE AIRDROP

On D-Day, 23 February, the amphibious raiders were the first to move, the amtracs plunging into Laguna de Bay at Mamatid at 0515 to arrive at Los Banos precisely at H-Hour: 0700. The fifty-eight amtracs (one had broken down; fifty-four would make the first assault) had to sail an 11.5 km course in total darkness, relying on compass and dead reckoning, with an initial dogleg to avoid Japanese observation posts.

B Company of the 1-511th had slept under the C-47s on Nichols Field, waiting for the pre-dawn preparations for the drop. Each of its soldiers had been assigned a specific mission once they landed, and was given a map of the camp area showing where they were supposed to move and the locations of the Japanese defences. In the words of one of its members, PFC Jim Holzem, 'For no amount of money could you have bought a seat on that plane from a Company B trooper. We had the feeling that this was why we had been training so hard and long, that this was the ultimate battle, the highlight of our combat careers.'[6] In addition to the attached machine-gun platoon and a squad of assault engineers, B Company would be accompanied by three volunteer Filipino guerrillas, each making their first parachute jump.

At 0640, a green flare rose from the operations van at Nichols Field and the nine C-47s carrying the airborne raiders took off in quick succession, forming up in a tight 'vee of vees' formation. The flight was a short one – twenty minutes at 300 m altitude over Laguna de Bay – just enough time for the paratroopers to check their equipment and then 'stand up and hook up'.

At 0658, the reconnaissance platoon elements marked the drop zone with two green smoke grenades to show wind direction. The drop zone secured by the reconnaissance platoon was a 900 m by 450 m field 730 m to the northeast of the camp, hemmed in by trees, power lines and railroad tracks.

Herbert Parker was in the lead C-47. 'As we crossed the edge of the drop zone, Don [MAJ Don Anderson] ordered the jump. I threw the switch that activated the green light over the rear cargo door. 1LT Ringler kicked out his equipment bundle and jumped. His troopers were right behind him.'

At precisely 0700, the C-47s arrived over the drop zone, changing formation to stack up in trail at 120–240 m, dropping the raiders in less than a minute with no injuries (despite two men landing in the trees and one in the power lines). They linked up with the reconnaissance platoon troopers, formed up and quickly moved towards the camp.

At the same moment as the raiders were jumping, flights of USAAF P-38 fighter-bombers hit Japanese positions around Los Banos, avoiding attacking the camp and incurring the chance for collateral damage. The machine-gun emplacements in the gravel quarry west of the camp were put out of action. The P-38s then kept a combat air patrol (CAP) over Los Banos for the rest of the day.

Inside the camp, the internees saw the air action as they were about to line up for the morning roll call and took cover. 'We ran back into the barracks. We lay on the dirt floor and pulled our so-called mattresses on top of us,' the Reverend R. Thomas Bousman later recalled.[7]

LIBERATION

Around the camp, the reconnaissance platoon troopers and their Filipino guerrilla allies saw evidence that the element of surprise had been maintained. The camp's Japanese garrison was, minus sentries, in formation for morning callisthenics at precisely 0700.

The first shot was from a 2.36-inch bazooka rocket launcher fired by 1LT Skau into one of the pillboxes at the main entrance to the camp, scoring a direct hit and destroying it. This was the signal for the force to open fire. Most of the Japanese fell in the initial volley, and then the attackers moved in. Not all of the scouts and Filipinos had managed to infiltrate into their attack positions in time, and they charged forward, firing, as soon as the C-47s came overhead.

Terry Santos recalled, 'As we charged the two pillboxes, the first bursts from the machine guns wounded troopers Call, Botkin and one of the Filipino guides . . . We knocked out the pillboxes. Then suddenly a third, unreported machine gun opened fire on us. We spotted this machine gun on a knoll near a large tree overlooking our exposed position. We kept it under fire until "B" Company troopers reinforced us.'

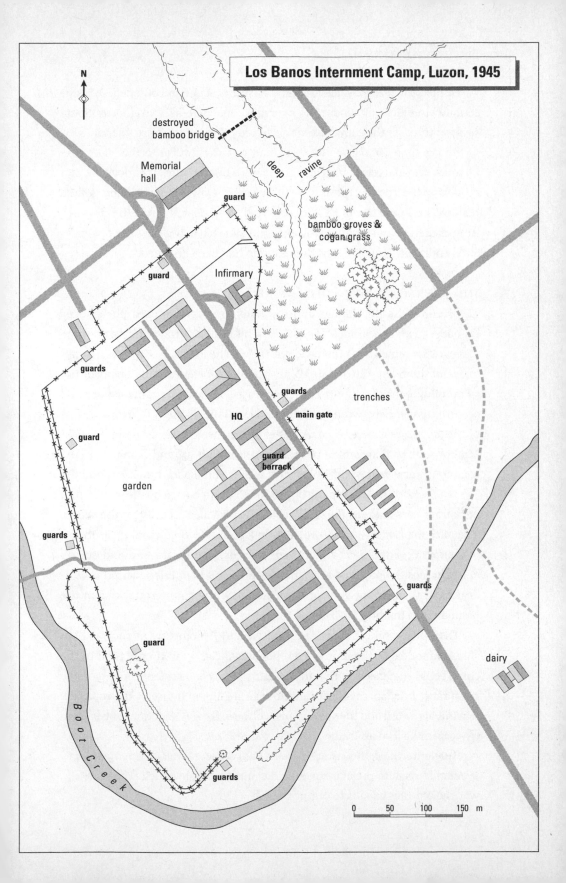

Los Banos Internment Camp, Luzon, 1945

N

destroyed
bamboo bridge

deep ravine

Memorial
hall

guard

bamboo groves &
cogan grass

guard

Infirmary

guards

guard

guards

garden

guards

guard

HQ

main gate

trenches

guard
barrack

guards

dairy

guard

Boot Creek

guards

0   50   100   150 m

Hunted down as they fled into their barracks, a handful of Japanese resisted long enough to die under the guerrillas' machete-like *bolo* knives. Some escaped through the camp to the south, only to run into more guerrillas.

By the time the parachute force had run the 730 m to the camp, the Japanese were largely defeated. B Company's 60 mm mortars knocked out a bunker by the front gate that was still resisting. Only a few surviving guards holding out in the prisoners' barracks had to be cleared out by B Company. Ringler then set out perimeter defences and started to organize the prisoners for withdrawal. By 0717, Los Banos camp had been liberated.

THE AMTRACS ARRIVE AT LOS BANOS

The reconnaissance platoon and the Filipino guerrillas used phosphorus grenades to mark a suitable landing beach for the amtracs. The first of nine waves of six amtracs hit the beach at 0659. The first objective was the Japanese positions at Mayondon Point. The coast-defence guns engaged the swimming amtracs without effect. One wave of amtracs came ashore and set up a roadblock between the Point and Los Banos, some 915 m away. Most of the Japanese defenders fled. Another amtrac wave inserted a roadblock at Matim, setting up defensive positions on the high ground dominating the road to Laguna de Bay. Other amtracs deployed the pack howitzers and the 1-511th's mortars. C Company of the 1-511th supported by the two 75 mm pack howitzers manned the roadblocks and provided security for the beach. That accomplished – with the remainder of the force coming ashore – C Company of the 1-511th moved towards Laguna de Bay and set up defensive positions against any Japanese attempts to interfere with the withdrawal. C Company was in position to delay any counterattack from the Japanese 8th Infantry Division.

The under-strength (fewer than fifty men) A Company of the 1-511th stayed mounted in the amtracs as they advanced 4 km up the road to the camp behind engineers with mine detectors. They encountered only sporadic resistance. A Japanese officer burst out of a Filipino house at the roadside, waving his sword and hauling up his trousers. He was shot down by a paratrooper in the lead amtrac.

Ringler recalled, 'It was at this time that someone yelled "enemy tanks". We had to react to the alert to defend against possible attack. The noise . . . was the amtracs headed to our positions.'

When the amtracs reached the camp, they found that 1LT Ringler had already started to organize the jubilant prisoners. They were milling around, greeting their liberators and pointing out where the surviving Japanese were hiding.

Guerrillas and paratroopers soon mopped up the area around the camp. A Company, dismounting from the amtracs, set up blocking positions. However, patrols away from the camp perimeter soon started drawing fire. The Japanese were obviously still in the area and awaiting reinforcements to counterattack.

BG Courtney Whitney, the guerrilla liaison chief from MacArthur's staff, had accompanied the raiders on the amtracs. He and another man dressed in civilian clothes met with the guerrilla leadership and seized several boxes of documents from the commandant's office – described by LTC Louis Walsh, a senior paratroop officer on an inspection tour who had accompanied the amtracs, as 'valuable State Department documents', believed by others to be records of Filipino collaborators and informers in the local area – and loaded them into one of the first amtracs out.[8] Whitney – who had kept a low profile throughout the operation to the extent of not giving his name to the raiders – was apparently also functioning as MacArthur's 'directed telescope', reporting directly to the top. This way, MacArthur was made aware of the planning and execution of the Los Banos raid without high-level interference.

LEAVING LOS BANOS

Command now reverted to MAJ Burgess. Some 1,500 former prisoners – women, children, sick and wounded – were quickly loaded into the amtracs, which had concentrated at the camp by 0830. The civilian internees insisted on carrying all their belongings – meagre enough, but a complicating factor – with them. Ringler reported to Burgess, 'My men can't get the people to head for the loading area. Most of them are cowering in their shacks and the barracks . . . It's chaos.'[9]

The camp was already on fire. Burgess ordered it to be burned down to get the internees moving towards the amtracs. 2LT Walter Hettlinger of the 1-511th set the fires. 'After the barracks started burning, it did not take long for the internees to leave and head for the parade field. The wind carried the fire to the next row of barracks, doing a very efficient job of helping the internees decide quickly what items they should carry out with them.'[10]

Burgess also commented: 'Internees poured . . . into the loading area. Troops started clearing the barracks in advance of the fire and carried out . . . over 130 people who were too weak or too sick to walk.'[11]

Reverend Bousman left along with his family: 'We climbed in, managing to stay together as a family in the crush of a happy crowd. Immediately the amtracs took off, taking us down the main highway, past the railroad station and . . . when we reached the beach, we kept on going.'

Japanese snipers fired on the column of internees and raiders heading for the beach, following the amtracs. They were suppressed by return fire from the 75 mm howitzers at the beach.

The amtracs followed a route back to the beach cleared by the airborne engineers, plunged into the water and started swimming for Mamatid. The Japanese at Mayondon Point opened fire with a machine gun, wounding two soldiers, three evacuees and a Filipino before it was silenced by the amtrac's .50-calibre machine gun. The remaining internees were marched to the beach to await the return of the amtracs. The three companies of the 1-511th – reinforced by the two pack howitzers – and the Filipino guerrillas formed a defensive perimeter around 500 remaining internees by 1200. They were soon under Japanese sniper fire, but there was no sign of the anticipated counterattack.

FOLLOWING UP SUCCESS

The force at Los Banos was unaware of the successful advance of the diversionary troops, spearheaded by the 1-188th Glider Infantry. The diversionary attack was also launched at 0700. Despite Japanese reinforcements in the forward area, the advancing 11th Airborne force soon crossed the San Juan River. By 0645 they had secured the Lecheria Hills and by noon had advanced to the Damplait River, encountering only light resistance. But a destroyed bridge over the river and the rough terrain, coupled with the certainty of a counterattack by the Japanese 8th Infantry Division, limited the overall speed of the advance. Regardless, the communications links between this force and the Los Banos raiders failed.

The original plan had been for the now reunited 1-511th to fight their way out of Los Banos overland to link up with the diversionary attack. However, when the amtracs returned after handing the first lot of internees over to XIV Corps at Mamatid, it was apparent that the entire raiding force could return on the amtracs with the remaining prisoners.

Burgess, concerned about a counterattack if the original plan was follow-ed, was unable to communicate with the diversionary attack force and did not know how far they had advanced. Burgess decided that the 1-511th would withdraw with the amtracs' second trip. LTC Gibbs, hearing Burgess's new plan, agreed.

At this point, Swing appeared overhead in an L-4 liaison aircraft. Swing had originally intended to accompany the amtracs, but due to travel delays from the divisional CP he had arrived after they had left. He had then gone to Soule's CP, where he borrowed one of the artillery-spotter aircraft.

The artillery forward observer accompanying Burgess, following stand-ard practice when one of these aircraft overflew an operation zone, switched to the day's air–ground liaison frequency, thus giving Swing a link to Burgess. Burgess explained the change of plan. Swing approved and reported that he would co-ordinate it with Soule. Swing asked Burgess if, given the tactical situation, they could convert the raid into an advance, progressing back up from the beach to Los Banos town and holding a defensive perimeter until ground forces linked up with them. Burgess was, however, wary of a coun-terattack by the Japanese 8th Infantry Division and his battalion did not have the equipment or supplies for a sustained action. No medical personnel other than aid men had accompanied the raiders; they had relied on evacu-ating casualties in the amtracs. In spite of the difficulties, however, Burgess's 'can-do' spirit prevented him from recommending the withdrawal to Swing. Instead, Burgess simply turned off the radio and proceeded to execute his new plan.[12]

At 1330, thirty-five amtracs returned from Mamatid for the second wave. They finished loading and left the beachhead by 1600. SGT Martin Squires recalled, 'Terry Santos and I were the last two Recon'ers to leave the camp and were on one of the last amtracs to leave shore. The Japanese were laying down fire on us as we left.'

The Japanese launched a counterattack during the withdrawal. Burgess recalled, 'When the last of us left in a group of about six amphtracks [amtracs], their deployed units of several hundred soldiers came forward in short rushes to fire small arms at us. Japanese artillery opened fire on the last few amph-tracks in the water, bracketing them but failing to hit any.'[13]

Despite fears that the swimming amtracs would be taken under heavy fire by enemy coastal positions, there was little Japanese resistance – easily answered by the amtracs' on-board machine guns – and the force was back at Mamatid by evening, the amtracs having successfully completed two round trips. One amtrac broke down on the return trip and was scuttled after its passengers and crew were transferred to another amtrac which came alongside.[14] For Reverend Bousman and the other internees, 'At the end of the journey, we found freedom and food.'

AFTER THE RAID

The Filipino guerrillas did not evacuate, but withdrew back to their bases in the hills, urging the civilian population in the Los Banos area to come with them. A few followed; most did not.

At this point – there was no need for a further advance as the raiders and internees had all been evacuated by amtracs – the diversionary force received orders from Swing to withdraw to defensible positions holding the bridgehead over the San Juan River and the Lecheria Hills. They registered their forward positions for defensive artillery fire before evacuating them. When the Japanese mounted a counterattack that night, the diversionary force was able to call down concentrations of XIV Corps artillery. The next day, the 1-511th took over the diversionary force's place in the line, while the 1-188th returned to the continuing battles around Manila.

It was only after the raid had been completed that it came to light that there had been no formal operations order written, as required, before the raid. Quandt and Burgess quickly wrote one and backdated it, to make it appear as if the entire raid had gone by the book. The raid had been a success largely through having a thorough plan, in spite of the lack of a formal detailed written order.

The operation resulted in the deaths of 243 Japanese. US casualties were two wounded at the camp, with an additional four killed and two wounded in the diversionary attack. Two Filipino guerrillas were killed and four wounded. Some 2,132 prisoners and internees – 1,583 of them American, nine being PoWs (nine of the eleven female US Navy nurses captured in 1942) – had been freed without loss.

In the month between the raid and the liberation of the Los Banos area by XIV Corps, the Japanese exacted revenge against the Filipino civilian population. The Japanese 8th Infantry Division massacred an estimated

1,000–1,500 Filipinos following the raid. The Los Banos Agricultural College was burned down. Whether this was in retaliation for the raid was never proven; the Japanese conducted a number of large-scale massacres without such provocation, especially in Manila. Warrant Officer Konishi, who had fled the assault at Los Banos, was particularly prominent in directing these atrocities, which earned him the death penalty in post-war war crimes trials, along with MG Masatoshi Fujishige, commanding general of the 8th Infantry Division.

Los Banos was not the only liberation mission carried out during the Second World War. In the closing days of the war and immediately after the surrender there was concern about a massacre of American prisoners or a hostage situation. Some operations, most notably the tank force sent on a liberation raid to Hammelburg PoW camp by Patton's Third Army, resulted in heavy casualties. Most liberation operations, however, went well, such as the Office of Strategic Services' (OSS) use of airdropped raiders to secure Allied prisoners in Manchuria and north China and then evacuate them by air before vengeful Japanese could harm them. Los Banos remained the model operation for decades to come.

LESSONS AND IMPLICATIONS

MacArthur ordered the Los Banos raid after receiving in-theatre intelligence. The imaginative plan conceived by MG Swing and the effective implementation of it by 11th Airborne Division headquarters staff made it possible. There was no time for any rehearsal. However, there was time on 22 February for the key leaders – of the C-47s and the parachute assault force, and of the amtracs and the amphibious force – to work out the details. The plans were made at the lowest feasible level. The decisions on the drop itself were made by Ringler and his USAAF counterparts. This willingness to delegate reflected the realities of wartime planning: planners and raiders alike worked together. The fact that the parachute assault force had been in ground combat until some thirty-six hours before the jump demonstrates how ably this raid was taken in stride by this highly proficient formation.

Higher headquarters, once orders were given for the raid, refrained from micro-management. The man on the scene – first Ringler, then Burgess – was in charge and able to adjust the plan to meet requirements, as when Burgess decided to withdraw the 1-511th in the second amtrac lift rather than move cross-country to link up with the 1-188th, as previously planned. While Swing and 11th Airborne staff had been critical to the planning and organization of the raid, they did not interfere with its execution. Swing wanted to look at the situation for himself, but refrained from second-guessing Burgess or Soule. The general accompanying the amtracs did not interfere with Gibbs' part of the mission. Nor did the high-level agendas of the Filipino guerrillas or the Army Air Force interfere with the planning or execution of the mission. Integration was key, and it worked. The C-47s, the P-38 fighters that provided CAP, the amtracs and the trucks to bring the rescued internees from the beach to medical care or a temporary camp were all where they were needed at the time they were needed.

The raid demonstrated the importance of surprise and of the ability of the raiders to project overwhelming force to achieve the objective, both of which were enabled by intelligence. The raiders were able to rescue the internees even though the Japanese 8th Infantry Division was between them and US main forces because they did not seek to engage that whole formation, only the guards at the camp. Air and amphibious movement provided the means for both surprise and mobility.

Intelligence was critical to the success of the raid. The escaped internees, guerrillas and the 11th Airborne's scouts provided detailed information about the Los Banos camp. Air reconnaissance provided information on Japanese troop locations. All these elements contributed to the successful IPB that made the raid possible.

Any raid is, by definition, a high-risk operation. But the likelihood of the massacre of the internees by the Japanese placed them in a high-risk position from the start. The Los Banos raid made effective use of US strengths and negated those of the enemy. By use of effective and actionable intelligence, the raiders had the element of surprise. The raiders, paratroopers and guerrillas were all combat veterans. They had the relative superiority over the Japanese in the Los Banos area throughout the raid. Even though the raiders were at the objective and then on the beach for several hours, longer than the half-hour normally considered the maximum for a successful raid, US control of the air limited the Japanese response to covert movement on foot under cover and sniping. Any large-scale movement of reserves to the area before nightfall would have been subjected to air attack.

Collateral damage – in the form of the Japanese massacres of Filipino civilians in the area after the raid – remains as a warning of an intrinsic limitation of liberation raids: if the enemy is not defeated, even if the raid is successful he may seek retaliation against others. With hindsight, reinforcing the victory gained at Los Banos with reserves and holding the terrain gained on 23 February would have made the raid an operational success in addition to the success of its assigned rescue mission. But with the heavy fighting in the Manila area occupying US resources, there was a reluctance to open a secondary action by holding Los Banos until a general advance could be ordered in March. Because much of the operation had been planned quickly and at the lowest possible level, no one in the process needed to consider the risks of subsequent Japanese atrocities against the local population. The guerrillas, for their part, assumed that the US would protect the local civilian population.

Years later, MAJ Vanderpool agreed that, in hindsight, Burgess had made the right decision when Swing asked him if he would convert his raid into an advance and hold Los Banos town. Even with the support of the guerrillas, the paratroopers with Burgess would not have been likely to prevail against the inevitable counterattack by the Japanese 8th Infantry Division. While MG Swing's idea was a good one, it had not been enabled by prior planning. Enabling the raiding force to hold ground would have involved a greater commitment of supporting assets – amtracs and C-47s – away from the main fighting near Manila. Supporting units, including medical assets, would have needed to be ready to go in. The plan had positioned the reserve – a key element in permitting the extraction of the raiding party in the event of a strong enemy response – to support an overland extraction, rather than having them ready and waiting to go in to reinforce Burgess by parachute or amtrac.

In the final analysis, however, it is difficult to argue with General Krueger's characterization of the raid. Los Banos itself was a textbook operation. The flexibility of a small, independent liberation force could, even in the context of a major operation – such as the liberation of the Philippines – yield success. It was to be many years before US forces were to enjoy similar success again.

CHAPTER 3 SUKCHON-SUNCHON, NORTH KOREA · 20–22 October 1950

The jump was outstanding – indisputably the best
combat jump the army had ever staged.

Clay Blair, *The Forgotten War.*

During the Cold War, liberation or seizure missions were often blocked by the realities of geopolitics. In October 1949, US Consul-General Angus Ward and other diplomats – effectively under house arrest since the Chinese Communists took Mukden in November 1948 – were subjected to a show trial there. President Harry S. Truman instructed GEN Omar Bradley, Chairman of the Joint Chiefs of Staff, to consider mounting a liberation mission to free Ward and his staff. Bradley's response was negative. He pointed out that such an operation could not be executed without a major military operation and a high risk of provoking all-out war, and that the safety of the hostages could not be assured. In the absence of an effective military capability, Bradley recommended instead the undertaking of negotiations to free the hostages. While the US considered a range of military options, eventually economic and diplomatic pressure was used rather than a liberation mission. Ward and the other diplomats were released in December 1949.[1]

Ironically, it was Truman's September 1945 disbandment of the wartime Office of Strategic Services (OSS) that in this instance limited both the intelligence available to Washington and the option to use force for a liberation mission without initiating a major conflict. US demobilization after the Second World War had cut back especially hard on SOF that could have been used for a liberation mission. In addition to the disbandment of the OSS, with its combat-proven capability for paramilitary action, the US Army had disbanded its Ranger battalions, Alamo Scouts and other SOF forces. The US

Air Force (formed from the Army Air Force in 1947) disbanded its Air Commando units. Consequently, the option of an SOF liberation raid to meet high-level direction was not available to the Truman administration. Later administrations would want to remedy this lack.[2]

The Angus Ward incident brought to light the problems of executing liberation and seizure missions in conditions short of total open warfare. However, the next time the opportunity for such missions emerged, there was already a war raging in Asia that negated such concerns.

KOREA, 1950

The speed and shock of the North Korean invasion of South Korea on 25 June 1950 and their subsequent advance to the US-defended Pusan Perimeter resulted in the taking of large numbers of prisoners. Many were Americans from the Korean Military Assistance Group (KMAG) or from the first forces hastily committed to the Korean conflict. US counterattacks found the bound bodies of prisoners murdered by the North Koreans as early as July 1950. Rumours that the North Koreans were slaughtering prisoners helped to build a sense of panic in some US units at the time, when the North Korean advance seemed like a juggernaut.[3] The North Koreans used prisoners for propaganda purposes, marching them through the streets of Pyongyang and broadcasting the first of a series of 'confessions' by prisoners urging United Nations (UN) forces to stop fighting in July. In August, GEN Douglas MacArthur, the UN commander, made a broadcast to the North Korean leadership with the message – reiterated in a leaflet drop – that they must halt these actions immediately or be held accountable.

The fate of US prisoners assumed increasing importance when the North Koreans were pushed back by UN forces following the US amphibious invasion at Inchon (15 September) and the breakout of UN forces from the Pusan Perimeter (22 September). The North Korean capital of Pyongyang – where intelligence sources reported that most prisoners were being held – became a UN objective in October. North Korean forces were pursued northwards.

The advance after Inchon and Pusan uncovered more evidence that the North Koreans had not taken MacArthur's demands to heart. In addition to the liberation of prisoners, therefore, capturing the North Korean leadership – seen as responsible for the conflict – became a priority issue, as it appeared that UN forces were mopping up opposition and that the conflict would soon be over.

THE RAKKASANS ARRIVE

The independent 187th Regimental Combat Team (Airborne) was hastily put together from the remnants of the stateside 11th Airborne Division. Nicknamed 'The Rakkasans' (from the Japanese word for parachute, acquired during occupation duties following the Second World War), the 187th was brought up from its weak pre-Korean-conflict strength with a mixture of replacements and veteran paratroopers from the 82nd Airborne Division before being deployed to Korea. It was commanded by COL Frank Bowen, who had served with airborne units in the Second World War, rising to the rank of brigadier general. The 187th was put through a brief unit-training programme – including a regimental airdrop – before deploying first to Japan, and then to Korea.

Additional USAF transport aircraft had arrived in Japan at Ashiya and Brady Air Bases in Kyushu. As with the 187th, their leaders included veterans of airdrops in all theatres during the Second World War. This shared expertise and personal knowledge made rapid planning and co-ordination easier.[4]

The 187th was airlifted from Ashiya AB in Japan to Kimpo airfield near Seoul, Korea, starting on 22 September. Within a few days, the 187th had defeated a numerically superior North Korean force to clear the peninsula between the Han River and the Yellow Sea. After this action was completed on 2 October, they were assembled south of Kimpo as a GHQ reserve formation to prepare for an airdrop or airlift mission as UN forces started their drive across the 38th parallel into North Korea. Morale soared when the unit was alerted for a jump.[5]

On 15 October, with UN forces within striking range of Pyongyang, MacArthur's G-3 (Operations) Staff in Tokyo recommended an airborne assault as part of a forthcoming attack. They identified the Sukchon–Sunchon area some 48 km north of Pyongyang as a key choke point, where they would be able to cut off the two main roads and their parallel rail lines heading north from Pyongyang to block the withdrawal of North Korean government leaders and military units. The westernmost road, running from Pyongyang through Sukchon some 40 km north, led eventually to Sinanju, the main road and rail crossing on the Chongchon River. Sunchon, 25 km to the east of Sukchon, was 48 km along the road between Pyongyang and Kunu-ri, another crossing point on the Chongchon.

In addition to blocking the routes, trapping key North Korean leadership personnel and liberating UN prisoners were also key objectives for the jump. G-3, citing 10 October intelligence reports, estimated that there were 1,400 prisoners in the Pyongyang area, including at least 1,100 Americans. Intelligence projected that the North Koreans would try to evacuate the prisoners with their retreating forces. Intelligence staff remained ignorant, however, as to where, when and how the prisoners might be moved. They could provide no further intelligence to the 187th, who would have to pick up their own intelligence on the ground from patrols and reports from friendly Koreans.

The staff of the 187th RCT and the USAF's Combat Cargo Command had been planning for airdrop missions since 2 October as part of the northwards advance. They had identified five potential drop zones north of Pyongyang. Before the final drop zone was selected, a number of key parameters were decided. Over the Air Force's objections, GHQ decided that the airdrop would be mounted from Kimpo airfield. It had been determined that eighty C-119 and forty C-47 transports would be required for the 187th's initial drop, with follow-up drops over the next two days. The Air Force was reluctant to bring so many transports forward to Kimpo – facilities were limited and they feared that the aircraft might be vulnerable to air attack while on the ground. GHQ, however, rejected the Air Force's idea to withdraw the 187th to Japan and mount the airdrop from there. It was determined that a minimum of seventy-two hours would be required to assemble the aircraft, perform maintenance and configure them for airdrops, deploy to Kimpo, load up the 187th and go into action. During that preparation period, the staffs would plan the operation, issue orders and brief the participants.

THE SUKCHON–SUNCHON AIRDROP

The 187th was put on alert for an airdrop on 15 October. The orders for Operation Hotdrop came from GHQ on 16 October. The 187th was to drop in the Sukchon–Sunchon area on 21 October (an objective changed to Anju on the 17th and back to Sukchon–Sunchon on the 18th). The primary mission was to cut the road and rail links to Pyongyang. The secondary mission was given in an order to 'capture important North Korean military and civilian officials and perform such PoW liberation raids as can be accomplished without jeopardizing the primary mission.'[6] Guidance as to how these objectives might be located was not provided. Reflecting the lack of intelligence, there were no specific liberation or seizure missions in the order. In the intelligence annexe of the operations order, recognizing the need for HUMINT to provide targeting for such raids, the 187th was reminded to question local civilians about fleeing officials or transported PoWs. How they would execute this instruction was left to the commanders on the scene, with only the organic intelligence assets of the 187th – meaning infantry patrols – to provide intelligence. COL Bowen ordered the staff of the 187th to begin planning their part in the operation.

The uncertainty of the situation and an intelligence picture limited mainly to air reconnaissance photos forced the planning to concentrate on the initial drop. The 187th's plan for the drop was ready on 18 October, calling for the 1-187th and 3-187th battalion combat teams (each with a reinforcing artillery battery) to drop at DZ William near Sukchon, some 40 km north of Pyongyang. The 2-187th BCT would drop at DZ Easy near Sunchon, 48 km northeast of Pyongyang and 25 km east of Sukchon. The 187th would take the towns of Sunchon and Sukchon on the day of the drop and then establish defensive positions on the high ground outside these towns to block the North Korean withdrawal. Linkup with advancing UN forces was anticipated within twenty-four hours of the drop and no later than forty-eight hours after it, and no resupply drops were scheduled after D+2.[7]

Once these positions were established, reinforced by follow-on airdrops, the plan was for the 187th to advance to carry out their dual mission as a blocking and PoW-liberation/Korean-leader-seizure force and link up with UN forces advancing overland from the south.

On 19 October, GHQ advanced D-Day to 20 October. This reflected slower than anticipated progress in the UN ground drive on Pyongyang. The new date was also intended to increase the chances of intercepting enemy officials and liberating PoWs. This caused frantic scrambling by the Air Force to make sure that the details of the planning were completed and that the required transports were available.

The Air Force was able to provide seventy-six of the planned eighty C-119s and all forty of the planned C-47s. The transports flew to Kimpo from their bases in Japan and were loaded with equipment at Kimpo on the evening of 19 October, while their crews went through final briefings along with the 187th. While there was no time for rehearsals or mission-specific training, sand-table models were built to brief paratroops and transport crews alike on the details of the drops. Even though the 187th and the Air Force transport units had been pulled together in ninety days and rushed to Korea, the leadership of both had worked together pre-war and had also had the benefit of a planning period before GHQ had given the orders for the drop. Most of the commanders and staff officers were veterans of the Second World War and had planned and executed similar operations. The 187th and the 314th Troop Carrier Wing had trained together in the US before deployment.

Take-off was scheduled for 0700 on 20 October, but delayed to 1200 due to poor visibility and rain. The C-119s led the formations, forty-eight planned for DZ William near Sukchon and twenty-eight for DZ Easy near Sunchon. The slower-cruising C-47s followed the big C-119s. The Cargo Combat Command's own command aircraft – a C-54 modified with extra aircraft and ground-unit radios – was on hand to direct the operation.

US Air Force fighters provided escort, and no enemy aircraft challenged the transports. US and Australian fighter-bombers attacked anti-aircraft positions that could engage the transports before they arrived over the DZs. Light bombers struck ground positions that could fire on the DZs. Abandoned anti-aircraft guns and a radar set were later found in the area.

The transports flew an indirect over-water route to the DZs, taking some ninety-five minutes, to reduce vulnerability to anti-aircraft weapons and increase the element of surprise. However, the over-water approach made visual alignment on the DZs more difficult. At 1405, the first sticks of the 187th jumped over Sukchon, with those at Sunchon starting a few minutes later. The drops were accurate, with troops jumping from 213 m and heavy equipment dropping from 457 m. There was no anti-aircraft fire. Once on the ground, the 187th encountered only light sniper fire.

SGT Donald G. Martin dropped as part of I Company of the 3-187th. 'It was a very good jump. Weather was excellent, good formation of the aircraft, all of our door bundles and monorail bundles were found, no jump casualties and light opposition to begin with.'[8]

Within an hour, the drops were completed. The transports flew back over Kimpo and then returned to Japan to prepare for the resupply missions. There were no combat losses. Six of the C–119s (but none of the highly

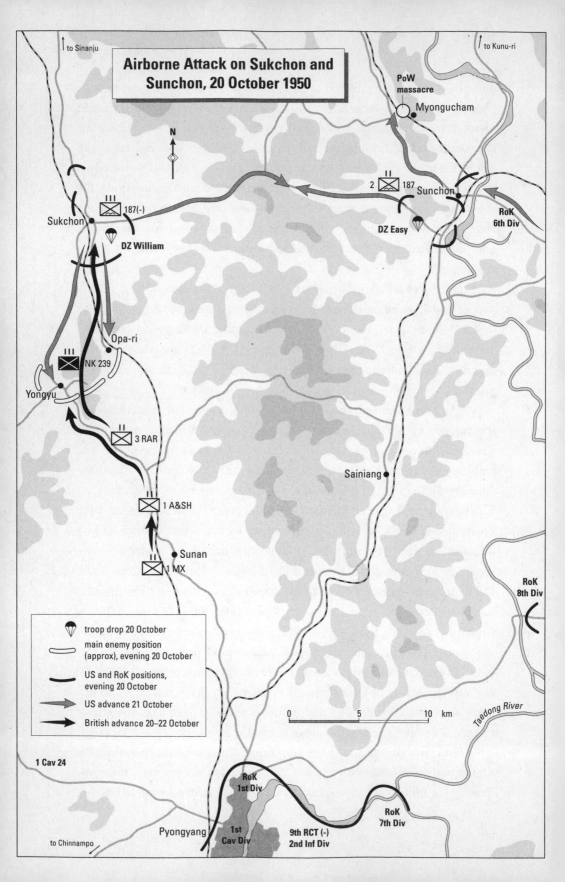

Airborne Attack on Sukchon and Sunchon, 20 October 1950

N

to Sinanju

to Kunu-ri

PoW
massacre

Myongucham

2 ☒ 187

Sunchon

III
☒ 187(-)

RoK
6th Div

Sukchon

DZ William

DZ Easy

Opa-ri

III
☒ NK 239

Yongyu

II
☒ 3 RAR

II
☒ 1 A&SH

Sunan

II
☒ 1 MX

Sainiang

RoK
8th Div

Legend

troop drop 20 October

main enemy position
(approx), evening 20 October

US and RoK positions,
evening 20 October

US advance 21 October

British advance 20–22 October

0   5   10   km

Taedong River

1 Cav 24

RoK
1st Div

1st
Cav Div

9th RCT (-)
2nd Inf Div

RoK
7th Div

Pyongyang

to Chinnampo

reliable C-47s) had to abort the mission due to operational problems. Following the troop drop came the heavy-equipment drop, including the 674th Airborne Field Artillery Battalion of eighteen 105 mm howitzers – the first time such big guns had been airdropped. Twelve landed successfully.

The parachute jump had a third, unspoken mission: providing good press coverage and demonstrating that the US Army was justified in continuing to include airborne forces in its order of battle. Jumping with the 187th were reporters who had been trained to accompany them. An Army camera team and additional reporters were also attached to the 187th. Those reporters and cameramen who did not jump with the paratroops were provided with a C-47 that circled the drop zones.

MacArthur – who recognized a good press opportunity when he saw one – was personally on the scene. He observed the airdrop from his own C-54, accompanied by his senior staff and Air Force counterparts. MacArthur then landed at Pyongyang airport – captured that morning – and announced to more reporters that the end of the war was at hand. COL Bowen's promotion back to brigadier general was announced to the press. Optimism pervaded the UN ranks at all levels.

THE 187th LANDS, 20 OCTOBER

On the ground, the 187th encountered little resistance.[9] The 674th Field Artillery (Airborne) landed to a scene described by 1LT Josiah A. Wallace Jr.: 'The sound of small arms fire was heard coming from all directions at the 1-187th, who had jumped five minutes earlier, destroyed [sic] the 75–90 North Korean soldiers who had the misfortune to be on the DZ. Those of the enemy that could, changed to civilian clothing and fled to the hills to the north.'[10]

At DZ William, the 1-187th moved north to clear the town of Sukchon and hold the high ground on Hill 97 to the east and Hill 104 to the north, sealing the routes north. Mortar fire, the 674th's howitzers and pre-planned airstrikes supported the capture of Hill 97. By afternoon, Sukchon had been taken. The 2-187th took the high ground around Sunchon and moved in to secure the town at 1830, only to find it already occupied by South Korean troops from 6th Republic of Korea (RoK) Division that had pushed north from Pyongyang. Instead, the 2-187th's E Company took the town of Changsan-ni, some 5 km east of Sunchon, and set up a roadblock at a nearby bridge on the Kumchon River. F Company pushed patrols to the northwest of Sunchon in search of US prisoners who were reported in the vicinity, but found only scattered North Korean sniper fire.

The 3-187th moved south from DZ William to secure the high ground. Gerald Krueger was a PFC in A Company, 127th Airborne Engineer Battalion, attached to the 3-187th. 'We assembled and picked up additional equipment that was dropped and started off . . . Resistance was light on the DZ.' [11]

K Company of the 3-187th advanced south during the day. They had to fight for Hill 163, forcing off a North Korean force that retreated east and south. Five Koreans were killed and forty-two captured. K Company then took up night positions on the high ground on the northern edge of the key town of Yongyu and Hill 163, some 3 km south of Sukchon. I Company, attacking on K Company's flank, moved into the hills from Opa'ri – 11 km south of Sukchon on the rail line – to hold the high ground. Patrols were sent out to block the railroad, where they ambushed retreating North Koreans.

It had been a good drop, followed by a strong advance. The towns of Sukchon and Sunchon were occupied. By nightfall the US troops had secured the high ground controlling the roads and rail lines, supporting blocking forces. North Korean troops offered light and scattered resistance; many, apparently demoralized fugitives from Pyongyang, were captured. But there were no officials among them, nor had any information been found regarding US prisoners.

The 187th was now in an intelligence vacuum. The intelligence annexe to the operational order had opened with the frank admission that it had 'no definitive information as to enemy units in objective area'. Nor did it provide information or guidance on how intelligence for the liberation mission might be obtained and exploited. The 187th's Intelligence and Reconnaissance (I&R) platoon had been committed first to secure a nearby dam after the initial jump and then to defend DZ William, so it was not available to patrol. The 674th had not received air reconnaissance photographs of the area before the jump and had been unable to prepare a target list. All patrolling ceased after dark – when the enemy started to move to avoid air attack – and the 187th pulled inside its defensive positions, covering the routes leading north with fire power.

THE SEARCH FOR US PRISONERS

Before dawn on 21 October, the 187th moved out from the positions it had secured at nightfall the previous day, but in the absence of fresh intelligence they had no way of knowing the locations of enemy units, officials or US PoWs. A follow-on airdrop – including 64 C-119s – was scheduled for 1000, with more on D+2 (the Air Force cancelled a second airdrop on 21 October due to a lack of rescue and fighter escort aircraft to support the drop). Pre-planned air strikes arrived in the area to support the 187th's advances to the north and south of its positions. An L-4 liaison plane flew in to carry away the correspondents' reports and film footage to Pyongyang so that news of the drop would reach the American (plus British and French) public in a timely fashion.

The 1-187th launched an attack to seize more high ground north of Sukchon. C Company patrols established communications with the other battalions. A and B companies captured Hills 142 and 126 respectively, against light resistance, then moved on to take Hills 73 (against increasing resistance) and 175 (unopposed). In the afternoon, the 1-187th was ordered to take the next ridge line to the north, hold it and dig in. The 1-187th set up blocking positions to prevent the escape of North Korean forces and to defend against attacks from the north by units aiming to aid cut-off North Korean forces in breaking through the US lines.

During the night, North Koreans had tried to infiltrate north through Sunchon to escape the 2-187th, leading to an hour-long firefight. At dawn, the 2-187th moved out from its positions on the hills overlooking Sunchon. They encountered only retreating stragglers and small North Korean units before linking up with both the rest of the 187th at Sukchon and the vanguard of the US 1st Cavalry Division, which was advancing from the south: Task Force Rogers, consisting of infantry from the 1-8th Cavalry and a company of M4 Shermans from the 70th Tank Battalion. The cavalry arrived at the 2-187th's positions – E Company's roadblock on the Kumchon River bridge south of Sinhung-ni, near Changsan-ni – carrying with them five former US prisoners they had encountered that morning south of Sukchon town, escapees from the last train heading north from Pyongyang.

In addition to the escapees, further HUMINT on the prisoners also arrived. A Korean made his way to the 2-187th's command post with more news of the prisoner train, claiming that the North Koreans had murdered the

200 Americans on board the day before near a railroad tunnel at Myon-gucham, some 8 km to the northwest of Sunchon. A patrol from F Company of the 2-187th mounted on the Cavalry's tanks and, under personal command of BG Frank Allen, assistant divisional commander of the 1st Cavalry, moved off in search of the enemy and US prisoners.

At 1500, they found them, near the point where the main rail line heading north from Pyongyang entered a tunnel near Myongucham, 6.5 km northwest of Sunchon. The 2-187th and 1st Cavalry troops found the bodies of sixty-six American prisoners, massacred the day before by the North Koreans, plus a further seven who had died of disease and starvation.

Neither the leaders of the 187th nor the 1st Cavalry had known anything about the train. It had sheltered in the tunnel during the airdrop before the massacre, which occurred at about 1000 on 20 October. While the 187th's war diary lamented that the weather delay may have prevented a timely rescue, the lack of actionable intelligence would have prevented any focused action even if the drop had occurred on time.

With the arrival of US troops, twenty-three survivors of the massacre – all starved, some badly wounded, two mortally so – started to come out of hiding. Survivors and friendly Koreans directed US patrols. Private Ed Slater had been bayonetted in the head and had found shelter with nearby Koreans. 'The door slid open and there stood the biggest master sergeant I had ever seen . . . He took me to see General Allen . . . we got into his jeep and went to where I had last seen Bob [another escapee]. Bob was still there and still alive.'[12]

Aided by local Koreans, the 2-187th and the 1st Cavalry were able to send the survivors back to Pyongyang for medical care by Air Force helicopter or in 1st Cavalry vehicles. The 2-187th encountered only light and sporadic resistance throughout the operation.

Advancing South Korean troops soon discovered the fate of the remaining prisoners in the Pyongyang area. In addition to some twenty fortunate Americans left behind in the capital when the North Koreans fled, they recovered forty-two escaped PoWs in the Kunu-ri area – 30 km north of Sunchon on the main road – on 22 and 23 October, before finding another massacre site with twenty-eight bodies beside the railroad 6.5 km north of Kujang-dong – a further 20 km northeast from the previous massacre site – and rescuing three more concealed survivors.

THE 3-187th's BATTLE, 21 OCTOBER

In the early morning of 21 October, the North Koreans, seeking an escape route to the north, probed the positions of the 3-187th, with K Company repulsing a company attack. The 3-187th received orders to send company-sized forces down the main road and railroad from Sukchon to Pyongyang. I and K Companies advanced southwards early on 21 October. The 3-187th found not US prisoners but more North Korean stragglers. The advance went well in the morning, and COL Bowen was on the scene to observe the results. Regimental headquarters confirmed that the 3-187th could advance clear to Pyongyang. But it did not provide any reconnaissance information regarding the situation beyond the view of each company's point rifleman.

It was only after noon that the 3-187th made contact with the rearguard of the North Korean Army, the 239th Security Regiment, dug in some 13 km south of Sukchon, in the Opa-ri–Yongyu area. The 239th, some 2,500 strong and heavily armed with AAA and mortars, plus towed and SP artillery, was the North Korean blocking force. Positioned to delay the UN advance northwards, its mission as a Pyongyang-based unit meant that it was manned with politically reliable troops who could be counted on to put up a fight. The North Korean regiment had chosen its own blocking position well, occupying positions on the high ground east of the town of Yongyu, south of Sukchon on the main road, the best defensive positions between Pyongyang and the Chongchon River.

I Company of the 3-187th, advancing south down the main railway line, pushed through Opa'ri, but at around 1300 hours, about 3 km north of Yongyu, it was hit by a powerful North Korean ambush – reflecting the poor tactical intelligence available to the Rakkasans on the ground that day. Mortars and concealed AAA positions that had survived the previous day's air attacks kept up a sustained fire against I Company.

The North Koreans followed up with a battalion counterattack, overrunning two platoons of I Company. The 674th Field Artillery's 105 mm howitzers fired several fire missions, but the North Koreans were soon too close to the US positions for this to continue safely. The artillery forward observer had to fight in self-defence.

After a two-and-a-half-hour firefight, I company was forced back to its positions of the previous night and nearby Hill 281. One of its medics, PFC

Richard G. Wilson, stayed behind with the rearguard to tend wounded and was killed while bringing them back. He was awarded a posthumous Medal of Honor. At the end of the action there were ninety reported missing from I Company, although many came in later. Faced with the tenacious resistance from I Company's rearguard, the North Koreans withdrew to defensive positions on the high ground around Opa'ri and nearby Sinopa.

K Company of the 3-187th was advancing down the main highway towards Pyongyang when it also, like I Company, encountered a dug-in North Korean force on the high ground north of Yongyu.

Bill Parsons was part of a platoon that found itself under fire from a North Korean SU-76 SP gun. His platoon sergeant sent out a request on the radio air support net and soon attracted overhead a flight of four F-51s from 77 Squadron Royal Australian Air Force. Parsons described the Australians' response: '"OK, Yanks, we have him spotted, pull in your heads and we will fix the bugger." With that, the entire flight peeled off and came down firing all the ordnance they had. One pass and we could hear the SP self-destructing in the distance.'[13]

Following this and other air attacks, the North Korean force, an estimated battalion, withdrew south and east of Yongyu. K Company advanced through Yongyu to Hill 63 and the high ground controlling the town. K Company found no fewer than thirty-four abandoned 82 mm mortars in Yongyu.

COL Bowen now contacted the 3-187th to inform them that British troops were approaching Yongyu from the south, advancing up the road from Pyongyang. K Company soon had visitors. The Deputy Chief of Staff of I Corps, COL Ted Unger, arrived to co-ordinate the linkup. At 1845, an officer and a sergeant from the 1st Battalion, Argyll and Sutherland Highlanders, sent forward from the advancing 27th British Commonwealth Brigade, linked up with K Company at Yongyu before the Rakkasans withdrew to night positions on the high ground outside town. The British 27th Brigade had been ordered to advance north from Pyongyang up the main road to Sukchon to link up with the US paratroopers. However, they were unable to provide the paratroopers with any better intelligence as to the location of prisoners or fleeing North Korean officials. Indeed, the paratroopers, for all their dearth of intelligence, had better information than the British, who had only received news a few hours earlier of the 187th's drop and that they would be linking up with them.

To the south, the bulk of the 27th Brigade heard the sounds of fighting and realized it had only been luck that had brought their advance patrol safely to rendezvous with the 187th. They would have to fight to link up the rest of their number with the paratroopers. In the late afternoon, the Argyll and Sutherland Highlanders, leading the 27th Brigade, advance-fought their way on to the hills south of Yongyu, overlooking the town. Having cleared the hills, the Highlanders took up night positions and prepared to resume the attack at dawn.

The 3-187th BCT had been heavily engaged all day. It was low on small arms ammunition and its mortars had fired off all their rounds. Resupply from DZs Easy and William was difficult and the battalion was not netted in to request a direct airdrop of ammunition. No US prisoners or North Korean officials were located in its sector. The numerically superior North Koreans resisted bitterly, and the lightly armed paratroopers were unable to defeat them in a day of hard fighting. Rather than being able to move out and search for prisoners and North Korean officials, the Rakkasans were forced to function as the anvil on which the North Korean rearguard was hammered by the 27th Commonwealth Brigade advancing north from Pyongyang.

LINKUP – 22 OCTOBER

The 3-187th – reinforced by additional personnel dropped at DZ William during the day of 21 October and 90 mm antitank guns sent south from the DZ – was hit during the night by North Korean forces advancing north. The remnants of the 239th Security Regiment were trying to break out. Companies K and L and the battalion headquarters took the brunt of the attack.

Gerald Krueger, an attached engineer, reported: 'About 3 or 4 a.m. I heard voices coming down the road towards our position. I thought they must be South Korean troops because they were not trying to be quiet at all. Captain Prendergass shouted a challenge. That's when the first shots were fired . . . The next four or five hours seemed like an eternity to me. I had fired so many rounds through my M1 rifle that I had oil oozing out of the wood stock . . . and was down to my last clip of ammo.'[14]

K Company repulsed its attackers several times. Its commander, CPT Claude K. Josey, was wounded in hand-to-hand fighting around the CP. However, after repulsing a third attack at 0230, the company was out of ammunition and had to withdraw.

The North Koreans attacked through the night. L Company and battalion headquarters also repulsed strong attacks, timed to coincide with smaller attacks on the 1-187th to the north. There were four organized attacks, lasting from 0015 until 1100. The 674th had moved all its guns out of range before dark and it was not until 0415 that they were able to answer the calls for fire with a two-howitzer battery. The North Koreans did not break through, but the 3-187th was almost out of ammunition and urgently requested relief.

At 0530, K Company recovered its wounded and commenced clearing out of Yongyu the surviving North Koreans who had re-occupied it.

At dawn on 22 October, the British 27th Commonwealth Brigade, advancing overland from the south, came up behind the North Koreans with the mission of breaking through to the 187th. Two companies of the Argyll and Sutherland Highlanders moved into the Yongyu area at dawn. By 0700 they were in Yongyu, joining Company K and COL Unger. At 0830, they were joined by British Brigadier Aubrey Coad, the 27th Commonwealth Brigade's commander.

Opening the road to the 187th would be the responsibility of the 3rd Battalion, Royal Australian Regiment. It was the 3rd RAR's – and the Australian Army's – first combat action in Korea. Moving through the Argylls at 0700, the Australians did not receive artillery support because of concern that it might imperil the 187th's forward positions. The RAR was reinforced by eighteen M4 Sherman tanks from D Company, US 89th Tank Battalion. They pushed north along the valley from Yongyu on the road and then deployed platoons for flanking attacks when they encountered North Korean resistance north of the town.

The 3rd RAR was able to seize a key position – an apple orchard with fields of fire controlling the main road north of the town – in a company attack. In the words of the US official history, the Australians 'jumped from the tanks and charged with fixed bayonets[15] into the apple orchard. They went into it with a dash that brought forth admiration from all who witnessed it. One American officer present told of seeing a big red-haired Australian jump into an enemy trench and come out after, his hands streaming blood from many cuts and his clothes slashed from head to foot. An inspection of the trench later revealed eight dead North Koreans there.'[16] The North Koreans suffered heavy casualties as they abandoned their entrenchments and tried to flee. 1LT William Weber recorded in the 3-187th's War Diary the final rout of the North Korean defenders: 'When the enemy withdrew it was in a state of disorder and rout with no apparent assemblance [sic] of organized withdrawal of any type.'

The rest of the 3rd Battalion RAR then consolidated the position. More Australian troops scaled the high ground to the east of the valley and secured it. The North Koreans soon staged strong breakout attempts to east and west – the road to the north was blocked by the main force of the 187th – but they were beaten back by the Australians. The 3rd RAR's command post repulsed a strong North Korean counterattack.

Resuming the advance, the Australians opened the road to the 187th by 1030. At 1100, the 89th's tanks and the 3rd RAR linked up with the 3-187th, arriving at the battalion CP just as the last North Koreans still remaining from the night's attacks were being driven off with the last of the 3-187th's ammunition. It had been a strong attack; LTC Delbert Munson, the 3-187th's CO, had been seriously wounded in the attack on the battalion CP.

The advancing Australians were followed by the 1st Battalion Middlesex Regiment. The Middlesex pushed on to Sukchon and set up a defensive position north of the town.

The Rakkasans had been relieved. They remained in defensive positions, policed the battlefield and undertook mopping-up operations over the next two days before moving back to Pyongyang on 25 October for a Bob Hope USO Show, hot showers and the hopes – soon to be dashed by the Chinese counterattack – of impending UN victory.

The 187th, supported by forces from the 1st Cavalry Division and the 27th Commonwealth Brigade, had engaged an estimated 6–8,000 North Korean troops, capturing 3,818 and killing an estimated 2,764. The 27th Brigade's attack killed over 200 and took 500 prisoners. Some 692 prisoners and 800 dead were the work of the 3-187th BCT alone. The 187th suffered forty-eight losses and eighty wounded in battle – mainly in the 3-187th – and fifty-eight jump injuries, one fatal.

FRUSTRATION IN KOREA
The operation itself had been planned and executed well without rehearsal, despite the lack of intelligence and the compressed timeframe, including

GHQ moving up the day of the drop to the 20th – had they not done so, they would not have caught even the North Korean rearguard. A much quicker and more precise operation would have been required to have liberated the last train taking prisoners out of Pyongyang.

The bulk of US prisoners had in fact been moved to the North Korean border with Manchuria during September. The surviving liberated prisoners who had been rescued by the 187th and the Cavalry reported that, unknown to US intelligence, two trains with the remaining 300 US prisoners had left Pyongyang on 17 October and, heading slowly north, had been in the vicinity of Sunchon when the 187th jumped. However, in the absence of fresh information, the 187th was unable to move out and liberate the prisoners until the North Koreans had staged their massacres and departed. The US, without intelligence on these moving targets, was unable to mount a timely liberation mission.

MacArthur had been unwilling to drop the 187th behind the North Korean Army primarily as a blocking force and secondarily as a rescue force until he believed that it could be relieved in a relatively short time. The lightly armed paratroopers, even with air resupply and the support of the US Air Force, would have run the risk of heavy losses had they tried to block the retreat of a desperate North Korean Army alone. However, with the North Korean Army already retreating beyond the Chongchon River to the north at the time of the drop, this concern proved to be moot. In the absence of specific intelligence, dropping the 187th earlier – even if this had been possible – would have probably only led to hard fighting and greater numbers of US casualties in a war that increasingly looked as if it would be won in a few months, regardless.

The 187th was, through no fault of its own, largely too late for both its primary and secondary missions. It was too late to intercept more than the 239th Security Regiment, the North Korean rearguard (though it needed the help of air power and the heavier 27th Commonwealth Brigade to defeat it) and stragglers. It was unable to capture any North Korean officials, who had already fled by the time of the jump. The surviving prisoners were rescued no faster than they would have been by the forces already advancing from the south.

COMMAND AND CONTROL

Committed as a GHQ reserve, the 187th was directly under the theatre CINC. MacArthur did not seek to micro-manage the 187th's operations. Indeed, after his press conference, he had little involvement in its operations at all. COL Bowen and the staff of the 187th were largely on their own, but once the drop was carried out, the operation devolved into three separate battalion operations. Bowen was dependent on reports by messenger and radio from the battalion and company headquarters – subject to terrain blocking – for his information of what was happening. He also had few sensors or weapons – other than the 105 mm howitzers – that could be used to support the troops in contact with the enemy. The 187th's own command and control was limited in its ability to react to changing situations. Even though regimental headquarters was aware that the 3-187th was hard-pressed, without motor vehicles – or helicopters – it was unable to commit a tactical reserve to support the 3-187th in a timely manner.

The planning for the 187th's mission reflected the hasty and improvised nature of the operation. Some elements were planned well, especially the airdrops and the air evacuation of wounded. Other limitations in command and control imperilled the mission. These included the inability of the 187th to modify the airdrop plan after the initial drop. There was no way for the 3-187th to directly request a priority airdrop when it was almost out of ammunition. Co-ordination with the 1st Cavalry Division and the 27th Commonwealth Brigade had to be improvised in the field. It was largely a matter of luck that fratricide incidents were avoided. As it was, the 27th Commonwealth Brigade was forced to break through to the 187th without using its artillery because it did not know where the 187th's forward positions were located.

INTELLIGENCE LIMITATIONS

The major oversight in the optimism prevailing at the time of this mission was how little US intelligence had been able to help the combat units. US intelligence preparation of the battlespace (IPB) (though the term was unknown in 1950) was limited to air reconnaissance of the drop zones and the immediate area. While US air superiority allowed photo reconnaissance over the 187th's area of operations before the drop – and this was critical to the planning that made it a success – it was not set up to provide time-critical surveillance of moving North Korean assets, whether PoW trains or the 239th Security Regiment. The limitations of air reconnaissance when its results could not be fused with those from other sensors were illustrated by the fact that the 187th dropped unaware of the presence of the train evacuating prisoners near the drop zone or of the North Korean AAA and mortars that ambushed the 3-187th the day after the drop. The North Koreans were beginning to demonstrate their expertise in camouflage and concealment. The ability to detect camouflaged positions and get the information beyond USAF headquarters in Japan (where the reconnaissance aircraft and photo interpreters were based) to troops on the ground in Korea in a timely manner was limited.

While friendly Koreans were able to provide local information, they first had to be found on the ground. The US SIGINT capability was only just becoming operational, and the US had been dependent on the limited South Korean SIGINT capability for the 187th's drop. There was nothing to compensate for the lack of the eyes-on HUMINT that had proven so vital at Los Banos. Hence both the prisoner train and the location and strength of the 239th Security Regiment came as surprises to the 187th and the forces moving overland to link up with them.

UN intelligence limitations were to be compounded over the next two months as the Chinese became increasingly involved in the war, finally launching a surprise counterattack that avoided detection by UN intelligence and was to retake Pyongyang and beyond. The intelligence limitations that left the 187th, in effect, blind beyond what its own patrols could learn once they hit the ground had also, in effect, left higher level command blind to the Chinese involvement in the conflict that emerged in the coming months.

There was little that the in-theatre leadership could have done about the lack of intelligence. It is difficult to project any IPB available in September 1950 that could have allowed the 187th to liberate the train carrying PoWs. Neither the intelligence sources nor the ability to direct force against a moving and time-critical target existed. With better intelligence, the 3-187th would not have walked into the North Korean ambush that decimated I Company and led to the unexpected pitched battle with the North Korean rearguard. The intelligence infrastructure was being improvised at the time, but it proved to be too late for the prisoner-liberation and enemy-seizure missions.

KOREAN LESSONS

The 187th was to jump again in Korea and gain further battle honours. The US revived its special operations capabilities to meet the challenges of the later stages of the war in Korea and the Cold War alike. In Korea, the US Army formed, committed to combat and then disbanded Ranger companies, with most of their personnel going to the 187th to replace the paratroopers that had carried out the Sukchon–Sunchon drop. Extensive raiding by both the military and the CIA (which during Korea had followed the OSS model by evolving a paramilitary operational capability in addition to intelligence-gathering and analysis) using US, British and Korean forces was carried out, but no US prisoners were liberated.[17]

The political importance of PoWs in Korea was clear throughout the conflict, with PoW-return issues being one of the critical elements in the long-running ceasefire talks that finally ended the conflict. It underlined that in a limited war, such as that in Korea 1950–53, the importance of prisoners as objectives and as sources of leverage will be magnified. The importance of prisoners meant that liberation missions could not be as peripheral to major operations as they were during the Second World War.

The importance of the PoW issue was underlined in 1952 when rioting Communist prisoners took senior US officers hostage at a prison camp on Koje Island off the Korean coast. A raid by the 187th to liberate the hostages was considered. Instead, the camp was assaulted by the 187th reinforced with forces from the 9th Infantry Regiment and the 64th Tank Battalion in a riot-control operation.[18]

The most long-lasting change was the emergence of the US Army Special Forces (who would not get their signature green beret until the early 1960s). This provided an institutional focus to bring together those who would be needed to train for, plan and execute the whole range of future SOF missions.

Korea saw the emergence of the helicopter as an important tool in SOF missions. They had been used, along with light aircraft, to evacuate the 187th's casualties, starting on 21 October. While short-ranged and unarmed in Korea, the helicopter soon demonstrated its ability in combat search and rescue (CSAR) missions, extracting aircrew, who would other-wise have been lost, from behind enemy lines or at sea. Within the next decade, the helicopter would have the benefit of improving technologies, including switching from piston to turbine engines. Greater power meant greater lifting capability (including the ability to carry weapons), greater reliability and longer range. After Korea, liberation and seizure missions would be able to take advantage of the helicopter's unique capabilities.

The advent of the helicopter meant that parachute drops would no longer be the primary means by which liberation or seizure missions would utilize the superior speed and mobility of aircraft to strike with surprise behind enemy lines. In the future, combat airdrops would be used primarily in 'forcible entry' situations, where paratroopers were dropped to seize an airfield or port where reinforcements could be brought in. But paratroopers still remain an important part of major armies worldwide. Even though a fully trained paratrooper costs about 110 per cent of the cost of a trained infantryman on an annual basis, the spirit and high morale of airborne units have given them a value above that provided by their ability to jump. Paratroopers are recognized as being élite infantry that can be used for a broad range of missions. Paratroops also provide the base for other SOF. The overlap between SOF and paratroops – shown by the commitment of air-borne units to liberation missions at Los Banos and Korea (and later Panama) – would continue.

CHAPTER 4 SON TAY, NORTH VIETNAM · 21 November 1970

Nothing could or would have stood in our way to successfully complete that mission except what we encountered – no prisoners at Son Tay.

SGT Joseph Murray, Son Tay raider.

The reconnaissance photographs brought in the first evidence. Images taken by high-flying US SR-71 reconnaissance aircraft of installations near the North Vietnamese town of Son Tay had shown the presence of escape and evasion symbols briefed to US aircrew. US prisoners held near Son Tay had made them. Under the eyes of North Vietnamese guards, they had arranged drying laundry and trodden out patterns in the dirt.

The prison compound itself was a small one, 42 m by 56 m, near the banks of the slow-moving Song Con River and its adjacent marshes. Behind 3 m high walls and concertina wire were barracks, a guardroom and 12 m high trees surrounding a small courtyard. Outside the prison compound itself were the guard force barracks, headquarters and support facilities. There were a number of other North Vietnamese military facilities close to the compound; the largest, designated the 'secondary school' for lack of any better intelligence, was also walled and located some 400 m to the south of the prison compound, separated from it by a canal. Other nearby facilities included an air defence training school and a power plant. Roads connected the area to the nearby town of Son Tay and a bridge over the river.

Repeated aerial reconnaissance missions over the Son Tay prison compound, about 35 km west of Hanoi, identified it as a potential objective for a rescue attempt. However, there were an estimated 12,000 North

Vietnamese troops near the camp and its location put it under the coverage of the enemy Hanoi air defences.[1]

THE PoWS IN NORTH VIETNAM

In the spring of 1970, over 450 US prisoners were being held in Southeast Asia, over eighty per cent of them in North Vietnam. It was known that North Vietnam was holding PoWs under terrible conditions. Reports of deaths in captivity were received in Washington. The prisoners personified the US commitment in Southeast Asia in a way that no institutions or individuals had ever done.

The North Vietnamese treatment of US prisoners had become a major issue in the frustrating process – through direct negotiations in Paris and other channels – to end the conflict. The Nixon administration put diplomatic pressure on North Vietnam to release the prisoners or provide information about them. The US delegation in Paris was instructed to raise the issue on a weekly basis starting in March 1970 – but without success.

The Nixon administration was still committed to 'Vietnamization' – shifting the burden of combat to South Vietnam – and was faced with the problematic combination of eroding political support at home and the need to continue working to defeat persistent communist military and political activity on the ground in Southeast Asia. The treatment of US prisoners in North Vietnam was a major issue with which the administration could rally US and world support. The prisoners consequently became a central US strategic issue, whereas in 1945 and 1950, prisoners and their liberation had been the concern of theatre commanders. Secretary of Defense Melvin Laird had established a team in 1969 to gather intelligence on PoWs and track their movements in North Vietnamese captivity, with the goal of making possible a liberation operation. In 1969, President Nixon asked the Department of Defense for 'unconventional rescue ideas'.

Compounding Washington's frustration at the worsening situation for US PoWs in North Vietnam were the results of the *Pueblo* crisis of 1968. On 23 January 1968, North Korea had seized the intelligence ship USS *Pueblo* on the high seas and held its crew for over a year until a diplomatic solution had secured their release. A liberation mission had not been regarded as feasible. The frustration over the *Pueblo* affair contributed to the pall of failure that hung over the Johnson administration as it left office in January 1969.

The Nixon administration that succeeded it was resolved to avoid the same fate. While a solution to the overall problem of the Southeast Asia conflict was seen as requiring a longer-term approach, the new administration was prepared to act to show that US force could be used to relieve the suffering of US PoWs. Washington wanted the raid.

The national command authority would have to be involved in any raid to liberate US prisoners because it would involve sending US forces, however temporarily, into North Vietnam. Both the Nixon and the Johnson administrations had resisted this step in the past, limiting such actions to non-US personnel, which at least provided some deniability. Now, the PoW situation provided motivation not only for a rescue operation, but for a raid that would increase the US pressure on North Vietnam. The political impact of a raid would be secondary to the liberation of US prisoners, but it would still be highly significant.

The willingness to put US boots on the ground – however briefly – in North Vietnam also distinguished this operation from previous prisoner-rescue operations in the 1960s. There had been forty-five raids on Communist prison sites in South Vietnam, Cambodia and southern Laos. These had not succeeded in freeing a single US prisoner who survived the liberation attempts (although over 300 South Vietnamese were liberated in these missions).[2] Such an approach – and outcome – would obviously be unsatisfactory for a strike against North Vietnam.

SOF FRUSTRATION

The planning of the Son Tay raid came as the Nixon administration was seeking to wind down a US military commitment in Southeast Asia that had built up throughout the 1960s.

The early 1960s had seen the renaissance of US special operations forces. The Kennedy administration's interest in limited wars in the developing world – as opposed to the Eisenhower administration's emphasis on 'massive retaliation' against Communist superpowers – led to an expansion of Army Special Forces (who still revere the president who gave them their green berets) and the re-establishment of the Air Force's Air Commandos. The US Navy formed the Sea-Air-Land (SEAL) teams for special operations. The Marine Corps strengthened the capabilities of its Fleet Marine Force and divisional-level reconnaissance units and took seriously the disciplines of low-intensity conflict. The CIA paramilitary capability increased. In Laos, the US adhered to a treaty banning the presence of foreign forces, consequently waging a covert war that stressed the use of SOF working with indigenous forces. There, as throughout Southeast Asia, the helicopter was key to mobility and resupply, making possible operations that would not have been feasible in the Second World War.

In the opening stages of the Vietnam conflict, SOF had been the US instrument of choice. Those days were long past in 1970. The Special Forces and other unconventional Army warriors had been overshadowed by the conventional US military forces that started to dominate the conflict in 1965.

The lack of a single US command for all the operations in Southeast Asia – divided between headquarters in Washington, Hawaii, Saigon and the embassy in Laos – undercut the effectiveness of SOF. There was no central command – or advocate – for them and their use, no source of expertise that high-level command could rely on or permit to strike at fleeting and time-critical targets without having to secure multiple clearances. Headquarters that had access to intelligence did not also have command of suitable forces to execute operations based on that intelligence. This was a critical reason why many liberation raids prior to Son Tay had failed.

The Air Force Air Commandos were pushed aside by an air war that stressed jet fighter-bombers. However, this change of emphasis did permit the development of one weapon of choice that would prove critical to future special operations: the gunship. This was a heavily armed version of a transport aeroplane – originally C-47s, then C-119s and finally C-130s – with aircraft and ground-unit radios, night-vision sensors and guns, lots of guns, positioned to be fired from the aircraft's broadside. The gunship would go into a banked turn, point a wing at the enemy and produce tremendous fire power, more accurate than any bomb. Originally armed with .30-calibre machine guns, by 1970 the Air Force had 105 mm, 40 mm and 20 mm cannon armaments in AC-130Hs. The Air Force also used long-range helicopter technology to expand the Aerospace Rescue and Recovery Service (ARRS). Their 'Jolly Green Giant' helicopters were a key part of air operations throughout Southeast Asia. The ARRS helicopters' success in rescuing shot-down aircrew from areas with dense enemy air defence coverage or close to enemy units showed that helicopter landings and pick-ups in enemy territory were feasible. The Navy also became highly proficient in CSAR operations. By 1970, saving individual Americans had overshadowed the original objective of saving Southeast Asia; it was not only politically accept- able, it also appeared to be achievable.

RAID PREPARATION

The Son Tay photographs and the proposals for a raid to free the prisoners were brought by the Air Force to the Joint Chiefs of Staff through US Army BG Donald D. Blackburn, Special Assistant for Counterinsurgency and Special Activities (SACSA), to the Chairman of the Joint Chiefs of Staff (CJCS), GEN Earle C. Wheeler. Blackburn was one of the Army's original special opera- tors – he had commanded Filipino guerrillas from 1942 to 1945. He had long been an advocate of integrating US special operations as part of the bombing campaign against North Vietnam, but had been turned down.

The Air Force's original proposal was to liberate a woodcutting detail of five PoWs from the Son Tay camp. Blackburn suggested that they go to the camp itself. 'We later learned of two prison camps which were on the western outskirts of Hanoi; one was at Ap Lo, the other was at Son Tay. I decided that we should make an attempt to rescue prisoners from these camps . . . It was at this point I went to see the CJCS, General Earle Wheeler, and proposed to rescue the PoWs from these two camps. To say the least, he was a little surprised at my proposal and wanted to know how many battal- ions it was going to take to do it. He pointed out the present mood of the country towards any activity in North Vietnam, bombing or otherwise. Naturally, he was a bit concerned about it, but I told him that there was no intention of going in there with a battalion. I was going in there with a small group of men and helicopters, and lift the PoWs out. Well, after discussing it for a while, he said, "Well, Don, if we don't try this, we'd be against mother- hood. We've got to have a good selling point on this. I want you to prepare a briefing for the Joint Chiefs of Staff [JCS]."'[3]

Wheeler was enthusiastic about the potential for a rescue and on 5 June, Blackburn briefed the proposal to the JCS. He was given the go-ahead to carry out a feasibility study for a raid. Blackburn was to act as the high-level advocate and implementer throughout.

A draft operational concept was prepared by SACSA, with the support of the intelligence community. A preliminary plan, codenamed Polar Circle, resulted in the feasibility study being briefed to the JCS on 2 July. The study recommended a raid to liberate PoWs. Intelligence information had shown that the Ap Lo camp had been closed, so the focus was now on Son Tay. The 2 July briefing led to JCS approval on 19 July of SACSA's plan for a raid. The new CJCS, ADM Thomas Moorer – replacing Wheeler – was convinced of the importance of liberating PoWs. He also placed considerable value on the secondary political mission, believing a raid would also 'convey to the North Vietnamese a hard lesson'.[4]

The JCS put in place a mission-specific organization for the rescue on 8 August. This action cut the Gordian knot of the convoluted command arrangements in Southeast Asia that had been fatal to previous potential rescue raids. The operation and the forces that were to carry it out were to be the first ever made directly subordinate to the JCS. They would not be subordinate to any intermediate command. This also ensured that the planning would be kept separate from the in-theatre SOF that had been associated with the previous failures to liberate live US PoWs, most notably the Studies and Operations Group (SOG) of US Military Assistance Command Vietnam (MACV). Unlike the previous raids, this one would be prepared in the US and only forward deployed right before execution. Unlike the previous raids, it would also be an all-US mission, minimizing the chance for compromise inherent in using allied assets.

Blackburn had wanted to command the operation himself, but it was pointed out to him that he was needed in Washington to make it possible.[5] Blackburn appointed as mission commander Brig. Gen. Leroy Manor, a combat veteran fighter pilot currently commanding the US Air Force Special Operations Group at Eglin AFB, Florida. His deputy was COL Arthur D. 'Bull' Simons, already a legend in the US Army's special operations forces, with Second World War service in the 6th Ranger Battalion in New Guinea and the Philippines, as well as more recent combat in Southeast Asia. Blackburn knew his reputation: 'When Bull Simons undertook an operation . . . the research and planning behind it were meticulous.'[6] Simons' choice for ground force commander was LTC Elliott 'Bud' Sydnor, another veteran special operations leader. To lead the assault team that would liberate the prisoners, Simons selected Special Forces veteran CPT Dick Meadows, who had operated under his command in Laos. There, Meadows had planned and executed the ground portion of a heliborne liberation mission using

Laotian forces that freed eighty-seven PoWs from a Pathet Lao prison camp (none of the prisoners were American).

Manor selected Lt. Col. Benjamin Kraljev Jr. as Chief of Operations (J-3) in charge of overall planning and Lt. Col. Warner A. Britton to be the helicopter element leader.[7] Like his ground force counterparts, Britton would select the personnel, train them, plan their use and then lead them on the raid. The chain of command was short, functional and well understood.

Together, starting in late July, they organized the Joint Contingency Task Group (JCTG), codenamed Ivory Coast. The feasibility study group transitioned to an operational planning staff that was to be given the maximum freedom of action by the JCS and SACSA. Manor commented that, 'We had practically a blank check . . . It is the only time in my thirty-six years of active duty that somebody gave me a job, simply stated, and the resources with which to do it, and let me go do it.'[8] They selected Son Tay as the objective of the raid after comparing other potential PoW camps as possible targets.

The high quality of the personnel involved – both in the planning and in the execution of the raid – reflected that while SOF may not have been a priority in Washington or Saigon, there were a lot of combat-experienced SOF personnel available. It was the decisions made in the early 1960s to revive US SOF that ensured the availability of such quality personnel in 1970. The lead time for training quality high-level personnel with the skills to plan and execute high-risk multi-service special operations is lengthy; the lead time for disbanding them or sending them away is instantaneous.

THE PLAN

The plan was based around the concepts of surprise and speed of execution. The intelligence evidence was that there were about sixty prisoners at Son Tay. The compound itself was surrounded by paddies where helicopters could land. The basic approach would be a surprise heliborne assault that would overpower the guards and lift out the prisoners before enemy reinforcements could arrive. The raid would be mounted from a US airbase in Thailand.

The planners put together a special operations version of a 'strike package' that would be able to carry out the mission in the face of North Vietnam's sophisticated air defences. Six US Air Force rescue helicopters – one HH-3 and five HH-53 'Jolly Green Giants' – would carry the raiders and five – one was to be abandoned – would extract them and any liberated prisoners. Providing close air support would be five US Air Force piston-engine A-1E fighter-bombers. The A-1Es would also provide electronic warfare support. Three would carry QRC-128 jammers for disrupting VHF radio communications, to prevent ground-controlled interception of the raid by the North Vietnamese Air Force. Providing in-flight refuelling for the helicopters were two Air Force HC-130P tankers. Navigation and communications for the formation would be handled by two MC-130E Combat Talon special operations aircraft, one leading the helicopters and the other the A-1Es. The MC-130Es would drop flares to illuminate the prison compound.

The numbers of aircraft were all selected on the basis of redundancy. For example, three HH-53s would be needed to lift out the raiders and prisoners; five were brought along, two to lift raiders, one as a gunship, and two as spare flare-dropping ships and to lift PoWs. In addition to the five HH-53s going along on the mission, there were two spares. The Air Force made sure that in total there were ten HH-53s ready for the mission on bases in Thailand. All the participants had too much experience in using helicopters under combat conditions to rely on them functioning correctly. However, each aircraft added to the force made it larger, more difficult to control and more likely to be detected. It also meant more aircrew had to be trained.

Integrated with the strike package that would go to Son Tay were other USAF aircraft that would support the raid. An EC-135 – a jet transport with long-range radios – would function as an airborne command post and com-munications relay, along with two EC-130E ABCCCs and one RC-135M Combat Apple COMINT aircraft, for monitoring both North Vietnamese radio transmissions and those of the raiding force. An EC-121T College Eye would provide radar coverage. Ten USAF F-4E Phantom fighters would block any interception attempts by North Vietnamese MiGs, especially during the egress. They would be joined by a flight of five F-105G 'Wild Weasels' to suppress air defences (a late addition to the operation plan by Manor). Ten KC-135 tankers would orbit to refuel the jets.

The planners counted on maintaining the element of surprise while the raiders were airborne through evasive routing, making maximum use of ter-rain shielding and low-level penetration. The North Vietnamese air defence radar network was set up to defend against US jet aircraft at high and medium altitude, and thus did not have complete low-altitude coverage. Fortunately,

US electronic reconnaissance had been refined throughout the course of previous air operations and gave the planners a good idea of the gaps in the enemy radar defences. However, some of these gaps were only intermittent, and each inbound flight would be required to keep precise timing.

Diversionary attacks were problematic because the US bombing halt against North Vietnam was then in effect. However, Manor had personally arranged – with PACOM's commander-in-chief's blessing – that Navy carrier aircraft would launch a strong diversion from the Gulf of Tonkin – dropping flares rather than bombs – to focus North Vietnam's air defences in the other direction while the raiders approached from over Laos.

The planners divided the Army raiders into three groups, each group carried in a separate helicopter. Redundancy was once again inherent in the planning: the mission could be carried out with any one of the three groups of raiders missing. When the helicopters arrived at the objective, the HH-3 Banana 1 would crash-land inside a small courtyard – surrounded by high trees – within the prison compound. The raiders on this helicopter – the fourteen-man assault group codenamed Blueboy led by Meadows and rein-forced by the helicopter crew – would have to alert the prisoners and release them from their cells while pre-empting any last-minute massacre attempt by their guards. The twenty-three-man support group codenamed Redwine plus Simons, codenamed Wildroot, in HH-53 Apple 1 and the twenty-man command group codenamed Greenleaf plus Sydnor, as alternative ground-force commander, in HH-53 Apple 2 would land outside the walls of the prison, secure the landing zone and then hold it. Ambush positions would be set up to block any potential enemy reinforcements from reaching the prison, with the aid of the supporting A-1Es. Egress was to be accomplished by blowing a hole in the wall of the prison compound. The liberated prison-ers and the assault force were to be loaded aboard within thirty minutes. The plan was designed to be fast in execution, simple, direct and – if not com-promised – was likely to retain the element of surprise.

The planners soon realized that the raid would only succeed in highly specific weather and lighting conditions. It required limited winds and rela-tively cloudless skies to permit formation flying and air refuelling. A quarter moon would provide needed light. This limited the planning to two 'windows' when the raid was likely to be feasible: 21–25 October and 21–24 November.

TRAINING AND REHEARSAL

A request for volunteers for an unknown, dangerous classified mission brought in 500 men at Fort Bragg, North Carolina. Of the 103 Army Special Forces personnel eventually selected, all but two were combat veterans. The USAF CSAR helicopter aircrew selected for the mission had an average of over 4,000 flying hours and all had combat experience. However, none had ever flown an air-assault mission, which would be very different from the CSAR missions they had been used to flying. Volunteers from units in the US and Southeast Asia were brought together for training at Eglin AFB, Florida.

The Army and Air Force components of the JCTG began repeated rehearsals and training at Fort Bragg and Eglin AFB by 20 August. A mock-up of the Son Tay camp was constructed at Eglin (and concealed from Soviet reconnaissance satellites). A detailed scale model was constructed and used by the command staff to war-game out alternative approaches to the raid.

In training, the different Air Force aircraft discovered the difficulties of operating together, especially during the low-altitude penetration phase. The MC-130Es had to cruise at 105 knots, with flaps extended, while the helicopters would try to follow in their slipstreams to keep up, with the A-1Es also throttled back to stay with the force. The lack of compatibility between the tankers and the helicopters was a major issue that had to be resolved by flight planning and rehearsal.

Manor and Simons briefed Laird of their confidence in the mission's success, based on training results, on 24 September. On 28 September – the day after the final plan for the raid had been briefed to the President and approved in principle – the training shifted from separate efforts at Eglin and Fort Bragg to joint operations at both locations.

Two all-night full-profile mission rehearsals were carried out (with JCS observers) when Air Force and Army components exercised together, with live fire, starting on 28 September and culminating in a full-scale rehearsal on 6 October. The ground phase of the operation was carried out in twenty-five minutes. By November, the raiders had practised their actions on the ground 170 times. The air elements of the force had flown 268 sorties and logged over 1,000 hours over seventy-seven days. Rehearsal and planning for unforeseen contingencies absorbed much of the time.

Despite the September go-ahead, the White House was concerned about the raid's potential impact on US diplomacy, most notably the rapprochement with China that was then being pursued through secret diplomatic channels. National Security Advisor Henry Kissinger wanted to push back the date of the raid, increasing the attendant risks of security compromise and prisoner movement.[9] This led to a White House decision – after checking feasibility with the JCS – to slip the proposed date for the raid from 21 October to 21 November. While the rescue element remained paramount in the minds of those training to carry out the mission, the use of the raid to make a policy statement was seen as an important goal in Washington.

Manor used the delay for additional training and equipment improvements, and to identify problems encountered in the full-scale rehearsal. The MC-130Es received state-of-the-art Texas Instruments FL-2B forward-looking infra-red (FLIR) equipment. The raiders received commercial Single-Point laser night-sights for their M16 rifles. Facilities for evacuating and caring for the PoWs – likely to be in bad physical condition – were expanded.

Repeated out-of-season typhoons moved through the target region. Rivers near Son Tay were rising, fed by rainfall from Laos resulting from US cloud-seeding and weather-modification efforts intended to slow the flow of North Vietnamese resupply to their forces in South Vietnam. The Son Tay planners were not aware of these weather-modification efforts or their potential impact on the raid, as both the raid and the weather-modification efforts were highly classified and compartmentalized activities.

Unknown to the Ivory Coast task force, imagery on the Son Tay compound was showing a decrease in activity. An SR-71 sortie on 3 October brought back photos that showed no sign of occupation, while other imagery showed continued occupation of the site by someone. US prisoners of war held at Son Tay had also sent out coded messages in letters home as to when they were to be moved. While US intelligence knew of these messages, the highly compartmentalized nature of the raid meant that this information was not available to the raiders.[10]

Despite the ambiguous intelligence, however, there would be no review of the plan or the intelligence that provided the basis for it – including the presence of prisoners at Son Tay. Fear of compromise led the JCS to turn down Manor's request for an outside expert review of the final plan.

On 8 October, Blackburn, Manor and Simons went to the White House. They briefed Kissinger and his military assistant, BG Alexander Haig, promising them a '95–97 per cent assurance of success'. Kissinger was enthusiastic. However, there were concerns that if the plan was compromised, the entire raiding force could be captured, leaving the North Vietnamese with even more prisoners. Simons' greatest fear was that the North Vietnamese had somehow learned of the coming raid and would have an overwhelming force set up in ambush positions. If no helicopter pick-up was possible, Simons planned to fight it out with the raiders' backs to the river. He realized that breaking up the raiding party and attempting to escape and evade (E&E) was unlikely to be successful. These were not idle concerns. Simons was aware that many US special operations in Southeast Asia had been compromised. The Soviet cryptological capability – enabled by the Walker spy ring and other Soviet intelligence successes that gave them access to US codes – would, in hindsight, have made such a compromise a substantial risk.

Following the briefing to Kissinger, Manor made a high-level trip to the area of operations, briefing Adm. John S. McCain Jr., the PACOM commander-in-chief, GEN Creighton Abrams, the commander in Vietnam, and GEN Lucius Clay, commander of the Seventh Air Force. Manor conducted in-depth planning with the Navy's Task Force 77, off the Gulf of Tonkin, for a diversionary strike.

DEPLOYMENT

After a final briefing directly to President Nixon and Kissinger – followed by a further meeting which included ADM Moorer as well as the Secretaries of State and Defense – a coded go-ahead message was sent to Manor to carry out what was now designated Operation Kingpin. The raiders received the go-ahead to deploy to Thailand from Eglin AFB, setting out on 12 November and arriving by 17 November.

While the final briefings were carried out in Thailand, more intelligence became available pointing to the likelihood that Son Tay was empty. There was a great deal of concern among the few officials in Washington that were aware of the mission, concern reflected in intelligence community briefings. A reliable diplomatic report was received from Hanoi that the prisoners had been moved, but this could not be confirmed by air photography. ADM Moorer personally went through photographs with senior intelligence officials. BG Blackburn and Defense Secretary Melvin Laird repeated these reports in person to the President on 18 November.

Laird had taken a hands-on role in the PoW issue. 'We knew the camp was active and had been for several years. The decision to execute was based on this intelligence. However, we knew there was a possibility there were no PoWs there. After all, we had no hard evidence of their presence, only indications from camps known to house PoWs that were similar to the conditions and activity found at Son Tay. The raiding force knew of this possibility also . . . The Hanoi information was simply not believable.'[11] Manor, Simons and the now-deployed task force were not informed of the Hanoi information.

On 18–19 November, more new photographs came in suggesting that Son Tay was empty. While the Defense Intelligence Agency (DIA) was now recommending that the raid be postponed, Blackburn was unconvinced by the new intelligence. Infra-red imagery showed the compound to be occupied, although it was impossible to tell whether by North Vietnamese troops or US prisoners. A follow-on reconnaissance sortie to provide conclusive evidence had to be cancelled due to bad weather. Blackburn told Moorer that 'with a 95–97 per cent confidence that the raiders could get in and out safely, it was worth the try even if the PoWs were not there.'[12] The DIA was won over. The Pentagon urged the White House not to cancel the raid.

Nixon gave the final go-ahead on 20 November, asking, 'How could anyone not approve this?' He had a final meeting with Laird, during which they reviewed the latest US-generated intelligence, and he was aware there was a 'fairly high confidence' that Son Tay was empty and that there was at best only a ten to fifteen per cent chance of even a few prisoners being there. It is uncertain in what context the President heard about the Hanoi information.[13] He heard a CIA estimate that up to ten additional PoWs had died in captivity. Nixon believed that the risks were acceptable and that the secondary political benefits of a successful raid made it worthwhile to run those risks even if there were no PoWs at Son Tay.

After receiving the high-priority JCS 'Red Rocket' message to go, Manor used his authority to bring forward the date of the raid to 20–21 November from 21–22 November, reflecting the likelihood of bad weather on the later date. Raiding and rescue forces, once assembled and rehearsed, can be wasting instruments. Once the force was trained and deployed, the decision-makers were soon presented with a 'use it or lose it' decision. If use was delayed, the chances for compromise and security leaks increased, especially if training was to continue in-theatre. The alternative – to discontinue training – would result in the force's capabilities being dulled. The decision to launch the raid was made with the full knowledge that keeping it in readiness for the next opportunity would prove difficult.

Manor chose to monitor the raid not from the EC-135, as had been planned, but from the plot room at the Monkey Mountain radar station near Da Nang in South Vietnam. He had radio links to the carriers, the EC-135 and the bases in Thailand. Another staff member had been dispatched to the US base at Yokota, Japan, to pass on intelligence from any last-minute SR-71 photos that might become available. But Manor made it clear that he would not second-guess Simons, who was in the field.

Simons pared down his force in Thailand, selecting fifty-six men to go on the raid from the 100 who had trained and deployed. The final briefing was given by Simons at the Takhli airbase theatre at mid-afternoon on 20 November, revealing the identity of the target that the force had been training for so long to raid. Up until that time, Simons, Sydnor and Meadows were the only soldiers who knew the identity of the target. 'This is something American prisoners have a right to expect from their fellow soldiers,' Simons told the raiders. Simons' briefing went on to stress the importance of decisive action, the need for rapid action on the ground, care of wounded, CSAR procedures and the need to fight together as a complete unit in case of disaster (a large North Vietnamese force waiting in ambush). At the end of the briefing, the troops gave Simons a standing ovation.[14]

Later that day, the raiders boarded transports for the flight to Udorn airbase, Thailand, where the helicopters and were waiting. Fifty-nine Navy aircraft on three carriers in the Gulf of Tonkin prepared to launch for the diversionary strike. The Air Force covertly brought CSAR forces to alert on air bases in Thailand, in case any of the raiders went down.

INGRESS

The helicopters, their MC-130E lead ship – the flare-dropper Cherry 1 – and the two HC-130P tankers Lime 1 and Lime 2 commenced their formation takeoff at 2256 (local time) from Udorn on 20 November, where the raiders had arrived earlier that evening from Takhli. Cherry 1 had its takeoff delayed by twenty-three minutes due to engine problems, but was able to catch up in flight. The five A-1Es, call signs Peach 1–5, and their MC-130E Cherry 2 lead ship had left their base at Nakhon Phanom at

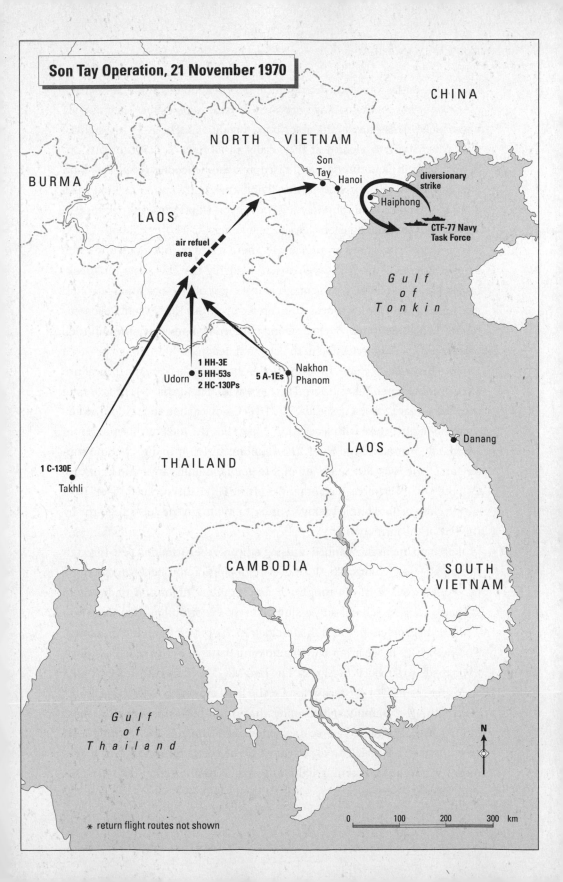

Son Tay Operation, 21 November 1970

CHINA

NORTH VIETNAM

BURMA

LAOS

Son Tay

Hanoi

diversionary strike

Haiphong

CTF-77 Navy Task Force

air refuel area

Gulf of Tonkin

1 HH-3E
5 HH-53s
2 HC-130Ps

Udorn

5 A-1Es

Nakhon Phanom

LAOS

Danang

THAILAND

1 C-130E

Takhli

CAMBODIA

SOUTH VIETNAM

Gulf of Thailand

N

0   100   200   300   km

* return flight routes not shown

2224. The entire force taxied, took off and formed up in total radio silence.

Once airborne, the package operated in total radio silence, just as they had trained. This proved critical for both formations. The A-1s lost sight of their MC-130E but rejoined at their cruising altitude of 2,590 m. An unknown aircraft flew through and disrupted the helicopter formation soon after takeoff. Capt. Jay Strayer was flying the right seat of Lt. Col. John Allison's Apple 2. 'We routinely fell into seven-ship formation, three helicopters stacked high on each side of the leading HC-130[P] at about 1,500 feet [457 m] AGL [above ground level]. There was a partial moon and some clouds that we climbed through when suddenly the call came to "break, break, break!" indicating someone had lost sight of the formation lead and we were to execute the formation break-up procedure. Each helicopter turned to a predetermined heading and climbed to a predetermined altitude for one minute then returned to the original heading.'[15]

The helicopters went through their rehearsed silent rejoin procedure after evading potential collision. The force was able to stay together despite the differences in cruising speeds. The HH-3, slower than the rest of the formation, had to cruise with 'everything open but the toolbox', its maximum speed only just above the HC-130P's stalling speed. It had to ride the slipstream of the HC-130P in an attempt to get additional range and knots. Lt. Col. Bill Kornitzer, aircraft commander of the HC-130P, recalled, 'The HH-3 stayed close behind our left wing in order to maintain the speed required by the rest of the formation.'[16]

Levelling out at the planned cruising altitude, the formation flew through the tops of low clouds. The low-level refuelling of the helicopters by the HC-130Ps over Laos – in rough air conditions, at night and under radio silence – was carried out successfully. The A-1E formation then joined up with the helicopters to travel the final leg to the prison as an integral force. The HC-130Ps broke away, one to a holding pattern, one to refuel at Udorn to be ready to support the egress. The two MC-130Es with their new FLIRs took over the lead of the formation for the final approach to the target.

Anything on a military helicopter that is not broken is going to break. Maj. Fredrick Donohue's Apple 3 experienced a transmission warning light *en route* to the target. The experienced flight crew, surmising that it was more likely that the warning light was malfunctioning than the transmission, elected – correctly – to press on regardless.

The F-4s and F-105Gs, having finished refuelling from the KC-135s, took up their covering positions, but the North Vietnamese air defences did not 'light up'. The careful planning based on thorough SIGINT IPB meant that the helicopters of the raiding force had been able to operate at 457 m above the ground rather than the extremely low terrain-following altitude that would have precluded refuelling. As the force approached Son Tay, the Navy diversionary operation had clearly succeeded in focusing North Vietnamese attention on the Hanoi–Haiphong area.

OBJECTIVE REACHED

The objective was reached at 0218 on 21 November.[17] Cherry 1, the lead MC-130E which was navigating for the helicopters at 152 m altitude, gave a final vector and then opened the show, climbing up to 457 m and dropping four flares and two pyrotechnic simulators on the 'secondary school' (to make any troops there believe that they were under attack). Cherry 1 then flew to an orbit point over Laos.

Cherry 2 came in next, leading the A-1Es, and dropped two napalm markers for their ground reference, then departed for a holding point 15 nmi west. Two HH-53s – Apple 4 and Apple 5 – waited for the order to drop additional flares (in case those from the MC-130E fizzled) or pick up liberated prisoners. They and three A-1Es pulled up and away into holding patterns over small uninhabited islands on a lake 7 nmi west of Son Tay. The remaining three HH-53s, the HH-3 and two A-1Es headed for the prison compound.

Apple 3, the lead HH-53 – which was to function as a gunship – was swinging into position for its firing run on the prison guard towers when, at the last minute, the crew realized they were lining up on the wrong target – the complex called the 'secondary school', 400 m south of the prison compound. They broke off the attack, still under radio silence, and, followed by the HH-3, made a firing run against the actual prison compound, which the crew spotted to the north. Apple 3 swept low over the prison compound between the high trees, its door gunners using three GAU-2B 7.62 mm miniguns, shooting down the two prison guard towers and spraying the guard barracks, as had been practised innumerable times at Eglin. It then broke away to a holding area, awaiting the order to return to pick up liberated prisoners.

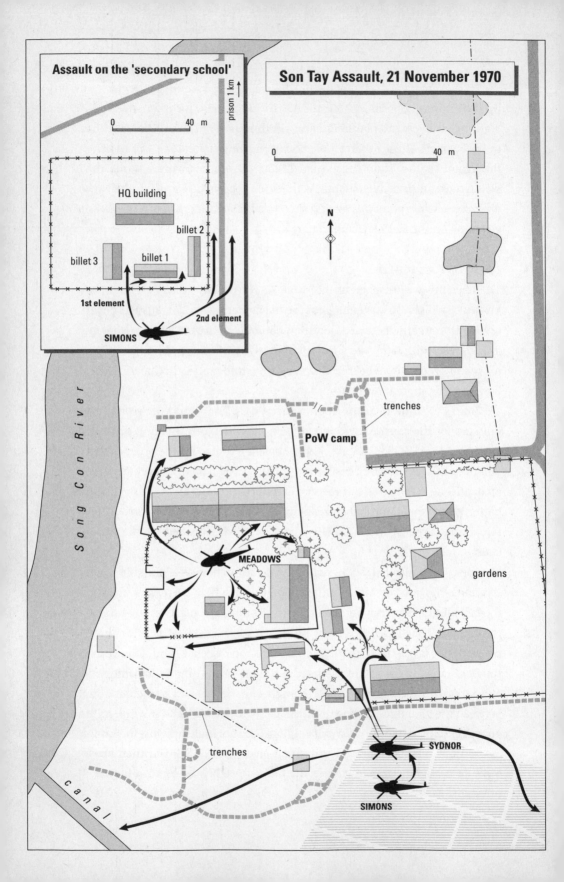

Assault on the 'secondary school'

Son Tay Assault, 21 November 1970

0 ——— 40 m

prison 1 km

HQ building

billet 2

billet 3

billet 1

1st element

2nd element

SIMONS

N

0 ——— 40 m

Song Con River

trenches

PoW camp

MEADOWS

gardens

trenches

canal

SYDNOR

SIMONS

Maj. John Waresh, one of the A-1E pilots, watched the attack from his holding pattern: 'A computer simulation could not have been better timed . . . The towers either blew apart or caught fire, as did the guard quarters.'[18]

Following Apple 3 to the prison compound was Banana 1, the HH-3 flown by Lt. Col. Herb Zehnder and Maj. Herb Kale. Its gunners opened fire with its M60 doorguns during the approach to the prison, and then the helicopter went into its controlled-crash-landing descent, spiralling down through trees and obstacles.

Any landing you can walk away from is a good one. Dick Meadows and his thirteen-man assault group and the helicopter crew – even the flight engineer who had broken an ankle during the landing – were able to grab their CAR-15s. The raiders stormed into the prison buildings. The helicopter crew guarded their flanks against North Vietnamese reinforcements and prepared to assist liberated prisoners.

Meadows announced impending liberation loudly through a bullhorn as two-man search parties fanned out through the compound. Surprised by the raid, only a few of the estimated fifty-five North Vietnamese soldiers in the compound resisted. About a dozen were quickly cut down. Most retreated into the darkness. The search parties opened locked cells with bolt cutters; all were empty.

The next two HH-53s, Apple 1 and Apple 2, carrying Simons and the support group and Sydnor and the command and security group respectively, were disorientated by the actions of Apple 3, which had been flying lead. As they recovered their night vision after the flash of the initial attack, the crew of Apple 1 landed not outside the prison, as briefed, but outside the 'secondary school' compound, 400 m south of the prison compound. This had been the compound Apple 3 had originally lined up to strafe, by mistake. Simons and the support group troops jumped out. Apple 1 quickly lifted off to the holding area 1.5 nmi west of Son Tay.

Apple 2 was on final approach to the same LZ when its crew realized that it, too, was in the wrong place. It abandoned its approach to the 'secondary school' and flew on north to the prison compound, its gunners engaging the remaining guard towers before putting Sydnor and the command and security group down into the planned LZ about 100 m from the prison compound's south wall, then joining Apple 1 at the holding area.

Sydnor, informed by the helicopter crew that Apple 1 was not where it was supposed to be, had only to come up on the raiders' tactical frequency and broadcast that Plan Green was in effect – an alternate plan that had been rehearsed many times – for the command and security group to secure the outside of the prison compound and the LZ without the help of the support group. Sydnor called on the A-1Es to supplement his reduced fire power. The two A-1Es that had accompanied the helicopters then attacked a nearby bridge with four white phosphorus bombs, then worked over the approach road with six Rockeye cluster-bomb units, further isolating the prison, before taking up a holding pattern around the napalm marker, waiting for any further call from the raiders. Sydnor and the command group moved swiftly to secure the LZ, seizing and securing the buildings that could be used to bring direct fire on it. They came under fire from scattered North Vietnamese. Security elements moved out to secure the area and set up ambush positions with claymores to defend against counterattacks. A pathfinder set up a beacon for pick-up in the LZ. The well-rehearsed teams of raiders encountered surprised North Vietnamese who were starting to resist. Detonation charges were used to drop a tower to clear the LZ.

While Sydnor and the command group were securing the LZ south of the prison wall, Simons and the support group were confronting the 'secondary school'. It turned out to be a barracks full of troops, blasted awake and grabbing AK-47s and bandoleers. Simons led his support group into an attack on the compound, shooting down enemy soldiers as they ran to entrenchments or opened fire from the windows and doorways of the buildings. The element of surprise was with the raiders. Accurate M79 40 mm grenade-launcher fire through the windows soon suppressed fire from the buildings. An M60 machine gun was used to silence firing from the west side of the compound. A fuel storage shed caught fire, illuminating the scene. Large numbers of the enemy – an estimated 100 – fell, with only one raider wounded. Simons led the attack into the 'secondary school' compound, clearing the billet at its southern end with grenades.

During an intense five-minute close-quarters firefight, the raiders thought the enemy were Chinese troops (they had been briefed to expect the Chinese line-of-communication and air-defence units that had in fact been in the area until shortly before the raid). They were big, tall men, fighting hard in the T-shirts and dark undershorts they had been sleeping in. They were most likely actually troops from the North Vietnamese 305th Airborne

Brigade, who were being trained for counter-special operations tasks in Laos.[19] In any event, Simons' attack put them out of action while the raiders were on the ground.

Within six minutes of its initial landing, Apple 1, recalled from its holding area, was back where it had dropped Simons off. The M60 gunner, Simons and his radio operators put down suppressive fire. The surviving defenders of the 'secondary school' compound were in no shape to interfere. Some nine minutes after H-Hour, after a short helicopter flight, Simons linked up with Sydnor in the LZ outside the prison walls. There was a brief exchange of fire between the two groups of raiders as they linked up, quickly halted without any casualties. The members of the command and support groups then carried out pre-briefed tasks: clearing a nearby pump house and demolition of a power station and poles (to clear the LZ).

Inside the prison, Meadows and his force searched the compound. It was empty of prisoners. Meadows' bullhorn echoed off empty walls as the search parties ran back to him to report that cells, bomb shelters and basements alike were all empty. Once this had been confirmed, at H+10 minutes, Meadows radioed a 'negative items' message to Simons, confirming that the 'items' were long gone. Pausing only long enough to destroy the remains of the crashed HH-3, Meadows led his force to rejoin Simons and Sydnor, exiting the prison compound at H+18 through a hole blown in the south-west wall by detonation charges. Having received the 'negative items' message, Simons made a radio call over the raiders' tactical net: 'Prepare to withdraw to the LZ for extraction. Command and assault groups exit on first extraction helicopter. Set up LZ security, command group to west, support to east.'[20]

EGRESS

As Meadows was leading his force to rejoin Simons and his support team, Sydnor's security perimeter around the main LZ saw a North Vietnamese convoy of four or five light trucks heading for the prison, apparently unaware of the situation. The lead trucks drove into an ambush with the raiders, who used 66 mm light antitank weapons (LAWs) to knock out the lead vehicles before withdrawing. The North Vietnamese were in no position to interfere with the withdrawal.

Two helicopters were called in to pick up the raiders at H+14 minutes. The inbound Apple 1 asked for a flare to mark the LZ; Peach 1 and 2 were called in to strafe as Apple 1 approached, hitting a bridge north of the prison. Peach 3 and 4 flew close escort for the withdrawing helicopters. Peach 5, navigation lights on, trolled for MiGs. Apple 1 landed at H+18, followed by Apple 2 at H+22 minutes, and by H+27 minutes had loaded all the raiders. Simons and the security elements were the last to leave, counted aboard to ensure no one was left behind. The total time on the ground had been twenty-eight minutes. Surprise had been complete, with only one minor gunshot wound sustained among the raiding force. Repeated headcounts, exchanged by radio, established that no raiders had been left behind.

Egress to Thailand, with North Vietnamese air defences now fully alerted, proved to be more problematic. Apple 3's rotor transmission warning light re-lit and this time an emergency was declared. There were radio reports of MiG fighters being scrambled against the raid, causing the helicopters to take evasive action, but none were encountered. At least sixteen SA-2 surface-to-air missiles (SAM) were fired at the force – mainly at the fighter escort – as it withdrew. One of the F-105G 'Wild Weasels' covering the raiders' withdrawal lost a confrontation with a SAM site, its two-man crew ejecting over Laos. The returning A-1Es peeled off from the Son Tay force and were able to set up a RESCAP over their position until reserve HH-53s Apple 4 and 5 could come in and pick the crew up, refuelling from an HC-130 on the way home.

At Udorn, the recovery base, the overall attitude was one of sadness at the mission's failure to rescue prisoners. The Air Force and Army raiders sat together on the Tarmac. 'We were all just sat mumbling to each other. No stories were being told. We had all just done it, seen it, or heard it and knew what had happened,' Maj. John Waresh recalled.[21]

The prisoners still in North Vietnam, however, were more enthusiastic when they heard about the raid. Lt. Col. Wes Schierman had been a prisoner for five years at the time of the raid, eighteen months of that at Son Tay: 'It was quite exciting. We didn't know exactly what it was all about. Eventually, we figured that out. We got some information from the outside that there had been a raid to rescue prisoners. We were ecstatic, of course, knowing that . . . The Son Tay raiders are our heroes, for sure.'[22] Moved out of reach of another raid, the prisoners would not be liberated until a peace settlement was made over two years after the Son Tay mission.

POTENTIAL FOLLOW-ON RAIDS

After returning to base, some of the raiders pleaded with Simons for a chance to go back the next night to another potential prison location. Surely, they said, the North Vietnamese could not move all their prisoners literally overnight. But this was, of course, impossible. The way that the Son Tay raid had been carried out ensured that it was not repeatable. The North Vietnamese were now aware of the tactics employed. The raid had achieved its success in execution in large part through meticulous target-specific planning and thorough rehearsal. There was no way that could be repeated. The raiders, Army and Air Force alike, dispersed and went back to their units. Blackburn was sent to an Army research and development position until his retirement six months later. It would be a long time before there was a special operator of his rank and experience working for the JCS.

As before Son Tay, in the years that followed there were liberation missions in South Vietnam, Laos and Cambodia, but never again in North Vietnam – although a number of such operations were proposed and planned. A large-scale liberation mission that would have involved the 82nd Airborne Division and US Special Forces groups making a large-scale raid against Hanoi itself was considered in Washington but never became a viable option.[23] There have been rumours and unconfirmed reports that Pathet Lao perception of an imminent liberation mission motivated a massacre of a number of allied PoWs, possibly in 1971.

In 1972, Operation Thunderhead, an attempt to liberate PoWs escaping from the 'Hanoi Hilton' prison in the capital, was called off. The PoW leadership – now concentrated together, possibly as a result of the Son Tay raid – thought it not worth the risk with the end of the war apparently near. One Navy SEAL, inserted to receive the escapees at the mouth of the Red River, was killed jumping from a Navy helicopter.

ASSESSING AN AMBIGUOUS RESULT

To the men planning the raid, the goal may have been focused on rescuing fellow American fighting men, but liberation missions cannot be disaggregated from their larger policy concerns.

The raid had failed in its primary objective of freeing prisoners. Most of the prisoners had in fact been taken out of Son Tay on 24 July. The remainder followed over the next two months. However, by demonstrating the vulnerability of dispersed camps, the North Vietnamese were encouraged in their new policy – which appears to have started before the raid – to concentrate their prisoners in the 'Hanoi Hilton'. They were forced to discontinue their repressive regime of solitary confinement.

In Washington, the impact of the raid – the first US ground force incursion into North Vietnam itself – had to be assessed in the broader terms of overall Southeast Asia policy. In Washington, elements that had seemed secondary to the raid planners were of paramount importance – in particular, demonstrating US resolve and threatening North Vietnam with targeted air-mobile attacks instead of a less-credible large-scale invasion.

In terms of its secondary objectives of sending a message to Hanoi on the prisoner issue and highlighting continued US resolve, there is no way of evaluating the effectiveness of the Son Tay raid. Hanoi and its supporters did not try to emphasize the raid as an example of US escalation, as they had with the recent US incursion into Cambodia. Most likely, the fact that the raid had succeeded so well was embarrassing enough for the North Vietnamese to let it pass. Initial US media treatment of the raid was largely negative. Opponents of Nixon's Vietnam policy held hearings on the raid in the Senate, but there was little enthusiasm for retrospective opposition to an operation intended to liberate US PoWs.

At a purely tactical level, the raid was a success, with over 100 enemy casualties inflicted without serious losses. It also demonstrated the US capability to plan and execute such raids. Son Tay served as a demonstration of what special operations could accomplish. It also illustrated the fundamental problems of such liberation operations. Planning for liberation operations must deal not only with the capability of captors to massacre their prisoners at the moment of rescue, but also with their ability to move prisoners in secret before planned raids can take place. The lengthy planning and execution required for the Son Tay raid could counter the first danger, but not the second.

Son Tay illustrated both the potential strengths and limitations of intelligence contribution to the success of rescue operations. Liberation missions require precise, accurate and timely intelligence in order to be successful. The raid owed its inception to reconnaissance photographs. The intelligence community was involved throughout the planning process. It provided indications that the prisoners might have been moved away, but no one was willing to halt the raid – with a good chance of success projected – as long as it remained possible that there were some prisoners still at Son Tay. However, the intelligence support of the raid did not pick up the presence of a substantial military force at the 'secondary school' compound. It was simply good fortune that Simons' support group came down there by mistake and was able to stage an impromptu *coup de main* to remove this unforeseen potential threat to the raiders' withdrawal.

Intelligence was also unaware that as a result of Operation Popeye, the US weather modification campaign over Laos, the level of the Song Con River had been raised in July. The river rose close to the prison walls and may have contributed to the evacuation of Son Tay camp.[24] While this is unlikely to have affected the final outcome – the North Vietnamese were already consolidating their previously dispersed prison camps before the flooding occurred – it does underscore the problems inherent in a situation where special operations are being planned alongside – but without knowledge of – other highly compartmentalized intelligence programmes intended to be kept highly confidential even within the intelligence community.

However, the results of the raid cannot be considered an intelligence failure. Blackburn thought 'the intelligence was absolutely superb'.[25] Even though the raiders did not know of the last-minute decision in Washington to go through with the raid, they knew as much about the objective as they could know in the absence of effective HUMINT.

The lack of HUMINT on the ground in the Son Tay area was a key limitation. About two months before the operation, the US was reportedly able to insert a single agent into the Son Tay area, but he had been unable to report back anything of value.

There was concern that HUMINT activity might compromise the raid. Blackburn commented, '[I] did learn that there was a CIA team that had gone across the Laotian border, but I didn't know what they were doing. They had come out of Laos and were operating in North Vietnam. I got a little disturbed about it because we were going to fly over Laos and land in North Vietnam shortly thereafter. And they were in an area that I would have liked to see quiet and not be disturbed.'[26]

There was no way that US intelligence assets could have confidence that the prisoners had been moved (as they proved to have been) or that enemy forces had occupied the 'secondary school' complex outside the prison. That considerable gaps remained in this knowledge underlines the risks inherent in any liberation mission – risks that cannot be compensated for even by the most responsive intelligence. Manor summed this up when he said, 'I can unequivocally state that, other than the absence of prisoners at the objective, there were no major surprises in the operation.'[27]

The Son Tay raid was the first combat operation ever to take place under the direct command of the Joint Chiefs of Staff. The command system was enabled by 'stovepipe' priority communications channels between the National Military Command Center in the Pentagon and the raiding force. Yet despite having this capability, neither the White House nor the JCS used this capability to micro-manage the mission.

Manor was effectively empowered to make plans and changes on the spot. This was demonstrated by his ability to set up and co-ordinate the Navy's diversionary air strikes, his decision to move up the date of the execution of the raid and to add a SAM-suppression component to the mission in the form of five F-105G 'Wild Weasels'. The one major failure is that, while Washington was willing to delegate effective decision-making responsibility, they restricted access to the most significant intelligence. Thus, Washington knew that it was much more likely that the prisoners had been moved than the raiders did. It is likely that Manor would have still gone ahead with the raid even if he had received this information, but the fact remains that he should have been empowered to make a fully informed decision.

The key men for both planning and execution – Blackburn, Manor, Simons, Sydnor, Britton and Meadows – were experienced special operators able to improvise a command structure for this one mission, pull together the force and integrate it through effective rehearsals. The raiders carried out their mission as briefed. Fortunately, at that time, the Vietnam War had provided these leaders with combat-proven Army and Air Force personnel, most of them also known personally to the leaders, from whom they could select to make up the force. Even when there was a problem – such as Simons' landing at the 'secondary school' – these experienced men were able to think on their feet and carry on with the objective of the mission.

In many ways, Son Tay was a success of planning. There was no area where it was likely to suffer single-point failure. The raid was basically 'conducted as planned'.[28] The joint integration was a success. Army and Air

Force – as well as the Navy diversion – functioned together. Effective planning compensated for limitations in equipment. The lack of long-range helicopter capability was worked around through effective rehearsal and provision of HC-130P tankers with trained crews. The importance of the rehearsals by the air and ground components – both separately and jointly – was demonstrated on the ingress to the target, when weather conditions would likely have forced the mission to abort had they not already rehearsed bad-weather, no-lights low-altitude refuelling under conditions of radio silence.

However, while the contingency that Simons most feared as a result of the experience of previous liberation missions in Southeast Asia – intelligence compromise – did not take place, the presence of what appears to have been North Vietnamese counter-SOF forces preparing for combat in Laos (rather than the Chinese air-defence or line-of-communication troops the raiders had been briefed to expect) made the potential for the raid turning into a deadly battle of attrition a possibility that no planning could have prevented.

The importance of rehearsal and training was demonstrated throughout, but so was that of luck. The unplanned attack on the 'secondary school' prevented a raid-reaction counterattack against the prison compound. Simons' group was able to defeat the force at the 'secondary school', then disengage and carry out the remainder of its original mission without prolonging the time the raiders spent on the ground. It functioned as a spoiling attack, preventing a reaction by the (presumed) North Vietnamese forces there. Luck compensated for the limits of intelligence.

Yet despite these successes, in some ways Son Tay was limited by its mission-specific *ad hoc* organization and command structure. It was one reason why the operation took so long to organize and prepare for launch. The Son Tay raid avoided OPSEC and command problems through its 'stovepipe' command requirements, which subordinated it directly to the JCS. At Son Tay, a mission-specific force had to be organized, trained, rehearsed and then disbanded after the operation. It was intended for a single operation against a single objective. There was no capability for repeated liberation missions or simultaneous liberation missions. As at Los Banos and Sukchon–Sunchon, repeatability and tempo were not considerations. The raid was intended from the outset to be a one-off. Blackburn later commented that 'if there had been an organization in being, one that was joint in nature, one that could be responsive to this type of operation, it wouldn't have taken as long. I've always felt there was a deficiency within our force structure in not having some organization on standby that can do this [kind of] operation.'[29] Such an organization would not emerge until the 1980s, motivated by later, more costly, setbacks. The lessons that would have prevented these future setbacks had been available from the Son Tay experience, but after Vietnam, no one noticed. After all, special operations, after Son Tay, were largely considered a thing of the past.

One aspect where Blackburn himself faulted the planning and organization of the operation was in failing to consider the press and public-relations impact. 'I think that the public relations side of this operation should have been made more deliberate because, regardless of the outcome, the American press was going to have its impact upon the populace. I felt that we could not just sit back and wait until the results of this operation were final before addressing these two aspects. In other words, an ounce of prevention is worth a pound of cure, and it turned out that the press was none too favourable . . . I still think for any such operations in the future, these points should be seriously considered.'[30]

However, Son Tay was only one of over 125 liberation missions launched by the US and its allies over the course of the Vietnam War. They liberated over 500 Vietnamese and recovered 110 American bodies. But no American prisoners were liberated and survived during these missions. Many of the other raids shared some of the reasons for their failures with Son Tay. Reaction times tended to be too long to utilize transient intelligence information. Many liberation missions that did not have the Son Tay raid's elaborate operational security were apparently compromised, through enemy HUMINT (widespread Communist infiltration of all allied forces and groups), COMINT (North Vietnam had an extensive if unsophisticated intercept and exploitation capability and US communications discipline was generally poor) and possibly Soviet-provided decrypts of US secure communications. This underlined the importance of operational security. Ironically, the manner of implementation of this lesson from Son Tay was to contribute to the failure of the Iran raid in 1980.

The US command structure, highly centralized, required high-level staffing and approval difficult to reconcile with the time-critical nature of liberation missions. Son Tay worked because no one micro-managed or second-guessed Manor. But the same could not be said for in-theatre operations. There was no single headquarters devoted to the liberation mission in Southeast Asia. There was no force or headquarters with access to resources, intelligence and the means of avoiding a fragmented and slow-moving chain of command. Inter-service rivalries, even when overlooked by those actually planning raids, were stirred up when plans were reviewed by higher headquarters, insisting that each service be involved or that preferred units or weapons be used. The divisions inherent within the US and allied governments and headquarters opposing an enemy that could easily move (and move prisoners) across international borders made it difficult to assign responsibility and maintain focus.[31] The US was never able to come to grips with the requirements for successful liberation missions during the Vietnam War.

It would be a long time before US SOF would again be as capable as they were at Son Tay. Once the Son Tay raiders were dispersed, they could not be called back. The capability was lost almost as thoroughly as if the force had been defeated. All SOF would be associated with fighting the wrong kind of war in Southeast Asia. It would require a number of setbacks and humiliations before US SOF and their missions began to receive once more the sort of resources that Manor and Simons were allocated in 1970. It would be even longer before liberation missions could be carried out by joint service forces and integrated with other theatre forces while maintaining OPSEC. To do so would require the putting in place – during peacetime – of a system for managing such operations, whereas the Son Tay raid relied on a few people with combat-honed skills brought together for a one-time mission.

CHAPTER 5 THE *MAYAGUEZ* INCIDENT, KOH TANG, CAMBODIA · 15 May 1975

*President Ford and Secretary Kissinger demanded
from the military a speed of performance that it could
not provide and forces were committed piecemeal and
pell-mell from different services and different doctrines
and unused to working with each other. There
were far too many cooks in this broth.*

VADM George P. Steele, USN, Commanding the Seventh Fleet, 1975.

The *Mayaguez* incident was resolved with a hastily mounted operation that used three simultaneous but uncoordinated raids to liberate a ship's crew and recapture the ship itself. The ship's crew was released unharmed by their captors during the course of the raid. The operation itself demonstrated many of the problems with US capability for liberation missions that were to be repeated in the Iran Raid in 1980 and on Grenada in 1983.

In 1975, the US armed forces were slowly recovering from the nadir of their post-Vietnam 'hollow forces' era, when the practices of assaulting unpopular leaders ('fragging'), widespread indiscipline and drug abuse that came out of the closing years of the Vietnam commitment had driven away quality personnel; others had retired or been lost to reductions in force. Decreased defence spending ensured that there was insufficient money to maintain equipment – much of it worn out during the Vietnam War – and train the new all-volunteer force that was emerging.

The US's three armed services – for they remained key in resource allocation as well as doctrinal development – invested in a capability for major conventional conflicts in response to the Soviet build-up that had started in the late 1960s. At that time, special operations forces and missions – including liberation and seizure missions – were largely viewed as part of the discredited, failed approach to war-fighting that had ended with the US ground force commitment to Vietnam. The cut-back in US SOF capability meant that by 1975 there was no joint service raiding force capable of executing liberation missions, nor anyone considering the doctrine and tactics for such missions.

US credibility – already damaged by the Watergate scandal that had led to Gerald Ford becoming President the previous year – had been further reduced by the fall of Indochina to the Communists in the spring of 1975. The White House was concerned that the US should not appear to be 'a helpless giant', an unreliable ally lacking resolve. The Soviet Union was already making statements about the change in the 'global correlation of forces' that would be implemented in the next few years with its deployment of SS-20 missiles in Europe and its increased military involvement in Africa. North Korean policies had become increasingly aggressive. It was feared in Washington that further military setbacks would encourage other challenges.

Such a challenge appeared a month following the final (April 1975) fall of South Vietnam, Laos and Cambodia to Communist forces. At 1414 local time on 12 May 1975, the US Sea-Land Lines merchant ship *Mayaguez* was seized by a Khmer Rouge gunboat in the Gulf of Siam. The ship's 225 containers held nonmilitary cargo. It was one of several merchant ships intercepted by the Khmer Rouge – already starting to exercise its destructive use of power – for penetrating their unilaterally extended territorial waters. Within the previous two weeks, a South Korean ship had been fired on and a Panamanian-flag ship seized and held for twenty-four hours in these waters. The *Mayaguez*'s radio officer sent several Mayday messages before the boarding party denied further communications. Captain Charles T. Miller and forty officers and seamen aboard were taken prisoner.[1]

WASHINGTON LOOKS TO LIBERATION – 12 MAY

Khmer Rouge gunboats were escorting the *Mayaguez* north, heading towards the mainland Cambodian port of Kompong Som (formerly Sihanoukville), when word of the seizure – but not the ships' post-seizure movements – reached the White House and the Pentagon. Three hours after it was seized, the Joint Chiefs of Staff authorized US Navy P-3B maritime reconnaissance aircraft to locate the *Mayaguez*. It was five hours after the initial seizure before the first reconnaissance mission could take off.

While the National Military Command Center (NMCC) in the Pentagon issued orders, US intelligence was unable to provide much in the way of information. It was uncertain where the ship and its crew were, or whether the *Mayaguez* had been seized on the orders of the Khmer Rouge regime or merely by a local commander taking independent action.

Heading towards the scene from the north end of the Lombok Strait were the aircraft carrier USS *Coral Sea* and its escorts. The guided-missile destroyer USS *Henry B. Wilson*, *en route* from Taiwan to the Philippines, had also turned towards the scene on hearing news reports. The destroyer escort USS *Harold E. Holt* and fleet replenishment ship USS *Vega* left Subic Bay. The carriers *Hancock* (at Subic Bay) and *Midway* and the amphibious warfare ship *Okinawa* and their escorts were also ordered to deploy. These were powerful forces, but the ships had been deployed for months covering the evacuation of Southeast Asia with limited maintenance. The *Okinawa* was limited to eighteen knots and the *Hancock* had an engineering plant malfunction. Neither could be in action within seventy-two hours. The *Holt* – closest to the scene – went to eighty per cent of maximum revolutions on its power plant to achieve twenty-four knots. The *Midway* and its escorts headed for the scene at twenty-five knots.

The crisis was in the geographical area of responsibility (AOR) of US Pacific Command (PACOM) at Pearl Harbor, Hawaii. PACOM appointed Lt. Gen. John J. Burns Jr., USAF, commanding general Seventh Air Force, based in Thailand, to be the on-the-scene commander. However, his headquarters never received formal operational control of all the forces involved, although Navy and Marine units were directed to respond to Seventh Air Force commands. Control was implied, but never spelled out. Burns chose to remain at his headquarters at Nakhon Phanom air base (AB), with its superior communications network to Washington and Hawaii.[2] This resulted in a disconnect on several levels: firstly, an Air Force headquarters in charge of an operation to be carried out primarily by naval forces; and secondly, a controlling headquarters at Nakhon Phanom while the forces that would be involved in the action were offshore or at U Tapao AB over 640 km away in southern Thailand.

The course of US actions for what was emerging as an international crisis were decided at the first National Security Council (NSC) meeting on 12 May, over six hours (Washington time) after the initial distress call. In order to secure the swift release of the *Mayaguez* crew, President Ford wanted the capability to execute a military option that would proceed in parallel with diplomatic actions.

Ford insisted that this must not become another *Pueblo* incident. This time, there was also no guarantee that the crew would simply be held prisoner. The first reports of the Khmer Rouge massacres were already circulating in Washington. Ford personally insisted that the safety of the crew be made a priority, even though Secretary of State Henry Kissinger – always a practitioner of *realpolitik* – and Vice President Nelson Rockefeller ('If we do not respond violently we get nibbled to death'[3]) argued that it had to be a secondary consideration to restoring US credibility through the use of military power.

The situation was clouded by lack of what Washington saw as strong diplomatic options. Ford directed that the US publicly condemn the seizure as piracy and appealed at high level to Chinese representatives in Washington, Beijing and at the United Nations, but these actions could not assure the responsiveness of the Khmer Rouge. The US had been forced to evacuate its embassy in Phnom Penh two months earlier. The Khmer Rouge did not have diplomatic relations with any major powers other than the People's Republic of China, nor had it previously shown much interest in communicating with the US or taking part in even indirect diplomacy.

This made a liberation operation the preferred option from the opening hours of the *Mayaguez* crisis. The Ford administration could not be seen to be implementing a sit-and-wait policy in what was emerging as a major crisis. Every day the military option was delayed increased the chance that the *Mayaguez* and its crew would be taken to the Cambodian mainland and massacred or at least concealed out of reach of liberation efforts. The lessons of Son Tay – where the prisoners were moved beyond the reach of rescue during a lengthy preparation for the raid – contributed to a perceived need for quick liberation in this situation. While never explicitly stated, Washington wanted the situation resolved within seventy-two hours. The actions discussed in the NSC meeting also imposed a key constraint on liberation operation planning: time pressure. On this occasion, there was time pressure involved in a way not seen in previous liberation missions.

In addition to avoiding the creation of more hostages – or corpses – the Ford administration was looking for a success to reassure regional allies that US forces were not inevitably going to become 'falling dominoes'. The priorities emerged as: first, recovery of the ship and crew; second, avoiding a hostage crisis; and third, demonstrating US credibility and resolve. Thus was the planning for a *Mayaguez* crew liberation operation initiated.

The White House made it obvious by its actions that even tactical decision-making was often in its hands during this crisis. Even before the initial NSC meeting, the *Holt*, steaming towards the scene from Subic Bay, received a message from a general in the White House situation room demanding its twenty-four knots be increased and that it cruise at 100 per cent power. The White House general did not realize that this would add only four knots to its speed, quickly drain its already low fuel reserves and greatly increase the chance of a machinery breakdown. (The *Holt* was a DE-1052 *Knox*-class destroyer escort, a versatile warship but of a class nicknamed a 'single screw whale', designed with minimal redundancy). Lack of fuel or a breakdown would mean that the *Holt* would not come into action at all; regardless of orders, it quickly had to reduce its cruising speed to twenty-one knots. The White House order was soon countermanded – President Ford, invoking his wartime naval experience, said he did not want the *Holt* 'dead in the water'[4] – but the Navy long remembered this incident.

IMPROVISING A CAPABILITY – 12–13 MAY

Following orders from the White House to put together a capability to rescue the crew and ship as soon as possible – yet without a precise deadline by which a capability was required – HQ Seventh Air Force in Thailand had to improvise a raiding capability from the primarily Air Force assets on hand. A scratch team of Air Force assets from Thai bases – rescue and special operations helicopters and Air Police – was put under the control of an improvised joint task force headquarters commanded by Col. Loyd Anders, deputy commander of the 56th Special Operations Wing. This team was ordered to be brought to readiness in case an emergency use of armed force to liberate the prisoners was required.

From bases elsewhere in Thailand, F-4E and A-7D fighter-bombers, AC-130A/H gunships and an EC-130E Cricket Airborne Command and

Control Center (ABCCC) (under Lt. Col. James Shankles and with an experienced Air Force battle-management team) were deployed to U Tapao. High-altitude U-2 reconnaissance aircraft provided imagery and functioned as radio relays. Tanker support – including HC-130s capable of refuelling HH-53 (but not CH-53) helicopters – was also put into place.

The critical resource was long-range heavy-lift helicopters. Every helicopter of this type in Thailand that could fly was committed to the mission. A total of sixteen US Air Force CH-53C special operations helicopters and HH-53C 'Jolly Green Giant' combat search and rescue helicopters were available. The helicopters were concentrated at the air base nearest the scene – U Tapao – from northern Thai bases. However, U Tapao was still 195 nmi distant from the scene.

The helicopters and their flight and maintenance crews had all been functioning at a high operational tempo in the preceding months, taking part in the evacuation of Southeast Asia. Immediately before being put on alert for the *Mayaguez* crisis, the CH-53Cs had been busy loading former South Vietnamese aircraft on to US ships to be removed from the region. They had experienced crews, good at covertly inserting small SOF teams behind enemy lines or saving shot-down aircrew but untrained in the company-size air assaults into 'hot' LZs that were the daily work of Army or Marine helicopter units. These helicopters would provide lift for a provisional 125-man rescue force improvised at U Tapao from the combined Air Police elements brought together from the USAF's Thai bases.

The Air Police provided an option for Washington to stage an immediate rescue mission, should that be required. The force was built around the 656th Security Police Squadron (SPS) at Nakhon Phanom AB. This unit had received training for a potential heliborne operation to rescue Americans from Phnom Penh, Operation Eagle Pull III, in April.[5] However, in the words of one unit NCO, Sgt. G. G. Browning, 'If the intent was for the SPS to assault Cambodian forces defending the *Mayaguez*, they were not prepared for their mission.'[6] Tragedy struck even as this force was being concentrated. On 13 May, a CH-53C carrying Air Police crashed *en route* to U Tapao, killing all twenty-three aboard – five crewmen and eighteen Air Police from the 656th SPS. This effectively decimated the Air Police contingent as a fighting force.

By the evening of 13 May, however, the Seventh Air Force was ready, with their improvised force, to launch a rescue if the order arrived. However, they lacked anything more than rudimentary intelligence on what to expect or the location of the *Mayaguez* crew. It was apparent to HQ Seventh Air Force that they were unlikely to have to mount the raid the next day. As a result, there was a chance that a force better suited for such an operation (and not decimated by a helicopter crash) could be rushed by air to U Tapao.

Burns asked CINCPAC for a force of Marines. This request was approved. The Marines at Okinawa and Subic Bay had been alerted on 12 May that they might be required to provide troops to recover the *Mayaguez* and its crew. Late on 13 May (local time), a composite battalion landing team of 1,100 Marines was ordered to be flown from Okinawa and the Philippines to assemble at U Tapao.

SHADOWING THE *MAYAGUEZ* – 13 MAY

First contact after the seizure came shortly after dawn on 13 May when a Navy P-3B maritime reconnaissance aircraft located the *Mayaguez* anchored off Poulo Wai island, 64 km from the Cambodian shore. The P-3B shadowed the ship and its escort of Khmer Rouge gunboats as they moved towards the mainland port of Kompong Som. However, rather than sailing there directly, they anchored off the nearby island of Koh Tang at noon. The P-3B got too close to the gunboats, escaping with a single .50-calibre hole in the fin.

Launched from Thai bases after the P-3B's reports were received, US Air Force fighters started to overfly the ship. Beginning during the afternoon of 13 May, the Seventh Air Force maintained a combat air patrol (CAP) of two F-4Es per half hour on-station to prevent the *Mayaguez* from moving and additional gunboats from providing reinforcements. USAF A-7D aircraft, acting on direct orders from the White House situation room – continuing in its *de facto* role as tactical headquarters for the incident – fired rockets fore and aft of the *Mayaguez* to discourage any further movement. Armed Khmer Rouge on board, fearing an attack, returned fire with Kalashnikovs.

RF-4C reconnaissance aircraft provided imagery, showing the gunboats alongside the *Mayaguez*. The CAP of F-4Es and A-7Ds was joined during the night of 13–14 May by USAF AC-130 gunships, with low-light televisions and infra-red sensors. The AC-130s kept a close watch on the *Mayaguez*. However, no one had located the crew.

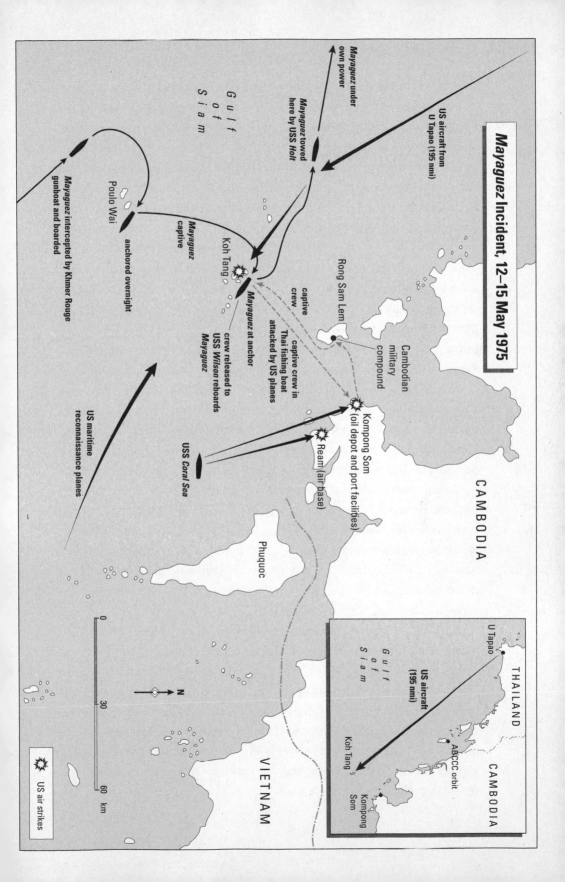

Mayaguez Incident, 12–15 May 1975

Gulf of Siam

Mayaguez under own power

Mayaguez towed here by USS Holt

US aircraft from U Tapao (195 nmi)

Mayaguez intercepted by Khmer Rouge gunboat and boarded

Poulo Wai

Mayaguez captive

anchored overnight

Koh Tang

Mayaguez at anchor

captive crew

captive crew in Thai fishing boat attacked by US planes

crew released to USS *Wilson* reboards *Mayaguez*

Rong Sam Lem

Cambodian military compound

US maritime reconnaissance planes

USS *Coral Sea*

Ream (air base)

Kompong Som (oil depot and port facilities)

C A M B O D I A

Phuquoc

V I E T N A M

N

0   30   60 km

US air strikes

Gulf of Siam

U Tapao

US aircraft (195 nmi)

THAILAND

CAMBODIA

ABCCC orbit

Koh Tang

Kompong Som

PLANNING LIBERATION – WASHINGTON, 13–14 MAY

The planning for a liberation mission continued throughout 13 May, limited by the lack of intelligence on the crew. US military planners thought they were either confined below decks or, more likely, had been moved ashore on to Koh Tang where there was a Khmer Rouge garrison of unknown size and weaponry. Other reconnaissance information – from the aircraft on-station, from high-altitude SR-71 reconnaissance aircraft and from 'national technical means' (satellites and SIGINT) – went to the higher headquarters and did not filter down to the forces standing by for a rescue attempt.

The planners worked in Washington, Hawaii and Nakhon Phanom, and a draft operational plan for a liberation mission was briefed to the NSC in Washington late on the evening of 13 May (it was already daylight on 14 May at the scene). Acting Chairman of the Joint Chiefs of Staff, Gen. David Jones, presented a series of options including raids on the *Mayaguez* and Koh Tang, air strikes, the dropping of mines or an amphibious attack against the Cambodian mainland. The potential forces involved included the USAF from Thailand (although the government in Bangkok was opposed to strikes against Cambodia's mainland being flown from its bases), the *Coral Sea*'s air wing once that vessel was in range (21 F-4Js, 24 A-7Es, 6 A-6Es with 81 precision-guided munitions in the magazine) and B-52s based on Guam.

Alternatives to a liberation operation were not thriving. The US became increasingly concerned that the absence of a Khmer Rouge diplomatic response (or even a statement disavowing the action) indicated that the Khmer Rouge leadership was intending to use the crew as hostages for long-term negotiations. Diplomatic efforts to reach the Khmer Rouge through China failed. In the US, bipartisan political support for military action to rescue the crew mounted.

The NSC meeting in Washington on the evening of 13 May bolstered the resolve for a liberation mission to be launched as soon as the forces in Thailand were ready. Kissinger's recommendation was, 'I would go for the island at daybreak of the 15th.' Ford was at first unsure – 'If you wait until the 16th, you have maximum capability . . .' Kissinger later responded, 'That is when the best forces will be available. But that has to be weighed against the other considerations for the twenty-four hours that you lose . . .' To this he later added, 'So we have to weigh the optimum military time against the optimum political time.'[7]

RUNNING THE BLOCKADE – 14 MAY

The morning of 14 May (local time) saw the US, in the absence of warships, forced to try to maintain a blockade using tactical aircraft to first locate and second prevent the *Mayaguez* crew from being taken to the mainland. These aircraft could make only limited use of their weapons for fear of injuring the captive *Mayaguez* crew.

The air presence around the island was increased. It now included an EC-130E ABCCC that was linked directly to the NMCC. The aircrew on the scene talked to the ABCCC, who talked to the Pentagon, who talked to Assistant National Security Advisor Lt. Gen. Brent Scowcroft in the White House, who talked to President Ford, who effectively made the decisions.

This difficult tactical situation and tortuous chain of command was put to the test early on the morning of 14 May. Three Khmer Rouge gunboats left Koh Tang, heading in the direction of the mainland. US A-7Ds fired warning shots and then engaged with 20 mm cannon. An A-7D and an AC-130H Spectre 41 used 40 mm cannon to run aground a Khmer Rouge patrol boat – a captured US-built *Swift* PBR design – off the eastern shore of Koh Tang. It was up to Ford to decide the next steps.

> SCOWCROFT Three little boats have taken off [from Koh Tang] towards the
> northeast. One boat has been sunk. The second has turned back. The third
> is continuing at full speed. If they [the aircraft] can't stop it any other way,
> we have no choice but to destroy it.
>
> FORD I think we have no choice . . . If we don't do it, it is an indication of
> some considerable weakness.
>
> SCOWCROFT No question about it.
>
> FORD I think we should just give it to them.

The order was passed back to the Pentagon and via the ABCCC to the pilots on the scene. Denis flight – four A-7Ds arriving on the scene – was directed to attack. Within ten minutes of Ford's order, the Khmer Rouge boat was sunk.

Following the air attack, a fourth, larger wooden Thai fishing boat headed for the mainland at about 0900 (local time). It was a four-hour trip to the Cambodian mainland. The initial strafing by A-7Ds was deliberately wide. Aircrew waved to 'possible Caucasians huddled in the bows'. To Capt. Ric Hunter, flying an unarmed F-4, 'They appeared to be Americans, doubled up in the schoolroom air-raid position with their hands protecting their heads. A few of them looked up as I passed overhead; I felt profoundly helpless.'[8]

A-7Ds fired rockets within 9 metres of the fishing boat's bow and stern and dropped CS gas bombs. Again, Scowcroft asked the President to make the tactical decision that would normally be made by a flight lead captain in a fighter cockpit or a colonel in the ABCCC and give the order to disable and possibly sink the fishing boat.

> FORD Well, I don't think we have any choice.
> SCOWCROFT If they get the Americans to the mainland they have hostages.
> FORD We have to predicate all these actions on the possibility of losing Americans.
> SCOWCROFT I will have them ask the pilot to do his best to stop it without sinking it.
> FORD I think that is right.

This time, however, the order to open fire was slower in being passed back to the aircraft on the scene. The order was apparently deliberately delayed in the Pentagon by the Secretary of Defense, James Schlesinger, who was concerned about harming the *Mayaguez* crew as collateral damage from an air attack.[9] As a result, there were no further attacks on the fishing boat, which arrived at the mainland port of Kompong Som about ninety minutes after Ford gave the attack order. It later proved to have been carrying the *Mayaguez* crew as prisoners.

This infuriated Washington. Kissinger complained, 'Now we are negotiating with the pilot.' Ford asked, 'I gave the order at the meeting to stop all boats. I cannot understand what happened on that order, because I heard it did not go out until 3:30 [Washington time 13 May].' 'It went out by telephone within half an hour after you gave it,' Schlesinger explained.[10]

PREPARING FOR ACTION – 14 MAY
Col. John M. Johnson, a staff officer for II Marine Amphibious Force, was dispatched to U Tapao from Okinawa with some five staff officers, arriving at 0730 (local time) on 14 May to take command of the Marines. There were no additional communications, reconnaissance, intelligence or ANGLICO (joint Marine–Navy gunfire and air-strike direction) personnel (other than

two air liaison officers) attached to the Marine force. Experienced Marine helicopter personnel were also conspicuous by their absence. Johnson was told that it was now thought likely that the *Mayaguez* crew was ashore on Koh Tang and that the mission now included raids on both the *Mayaguez* and the island. His command was as much a scratch formation as one the Air Force had assembled the day before. Designated Task Group 79.9, the Marines came from two different battalion landing teams (BLTs) – Company D of the 1st Battalion, 4th Marines, from Subic Bay and elements of the 2nd Battalion, 9th Marines, from Okinawa. Lt. Col. Randall Austin of the 2-9th was in overall command, putting his executive officer, Maj. Raymond Porter, in charge of the company from Subic Bay.

These Marines were not a special operations force, or even well and fully trained. The 'hollow forces' era had led to difficulties in recruiting and retaining skilled personnel at all levels. It had also provided inadequate operations and maintenance funding for spare parts and training. The 2-9th had sent home most of its experienced Marines after the evacuation of Southeast Asia and had been topped up with recent recruits just out of stateside training. It had been in the middle of its training cycle and was deployed in an exercise area on Okinawa when called back to base to get ready to deploy to U Tapao. The 1-4th was in better shape as far as trained personnel were concerned.

Since Washington was insulated from the realities of these limitations by a lengthy reporting chain, those at the top lacked an effective understanding of what the force on the ground might actually be capable of doing. The Marines' chain of command made no effort to ensure that the force they were sending on this mission was the most capable available in the Western Pacific. The mission could have been assigned to the more experienced and better trained 1-9th Marines BLT, which in fact was the unit that was designated as PACOM's primary force for West Pacific air-deployment contingencies, but these Marines were at the end of their deployment and it was decided not to retain them in theatre. The planners in Washington, Hawaii and Nakhon Phanom were not aware of the state of the Marines' training, that there were better-trained units available or that partially trained Marines were being sent in response to the urgent tasking.[11]

Porter and the company from Subic Bay arrived at U Tapao at 0430 (local time) on 14 May. Twelve volunteer sailors from Military Sealift

Command ships – half civilian, half Navy – accompanied them to get the *Mayaguez* underway if required. The 1-4th Marines – joined by Austin at 0945 as the 2-9th began to fly in – met with the Seventh Air Force staff representatives forward deployed to U Tapao. They thought the Navy would be out of the picture until the next day and did not include them in the plans, which were based on the expected orders for an immediate launch.

They were told they would be carried to the *Mayaguez* on Air Force helicopters that morning. Porter consulted with Seventh Air Force staff, the Air Force helicopter pilots and the sailors. The RF-4C photos showed the *Mayaguez*'s decks still covered with containers. These would not support the weight of a helicopter. The Marines would have to use hastily improvised equipment to jump or rappel from hovering helicopters on to containers, and then lower themselves on to the deck. At noon, D Company boarded the helicopters and waited for the order to launch.

By 1300, with D Company still waiting in the helicopters, the word came down that Koh Tang would also have to be raided in an effort to secure the *Mayaguez* crew. But the order from Washington to 'go' still did not arrive. The 2-9th had finished flying in by 1300. At 1400, with insufficient daylight left for the operation, D Company secured from the helicopters. The rest of the day was devoted to getting the Marines and Air Force helicopters ready and mission planning dominated by top-down direction from Washington and Hawaii.

Despite an effort to use every possible source, there was still an almost total dearth of IPB. In the afternoon, Austin and three other officers from the 2-9th flew over Koh Tang in a light transport aircraft. Without sensors other than a pocket camera and unable to go lower than 1,830 m because of concern about AAA, the only possible helicopter LZs appeared to be on the beaches. The vegetation looked dense and it would limit visibility to 1.5–4.5 m. Lacking sophisticated cameras, they were unable to produce detailed aerial photography to compensate for the absence of grid maps of the island. Ten USAF RF-4C photo recon missions were flown, but these concentrated on the ship and produced only a few unclear photographs of the island, which also failed to compensate for the lack of maps or intelligence.[12] Air photos of the defences on Koh Tang were provided to the Marines only at the last moment, when it was too late to change the top-down directed plan.

Koh Tang itself was relatively flat, heavily forested except for the beaches and some 7 km long. Most of the interest was at the northern tip of the island, where there were Khmer Rouge huts and a camp. The Khmer Rouge had cleared away some of the vegetation in the 350 m neck between the two main beaches, east and west, near the northern tip of the island.

GIVING THE ORDERS – WASHINGTON, 14 MAY

Starting at 1537 on the afternoon of 14 May, Washington time, the NSC revisited the options on which they had been briefed the day before. Attempts to get the UN to intervene with a diplomatic approach fared no better than the earlier approaches via the Chinese. In the meeting – in the absence of any of the official participants raising the question – the White House photographer (who had served in Cambodia) interjected the question of whether the Khmer Rouge leadership in Phnom Penh was behind the capture of the *Mayaguez* and whether it may have been too disorganized or ignorant to respond to the diplomatic overtures. The assembled NSC heard out the photographer and then considered the options.

While it was thought that at least some of the captives may have been brought to the mainland on the fishing boat the day before, others might still be below decks on the *Mayaguez* or on Koh Tang. Jones stressed that another twenty-four hours would give more time to plan – so far there had only been limited training and planning time available to the Thailand-based Air Force helicopters and the Marines, and they had dealt only with getting a boarding party on to the *Mayaguez* – and would allow additional forces to participate. The *Coral Sea* would be in range later that day, and would be joined by other carriers. A further delay – to 16 May – would allow the *Coral Sea* to serve as a helicopter carrier for two companies of Marines and their Marine helicopters (and air-assault-trained aircrew) ferried from the USS *Hancock*, which was heading for the scene from Subic Bay. The *Midway*'s air group would also arrive in range by 16 May. A further two days' delay would bring the USS *Okinawa* within range, supplying more Marines and helicopters.

Despite the lack of intelligence, the national command authority was reluctant to make any decisions that might lead to additional risk to the *Mayaguez* crew or lead to US casualties before the raid. US Navy SEALs based in the Philippines (Delta platoon of SEAL Team 1) advocated that they be dropped in the area to provide clandestine reconnaissance. This was not approved. The *Coral Sea* battlegroup asked for permission to fly low-level reconnaissance sorties over Koh Tang before the raid. This was not approved either.

The President and the NSC may not have realized how improvised the in-theatre planning was or how limited the on-the-scene intelligence. The operation was high-risk – limited mission rehearsals, limited intelligence and a total absence of maps compounded the situation – but this was not a decisive factor in the timing of the mission. The President's decision was that however advantageous additional delays might potentially be, they could not be justified militarily or politically. While a senior Chinese diplomat had reported that the ship and crew were expected to be released soon, this did not sway the decision-makers in Washington: there was no faith in Khmer Rouge reliability and there were fears that they might simply be stalling for more time to move the crew inland.[13]

The decision was made for immediate raids to be launched against the *Mayaguez* and Koh Tang. They would be supported by air strikes from the *Coral Sea* on the mainland at Kompong Som. Options for the mining of mainland ports, the use of Guam-based B-52 bombers – a dozen were on alert – and amphibious actions against the mainland were revisited and rejected. The President's order for immediate use of military force was given at 1645 Washington time.

Both Jones and PACOM requested a twenty-four-hour delay, to allow Marines from Thailand to link up with the Marines and helicopters from the *Hancock* on board the *Coral Sea* on 16 May. The White House, afraid the *Mayaguez* crew would disappear into Khmer Rouge territory inland, stayed with the original order for action on 15 May.

FINAL PLANNING – 14–15 MAY

At this point, the disconnects between the forces on the scene and the planners became critical. The Marines and Air Force helicopter crews just about had time to read the different parts of the orders as they rolled off the secure teleprinters before they were ordered to go. Only at the last minute did U Tapao learn that the Navy would have surface warships off Koh Tang the next morning. The disjointed planning process – in Washington, Hawaii, Nakhon Phanom and U Tapao – was not even using all the assets available on 15 May. No forward air controller (FAC) aircraft were scheduled to cover the raids, and no on-call close air support was to be provided. Johnson asked for USAF OV-10s with FACs to cover the Marines' insertion. This was not acted upon.[14]

The command and control arrangement reflected the improvised nature of the operation, the hasty planning and the need for multi-service involvement. The plan called for Burns at Seventh Air Force HQ at Nakhon Phanom to maintain command and control of all aspects of the operation. Cricket, the EC-130E ABCCC with Anders aboard, would provide on-scene command and control for the three raids. However, there were no Marine or Navy officers on board the ABCCC. Further reducing the ABCCC's situational awareness, it was to orbit 90 nmi north of Koh Tang, out of sight of the situation, to enable it to maintain its radio links with Nakhon Phanom. Anders was designated the airborne mission commander (AMC), the focal point of all on-scene activities, for the duration of the mission. But the warships participating remained under the operational control (OPCON) of PACOM's commander-in-chief and would not be integrated with the ABCCC, which was not expecting to hear from them.

With the location of the prisoners unknown, there was no way to secure their safety as quickly as possible during the operation. The plan sought to minimize the risks to the prisoners by making three simultaneous initial strikes. Of the fifteen surviving helicopters in Thailand, only eleven were available to insert Marines on to the *Mayaguez* and the two landing zones – east beach and west beach – on Koh Tang. (Proposals to use massive 6,800 kg BLU-82 'daisy-cutter' bombs to blast LZs out of the jungle were rejected due to fears of imperiling the as yet unlocated *Mayaguez* crew.) Johnson, concerned about possible HMG positions spotted in low-quality air reconnaissance photographs, asked for fixed-wing air attacks around the LZs to suppress defences. This was not approved either, apparently also due to collateral damage concerns, but neither the Marines nor the helicopter crews were so informed.[15] Even the precision fire power of the AC-130s was not included in the plan due to collateral damage concerns.

The final plan was highly specific, with different elements of it coming to U Tapao from Washington, CINCPAC at Pearl Harbor and HQ Seventh Air Force at Nakhon Phanom. Changes were made at different levels. The decision was made to divide the force. Of the eleven available helicopters, three would carry the boarding party to the *Holt*, two would be reserved for

CSAR use and eight would insert the first wave of Marines, from the 2-9th's G Company, on to the island. The limited initial force would have to be divided three ways without the potential for mutual support and with limited potential for reinforcement or evacuation until later in the day. Launching three raids at the same time stretched the limited helicopter lift assets available, complicated the planning process and stressed the improvised command and control arrangements. However, it was thought to offer the best chance to keep the *Mayaguez* crew out of harm's way. In addition, the *Coral Sea* would launch four bombing strikes on military targets on the mainland. No pre-assault air strikes were permitted for fear of injuring any of the crew who might be on the island. Air Force tactical aircraft would provide air cover for the raids on an on-call basis from Marines on the ground. The Marines and Air Force held a final planning conference at U Tapao at 1900 local time. Lt. Col. Shankles, the ABCCC crew and the forward air controllers (FACs) that flew the high-endurance OV-10 twin-turboprop aircraft – the Air Force's experienced 'battle managers' – were not brought into the planning process even though they were standing by at U Tapao.

When it became known (at about 2200 local time at U Tapao) that the *Holt* would soon become available, it was decided at the planning conference that after Marines from D Company and the volunteer sailors were put on board the *Holt* by Air Force helicopter to reinforce its crew, the *Holt* would assist in the seizure of the *Mayaguez* by coming alongside and putting over a boarding party (reminiscent of how HMS *Cossack*'s sailors boarded the German oiler *Altmark* to liberate British prisoners in 1940). While the Marines in Thailand had been rehearsing a direct helicopter assault landing on the *Mayaguez*, aiming to overwhelm any Khmer Rouge prize crew before any prisoners on board could be harmed, CINCPAC had changed this, possibly reflecting the 'rice bowl' concerns that dominated the Navy's surface warfare community. The Marines would instead fly to the *Holt* by helicopter and then board the *Mayaguez*. Unlike a heliborne assault, this was obviously not going to be a swift action that could pre-empt any violence against prisoners, and consequently the planners were now counting on large-scale use of tear gas delivered by Thailand-based USAF A-7s to incapacitate any Khmer Rouge guards on board the freighter. The revised plan also reflected concerns regarding the vulnerability of the helicopters to any Khmer Rouge with light weapons on board the *Mayaguez*. Certainly, there were no objections from the Marines and helicopter crews at U Tapao.

However, the *Holt*'s ability to back up a boarding party was limited. Its only integral gun – a five-incher (12.7 cm) in a turret – had broken down (reflecting its lack of redundant systems) and it depended on repairs jury-rigged by the crew. The *Holt*'s only usable weapons appeared to be the two M60 machine guns taken from the arms locker and mounted on the bridge wings and sailors with M14 rifles. President Ford commented, as the options for a boarding party were being reviewed in Washington, 'Unless sailors are different now, they are not good boarders.'[16]

At the same time as the boarding party would fly to the *Holt*, Marines from the 2-9th, lifted by Air Force helicopters, were to land simultaneously on Koh Tang at an eastern LZ on the beach on the cove side of Koh Tang (where the Khmer Rouge compound was located) and a western LZ on a narrow spit of beach about 350 m behind the compound on the other side of the island. A platoon-sized force would land on Koh Tang's western beach LZ at the point where there was a man-made cut across the dense vegetation. These soldiers would act as a blocking force. The main force – the rest of G Company, the BLT command group and an 81 mm mortar section – would land on the eastern LZ. They would drive across the narrow neck of the island and sweep through the collection of huts that were thought to be the likely location of the *Mayaguez* crew if they were on the island. The Marines hoped to surround the compound. They would then use loudspeakers (the US Army would provide Cambodian language specialists) to demand the release of the prisoners. If the advance on the compound did not lead to the release of the prisoners, the Marines would then sweep the island (some 7 km long and about 1.6 km wide at its thickest point) reinforced by a second wave of troops – E Company of the 2-9th, picked up at U Tapao by helicopters returning from the first wave. It would, however, take four and a half to five hours for the helicopters returning after the first wave to be able to bring in any reinforcements or evacuate casualties. The plan depended on the original estimate of the threat force – a weak militia platoon – being accurate (and the men at U Tapao had no inkling that this estimate was not believed accurate in Washington, Hawaii or Nakhom Phanom). 1Lt. Gary Weikel, an HH-53 co-pilot, heard the briefings at U Tapao and observed, 'After all the city evacuations, I felt pretty comfortable that this was a piece of cake.'[17]

Other key information was also held at high level and not given to the rescue force at U Tapao. AC-130s had reported the locations of several heavy-machine-gun positions on Koh Tang, located through their night-vision optics. Two HH-53Cs dispatched (unsuccessfully) to rescue the crews of the Khmer Rouge boats sunk off Koh Tang by US aircraft the preceding day reported being engaged by what appeared to be 23 mm tracers from the island. This information had gone up the chain of command to Seventh Air Force HQ at Nakhon Phanom, then to CINCPAC and finally to Washington. There the information remained, unknown to the rescue force offshore and at U Tapao, including, most significantly, the USAF helicopter crews (they were in crew rest status on 14 May, rather than participating in the frantic last-minute planning). On 14 May, even though refined DIA intelligence estimates – which had the benefit of all-source intelligence – put the Koh Tang defenders at a 200-man strong regular Khmer Rouge reinforced company or under-strength battalion with heavy weapons (PACOM intelligence estimated half that size), the rescue force was provided only with earlier estimates that the island was defended by a weak eighteen-to-twenty-man militia platoon armed only with rifles. No one thought to provide the rescue force with the latest intelligence. Instead, it was intended to enable a strongly top-down controlled plan designed to centralize as much of the operation as possible as high up as possible.

BOARDING PARTY – MAY 15

Shortly after dawn (local time) on 15 May, air strikes from the USS *Coral Sea* began attacking mainland harbour facilities and an airbase. The carrier air wing planned to launch four strikes against the mainland at ninety-minute intervals while maintaining a CAP – the Khmer Rouge was known to have captured three AT-28 piston-engine combat aircraft based at Kompong Som and these could be reinforced by airworthy remnants from some 100 AT-28s abandoned at Pochentong Airfield near Phnom Penh when it fell.[18]

On the morning of May 15, the *Mayaguez* remained anchored off Koh Tang. The first step was to bring the boarding party to the *Holt*. At 0400, three USAF HH-53Cs – Jollygreens 11, 12 and 13 – launched from U Tapao. Arriving over the *Holt* at 0550, they approached one at a time – the process required half an hour – and offloaded fifty-nine Marines, the boarding party, an Army translator, a naval detachment and the volunteer civilian sailors

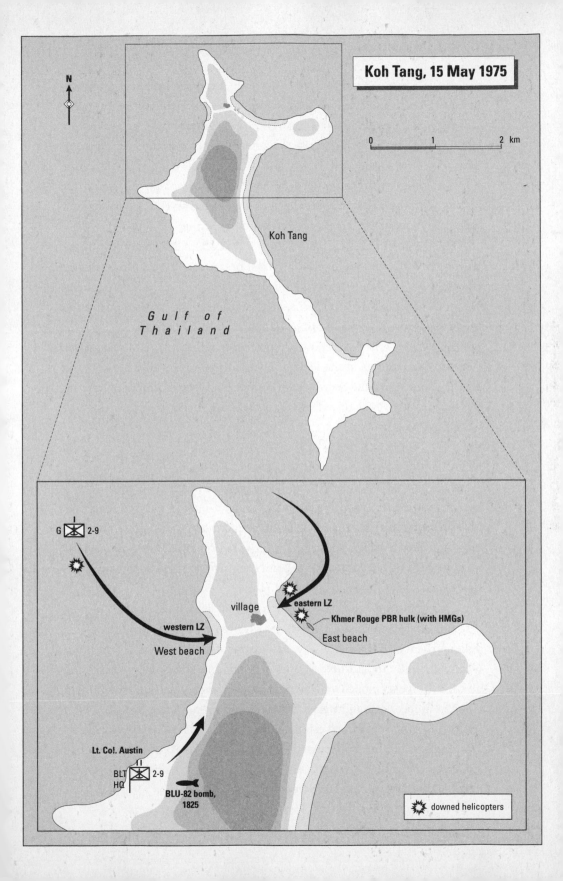

Koh Tang, 15 May 1975

0   1   2 km

N

Koh Tang

Gulf of Thailand

G ⊠ 2-9

village

eastern LZ

western LZ

Khmer Rouge PBR hulk (with HMGs)

West beach

East beach

Lt. Col. Austin

BLT HQ ⊠ 2-9

BLU-82 bomb, 1825

✸ downed helicopters

to sail the *Mayaguez* out of danger, plus an Air Force explosive ordnance disposal (EOD) team. This in itself was a dangerous operation, as the *Holt*'s helicopter pad was too small for the HH-53Cs; only one of the big helicopters could approach the warship at a time, and then could only set down one landing gear at a time.

With the boarding party aboard, the *Holt* started for the *Mayaguez*, 24 km away. The helicopters headed back to refuel from an HC-130 tanker and then to U Tapao to pick up the second wave of Marines.

The *Holt* approached the *Mayaguez* at 0710, about 2.7 km off Koh Tang, within range of heavy weapons from the shore. A-7Ds dropped CS bombs on board the *Mayaguez* just before the *Holt* came alongside. With the traditional command 'boarders away', Marines wearing gas masks crossed over on to the *Mayaguez* and passed mooring lines across.

The well-organized search was completed in an hour. The *Mayaguez* was deserted. No clues as to the location of the crew were found aboard. The *Holt*'s sailors joined the boarding party and its volunteer sailors to light up the engines. By 0822 the *Mayaguez* was secure, being towed by the *Holt* until it got underway.

ASSAULT ON KOH TANG, 15 MAY – THE EASTERN LZ

At 0607, the assault on Koh Tang commenced with the first wave of 179 Marines launched from U Tapao AB expecting only light resistance. The helicopters approached the beach LZ one at a time in a straight-in low-level approach from seaward. Before landing, the helicopters slowed to a hover at an altitude of 6–9 m and turned to point their rear passenger ramps towards the tree line before descending one at a time.[19]

Waiting for the helicopters in the tree line, disciplined enough to hold their fire, were an estimated 150–250 Khmer Rouge armed with AK-47s, light and heavy (.50 calibre, 12.7 mm and probably 14.5 mm) machine guns, 60 mm and 82 mm mortars, 57 mm, 75 mm and 106 mm recoilless rifles and RPG-7 rocket launchers. The men and weapons were dug in, with gun pits and timber and sandbagged bunkers. The strength was probably what the DIA in Washington had estimated it would be.[20] Yet even decades later, the strength of the defence remains unconfirmed. Some Khmer Rouge survivors claim the defenders, the 450th Battalion, had only eighty-five combat-effective men available on 15 May.[21]

At the eastern LZ, the Khmer Rouge held fire until the lead CH-53C, Knife 23, flown by 1st Lt. John Shramm, started to take off after landing a platoon of twenty-one Marines from G Company of the 2-9th. The opening volley hit the tail rotor, separating the tail boom and sending the helicopter plummeting down into the surf just 6 m from the beach. There was no fire and the five-man Air Force crew was able to dash for nearby rocks and trees on the beach to join the Marines. The co-pilot was able to contact the remaining helicopters on his survival radio.

Knife 23's wingman, Knife 31, was following in trail, carrying its own load of Marines towards the beach. It was hit by an RPG-7 round, which exploded a fuel tank (CH-53Cs lacked the HH-53's self-sealing external tanks). Knife 31 crashed – returning fire from its miniguns and with hand-held weapons – in the surf just off the LZ. The helicopter caught fire on impact. Seven Marines, two Navy aid men and the Air Force co-pilot were killed. As the survivors struggled out of the burning helicopter, the Khmer Rouge machine guns opened intense fire. Three Marines were killed in the surf, showing the remainder that the only hope for survival was in heading out to sea. Sgt. Jon Harston, Knife 31's flight mechanic, although wounded, pulled three Marines from the burning helicopter. He then re-entered the burning CH-53C to rescue another wounded Marine and then guided them away from the island. The survivors of the crash – ten Marines and three members of the helicopter crew – managed to stay afloat. Knife 31 had carried the Marine air liaison officer, who kept directing aircraft while floating in a life jacket. Flights of A-7Ds passed overhead, but few were able to attack because of uncertainty as to the locations of survivors or Khmer Rouge positions. Those that did attack were limited to 20 mm strafing. Onboard Knife 31 and in the surf, thirteen aircrew, Marines and Navy corpsmen lost their lives.

The other helicopters heading for the eastern LZ were called back. 2Lt. Michael Cicere, the Marines of the 3rd Platoon, G Company, 2-9th and the crew of Knife 23 were on their own. Soon two of the Marines were hit and wounded by Khmer Rouge fire.

THE INSERTION – WESTERN LZ
The western LZ was a small strip of beach, and only one helicopter could land at a time. The lead helicopter, CH-53C Knife 21 unloaded twenty-one

Marines from G Company of the 2-9th at 0615 on to the still-quiet beach while wingman Knife 22 waited its turn nearby. Then the Khmer Rouge opened fire.

Knife 21, on the ground as the first volley struck it, managed to struggle into the air on one engine. It barely cleared the tree line. Knife 22 came to its aid, closing with the Khmer Rouge positions, firing its on-board mini-guns and drawing fire. Knife 21 was able to get only a mile offshore before crashing.

Capt. Terry Ohlemier, flying Knife 22, now had to decide whether to try to rescue the crew of Knife 21 or to deliver the Marines on board to reinforce those who had been brought in by Knife 21, now pinned down on the beach by the Khmer Rouge. Ohlemier decided on a single-ship air assault, circling back for another pass, bringing Knife 22 through heavy machine-gun fire and towards the western LZ. The Khmer Rouge shifted their fire away from the Marines on the beach to the approaching helicopter. After making two attempts to land, Knife 22 suffered a ruptured fuel tank and lost an engine. Ohlemier could see that going into a hover to attempt to land would have been suicidal. Knife 22 staggered back to an emergency landing in Thailand. Its Marines were still aboard – including Capt. James Davis, G Company's commander, who was intended to be in charge of the western LZ – and were now out of action. The LZ was now held by a single helicopter load of unsupported Marines.

THE FIRST WAVE GOES IN

At this point, four of the eight helicopters of the first wave were down or out of action. Anders, aboard the ABCCC, told the remaining four helicopters of the first wave that had been heading for the eastern LZ to use the western LZ. The four helicopters arrived in time to see Knife 21 ditch and Knife 22 make its single-handed assault at the western LZ. They could see that the overlapping fields of fire from heavy machine guns made any reinforcement of the Marine platoon holding the eastern LZ impossible.

Following orders from Cricket to go in from their holding points at 0620, the rest of the first wave arrived over the western LZ. Knife 32 came in first and then peeled off to pick up Knife 31's crew. It took twenty minutes to winch up three men. Following this, it came into the LZ, miniguns and hand-held weapons blazing. Despite sustaining over seventy-five hits – including an RPG grenade – Knife 32 managed to land and was able to insert thirteen to fifteen Marines. Knife 32 was then able to take off and fly back to U Tapao for medical treatment of a crewman and a Marine wounded during its approach to the LZ. Knife 32 was so badly shot up that it was grounded on arrival at U Tapao.

The remaining three first-wave helicopters, seeing the punishment Knife 32 received, stood back and circled, talking to the ABCCC and among themselves to figure out what to do next. Air Force A-7Ds made strafing passes on suspected Khmer Rouge positions, but they were limited by a lack of radio contact with the troops on the ground. HH-53C Jollygreen 41 approached, coming directly to the western LZ. Heavy machine-gun fire perforated its fuel tanks before it abandoned the approach. HH-53C Jollygreen 43 diverted to a stretch of beach some 1.2 km south of the western LZ, landing twenty-nine Marines including Austin, his command staff and an 81 mm mortar platoon at an unplanned location. They had only four rifles between them. HH-53C Jollygreen 42 then tried its luck at a one-ship air assault on the western LZ. It managed to fly through the fire, land and unload its Marines before being hit by a mortar barrage while taking off. Damaged by mortar fragments, it staggered off to Thailand. Jollygreen 41 came around again for another approach to the western LZ, leaking fuel, closing with the Khmer Rouge machine guns before breaking off to refuel at the HC-130.

The first wave had been intended to insert 179 Marines. It had managed to insert about 100 – plus five Air Force crewmen – divided in three positions: the eastern LZ, the western LZ and Austin's position south of the western LZ. All except Austin's force were pinned down and under fire.

Around the western LZ, the Marines, under 1Lt. James Keith, the G Company executive officer, first organized themselves in a defensive perimeter and then started to move out and take the offensive. The most intense fire was coming from bunkers to the south of the LZ. A platoon engaged the bunkers. At the same time, an attempt by a squad to advance from the western LZ perimeter to link up with Austin's force to the south was promptly ambushed when it left the beach and entered the dense vegetation, leaving one Marine dead (lost to a mine) and five wounded. Concerned that these forces could be vulnerable to enfilade fire, Keith pulled them back inside the perimeter. The perimeter was secure, but under relatively constant sniper fire. The Khmer Rouge launched a local counterattack, but were repulsed by the Marines. Much of the fighting consisted of close-range grenade duels. The Marines soon found that they could scoop up Khmer Rouge grenades and toss them back before they exploded.

THE FIGHT ON KOH TANG – MORNING, 15 MAY

The destroyer *Wilson* arrived off the western LZ at Koh Tang at 0700. The situation was obviously bad, with smoke rising from the shot-down helicopters. Checking in with the ABCCC, the *Wilson* was told to orbit at 3,048 m – Anders thought it was an aeroplane. It was another incident that would be retold in wardrooms for a generation. With no naval officers on the ABCCC, no one had any idea how to integrate the unplanned arrival of the destroyer into the operation.

CDR John Rodgers, captain of the *Wilson*, decided to act independently. Moving slowly to 1,000 m offshore, the *Wilson*'s lookouts spotted the remaining survivors of Knife 31. To Rodgers, the swimming survivors 'appeared to be coconuts in the water off the island'.[22] The destroyer came to a stop to rescue them. However, without radio communications with the Marines or any idea as to where enemy positions might be, the *Wilson* could not use its five-inch guns to support the Marines ashore.

The first priority, ordered by Anders in the ABCCC, was to evacuate the Marines in the eastern LZ. Jollygreen 13 – a boarding-party helicopter now refuelled from an HC-130 – made a lone run into the Khmer Rouge fire. Landing on the beach, it became apparent that none of the Marines would survive a run for the helicopter. Jollygreen 13 caught fire and took off without any Marines making it aboard. Jollygreen 13's crew managed to extinguish the fires and make it back to Thailand, but the damaged helicopter was out of action.

The Air Force started attacks with A-7Ds, F-4Es and AC-130s, hitting targets on the island. Lacking radio contact with the Marines on the ground or the direction of a forward air controller (FAC), they could not strike close enough to the Marines to knock out the machine guns and RPGs in the tree line that had shot up the helicopters. They first worked over the eastern LZ force, starting as soon as Jollygreen 13 was out of danger, and then shifted their fire to the western LZ.

1Lt. Keith and the Marines in the western LZ were now able to contact an Air Force FAC in an F-4E. This aircraft – and its successors when it left to refuel – was now able to direct the fire of the AC-130 against the positions that had been keeping the Marine perimeter under fire. However, even with an FAC now in contact, the Khmer Rouge were still so close to the Marines that they could not be engaged with bombs, only the more accurate cannon on the AC-130. Capt. Barry Cassidy, the Air Liaison Officer (ALO) with Austin's force, was in touch with different Air Force tactical aircraft as they came on- and off-station. While it was a slow process to orient them, these aircraft could be directed against targets a safe distance away from the Marines.

Khmer Rouge counterattacks kept up the pressure on the Marines' western LZ perimeter. Spectre 61, a 105 mm-armed AC-130H able to strike close to the Marines, helped to break up the attack with accurate gunfire. Its 105 mm cannon was able to crack open Khmer Rouge bunkers with overhead cover. As the AC-130H engaged Khmer Rouge positions, the ABCCC sent in the last helicopter from the first wave, Jollygreen 41, now refuelled.

With covering fire from Spectre 61, Jollygreen 41 landed in the western LZ on its fifth attempt at about 0930. While unloading, it was caught in a Khmer Rouge mortar barrage and had to take off before the last five of twenty-seven Marines on board could jump off. Jollygreen 41 made it to a tanker to refuel and then returned to Thailand. Spectre 61, out of ammunition, followed at around 1000. It would be late afternoon before, on Washington's orders, the AC-130s would return to the fight.

All levels of command – Seventh Air Force, CINCPAC, the NMCC at the Pentagon and the White House – were overloading the radio channels with demands to know about the *Mayaguez* crew and the situation on the ground. This flood of communications prevented the ABCCC from maintaining a communications link between Col. Johnson back in U Tapao, Thailand, and his Marines on Koh Tang. Johnson had to rely on verbal reports from returning helicopter crews.

At U Tapao, the five helicopters of the second wave – Jollygreens 11 (which had escorted a damaged helicopter back after refuelling from a tanker), 12 (which had also carried the boarding party) and 43, Knife 51 and Knife 52 (which had accompanied the first wave as CSAR helicopters) – were loaded with a total of about 127 Marines (including those who had returned to U Tapao on damaged helicopters) and took off individually between 0900 and 1000 as soon as they were ready to go.

RECOVERING THE *MAYAGUEZ* CREW – MORNING, 15 MAY

At about 0800, a P-3 spotted a small boat exiting Kompong Som harbour. Visual identification determined that the *Mayaguez* crew was on a Thai fishing boat waving white flags. The boat finally approached the *Mayaguez* and the *Wilson* intercepted it. The destroyer kept its guns trained on the boat until a positive identification was made. A voice through a loudspeaker on the *Wilson* proclaimed, 'Crew of the *Mayaguez*, welcome aboard.' They had been rescued some sixty-five hours after being taken captive. The *Wilson* brought the crew back to the *Mayaguez*. Within a few hours, the *Mayaguez* was under way with her own crew, under her own power.

The *Mayaguez* crew reported that on the night of 13 May they had slept on fishing boats offshore of Koh Tang and, after they had been brought to the mainland, they had slept in an abandoned village. They had been transferred, on 14 May, to a Thai fishing boat, the crew of which had been held by the Khmer Rouge for more than five months. The fishing boat had put to sea without explanation earlier on the morning of 15 May, only to see the Khmer Rouge guards leap from the fishing boat to the escorting gunboat, which quickly sailed the other way.

The ABCCC, on hearing the news, turned around in midair the five-helicopter second wave of reinforcements – most of E Company of the 2-9th. Col. Anders ordered the helicopters back to Thailand to unload and prepare to extract the Marines. The ABCCC also passed the news to Washington, which in turn cancelled the *Coral Sea*'s planned fourth air strike on mainland targets. In addition to hitting the three AT-28s, six transports and three other aircraft at Kompong Som's Ream air base and sinking another gunboat at its Phumi Phsar naval base, *Coral Sea*'s aircraft had struck a rail yard, port facilities and an oil-storage facility.

Johnson, now monitoring the Marine tactical net at U Tapao, knew that his men on the ground were hard pressed. He countermanded Anders's orders and instructed the helicopters to carry on to Koh Tang with their much-needed reinforcements. High-level headquarters quickly backed up his decision.

THE SECOND WAVE LANDS – AFTERNOON, 15 MAY

Austin, his command group and the 81 mm mortar platoon, landed to the south of the western LZ perimeter by Jollygreen 43, fought their way through. They advanced slowly and carefully, co-ordinating their movement with the Marines in the western LZ and taking advantage of Spectre 61's destruction of bunkers and disruption of the Khmer Rouge counterattack. They had knocked out several Khmer Rouge log bunkers and snipers firing from spider holes. Their slow advance reflected the lack of maps. Using fire-and-movement tactics supported by the mortar platoon, they had avoided suffering any casualties.

The Marines advanced on the ground from the southern edge of the western LZ to prevent the Khmer Rouge from blocking the command group's linkup. The Marines moved against the Khmer Rouge positions using classic fire-and-movement tactics, supported by covering fire from their M60 machine guns, now running short on ammunition. Some Khmer Rouge manoeuvred to gain enfilading fire on the Marines, only to find themselves vulnerable to fire from the command group, which broke through at about 1245.

A second attempted Khmer Rouge counterattack was broken up by Marine fire and nearby air strikes. A 106 mm recoilless rifle and two Khmer Rouge bunkers to the north of the perimeter had been knocked out and taken; others were kept under suppressive fire. However, the Khmer Rouge still kept up their fire and held the tactical advantage.

The linkup was followed by the arrival of the second wave of helicopters. They tried the eastern LZ first, reflecting Anders's earlier judgement that the situation there was the most critical. Knife 52, leading the assault, was shot up so badly on its approach that it had to return to Thailand for an emergency landing. It was unable to land its twenty-seven Marines.

Other helicopters approached the eastern LZ before the ABCCC diverted them to the western LZ. At the western LZ, Khmer Rouge fire had slackened after the defeat of the counterattack. The remaining four helicopters of the second wave, landing in turn, made it into the western LZ. They unloaded over 100 Marines and were able to take away some of the wounded. With them came the news that the *Mayaguez* crew had been rescued and that the next step was to be extraction.

This changed the mission for the Marines on Koh Tang. Until then, they had been trying to move out from the LZs to sweep the island, according to the plan. Now the mission became simply to hold position until extracted. While the forces at the western LZ, now reinforced and linked up, could hold on through the night if required, there was concern about the platoon still holding on at the eastern LZ. Austin, in contact with the ABCCC and, through that, with the Seventh Air Force HQ at Nakhon Phanom, insisted that the entire extraction, if ordered, had to be completed in rapid sequence so that the Khmer Rouge could not mass forces and overrun the rearguard.

EXTRACTION – EASTERN LZ – AFTERNOON, 15 MAY

At 1415, the extraction began. The beleaguered Marines on the eastern LZ would be the first to be brought off; the arrival of the second wave had ensured that the western LZ perimeter, now reinforced, could hold on through the night if need be. The pinned-down platoon on the eastern LZ was at greater risk as their ammunition ran low. Two helicopters returning from the second wave, Jollygreens 11 and 43, had remained behind when the others returned to base, performing CSAR duties. Unknown to Austin at the western LZ, they were now ordered by HQ Seventh Air Force to go into the eastern LZ and extract the Marines. The decision to evacuate the eastern LZ was made by Burns in Nakhon Phanom, without consulting or informing any of the Marine commanders.

The *Wilson*, having put the *Mayaguez* crew back aboard their ship, came in close offshore, engaging targets with its two 12.7 cm guns. But it was limited as to the targets it could engage because of the lack of a grid map of the island and uncertainty as to the location of the Marines and shot-down helicopter crews. The *Wilson* even armed its gig and put it nearer to the island for fire support and to pick up any Marines who might have to swim offshore. USAF A-7Ds made close-in attacks with CS gas bombs, hitting as close to the Marine positions as they could.

Under the cover of the air attack, the two helicopters approached the eastern LZ in trail formation at about 1415. The lead, HH-53C Jollygreen 43, was hit by concentrated Khmer Rouge fire and was badly damaged. Lt. Col. Austin described what happened: 'As he [the first HH-53C] settled into the shallow water at the edge of the beach he was greeted by an almost unbelievable hail of SA and AW fire from the ridge to our south and east. Tracers streamed into the perimeter and bounced around like flaming popcorn. The pilot set his aircraft down and took his share of the fire without flinching. As he lifted off, the next aircraft, whose reception by the Khmer Rouge was just as warm, moved into the zone.'[23]

Leaking fuel, Jollygreen 43 headed off to the nearest possible recovery point, the carrier *Coral Sea*. Jollygreen 11 aborted its extraction attempt to fly along with Jollygreen 43, in case it could not make it to the carrier.

The extraction attempt had, however, revealed more Khmer Rouge positions. They fired on the *Wilson* from the island and from the wreck of the *Swift*-class gunboat that had been knocked out the previous day – a twin .50-calibre machine-gun mount was still above water and operational. This weapon – it had accurately engaged the helicopters approaching the LZ – was knocked out by the *Wilson*'s gunfire.

OV-10 Nail 68, flown by veteran USAF FAC Maj. Robert Undorf, arrived along with his wingman Nail 47, replacing the relays of F-4Es and A-7Ds that had been filling the FAC role earlier in the day. Undorf was able to organize the air battle, bringing an AC-130H against the gun positions near the eastern LZ.

Meanwhile, on the *Coral Sea*, Jollygreen 43's crew and Navy mechanics worked frantically to repair the helicopter. Jollygreen 43, thought permanently out of action, was ready for another mission by 1700.

Another extraction attempt at the eastern LZ started around 1730 – again, ordered directly by Burns without reference to the Marines. This time it benefited from Khmer Rouge positions being hit by attacks directed by the forward air controller – engaged either by USAF fighters, an AC-130 or the *Wilson*'s guns. No one had grid maps of the island. The *Wilson*'s gig came close inshore again to rescue any shot-down helicopter crew or Marines left on the beach. Nail 68 used white phosphorus rockets to mark the Khmer Rouge positions for Buckeye flight, four F-4Es attacking with rockets and bombs as close to the LZ as safety allowed. The *Holt* arrived to join the *Wilson*, but was still unable to use its 12.7 cm gun.

HH-53C Jollygreen 11 – which had been flying CSAR duties since covering the withdrawal of Jollygreen 43 – went in first, with two wingmen in close formation providing suppressive fire, trying to get as close to the Marines and airmen on the beach as possible. The Marines made an orderly withdrawal, keeping up the fire on the Khmer Rouge within grenade range. Jollygreen 11 used the *Wilson* to mask its approach, then did a high speed run-in to the LZ. 'The survivors popped the red smoke. We saw exactly where to go. We backed in under some pretty heavy fire,' said 1Lt. Weikel.[24]

As Jollygreen 11 hovered – the wreck of Knife 23 blocked it from landing

– and loaded the Marines and airmen aboard, the Khmer Rouge launched an immediate counterattack, trying to overrun the helicopter. The attackers were cut down by the miniguns of the supporting helicopters. One got close enough to hurl a grenade at Jollygreen 11 before being killed.

As the damaged Jollygreen 11 headed off to the *Coral Sea* with its relieved Marines and airmen, FAC-directed fighter-bombers worked over the eastern beachhead area before another helicopter, Jollygreen 12, came in to look for anyone left behind by Jollygreen 11. All Jollygreen 12 found was enough surviving Khmer Rouge fire power to riddle it and send it back off the *Coral Sea*. Both helicopters were out of action. This left only three helicopters – Jollygreen 43, Jollygreen 44 (inbound from U Tapao after being unable to launch for the first or second wave) and Knife 51 – to extract the Marines at the western LZ.

Arriving over the island were five C-130 transports, one carrying water, medical supplies and ammunition to be airdropped to the Marines, the others, Klong flight, carrying 6,800 kg BLU-82 fuel–air explosive 'daisy-cutters'. Once detonated, they were the nearest thing available to a nuclear explosion, designed to level all trees over a 50 m radius to clear landing zones. One 'daisy-cutter' was dropped at 1825 for psychological effect south of the major fighting – to avoid potentially hitting Marines – as another extraction attempt was launched at the western LZ. The Marines, who had been given no prior warning of its use and had not been told to expect it, could only watch in awe.

EXTRACTION – WESTERN LZ – EVENING, 15 MAY

Night was starting to fall at about 1830 when a helicopter, Knife 51, ran the gauntlet of fire into the western LZ, guided into the LZ by Marines with flash-lights. The Marines ashore thought it was a resupply mission; they had not been told they were to be extracted. Burns had issued the order at 1717 without informing any of the Marines. Neither Johnson at U Tapao or Austin on Koh Tang were informed of a planned extraction time.

The Marines on the ground were already organized either to hold through the night or withdraw and they hastily improvised a withdrawal plan, loading the wounded first. The first helicopter, Knife 51, was soon loaded and *en route* to the *Coral Sea*.

At 1900, two more helicopters – Jollygreen 43, back from the *Coral Sea* with improvised battle-damage repairs, and Jollygreen 44 – narrowly missed colliding as they approached the western LZ. They were met with heavy fire. The Khmer Rouge muzzle flashes were spotted by the OV-10s. Nail 68 – now joined by a third OV-10, Nail 69 – was able to direct an AC-130H against the sources of fire while at the same time directing F-4Es and A-7Ds on strafing attacks. With the air attacks as cover, the helicopters were able to load, one at a time, at the western LZ. Jollygreen 43 took its load of Marines to the *Coral Sea*, Jollygreen 44 diverting to the *Holt* for a quicker turnaround.

Now there was only a rearguard holding on to the western LZ in the dark. The Marine riflemen in the rearguard may have been green and only partially trained, but there was no panic or rushing for helicopters or the beach. They held on and followed the improvised orders. The danger was that the Khmer Rouge might launch a counterattack – as they had at the eastern LZ – and overrun the rearguard or infiltrate into positions where they could engage any incoming helicopters while being too close to the Marines to be attacked by aircraft. The *Wilson*'s gig again moved close inshore to support the rearguard and offer the chance of rescue over the beach if the helicopters did not get through.

Soon after 1900, radio contact was lost with the rearguard. It was thought that it had been overrun until contact was re-established at 1925. The Marines called for immediate evacuation and set out a strobe lamp to mark their position. With Spectre 11, an AC-130, providing support, Jollygreen 44 – back from the *Holt* – came in at 2000 and loaded successfully.

There were now twenty-nine Marines remaining in the LZ. One last helicopter, Knife 51, supported by AC-130 fire, came in at 2015, and loaded what they thought were the last of the Marines. Overlooked was the body of the only Marine to be killed in ground combat on Koh Tang (his body, buried by the Khmer Rouge, was recovered in the 1990s). Other helicopters and fighter-bombers attacked the Khmer Rouge in support. The helicopter used its miniguns. Covered by this fire power, two Marine officers and an Air Force pararescueman who had flown in on Knife 51, a veteran of Son Tay and many crash-scene inspections, made a final check of the evacuated Marine positions. They returned Khmer Rouge fire. With the AC-130 providing supporting fire, they ran aboard the departing helicopter.

Part of the rear guard protecting the perimeter during the final evacuation was a three-man machine-gun team. They had run out of ammunition and were ordered to evacuate on the last helicopter. It was their last contact. The Marines and airman who had made the final sweep of the beach before boarding the helicopter were unable to locate them, and they were declared Missing in Action. In fact, they had been left behind in the withdrawal, abandoned to the Khmer Rouge. It was only discovered years later that they had in fact escaped from the beach and had evaded the Khmer Rouge on Koh Tang for up to ten days before they were hunted down. They were either killed on Koh Tang or taken back to the mainland and executed.[25]

SMOKE RISES FROM KOH TANG

The next morning, the *Wilson* sailed around the island, using its loudspeakers to try to make contact. The Khmer Rouge held their fire. There were proposals for Navy SEALs to go back to Koh Tang to try to recover the dead and missing and to destroy the shot-down helicopters, either unarmed under a white flag or through clandestine infiltration, but neither approach was approved.[26] It was thought that the three missing Marines were dead. A return to Koh Tang might mean more casualties. It would also undercut the effect of a military success that Washington had considered one of the key reasons behind its policies. It is unlikely that the White House ever learned of the three abandoned Marines or their fate. They were not mentioned in the immediate post-battle accounts.

The US left behind more than those killed in the shot-down helicopters plus one killed in action and the three overlooked Marines on Koh Tang. The US losses incurred during the raids were eleven Marines, two Navy aid men and two Air Force personnel dead and over fifty wounded. Four helicopters were shot down. The pre-operation helicopter crash added more dead. The fallen of the *Mayaguez* incident are honoured on the Vietnam War Memorial in Washington, engraved at the tail end of the commitment, symbolically closing the door. It was the last US combat operation in Southeast Asia, a coda to a commitment going back to 1945 and including the longest war in American history. Kissinger summarized: 'We had entered Indochina to save a country and ended by rescuing a ship.'[27]

Khmer Rouge losses were unknown but were likely heavy – 100 killed and wounded on Koh Tang according to US estimates, fourteen dead and over fifteen wounded according to Khmer Rouge veterans. In addition to the boats attacked near the island, others were sunk near the mainland by *Coral Sea's* aircraft on 15 May. A total of eight to ten Khmer Rouge boats were destroyed.[28]

In retrospect, the US could have suffered much worse losses. That the *Mayaguez* crew was released alive was a Khmer Rouge decision. Four months after the incident, the Khmer Rouge claimed the incident had been a result of an unauthorized action by local commanders who had been instructed to guard against Vietnamese incursions and that the crew was released as soon as the leadership heard about the seizure in the news media and could issue appropriate orders.[29] There are many scenarios – additional companies of troops on the island, a few man-portable surface-to-air missiles, a final counterattack against the Marine rearguard while they were out of radio communication – that could have turned a hard-fought mission into disaster. There was, with the limited IPB and key mobility assets (the finite number of helicopters) available, no way that the planning and execution of the mission could have guarded against them.[30]

MISSION ACCOMPLISHED

In a liberation (or seizure) mission, Clausewitz's 'centre of gravity' remains the people to be saved (or captured). Otherwise, they are likely to end up dead. Planners need clear guidance on how this is to be reconciled with other objectives, such as demonstrating resolve, psychological and morale effects, or inflicting casualties. Dr. Kissinger and Vice President Rockefeller stressed that the latter considerations were actually more important for national strategy.

In terms of carrying out President Ford's primary mission of recovering the *Mayaguez* crew alive, the liberation operation was a success. It is only hindsight that makes it appear likely that the Khmer Rouge *ex post facto* explanation was correct and they would have been released (as had the Panamanian-flag merchant ship detained earlier) – along with the Thai fishing boat crew – rather than disappearing into the Khmer Rouge genocide machine, even had there been no military operation. However, the fact that the Khmer Rouge was willing to release the crew in the face of the US build-up of forces in the region suggests that the option for projecting military power was critical to that mission success. The fate of Americans who fell into Khmer Rouge hands when military operations did not appear imminent is suggested by that which befell the three abandoned Marines and, in later years, other civilian sailors.

The success of the objectives stressed by Kissinger and Rockefeller – demonstrating US power and will not only to the Khmer Rouge but to a broader audience – is more difficult to evaluate. The decision to act militarily appeared popular both domestically and internationally, a change from the near-constant litany of defeat and humiliation that had been directed at this administration and its predecessor. The political dimension of the raid was critical, even more than that of the Son Tay mission, influencing the planning, timing and executing of the operation. The degree of high-level decision-making (and interference) was unprecedented. It reflected the political needs of the national command authority (NCA) as well as their post-Vietnam distrust of military decision-making.

The lessons of the *Mayaguez* incident include not only the need for high-level decision-makers to be aware of the potential cost to those on the scene of top-level micro-management of complex tactical operations, but also for those on the scene to be aware of the political imperatives as seen by those making top-level decisions. As is so often the case, a dominant (and perhaps inapt) historical analogy – in this instance the *Pueblo* incident and the subsequent holding of US prisoners by North Korea – helped to drive the political decision-making in Washington. At other times during the 1970s – the Israeli raid on Entebbe, the SAS at the Iranian embassy in London – SOF were not subject to micro-management even in politically sensitive situations because the political leadership personally knew and trusted the SOF leadership. That sort of personal knowledge or trust did not exist between the US NCA and the multiple layers of command in Hawaii, Thailand, the ABCCC and on Koh Tang. Nor did the men hastily pulling together a plan in diverse locations know how important the seventy-two-hour figure was to Washington and how they needed either to accommodate it (as they did) or to tell Washington what they needed to hear to extend their deadline.

Politics included inter-service politics. The Navy, Marines, Air Force, even the Army, all wanted to have 'their' part in the mission. The local command headquarters, Seventh Air Force, knew all about air campaigns and combat search and rescue, but little about special operations. There were no SOF involved in the planning or IPB processes. Specialists in mission execution – the SEAL Team at Subic Bay and the ABCCC crew at U Tapao – were not involved in the hastily improvised process either.

Time proved to be the key determinant of the results. Washington insisted on a quick response – before the crew could be carried off to the Cambodian mainland or massacred – that could not be reconciled with the careful planning normally associated with successful liberation missions. There was no time for the in-depth preparation that characterized the Son Tay raid or liberation operations intended to free prisoners being held in camps that are not likely to move. There was very little time to plan or rehearse. Because the helicopters had to forward deploy from U Tapao and the Marines had to fly in from Subic Bay and Okinawa, there was no time for these two elements to train together before the operation. The fact that the operation was carried out in what amounted to an IPB vacuum – due to the failure to ensure that the raiding force had full access to intelligence – brought the operation close to disaster.

The time available for the liberation missions – of crew and ship – was closer to that allowed for a CSAR mission, but this operation lacked the clear and direct command and control of a CSAR mission, the highly trained specialist execution and the effective tactical doctrine developed over years of conflict. By 1975, the US was good at CSAR because it had much experience in that mission area. A quick-response liberation mission was something that neither headquarters nor war-fighters had given much consideration to or had trained to carry out.

The plan that emerged was a compromise intended to keep all the (US) parties happy, and it nearly resulted in failure. The plan depended on the assumption that Koh Tang was weakly held, even though Washington and PACOM's intelligence estimates did not support this assumption. The plan disregarded many of the requirements for any successful raid. At no time did the raiders have a 'relative advantage' over the Khmer Rouge. Speed, surprise or weight of numbers are normally the ways in which a raid ensures such an advantage, with overwhelming fire power being an alternative. The plan for the *Mayaguez* raid had none of these. There was no deception or surprise that would have reduced the risk of this mission turning into a miniature battle of attrition. At no time, either through surprise, deception, information warfare or suppression, was the US able to make it impossible – or even difficult – for the Khmer Rouge to resist the raid. The shortage of helicopters meant that the US could not achieve the presence of an overwhelming force in the key opening stages of the raid. The tactics – of having one helicopter at a time literally backing into the enemy positions on the beach – would have been recognized as ineffective and, even worse, suicidal, by any helicopter unit trained in air assaults into 'hot' LZs. By the time the second wave of helicopters could bring in more Marines, they could not mass enough ground fire power to force the Khmer Rouge to retreat.

Compared with Son Tay, the *Mayaguez* operation was lacking in IPB, planning, training, rehearsal, co-ordination, effective command and control and personnel.

The limitations on available intelligence were the source of many of the constraints in planning and executing the operation. The lack of maps undercut both planning and execution. The lack of a firm location for the *Mayaguez* crew undercut any planning efforts. The fighting on Koh Tang was not focused on the centre of gravity – the likely location of the *Mayaguez* crew – but on the likely enemy location. These intelligence limitations followed from the availability of only limited air reconnaissance and the lack of HUMINT information about the Khmer Rouge in general and their operations on and around Koh Tang in particular. SEALs or Marine Recon could have provided eyes-on-target reconnaissance, but these were not used for fear of compromising or undercutting diplomatic efforts.

As it was, only limited air flyovers of the island were possible to provide intelligence. However, as the intelligence picture was developed over the course of the crisis, the latest and best information was held at the top, especially in Washington but also at HQ Seventh Air Force. It was not made available to those planning or executing the raids.

The ability to use fire power to compensate for other limitations in the operation was restricted. The ability to use non-lethal riot control agents – explicitly authorized by the President – gave some capability but did not prove to be significant in the combat operations. The importance of avoiding collateral damage in liberation missions was again underlined. The uncertainty as to the location of the *Mayaguez* crew led to limitations on US fire power in the opening stages of the operation. A suppressive air strike before the helicopters came in with the first wave would have been standard tactics in Vietnam, but here it was not considered feasible, an assumption that does not stand up in hindsight. Even once the location of the crew was known, limited IPB, the lack of maps and uncertainty as to Marine positions and the location of the crews of shot-down helicopters limited the use of both US air power and naval gunfire. The failure to have fire power available on call and

ABOVE The LVT-4 amphibious tractor or amtrac – nicknamed 'Alligator' in US service – made the Los Banos raid possible. *US National Archives*

MG Joseph Swing (front right), commanding general of the 11th Airborne Division and planner of the Los Banos raid, and LTG Oscar Griswold (centre), commanding general of XIV Corps, host GEN Joseph Stilwell (left). *US National Archives*

RIGHT Nuns liberated at Los Banos are driven to shelter at Mamatid. At Los Banos, the sight of these same nuns being loaded aboard an amtrac named the 'Impatient Virgin' provoked much mirth among the paratroopers. *US National Archives*

The 1st battalion Middlesex Regiment relieves the 2-187th at Sukchon, 22 October 1950. *US National Archives*

The Rakkasans getting ready to load onto C-119 transports at Kimpo airfield, 20 October 1950. *US National Archives*

Rakkasans jump from C-119s over DZ William, 20 October 1950. *US National Archives*

The missed objective: UN PoWs exhibited by the North Koreans in Pyongyang, 1950, before most were taken northwards or murdered. *US National Archives*

RIGHT A USAF air reconnaissance photo of Son Tay. The camp was in the middle of an area thought to be full of North Vietnamese – and possibly Chinese – troops. *US National Archives*

15 May 1975 – Boarders away! Marines, and sailors from the USS *Harold E. Holt*, board the deserted SS *Mayaguez*. *US National Archives*

BRIDGE

SON TAY POW CAMP
(POST-ASSAULT)

SON TAY POW CAMP

SON TAY CITY

U/I LIGHT INDUSTRY

SECONDARY SCHOOL

FOOT BRIDGE

ABOVE The situation plot is manually updated in the ABCCC, the 'back end' of an EC-130E. From this position Col. Anders and his (Air Force) battle managers fought the battle on Koh Tang. *US National Archives*

A Marine searches the deserted *Mayaguez* to make sure that there are no Khmer Rouge hidden on board. *US National Archives*

NO.1
S.S. MAYAGUEZ
50 PERSONS
840 CU.FT.
WILMINGTON DEL.

ABOVE LEFT Jimmy Carter delivers a speech after visiting the wounded of the Iran Desert One disaster at Walter Reed Army Hospital. *US National Archives*

ABOVE RIGHT The carrier USS *Nimitz*, from where the Iran raid's helicopters took off, refuels in the northern Arabian Sea. The number and type of helicopters that could be kept on the hangar deck of the *Nimitz* was a key constraint in planning the raid. *US National Archives*

OPPOSITE TOP Grenada: a US Army Ranger guards Cuban 'construction workers' taken prisoner in the fighting on D-Day at Point Salines Airport (seen in the background). *Department of Defense*

RIGHT Paratroopers from the 82nd Airborne, heavily laden as a result of the Rangers' reports of unexpected opposition at H-Hour, move out from Port Salines on D-Day to secure the rest of Grenada. *Department of Defense*

ABOVE M102 105 mm howitzer of the 82nd Airborne in action on Grenada. These guns supported the successful liberation mission at Grand Anse on D+1 and the disastrous raid at Calivigny on D+2. *Department of Defense*

Mogadishu, 1993: 10th Mountain Division soldiers move through a residential street in the Bakara Market district. These troops carried out several seizure raids before the arrival of Task Force Ranger and then extracted Task Force Ranger during the decisive battle of 3–4 October. *Department of Defense*

the late arrival of the FACs in the OV-10s – a direct result of poor planning for the use of these key assets – brought the operations close to disaster. Massive fire power was not feasible, but it would have been possible to have accurately directed fire power on call with better planning.

The improvised nature of the chain of command, down to the Marine's scratch task group, compounded the limited time available for planning and rehearsal. High-level intervention by the NCA undercut the effective co-ordination of the ABCCC to link together the different elements of the operation, especially in the opening hours when neither Johnson nor Austin was in position to give orders to the Marines on the ground. It is unlikely that the order to turn around the second wave of helicopters would have been given had there been a senior Marine on the ABCCC who could tell from the radio traffic the dire need for those reinforcements on the island.

The lack of communication between Air Force fighter-bombers and the Marines limited the effectiveness of US air power. Helping to save the situation were Marine officers – pinned down under fire or floating in life jackets – who were able to improvise communications, and Air Force air–ground specialists – the FACs and AC-130s – with reliable radio links.

As at Son Tay, the capability of the CH-53-series helicopter – its carrying capability, range and reliability – made the liberation operation possible. Koh Tang further illustrated the importance of these helicopters for liberation operations. There would have been no way to carry out the mission without them. But its limited range, carrying capacity and, especially in the case of the CH-53Cs, survivability, imposed serious operational constraints on the planners.

Ironically, the Khmer Rouge had reinforced Koh Tang before the *Mayaguez* incident because they were concerned about a potential North Vietnamese (or Thai) move against the island. The Khmer Rouge, aware that the Vietnamese had captured lots of helicopters, had positioned their machine guns to engage a heliborne assault.

The tragic conclusion was the three rearguard Marines being left behind. Raiders leaving people behind during extraction is the sign of inexpert execution, as demonstrated by the British at Bardia in 1941 and the USMC Raiders at Makin in 1942. One reason raids are meticulously planned – rather than improvised to achieve a quick reaction like CSAR – is to make sure that no one is left behind. Leaving raiders behind to the Khmer Rouge was a result not of the quality of the troops – the helicopter crews and Marines did all that could have been expected of them – but of the improvised nature of the operation and the divided and heavily overcentralized command.

While the personnel in Son Tay were literally hand-picked by the leadership, those involved in the *Mayaguez* operation were those who could make it to U Tapao in time. The Air Force helicopters, for all the bravery of their crews – recognized by four Air Force Crosses – were asked to perform air-assault tactics in which they were not trained. The Marines – even the partially trained riflemen of the 'hollow forces' era – were forced to carry out their mission under heavy fire, and the command system failed to ensure that a better-trained unit was sent into harm's way even when one was available. Once again, courage and improvisation could not by themselves bring victory in the face of modern weapons, especially without fire power, numbers, darkness, deception, speed or surprise to provide cover. Good fortune was what kept the crew of the *Mayaguez* and most of the raiders alive at the end of the day.

CHAPTER 6
IRAN · 24–25 April 1980

To you all, from us all, for having the guts to try.

Message to the returning Iran raiders,
Masirah, Oman, from UK military personnel.

The Iran raid failed – incurring heavy casualties and high political costs – long before it was in a position to liberate any hostages. Special operations forces were asked, through an admittedly high-risk operation, to produce results that diplomacy had been unable to achieve. The determination and courage of those who planned and went on the mission were just as evident as the elements that failed.[1] The lessons of the Iran raid – reinforced in the years that followed – were to be a prime motivating force behind reforms to US SOF and to US capabilities to carry out liberation and seizure missions.

NEW MISSIONS AND FORCES
In the years between Son Tay and Iran, special operations forces changed in response to the rise of international terrorism. Throughout the Middle East and Europe, governments were challenged by the Palestine Liberation Organization (PLO), the Irish Republican Army (IRA), the Red Army Faction, the Red Brigades and many other ideological, ethnic and nationalist-based terrorist groups. The cultural and political upheavals in the West – compounded by the global energy crisis of 1973–4 – convinced many terrorists that, in the absence of any effective will or capability to counter them, they could attack the capitalist world much as their idol Che Guevara had said his *focos* would: a small vanguard could overturn a rotting regime without the lengthy Leninist organization and preparation.[2]

Many of the terrorists' successes in the 1970s seemed to confirm their power, even if not the imminence of their success. Airline hijacking and kidnappings became prime terrorist tactics. Multiple hijackings to Jordan had started the PLO's 'Black September' in 1970; the US military soon became conscious of its lack of a force to respond to such actions. The US had to improvise a plan – fortunately never used – for European-based airborne units to liberate the US embassy in Amman, Jordan, if terrorists seized it.[3] The PLO's murder of kidnapped Israeli athletes in Munich in 1972 underlined the inadequacy of the improvised German special operations response.

The terrorist threat became a focus for Western development of a special operations response. A nexus of hostage-liberation missions marked a turning point: the Israeli raid on Entebbe, Uganda, in 1976; the operations in Djibouti, East Africa, by the French GIGN in 1976; and in Mogadishu, Somalia, in 1977 by the German GSG-9 with British SAS advisors. A day after Mogadishu, US Defense Secretary Harold Brown received a memo from President Jimmy Carter which ended with the order to 'develop similar US capabilities'. Successful special operations direct actions showed that the West had the will and capability to defeat this element of the terrorists' tactics. The United States did not have to deal with a direct terrorist threat to its homeland, but did realize that terrorism was a part of the modern world and that a capability to counter its effects was both a military and political necessity. Turning this need into a capability proved to be more difficult.

Since the US was now concerned with an increasing Soviet threat and would no longer be fighting counter-insurgency conflicts in the Third World, special operations forces were considered peripheral. The military services – at that time each responsible for funding their own special operations forces – had been reluctant to devote a share of their limited funding and quality manpower to special operations, which was seen as a relic of the Vietnam era.

The US Army, institutionally on the side of its big battalions, was reluc-tant to devote resources to a mission it saw as peripheral. The US Army has always preferred to liberate prisoners by winning wars rather than through raids, just as the Air Force has preferred to liberate prisoners by bombing the enemy into surrender and the Navy by controlling the sea lanes. The US Army disbanded four Special Forces Groups (SFG). Another, 7th SFG, escaped disbandment only after a strong lobbying campaign in 1979 by special forces officers and congressional allies. All the surviving special operations units were severely understrength. Other services also cut back. The US Air Force's 1st Special Operational Wing had such low readiness that it was unable to get any aircraft airborne one night during an operational readiness inspection.[4] The SEALs remained in the order of battle only because of their utility to naval operations – for example, their ability to attack enemy bomber airfields or scout invasion beaches.

US special operations forces shared their parent services' initial suspicion of the counter-terrorism mission. However, in the post-Vietnam era, the counter-terrorism mission provided a *raison d'être* and a justification for funding being made available to maintain special operations force structure. However, US special operations forces did not adopt the model of the British SAS, which had shifted from its traditional primary raiding role to embrace a counter-revolutionary warfare role over the course of the 1970s, undergoing an intellectual transformation to understand the distinct challenges presented by terrorism and revolutionary warfare. Rather, the US military viewed the new threat as a tactical problem requiring weapons, tactical solutions and, eventually, specialist operators to apply them.

The counter-terrorist mission was deemed to call for special teams, for a war that would be fought by small-scale sub-units. Soon, Army special operators were issued with flash-bang 'stun' grenades and silenced rifles, and were practising hostage-rescue techniques in close-combat houses built in Fort Bragg, NC, where simulated terrorist pop-up targets emerged from among silhouettes of bound hostages. Navy SEALs practised boarding and recapturing hijacked merchant ships.

The role that these specially trained forces would play in the larger national security strategy was a question too difficult to answer in the 1970s. The new capabilities were regularized and institutionalized in new forces. The Navy formed SEAL Team Six, specialists in maritime counter-terrorism and hostage rescue. The US Army initially formed a dedicated Special Forces counter-terrorism command, Project Bright Light, which was eventually supplanted by what became known as the 1st Special Operations Forces (Airborne) Detachment Delta. It was usually known as Delta Force.

DELTA FORCE

COL Charles 'Charlie' Beckwith, a much-decorated Special Forces Vietnam veteran, formed Delta Force, and its existence remained nominally classified. The personnel for Delta came largely from Special Forces, but there were also other influences. Beckwith had served under Bull Simons of Son Tay fame in Laos and was a veteran of special operations throughout Southeast Asia. An Anglophile with a Texan drawl and cowboy ways, he had undertaken an exchange tour with the British SAS and had learned that it was possible for a modern democracy to have an effective military counter to terrorism and revolutionary warfare. Increased US–Israeli defence co-operation post-1973 brought lessons from that direction as well, especially after the 1976 Entebbe raid. Charlie Beckwith set out to apply these lessons in the US. Delta is organized into squadrons and troops, like the SAS, rather than groups and detachments, like Special Forces. Like the SAS, Delta is built around the four-man team, the minimum needed to clear a room or maintain an observation post.

Delta was controversial. While Beckwith enjoyed high-level institutional support – most notably from Army Chief of Staff GEN Edward C. Meyer and Training and Doctrine Command (TRADOC) Commander (and leading Army reformer) GEN William DePuy – many in the Army wanted to stay away from the counter-terrorism mission. Special Forces wanted Bright Light to retain the mission. The creation of Delta provided a cadre of professionals able to use multiple tours to literally write the book on the tactics and techniques of liberation and seizure missions. It also made available to the national command authority a force capable of carrying out these missions that would not be subject to the turbulence, training cycles and other commitments affecting the other units that could be given over to these missions.

THE RANGERS

The Army wanted a stronger direct-action special operations capability. This led to the organization of two US Army Ranger battalions (a third and a regimental headquarters were added later, in the 1980s). Originally organized for rapid strategic reaction rather than raiding, Ranger battalions were recreated, specializing in forced entry via parachute, air landing or amphibious insertion as part of the US's power-projection capabilities. Forced-entry operations – the seizure of airfields for use by heavier follow-on forces – soon emerged as a Ranger speciality. The Rangers would, as their Second World War predecessors were intended (but rarely able) to do, literally 'lead the way', seizing and securing airfields, ports or beachheads for heavier follow-on forces. They did not have the Special Forces capability to train foreign troops or perform the patient, slow work of bolstering foreign internal defence.

The Rangers were light infantry, and when the first two battalions were formed, their heaviest weapons were 60 mm mortars and 90 mm recoilless rifles. They were trained in night operations (in 1974 the US Army still operated primarily by day as they had in Korea in 1950). They were obviously organized to use speed and surprise rather than fight battles of attrition.[5] Since 1974, the Rangers have evolved into large-scale (company- to regiment-sized) direct action special operations specialists, carrying out forced-entry attacks, raids and security and reinforcement missions in support of other US SOF.

The formation of the Ranger battalions was controversial, some critics seeing them as absorbing trained, motivated enlisted personnel, who at that time were rare in the Army's line battalions. The Rangers soon developed their own *esprit de corps* and mystique, comparable to that of the Special Forces. Intense training for the coveted Ranger tabs soon attracted recruits who would never have joined the 1970s-era 'hollow army'. This enabled the Rangers to pick and choose from recruits. Some were exceptional – two early-enlisted Rangers had PhDs – and the rest were well above average, scoring equally in aptitude testing with the personnel in the best signal and military intelligence battalions.

HOSTAGES AND PLANNING

The war you get is seldom the war you trained for. No US service saw Iran as a major area for potential US involvement – except as a market for US military hardware and as a duty station for US military trainers and advisers – until January 1979. The turmoil following the sudden abdication and flight into exile of Shah Mohammed Reza Pahlavi, the longtime ruler of Iran and staunch US ally, brought to power anti-American fundamentalist Shiite Muslim clerics led by Ayatollah Ruholla Khomeini. On 4 November 1979, two weeks after President Jimmy Carter had allowed the former Shah to enter the US for medical care, 3,000 Iranians – Revolutionary Guards and 'student' radicals – invaded the US Embassy in Tehran and seized it, holding sixty-six Americans, mainly diplomats, hostage. Chief of Mission L. Bruce Laingen and two aides were held separately at the Iranian Foreign Ministry. Khomeini and his supporters repeated demands that the former Shah be returned for trial.

It became apparent that the Iranian government would not release the hostages despite a large-scale diplomatic effort by the US and a wide range of friendly countries to free the hostages. It was unclear whether the hostages were being tortured or readied for execution. Within hours, the newly operationally certified 120-man Delta Force was on full alert. What it lacked was a plan, actionable intelligence or an effective capability.[6]

An earlier private-sector liberation mission to Iran had succeeded. When the Iranians had jailed two employees of the US firm Electronic Data Systems, its owner, eccentric Texas billionaire (and future part-time presidential candidate) H. Ross Perot, enlisted Bull Simons, then a retired colonel, to liberate them. With a blank check from Perot, Simons travelled covertly to Iran, arranged a jailbreak and – by the end of February 1979, seven weeks after Perot had called him – had the two Americans safe. It was Simons' last op. He died three months later from heart failure.[7]

On 6 November 1979, President Carter directed the Joint Chiefs of Staff to start working on a liberation plan. In response, the Chairman of the Joint Chiefs of Staff (CJCS), Gen. David C. Jones – who had filled in as acting Chief of Staff in the opening days of the *Mayaguez* crisis – directed the J-3 (Operations) section of the Joint Staff to initiate contingency planning.

Carter, facing a re-election battle in 1980, strongly favoured a diplomatic solution. Many of his advisers and cabinet officials – most notably Secretary of State Cyrus Vance and his deputy, Warren Christopher – were also opposed to the use of force. However, despite this, National Security Advisor Dr. Zbigniew Brzezinski, on his own initiative, directed the Pentagon to begin planning for a rescue mission and retaliatory strikes.[8] Brzezinski became the main conduit for the issue between the White House and the Pentagon. The lack of intelligence on the situation in Tehran – who was holding the hostages, where and how – precluded effective planning for a liberation mission until the intelligence picture could be pieced together from multiple sources over a matter of weeks.

As planning started, Carter pledged that there would be no White House interference. He did set parameters: a high probability of success, minimize collateral damage, maximize security, keep the force as small as possible, avoid actions that would cause a permanent estrangement from Iran or drive them towards the Soviets.[9] Until the US broke diplomatic relations with Iran in April 1980, the plan for the raid was to have a 'firebreak' at every step so that it could be halted short of execution. Concerns that Iranian moderates – though this group was never defined or identified – should not be marginalized by any US military action remained strong.

On 12 November, the CJCS established a small, secretive planning group for the operation, dubbed Rice Bowl, to study American options for a liberation effort. The codename of the operation itself – though intended to fit a cover story that the planning was for humanitarian relief in Southeast Asia – was a reference to the parochial interests of each of the services. The planners would not 'break the rice bowl' of any service by excluding them from the mission and thereby removing the justification for each service to have its own special operations capabilities and the associated funding.

The JCS's Crisis Action System (CAS) was not used to minimize the personnel involved. Following the Son Tay model, a secret Joint Task Force (JTF) – 1-79 – was set up, responsible directly to the Joint Chiefs of Staff. This would be an *ad hoc* mission-specific organization.

On 12 November, Jones selected Army MG James Vaught, a veteran of three wars, to command the JTF. Though an Airborne Ranger, Vaught had no command experience with joint or special operations. The services did not have many senior officers drawn from the special operations community – few, if any, were promoted above field grade – and there were no specialized special operations staffs. The experienced operators that had emerged from the Vietnam war and had planned and executed the Son Tay raid had largely retired or been separated from the military during the post-Vietnam reductions in force.

As a result, Vaught had to improvise a planning team and an operational headquarters. Vaught had to set up an *ad hoc* organization responsible for pulling together intelligence as well as disparate units and capabilities into a coherent whole while carrying out a complex planning process without the benefit of any existing contingency plans.[10] Because of the need for extreme secrecy, he was denied the use of any existing JCS or service organizations. Vaught had to deal with all these aspects himself, and he lacked assistance –

a formal deputy, USAF Lt. Gen. Philip Gast, was designated fewer than two weeks before the raid took place. Up to that point, Gast – who outranked Vaught – had been functioning as an adviser to Vaught on the region because of his recent service in the Tehran embassy.

The chain of command that emerged was neither direct nor effective. While Vaught's direct access to the national command authority was backed up by effective command and control arrangements, the command and control of the force under him reflected the improvised multi-service nature of the operation, the shortage of skilled special operations planners and the desire to minimize the numbers involved. There was no staff to deal with intelligence, logistics, training, planning and operations.

Vaught brought in as *de facto* air component commander Col. James Kyle, a veteran Air Force special operations officer and MC-130 Combat Talon pilot. COL Charlie Beckwith was brought in as Delta Force commander and ground component commander.[11] Selected to lead the helicopter element was Marine Lt. Col. Edward Seiffert, an experienced CH-53 pilot who had flown long-range search-and-rescue missions in Vietnam and had considerable experience flying with night-vision goggles. Beckwith described Seiffert as 'a no-nonsense, humourless – some felt rigid – officer who wanted to get on with the job'. But Seiffert was not in charge of the training of the helicopter pilots. That was the responsibility of a more senior Marine officer – a helicopter pilot with regional expertise, Col. Charles Pitman, was brought in as a 'consultant'. He effectively – although not formally – assumed control of the rotary-wing element of the operations. It was determined that Seiffert would be responsible to Pitman for the execution of the mission but that all tactical decisions in the air would be Seiffert's responsibility as flight leader.

Training of air (fixed wing at Hurlburt Field, Florida, helicopter at Yuma, Arizona) and ground (mainly at Fort Bragg, NC) elements started in mid-November. A select team from the Air Force Weather Service was formed to provide forecasting support to the planners.

PREPARING THE PLAN

The scope of planning and organizing a rescue attempt from Tehran made the Son Tay raid look like an exercise in minor tactics by comparison. Tehran was remote from friendly countries and surrounded by desert and mountains. The embassy where most of the hostages were being held was in the heart of a congested city of four million people.

The planning was interrupted some two weeks after it began by an order from the White House, concerned that a leak about the mission might undercut diplomatic efforts. This sent a mixed signal to the planners and cost them a significant amount of time before efforts were restarted.[12] The planning was being undertaken in an atmosphere of concern over operational security. Brzezinski was also concerned about leaks.[13] Soviet intelligence was believed to have US actions towards Iran as their second collection priority after strategic nuclear posture. Security was intense, making the planners and the force reliant on *ad hoc* arrangements, including the collection of intelligence. Only a select few knew the entire plan.

Initially, the core planning group considered a direct assault on Tehran. Air Force SOF helicopters had deployed to Turkey in February in the immediate wake of the hostage crisis, but the potential for their use in such a mission was undercut when their presence was leaked to the press by Turkish officials.[14] An airborne assault – with fighter escort and preceded by defence-suppression aircraft – was proposed next, which would drop paratroops and vehicles over the embassy in Tehran. Another force would drop and seize an airfield outside Tehran. The force dropped on the embassy would then, with air support, fight their way to the airfield to be picked up. Complicating the planning was the fact that in addition to the sixty-six hostages held at the embassy (eventually reduced to fifty-three by April due to Iranian releases) there were a further three diplomats being held at the Iranian Ministry of Foreign Affairs. Beckwith eventually ruled out a parachute drop as a way of inserting raiders directly into Tehran.

Helicopters – a heliborne raid was selected as the primary planning option by the CJCS on 19 November – were seen as the best option for reaching Tehran, despite the doubts Beckwith and other Vietnam veterans had about their reliability. Jones ordered six Navy RH-53D helicopters deployed to the carrier *Nimitz* in the Indian Ocean (two more were to follow months later).

Initially, the raid was to involve eighty raiders in four helicopters.[15] The numbers grew as additional intelligence was received and as planning and training progressed. When it was learned that many of the hostages were being held dispersed throughout the large embassy chancellery building, the numbers increased to ninety raiders and six helicopters.[16]

By March 1980, the evolving plan would include aircraft and aircrew from all four services flying eight types of aircraft (including eight RH-53D helicopters, four MC-130s, three EC-130Es, three AC-130s and two C-141s) into Iranian airspace, with many more in support or standing by. The plan relied on covert operators being infiltrated into Tehran ahead of the actual assault, gaps in Iranian radar coverage and the desolate nature of much of the surrounding countryside. The distance to the target, the lack of needed intelligence and the 'rice bowl' requirements to involve all services led to the planners evolving a complex and admittedly high-risk plan that depended on many different independently organized and trained components working together perfectly.

The heart of the ground raiding force would be Delta Force. The USAF's special operations forces would provide the C-130-series aircraft. Multiple helicopter types were evaluated for the mission. It had been proposed originally that the Air Force HH-53-series Pave Low special operations helicopters and their experienced crews would carry out the rotary-wing portion of the plan. Objections were raised, however, that since the plan required the helicopters to be launched from an aircraft carrier off the Iranian coast, the presence of the Air Force helicopters – with their distinctive nose radomes for protecting terrain-following radar – would violate operational security. The latest version of the Pave Low's electronics were not fully tested – reflecting the low level of SOF funding available before the raid – and the helicopter itself had not been qualified for carrier operations. It lacked folding rotors for below-decks stowage. The problems of refuelling these helicopters from C-130s at low altitude were also raised, although this had been done successfully in the Son Tay raid.

Instead of the Air Force helicopters, Navy RH-53D Sea Stallions – used as airborne minesweepers – were chosen because their presence in the region could be explained by the need for US forces to have a minesweeping capability. The Navy helicopters and their crews were both carrier-qualified. The RH-53D also had folding rotors and tail sections and could therefore be forward deployed in squadron strength on a carrier without interfering with other air operations. Their on-board electronics would not interfere with other Navy systems. The Navy and Marines also wanted to make sure that they were institutionally represented in the raiding force. RH-53Ds were not configured, nor their crews trained, for air refuelling.

This committed the raid to covert on-the-ground refuelling in Iran, with fuel either parachute-dropped or air-landed near the helicopters by fixed-wing transport aircraft. The latter approach was approved on 27 December. There had not been a long track record of using such tactics in successful raids. However, the US had studied this capability for years, especially during the 1950s and 1960s when it was thought that an attack on the Soviet Union would lead to US bombers – at that time the primary nuclear weapons delivery system – having to recover at airfields that had avoided Soviet nuclear strikes. Some of these could be in neutral countries or within the Soviet Union itself, secured by special operations forces. More recently, US Army heliborne forces had looked at using forward FARRPs to enable operational manoeuvre into enemy rear areas (as the 101st Air Assault Division would eventually do in 1991). The concept seemed feasible.

INTELLIGENCE

Intelligence – especially the all-important human intelligence – was weak. Most of the US HUMINT operations that remained inside Iran had been run from the embassy, and the Iranians had effectively closed down these operations. By the time of the raid, they were 'rolling up' the US HUMINT assets whose identities were revealed by captured documents.

While they received CIA and NSA reports directly, the raid's planners lacked detailed information on the numbers and locations of the Iranian guards and, most importantly, on the location of the hostages. This information was unlikely to be gained through the National Technical Means – the big eye and the big ear – on which US intelligence had come to rely. These facilities could not tell what was going on inside the compound. More importantly, they could not provide either decision-makers or planners with insights into the intentions of the hostage-takers – whether they were looking to slaughter them all or release them in a show of mercy.

Beckwith was desperate for information about how the hostages were being held. He had requested covert reconnaissance by Delta personnel and had been denied. Without this data, Delta had to plan to search up to six buildings in the embassy compound where the hostages might be held. That required Beckwith to increase the size of his assault force, which meant more helicopters were needed. That the intelligence community was able to provide as much covert capability inside Iran as it did by the time of the raid was a tribute to them, but limited HUMINT meant that planners and raiders alike would literally be going into the embassy blind. That, in turn, would shape the size and scope of the raid. The plan required a US covert on-the-ground capability to support the raiders. This in turn required the infiltration of agents to replace the assets 'blown' by the fall of the embassy. The CIA had also been given the mission of obtaining detailed intelligence about the hostages' location and preparing to support the raiders.

In addition to CIA assets, there was a separate covert military HUMINT effort inside Iran led by retired MAJ Dick Meadows, who had stormed the prison compound at Son Tay. Operating under neutral passports, Meadows and three Army and Air Force NCOs independently verified CIA-provided intelligence and set themselves up to receive the raiders inside Iran. The presence of competing covert capabilities reflects the mutual lack of confidence between the military and the CIA.[17]

THE IRAN RAID PLAN

The plan for the Iran hostage raid that emerged was a complex two-day multi-phase effort. It was heavily dependent on the unverified – and unverifiable – assumption that large heliborne forces could penetrate Iran, refuel and camouflage themselves until their final strike to liberate the hostages. The decision to rely on this assumption was seen as reasonable by those Americans with in-depth knowledge of Iran – the relationship between the two countries had been a close one under the Shah – and reflected the poor internal communications in Iran, the disruption of the Iranian military caused by the Islamic revolution and the fact that the raiders would use the same equipment as the Iranian military and would only be apparent as a US force when it was too close to matter.

Phase One called for two air packages – the fixed-wing package carrying the raiders and fuel for the helicopters, the rotary-wing package flying empty – to penetrate Iranian airspace, undetected, at low level on the first night. Three MC-130s were to fly from the island of Masirah, off the coast of Oman, more than 1,600 km to Desert One, an abandoned unimproved airfield near Tabas in Iran's Dasht-e-Kavir desert, 420 km southeast of Tehran, which had been selected by MG Vaught on 7 April. The lead MC-130 would use its

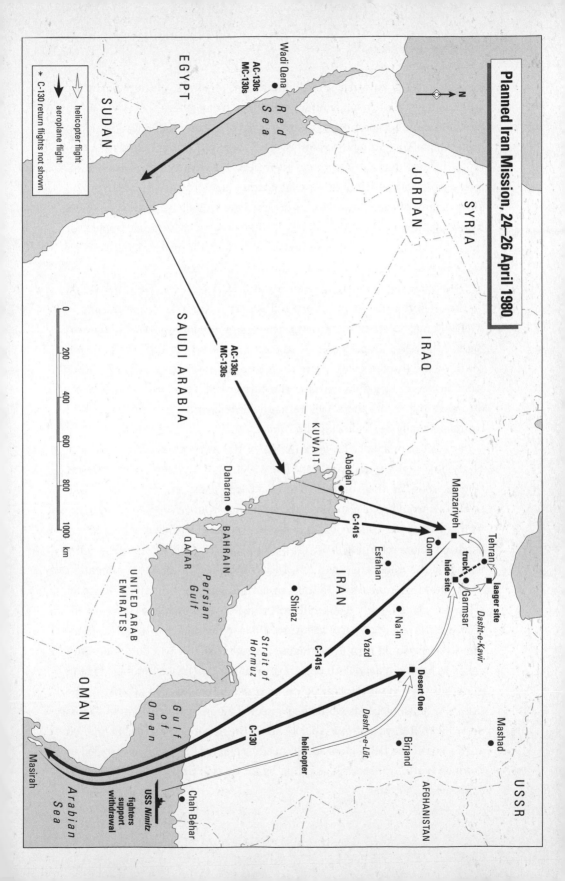

Planned Iran Mission, 24–26 April 1980

N

* C-130 return flights not shown
aeroplane flight
helicopter flight

EGYPT

SUDAN

Wadi Qena
AC-130s
MC-130s

Red Sea

JORDAN

SYRIA

IRAQ

SAUDI ARABIA

AC-130s
MC-130s

0
200
400
600
800
1000
km

KUWAIT

Abadan

Dahran

BAHRAIN

QATAR

UNITED ARAB
EMIRATES

Persian Gulf

C-141s

Qom

Esfahan

Shiraz

IRAN

Na'in

Yazd

Manzariyeh

Tehran
truck
hide site

Dasht-e-Kavir

laager site
Garmsar

Mashad

USSR

AFGHANISTAN

Birjand

Desert One

Dasht-e-Lut

C-141s

C-130

helicopter

Strait of Hormuz

OMAN

Gulf of Oman

Masirah

Arabian Sea

Chah Behar

USS *Nimitz*
fighters
support
withdrawal

forward-looking infra-red (FLIR) and radar to check the airfield before landing. It would then land and set up a tactical navigation (TACAN) beacon for the remaining aircraft to home in on. They would offload the raiders: ninety Delta Force troops (reinforced) and forty-two others including a separate thirteen-man Special Forces team, USAF Combat Controllers, volunteer translators (including several former senior Iranian officers and government officials) and twelve truck drivers. Following the MC-130s would be three EC-130Es modified as tankers to carry fuel and supplies for the raid, which would later be loaded on board the helicopters. Another MC-130 and an EC-130E would fly part way as spares.

The MC-130s carrying the raiders and EC-130Es carrying fuel would land at Desert One, set out a ground security perimeter using a force of twelve Rangers carried in for that purpose and prepare to refuel Bluebeard flight,[18] the RH-53D helicopters flying in from the carrier USS *Nimitz* 80 km south of the Iranian coast, more than 965 km from Desert One. Another Navy task force, organized around the carrier USS *Coral Sea*, would stage a diversion to 'peel off' the Soviet 'tattletale' intelligence-gathering ships that would normally be shadowing the *Nimitz*.

Phase Two would begin once the RH-53Ds were refuelled, before dawn on the first night of the operation. The MC-130s – two were to leave Desert One as soon as they unloaded to make room for the RH-53Ds – and EC-130Es would return to Masirah, refuelling from KC-135s *en route*. The twelve 'Desert Rangers' would collapse the security perimeter as the raiders departed before returning to Masirah on the last EC-130E out. The RH-53Ds would fly the raiders, picked up at Desert One, to 'Desert Two', a location about 80 km southeast of Tehran, in a wadi outside the city of Garmsar. There they would rendezvous with covert agents and their assets already in-country. The reception party agents would lead the raiders to a safe location. The RH-53s would then fly to 'Figbar', another site nearby, and hide until called in by the raiders. Both positions would be heavily camouflaged using materials carried on the helicopters and would be guarded against intrusion. The helicopter hide would be protected against air detection by teams armed with Redeye man-portable SAMs. If the mission had to be abandoned at this point, the helicopters would need to call for fuel to be airdropped to them by C-141 transports – standing by for this contingency – to be able to exfiltrate from Iran.

Phase Three was the rescue itself. The raiders and the helicopters would spend the daylight hours of the first day of the raid in their concealed positions. Iranian vehicles – six Mercedes trucks – procured and concealed by the covert agents would be brought out of their hiding places and driven towards the raiding force's concealed location. There would have been an opportunity for last-minute observation of the objectives, possibly via a daylight command reconnaissance by the raiders' leaders. On the second night of the raid, under the cover of darkness, the raiders would board the vehicles and head for 'The Mushroom', a Tehran warehouse to be used as a staging area for their assault on the US embassy compound (where fifty-three hostages were being held) and the Foreign Ministry building, where Bruce Laingen and two other US diplomats were being held captive. Another force would secure the pick-up zone.

Later that night, the raiders would be driven to the embassy in the Iranian vehicles, getting through Iranian checkpoints by pretending to be an Iranian military operation. The column would then split, with the thirteen-man SF force heading for the Foreign Ministry.

The main force would first infiltrate – with the aid of pro-US guards among the student militants – and then assault the embassy. Power and telephone lines would be cut. H-Hour would be at 0010. Two forty-man elements, Teams Blue and Red, would search and secure the eastern and western sections of the compound. They would rely on the element of surprise, demolitions and stun grenades to prevent a massacre of the hostages before they could be rescued. Blue would release prisoners in the Deputy Chief of Mission's house, the ambassadorial residence and the chancellery, all on the eastern side of the embassy compound. Red would clear the staff cottages and commissary on the western side of the compound. Translators dressed in Iranian uniforms would issue misleading orders to any enemy forces arriving on the scene. The thirteen-man White Team, heavily armed with light machine guns, would provide security.[19]

Hammer Flight of four Egypt-based AC-130s would support the assault. They were to be relied on to keep troops and mobs away from the Amjadieh football stadium where the raiding party and helicopters would rendezvous and to suppress action by the Iranian Air Force from nearby Mehrabad Airport.

After the raiders had freed the hostages, they would rendezvous with four RH-53Ds – flown from their concealed position outside of Tehran – at the nearby (500 m distant) Amjadieh football stadium. The raiders would lead the hostages there, exiting through a gap blown in the embassy compound wall. Each pair of helicopters would leave a holding point and move in to the LZ. The stadium pick-up was seen as the highest-risk part of the operation. If the Iranians were able to rush troops to the scene, it could end up as an Alamo-style defence, with the raiders holding the perimeter with the help of AC-130s. If the helicopters suffered losses and there were not enough to lift out the raiding force, there was an overland escape and evasion plan in place.

The thirteen–man Special Forces team would rescue the three Americans held in the Foreign Ministry (this second separate force was a late addition to the plan) and would be picked up from a park's athletic field near the foreign ministry by a fifth RH-53D, with the sixth as a back-up.

Phase four was the extraction. The first step was to secure the pick-up point while the ground action in Tehran was in progress. Four MC-130s would again penetrate Iran from Egypt. They would land a seventy-five-man reinforced Ranger company (with USAF CCT), using M151 gun jeeps and motorcycles for mobility, on the disused Manzariyeh airfield, about 80 km southwest of Tehran. The Rangers were to parachute in if the runways were blocked or the defences were alerted. They were to hold the airfield until the liberated hostages and the raiders arrived from Tehran.

Two C-141s (one, codenamed Electrode, configured as a hospital ship) would fly in from Saudi Arabia and land at Manzariyeh once the Rangers had secured it. These aircraft would ferry the hostages and raiders back to base after destroying the helicopters. The AC-130s would cover the final evacuation of the Rangers on MC-130s before egressing. An escort of four Navy F-14A or F-4N fighters from the carriers *Nimitz* and *Coral Sea* would provide air cover inside Iran, while others would fly a combat patrol along the Iranian border, ready to render assistance against any air threats.

Python Force, a ninety-man unit of Force Reconnaissance Marines, was the back-up extraction force, waiting with helicopters and C-130s in western Turkey. They would go in for CSAR if any aircraft were shot down or head directly for Manzariyeh, Tehran or Desert Two if reinforcements were needed.[20]

Vaught would accompany the C-141s on the extraction phase of the mission, but aside from that he would remain at his headquarters at Wadi Qena airfield in Egypt. No overall commander would be with the operation throughout.

The plan was subjected to an in-depth review by a 'murder board' drawn from among the JTF planners themselves. While realizing that it was difficult to critique their own work, the high classification of the plan prevented it from being reviewed by experts who had not themselves participated in the planning. The 'murder board' review approved the plan. However, security constraints prevented the board from carrying out a comprehensive readiness evaluation or reviewing the training of the force.[21] The *ad hoc*, decentralized and highly compartmentalized nature of the training and planning led to a situation where no one had a coherent picture of the JTF's full capability or the entirety of the plan.

This brought into question one of the key principles of special operations, which is that those who will carry out the mission need to be involved in the planning as well. According to one MC-130 co-pilot, 'only a couple of navigators were permitted to review the plans prior to mission briefs. This is one area where we felt security was taken too far. We had some very qualified planners filling aircrew positions.'[22]

Complicating both the planning and the training for it was the fact that no timeline or target D-Day was established at the outset. Rather, the forces had to be ready to go at almost any time, in response to any potential threats to the lives of the hostages that might emerge. It took several months for Operation Eagle Claw (with a target date of 24–25 April not being set until 12 April) to emerge as something the Joint Task Force considered a workable plan. The locations for launching and supporting the raid would not be known until after many months of intense diplomacy. Only in the final stages of planning did Vaught find out that the force could launch from a base in Oman.

All of the diverse operational elements had become confident of their ability to carry out the mission. Jones briefed this plan to President Carter and his national security team on 22 March. Jones had confidence in the plan. The President found the plan 'feasible', but noted that it was exceptionally complex and that making each of the elements work together on time gave him concern.[23] Brzezinski wanted the rescue to be integrated with larger retaliatory strikes against Iran. This would add to the secondary mission of demonstrating US will and capability and, if the raid failed, it could be presented as but one part of a larger successful operation. Although this had support from the Secretary of Defense and the Director of Central Intelligence, Carter elected not to integrate the raid with broader operations.[24]

Secretary of State Cyrus Vance remained opposed to any military action, so much so that Jones directed that the State Department be kept out of the loop on the planning of the raid.[25] Vance argued that the hostages – mainly State Department personnel – were more likely to be killed in a liberation attempt than by Iranian execution or mistreatment. He was also concerned that if the mission were successful, the Iranians would replenish their stock of hostages from the 200 Americans then in Iran, a number of whom were covert US agents. He thought that an embarrassing defeat of Iranian forces in the course of a successful raid might drive revolutionary Iran in the direction of the Soviet Union. However, in spite of his reservations, Vance did not try to kill the raid by leaking plans to the press.

TRAINING

Concurrent with the planning process, from November to March, the different elements of the force trained hard under conditions of strictest operational security, which mandated that each element train separately. Over the five months between November and March, the preparation for the rescue attempt was complicated by the strict security concerns. Just as the Joint Chiefs and the Carter administration's national security team were unable to turn to outside experts to evaluate the plan because of security requirements, the training and co-ordination of the different elements of the raiding force was also limited and highly compartmentalized. The Marine helicopter crews trained initially at their home base of Yuma, Arizona. The members of Delta Force did most of their five months of thorough training at their specialized facilities in Fort Bragg, North Carolina. Special Forces personnel – from the Berlin-based SF Detachment A – trained in Europe. The Air Force crews that would take part in the mission trained in Florida (MC/EC-130s) and Guam (AC-130s).

Training of the helicopter crews continued at the Marine base at Twenty-Nine Palms, California, in late November and presented several problems. During the training phase, two different officers assumed that they were in charge of the highly compartmentalized training program.[26] Initially, the RH-53Ds were trained with their specialist minesweeper crews. The Navy, due to security restrictions, had thought the requirement for RH-53D aircrew was for minesweeping. Consequently, they supplied aircrew with lots of minesweeping experience but none in special operations. The first change was to add Marine co-pilots with experience of land-assault missions. That combination soon proved unworkable. Many of the Navy pilots were untrained in long-range low-level flying over land, at night, using first-generation PVS-5 night-vision goggles. Their skills at airborne minesweeping were needed elsewhere. Following the first integrated JTF training on 18–19 December, Vaught decided to replace nine of the helicopter pilots.

In December, Marine helicopter pilots with experience in night-time low-level flying replaced most of the Navy pilots. Some of these had to be replaced in turn. As a result of security restrictions, the importance of the mission was not revealed to the Navy or the Marines. The helicopter aircrew sent to train for this mission were thus not necessarily the best available. Some, in classic military fashion, appear to have been those that their units wanted to be rid of. Some of the raiders, who had wide experience of heliborne operations, considered them to be the worst pilots they had encountered.[27] In the words of one MC-130 co-pilot, 'We all had serious doubts concerning the abilities of the chopper pilots. Based on what we saw they were the only weak link in the chain.'[28]

The RH-53D minesweeper helicopters, however, would remain. The eight helicopters were already on board the *Nimitz*, being maintained and operated by their owners, Navy Minesweeping Squadron HM-16. They were supported by one or two Sikorsky factory technicians, but the carrier lacked many of the more sophisticated tools associated with depot-level maintenance, such as x-ray equipment to inspect rotor blades for hidden cracks. However, only two of the helicopters were past due for such maintenance.[29] The helicopters proved relatively complex but reliable, with an abort rate of 6.3 pre-flight and 3.8 in-flight aborts per 100 hours.[30] The raiders trained on a mixture of CH-53A, CH-53D and RH-53D helicopters as stand-ins. Consequently, they did not get to know the specific handling qualities or reliability of the helicopters they would be flying on the raid.

Beckwith realized that the decision to launch and the timing of any action would 'always [be] a political decision, it's not, nor should it be, a military one'.[31] The constant pressure – expressed through Brzezinski but coming from the White House – to get the raiding force ready early and remain ready to act if the situation changed affected the helicopter force. Had the military known going into the training process that they would have more time, they could have selected helicopter pilots from a broader group and trained more crews.[32] Eventually, of the sixteen helicopter pilots to launch, twelve were Marines, three were Navy, and one was Air Force. Unlike Delta Force and the MC/EC-130 crews, the helicopter crews were not special operations personnel and were not merely refining skills in their primary mission area, but learning new ones. It is not surprising that the helicopter aircrew never acquired the high degree of cohesion required for such a mission.[33]

Beckwith and Seiffert had agreed that they would need a minimum of six flyable helicopters at Desert One for the mission to continue. Beckwith had asked for ten helicopters on the carrier to cover possible malfunctions, but the Navy claimed they could not store more than eight on the hangar deck of the *Nimitz* without interfering with its operational capability; in reality twelve helicopters could have been stored on the hangar deck and used for the mission.[34] During the planning, the use of an MC-130E pathfinder for the helicopters, as in the Son Tay raid, was considered. Despite its success then, it was thought that the improved on-board navigation systems of the RH-53Ds would make this unnecessary.

The helicopter pilots were not the only training issue. The thirteen-man Special Forces team intended to liberate the hostages held in the Foreign Ministry building was being trained separately from the rest of the ground raiding force, in Germany. This reflected not only the limited size of Delta Force but also Special Forces leadership's distrust of Beckwith. Due to both operational (Delta was new, unproven and stretched too thin) and 'rice bowl' concerns, they had to be included. They would only join up with Beckwith immediately before the operation.

The range of forces and capabilities required to carry out the plan was staggering in its scope and complexity. It was hoped that this would be mitigated by training: the refuelling of helicopters at Desert One was rehearsed repeatedly until it was thought that it could be accomplished in forty minutes. But how the different elements of the plan would interact remained uncertain.

The fourth JTF training exercise on 26–27 February 1980 was the first limited rehearsal that brought together MC/EC-130s and RH-53Ds, and it revealed a host of problems. To one MC-130 co-pilot, 'There seemed to be some confusion as to where each chopper was supposed to land once it arrived in the area. Radio transmissions became excessive as the ground controllers attempted to talk the choppers into position. The whole process consumed far too much time. We were concerned because the chopper supposed to marry up with our aircraft never did arrive. The mission commander finally put the exercise on administrative hold. I remember thinking that if any high-level official was watching this drill, we were in trouble.'[35]

A proof-of-concept operation involving two C-130s and four RH-53Ds – a fraction of what the actual raid would require – was held in the US on the night of 13–14 April and judged satisfactory. This second rehearsal, like the first, used a paved runway rather than a sand one to prevent damage to the aircraft. This time, it seemed to the MC-130 co-pilot who had been critical of the helicopter performance on the previous exercise that, 'the second practice went very well. All the components went according to plan, even the choppers. Our radio chatter was eliminated. We felt good about it.'[36] But time and OPSEC constraints prevented a full-scale 'real-time' rehearsal of the plan.[37]

In March, after five months of planning, organizing, training and a series of increasingly complex individual rehearsals, Kyle was able to say: 'The ability to rescue our people being held hostage, which didn't exist on November 4, 1979, was now a reality.'[38]

Yet the participants still felt unease. One MC-130 co-pilot recalled, 'Our briefing dealt solely with C-130 operations. Other participating units briefed at separate locations. This stuck me as being unusual for a joint operation, but we were told that it was due to OPSEC requirements. With the exception of one representative who attended our briefs, we would never have face-to-face contact with the participants from the other services.'[39]

In the end, the raiding force was denied the one thing that is considered vital to success in any other comparable activity: a full-scale dress rehearsal (plus the all-important debrief) and the chance to implement corrections. The force command structure was only rehearsed once. The two partial rehearsals had been held in darkness for OPSEC reasons and training realism but there was no attempt to hold a face-to-face critique involving all the participants.[40]

THE TWIN OTTER RECONNAISSANCE

The decision to plan for an on-the-ground refuelling inside Iran meant that the raiders had to know in advance whether the selected landing ground would support the weight of the heavily laden EC-130 tankers. This intelligence was considered so important that high-risk reconnaissance that could compromise the whole operation was undertaken. Carter delayed authorizing the flight.[41] He turned down requests for such a mission on 28 February and 7 March before finally approving one on 22 March.

On the night of 26–27 March, a CIA Twin Otter flew into Desert One. USAF Combat Controllers carried out a specialist airfield survey mission, checking the surface and inspecting the field on light dirt bikes. They planted well-camouflaged landing lights that could be remotely activated by a signal from incoming MC-130s to help guide the force in. The survey proved successful – Desert One would support the tankers.

There had been concern that Iranian air-defence radar might detect the raiders as they penetrated. The Iranians had fifteen air-defence radars, US and British designed, but many were unreliable and the US was aware that low altitude coverage was limited. Regardless, the task force aircraft were modified with active and passive countermeasures. Reflecting these concerns, the Twin Otter had also been fitted with ELINT equipment, which had revealed no signals below 915 m and only a few above that altitude. A low-altitude penetration seemed viable.

However, the delay in the Twin Otter flight had reduced its impact on the raid. There was now even less time available to adjust planning or training, and the timing of the raid could not be brought forward to take advantage of longer nights and cloud-cover weather conditions.

THE DECISION TO GO

The diplomatic track to freedom for the hostages continued to fail. Egypt's President Anwar El Sadat warned Carter that the US regional position was eroding because of what was perceived as 'excessive passivity'. On 11 April, Carter realized that the raid was his only remaining hope: 'I told everyone that it was time for us to bring our hostages home; their safety and our national honour were at stake.' On 12 April the CJCS instructed Vaught to finalize the planning, and 24 April was fixed as the target date for the operation.

The high-stakes nature of the raid was apparent to the President's inner circle. Presidential Press Secretary Jody Powell said after the 11 April meeting, 'If we can bring our people out of there, it will do more good for this country than anything that has happened for twenty years.' Defense Secretary Harold Brown agreed, adding, 'If we fail, that will be the end of the Carter presidency.'[42]

Yet while Carter had lost hope of a diplomatic solution, his heart was never truly in the option of a liberation mission. On 16 April, following a day of briefings at the Pentagon, Jones, Vaught and Beckwith briefed Carter at the White House on the status of the rescue attempt and restated their confidence in their ability to pull it off. Carter told Beckwith: 'I do not want to undertake this operation, but we have no other recourse . . . We're going to do this operation.' Carter then told Jones: 'This is a military operation; you will run it . . . I don't want anyone else in this room involved.'

Almost immediately, forces began to move to their jump-off points. By 24 April, forty-four aircraft were poised at six widely separated locations to perform or support the rescue mission. The RH-53Ds were already on the *Nimitz*, where they had been stored for months, but a frantic effort brought them up to what Seiffert and the Navy insisted was top mechanical condition by launch day. Delta Force and many of the Air Force aircraft staged briefly through the Soviet-built airfield at Wadi Qena, Egypt, on their way to Masirah. Wadi Qena would serve as Vaught's headquarters for the mission. KC-135 tankers would operate from Egypt, C-141s from Saudi Arabia.

While at Wadi Qena on 23 April, the task force received an intelligence report that fifty-three hostages were being held in the embassy's chancellery. This was 'the cook's report'. The cover story for the information was that a former embassy cook had had a chance contact with a CIA agent while both were leaving Iran. The information was passed to the leadership of the JTF, but the CIA did not divulge its source.[43]

Because Beckwith was not told the source of that information – and because he could not evaluate it personally – he did not trust it enough to reduce his assault force. He had to have enough troopers available to search the entire embassy compound for prisoners, if necessary. He also knew that even if most of the prisoners had been concentrated in the chancellery, there were still likely to be some held separately either under interrogation, sick or being punished. Beckwith would leave no one behind. While intelligence showed that the guards at the embassy were no longer as well armed or as alert as they had been in the opening days of the hostage crisis, Beckwith was concerned with the need to hit with speed and overwhelming force to maintain the element of surprise.[44]

The next day, the raiders and the EC-130Es flew on to Masirah. The helicopter crews were waiting on the *Nimitz*. Vaught received the final weather report: it promised virtually clear weather. Vaught then sent a message to all units: 'Execute mission as planned. Godspeed.'

LAUNCH

The mission started at twilight on 24 April. One MC-130 co-pilot recalled the scene at Masirah: 'The maintenance troops lined the taxiway as the 130s lumbered towards the runway. They were waving wildly and giving the thumbs-up sign and salutes. Their enthusiasm was contagious. I remember the pride I felt as I taxied by them.'[45]

Kyle and Beckwith flew out of Masirah on the lead MC-130 Combat Talon, about an hour ahead of the rest. The three MC-130s of Dragon flight carried the raiding force as well as fuel-pumping equipment on the 1,600 km flight to Desert One. Three modified EC-130E tankers followed them, each equipped with two 11,300 litre fuel tanks. A near-collision between two aircraft as they were positioned for take-off delayed the force only by five minutes.

On the carrier *Nimitz*, hours before the mission was to begin, a sailor accidentally hit a fire-control switch, dousing five of the RH-53D helicopters with sea water and foam. The helicopters were cleaned and inspected with no obvious damage found. The helicopters, despite their months at sea, 'were in as good condition as any they had flown,' resplendent in new desert camouflage paint that made them look like Iranian helicopters.[46]

At 1905 on 24 April, Seiffert, in Bluebeard 1, led the eight RH-53Ds of helicopter force Bluebeard from the *Nimitz*. The Bluebeard helicopters headed to the Iranian coast, 96 km away, on the first leg of a 965 km trip. They crossed the coastline at an altitude of 30 m.

The RH-53Ds had been fitted in December with OMEGA and PINS (precision inertial navigation system) advanced navigation systems. However, there had been limited stateside training (only a single training helicopter had been similarly modified). The pilots found the new systems unreliable and were relying mainly on dead reckoning and visual navigation as they cruised at 60 m, using night-vision goggles for external reference.

About two hours into the mission, Bluebeard 6 was lost.[47] A warning light signalled that a rotor blade had cracked. It was forced to land in Iran, accompanied by Bluebeard 8. The crew – who had trained for the mission on CH-53 versions – was unaware of the RH-53D's improved rotor blades and that no cracked rotor had ever failed up to that time. The Marine crew was familiar with their versions of the basic CH-53 with older rotor variations, where such massive failures were possible. The crew visually inspected the rotor and decided to abandon Bluebeard 6. The crew, quickly gathering up all of the classified materials, boarded Bluebeard 8 and pressed on. They had no way to destroy the helicopter, as the planners had decided against carrying self-destruction devices for such contingencies. Bluebeard 6 was left intact for the Iranians to recover. Bluebeard 8 was now twenty minutes behind the rest of the formation.

The lead MC-130 descended 122 m while crossing the Iranian coastline between Chah Bahar and Jask at dusk. It had climbed back to 610 m when, about 160 km into Iran, it ran into a thin cloud that reduced visibility but was not otherwise a problem. The cloud was a mass of suspended dust, a *haboob*, common in the Iranian desert. According to the co-pilot of Dragon 3, 'Our visibility began to deteriorate rapidly. Our "clear and a million" night quickly turned to "zero-zero."'[48]

Air Force Air Weather Service experts supporting the mission could not provide a detailed forecast due to the lack of ground sites in the area, but they knew such a condition was likely. This information had not been passed to the compartmentalized mission crews due to security considerations. It remained in the weather annexe of the operational plan. The Air Weather Service, due to security compartmentalization, was unable to brief the aircrews. The intelligence officer filtering the information was not a pilot and did not know that the *haboob* weather information was important. Due to security concerns, the time-honoured tradition of giving the flight crews direct access to the weather forecasters was quashed.

Kyle, penetrating at 305–915 m in a modified terrain-following flight profile, considered sending a warning to the helicopters but decided that the condition was not significant, which it was not to his MC-130s.[49] When the MC-130 ran into a much thicker *haboob* cloud later, Kyle did try to alert

Seiffert, but the message never got through because of problems with second secure radio communications. Assured communications – assumed by the planners – was the second system to fail after the OMEGA/PINS.

As the helicopters penetrated at low level – much lower than the MC-130 – *en route* to Desert One, they encountered the thickest part of a *haboob* about three hours into the flight. Because they had not been briefed on the condition, they did not know what to expect. Unlike the C-130s, they were unable to fly over the worst of it.

Had the helicopter pilots been involved in the planning process and known that the Twin Otter SIGINT had found little low-altitude Iranian radar coverage – which was reflected in the higher penetration altitude approved for the MC-130s once they crossed the coast – they would not have unquestioningly accepted having to fly at or below 60 m to avoid radar. This limitation forced them to cruise inside the *haboob*. Flying in formation and visually navigating at 60 m while wearing the NVGs was fatiguing and highly difficult even for the skilled helicopter crews. The helicopters broke out of one cloud after thirty minutes only to re-enter a second, thicker one.

The flight was forced to separate. Seiffert in Bluebeard 1 and another helicopter decided to climb to 150–300 m to get above the worst of the dust. The other helicopters held to the pre-briefed altitude. The helicopters lacked secure radios – only Bluebeards 1 and 5 had SATCOM – that could communicate through the formation, so a rejoin was not possible. This reflected concern over enemy SIGINT capability, even though the Twin Otter mission data, the low-altitude flight and the rugged terrain made such interceptions unlikely. Indeed, the MC-130 electronic warfare officers had planned at flying up to 1,524 m if required.[50]

The flight conditions started to erode the helicopter formation. An electrical power source on Bluebeard 5 overheated, knocking out the gyro compass, horizon indicator and the cockpit lights. The crew – Col. Pitman was flying right seat – aborted back to the *Nimitz*, landing with fuel tanks dangerously close to empty. Bluebeard 5 maintained radio silence, so the rest of the formation did not know that it had turned back. Bluebeard 5's crew did not know that they were only about twenty-five minutes from clear air, which prevailed all the way to Desert One, because the reports from the lead MC-130 had not been sent correctly. (The Bluebeard 5 crew later said that, had they known this, they would have pressed on to Desert One. This was yet another example of intelligence information not being available to those who needed it in order to make decisions.) Bluebeard 2's secondary hydraulic pump burned out and failed after a leak in the system, but it pressed on using its primary system. None of this was known to Bluebeard lead, due to radio silence. The mission was now down to the minimum six helicopters.

ARRIVAL AT DESERT ONE

Kyle and the command group in Dragon 1, the lead MC-130, landed at Desert One at midnight. The concealed runway lights had been turned on as planned. The US Air Force Combat Control Team set out a portable TACAN navigation system and additional runway lights. Rangers and Delta Force perimeter security elements secured the field, blocking the dirt road that traversed the site. Kyle was supposed to establish SATCOM contact with Vaught immediately, but the shock of the rough field landing had disabled the equipment. He was limited to sending brief, coded high-frequency radio signals until Beckwith arrived with the backup SATCOM.

Dragon flight, consisting of the two remaining MC-130s, soon landed, bringing in Beckwith and the rest of the ground raiding force, followed by the three EC-130Es within an hour. Dragons 1 and 2 took off, empty, once they had unloaded. Dragon 3, tasked as a back-up tanker, remained. The remaining aircraft were carefully positioned to refuel the helicopters, which were scheduled to arrive twenty minutes later. To reduce the chance of malfunction and provide ground power, they kept their engines idling. According to the co-pilot of Dragon 3: 'We had been on the ground almost two hours and still no choppers. Where the hell were they?'[51]

The planners had been concerned about the possibility of SIGINT detection but had gone ahead and selected the Desert One site despite its proximity to a road, hence increasing the likelihood of early compromise. Within minutes, the raiders found that the road was not as deserted as intelligence reports had assured them it would be. Traffic – pilgrims and fuel smugglers especially – often travelled by night to avoid daytime heat. But the plan had provisions for dealing with vehicular traffic. Delta troopers stopped and detained an Iranian Mercedes bus carrying forty-four people at one end of the site. One of the passengers shouted a welcome in English to the 'Yanks'.

At the opposite end of the field, Rangers had to fire a 66 mm LAW anti-tank weapon into a gas tanker that refused to stop. The driver of the tanker leaped out of his burning vehicle and into a pick-up that was following and vanished into the darkness. But they had seen nothing that would have compromised the mission, nor anything to suggest that the men and aircraft were American rather than Iranian.

Kyle thought compromise was inevitable. Beckwith, however, thought that the truck likely belonged to a fuel smuggler – hence the presence of a fast escape vehicle, standard rum-runner tactics – and was unlikely to report the encounter. Kyle was persuaded to continue with the operation, relying on SIGINT to alert them if the Iranians were heard to pass warning messages.[52]

The delay in the arrival of Bluebeard flight was ominous. Finally, the helicopters arrived at Desert One. To Beckwith, they seemed to come in from all points of the compass, over an hour late, arriving at 0105. They counted them all in: only six, the minimum required for the operation. However, if they could be refuelled in forty minutes as in rehearsal, the raiders could still be lifted to their hiding positions before dawn.

Bluebeards 3 and 4, first to arrive, were positioned behind EC-130E Republic 4 on the northern edge of the airfield, experiencing 'brownout' conditions due to flying sand and dust. Bluebeard 3 had a flat nosewheel and had to hover-taxi. Bluebeard 8, next to arrive, was marshalled behind EC-130E Republic 5, on Republic 4's right wing, north of the road. Bluebeard 7 went behind Republic 5, south of the road. Last to arrive were Bluebeards 1 and 2. Bluebeard 1 was positioned north of the road behind EC-130E Republic 6. Bluebeard 2 went to the left of Bluebeard 7, behind Republic 5. As the helicopters struggled through unexpected deep sand to get into position behind the tankers, Bluebeard 2 shut down its engines to check its hydraulic system after getting into position behind EC-130E Republic 5.

The situation on the ground was one of confusion. The M/EC-130s, idling for over an hour, had blown up clouds of dust, reducing visibility. There was no identifiable or briefed command post for Kyle. Key personnel wore no distinguishing insignia, but rather sterile fatigues or flight suits. The helicopter crews did not understand who was in charge or know who Kyle or Beckwith were. The noise from the engines and the swirling sand and dust made communication difficult and limited visibility. The operation was experiencing complexities never anticipated during training.

As the helicopter crews inspected their sandblasted aircraft, a new problem arose which quickly attracted all the senior leadership at Desert One. Bluebeard 2's secondary hydraulic system remained inoperative. The pilot was willing to carry on with only his primary flight control system, but Seiffert overruled him. Despite Kyle's entreaties, Seiffert refused to let the helicopter proceed, warning that flying with only one system operational at such a heavy weight (due to taking off from Desert One full of troops and fuel) and high temperature could result in a control lockup and a crash that would kill not only the crew but the raiders on board. (Bluebeard 5's earlier decision to abort had been similarly influenced by recognition of the need to abandon rather than risk a failure when fully loaded.)[53]

Kyle, reluctant to abort the mission, then asked Beckwith if he could reduce his assault force to go with five choppers. Beckwith was equally adamant about not changing his plans – meticulously prepared – to allow the raid to proceed with five helicopters.

FAILURE IN FLAMES
Even though Kyle had been designated Desert One on-site commander – a fact that had not been briefed to the aircrew – there was only one single commander for the raid. That was Vaught, back in Egypt. Kyle could not command Seiffert or Beckwith. Faced with an impossible situation, Kyle said, 'Sir, my recommendation is that we abort.' Beckwith blurted out, 'There's just no way.' Kyle then notified the Pentagon of the situation via a secure SATCOM link. Kyle also informed Vaught of the situation by satellite radio. Vaught called the Pentagon, also requesting guidance on what to do with the Iranian bus and its passengers.

The word was relayed to Jones and the Secretary of Defense, Harold Brown, at the Pentagon. 'I think we have an abort situation,' Brown informed Carter. Brzezinski recommended that they go with five helicopters only if 'the field commander' recommended it.[54] After Brown explained the decision as that of the on-scene commander, Carter simply responded, 'Let's go with his [Brown's] recommendation,' then 'hung up . . . put his head down on top of his desk, cradling it in his arms for approximately five seconds,' Brzezinski recalled.[55]

It was even worse at Desert One. 'The crew was dumbfounded. We had never, ever, considered aborting.'[56] The order to abort was received at Desert One about twenty minutes after it was requested from Washington. Kyle was left with the unrehearsed job of getting everyone out of Iran. The bus and its passengers were to be released and Bluebeard 2 destroyed.

As a result of the extended wait for the helicopters, one of the EC-130Es, Republic 4, idling while waiting for the delayed helicopters, was now running low on fuel and needed to leave soon. To allow that tanker to move, Kyle directed Marine Maj. James Schaefer to reposition his helicopter, Bluebeard 3. With a damaged nose wheel, Schaefer's helicopter could not taxi over the sandy terrain. It was decided to hover-taxi Bluebeard 3 to its new position. A ground guide with a lighted wand was positioned between it and the C-130. As it lifted off to move, the helicopter stirred up a blinding dust cloud. The RH-53D slid sideways.

Hit by the force of the sandstorm created by the helicopter's downdraft, the ground guide staggered back towards the EC-130E. He was still holding his wand, so the RH-53D followed him. The movement of the hover reference point placed Bluebeard 3 in a position where getting above the EC-130E and hovering was impossible, requiring more power than its engines could produce.[57]

The co-pilot of the remaining MC-130, Dragon 3, watched as 'the helicopter pilot drove his craft into a stationary EC-130. I watched him do it.'[58] Bluebeard 3's rotors sliced into the EC-130E, igniting a raging fire. SGT Mike Vining was in EC-130E Republic 4. 'Instantly there were flames everywhere. The only door we could use was the right rear paratrooper door. Being near the front I was nearly the last person to evacuate. I did not think it was possible to get out of these alive. While there was considerable confusion, there was no panic.'[59]

Munitions in both aircraft cooked off, but the raiders managed to get out of the burning EC-130E. Secondary explosions sprayed hot fragments at nearby aircraft – damaging three helicopters – and personnel. Quick action prevented the disaster from spreading. Two survivors from the EC-130E and the RH-53D, both badly burned, were put aboard the departing MC-130 in the care of the Delta Force medics. By the light of the burning aircraft, Kyle gave the orders to marshal and launch each of the surviving EC-130Es.

It seemed to the co-pilot of Dragon 3 that 'the decision was made to abandon the helicopters and put their crews on the remaining EC-130s. Time was becoming a factor, not only for fuel but for darkness as well. Still, nobody panicked. The CCT [combat control team] had complete control of

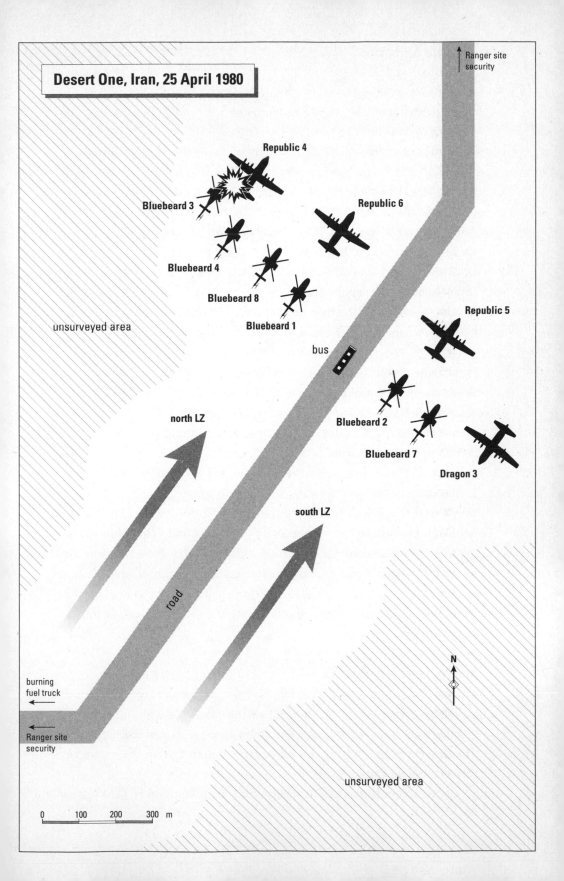

the situation and began to load the aircraft. The primary concern of the leaders was that we didn't leave anyone behind. We could not rush too much and forget someone.'[60]

In the organized but hurried evacuation, no living Americans were left behind. However, eight bodies were left in the two burning aircraft – there was no way they could be extracted from the fires that would continue to burn well into the next day – along with the five surviving helicopters. Two helicopters were 'sanitized' before being abandoned; three were not, due to their proximity to the fire, and so were captured with all their contents. Undestroyed operational plans included the identity and location of the covert agents pre-positioned in Iran.

The planning for the mission had not considered the need to take off from Desert One with fully loaded EC-130Es. Dragon 3 was second to take off. Its co-pilot, encouraged by seeing Republic 6's successful take-off, soon found more problems. 'The takeoff roll seemed to take forever. The airspeed slowly climbed towards takeoff speeds. We were looking for 90 knots. I called it off: 40, 50, 60, 70, 75, 80, 85 . . . 85. We had stopped accelerating. The tires were digging into the sand and we were running out of desert . . . Somehow we got airborne.'[61]

Once airborne, Kyle called Vaught and asked for an air strike to be launched from the *Nimitz* to destroy the helicopters left behind at Desert One. Carter told Jones, 'Now, David, one thing we don't want to do is compound the problem by having a major air battle over Iran.' The White House, following recommendations from Vaught and the CJCS, decided against the air strike.[62] Carter cited collateral damage concerns: 'Let's not do it, because if there're hundreds of Iranians all over those helicopters looking at them as a curiosity . . . you know they're going to wind up with a bunch of Iranian casualties.'[63]

THE END OF THE MISSION

There was no shortage of blame. The total monetary cost of the mission was estimated at $25 million, $193 million if the value of the lost aircraft were taken into account. But the political and diplomatic costs were much higher.[64] The press coverage was extensive and negative, reflecting the inherent impact of such operations.

Carter accepted total responsibility, knowing this would be held against him at the polls in November. Cyrus Vance resigned in protest.[65] Congress – even the intelligence oversight committees had not been informed before the raid – was highly critical. Dick Meadows and his assets inside Iran were warned by a radio message and were able to escape and evade the Iranians before they could be picked up. CIA assets also had to E&E.

The Iranians, after reading the planning documents – and then publishing them in book form – moved their prisoners frequently and kept them dispersed. They claimed to have flown at least one of the RH-53Ds away from Desert One; it was the only part of the JTF to reach Tehran.[66]

A second Iran raid, codenamed Honey Badger, was soon in planning. Vaught was put in charge of it within days of the Desert One fiasco, with Air Force Maj. Gen. Richard Secord – a veteran of Southeast Asian liberation missions – as his air operations deputy and Col. Robert Dutton as the operations officer (J-3). No fewer than ninety-five helicopters were incorporated into the new plan. It was to use US Air Force CH-53 Pave Low special operations helicopters refuelled in midair for insertion. Two Ranger battalions would seize Meharabad Airport for use as a helicopter base. Two companies of UH-60A Black Hawk helicopters from the Army's newly formed special operations aviation force, Task Force 158 (to be renumbered TF 160), would also take part. OH-6A light observation helicopters were modified to be used as AH-6A 'Killer Egg' attack helicopters. CH-47s were modified as tankers for on-the-ground refuelling. Pickup would use three 'Leapfrog' C-130s codenamed Credible Sport, capable of near-vertical takeoff through massive use of rocket-assisted take-off (RATO) motors. But training was delayed by the non-fatal crash of one of the C-130s (the RATO went off at the wrong time) and a fatal helicopter crash.

Honey Badger went through ten major exercises between April and November 1980, each representing a different rescue option reflecting the varying information on where and how the hostages were being held. The Iranians were moving the hostages frequently between hidden locations and obtaining adequate intelligence was problematic.

The second Iran raid ended up being overtaken by events. The US hostages were to spend the remaining days of the Carter presidency in captivity, only being released on the day Ronald Reagan was inaugurated as President.[67]

THE HOLLOWAY COMMISSION

The débâcle at Desert One was subjected to a formal review rare in special operations. A board of three retired and three serving flag officers, representing all four services, chaired by retired ADM James L. Holloway III, was empanelled. The panel included veteran special operators including Leroy Manor, who had organized the Son Tay raid, then a retired lieutenant general. It was given access to the records of the operational planning.

The Holloway Commission concluded that the concept and plan for the mission were feasible and had a reasonable chance for success. However, 'the rescue mission was a high-risk operation . . . People and equipment were called upon to perform at the upper limits of human capacity and equipment capability. There was little margin to compensate for mistakes or plain bad luck.'

The Commission's report listed twenty-three areas 'that troubled us professionally about the mission-areas in which there appeared to be weaknesses'. The major criticism was leveled at the '*ad hoc*' nature of the task force and its improvised mission-specific headquarters, the lack of comprehensive full-scale joint training and rehearsals, an improvised chain of command the Commission felt was unclear and an emphasis on operational secrecy it found excessive. The force had been organized from scratch, and in the final analysis its cohesion and command control processes had been found wanting.[68]

The Holloway Commission emphasized the lack of rehearsals – especially a full-scale one involving the entire force – as critical to the ultimate failure. 'Forces were so interdependent that complete force integration was essential', yet there was never a full-scale joint rehearsal. If one element was lost or failed, the remaining force could not carry on by itself.

Equipment and organization were ruled adequate. The decision to organize the raid with ground refuellings and hides rather than the air refuellings of the Son Tay raid was identified by the Holloway Commission as contributing significantly to the ultimate disaster at Desert One. As a result of the limitations of the RH-53Ds' range and speed, the rescue had to be performed in stages. Each stage increased geometrically the chance that something would go wrong. The overall incapacity of the US military during the 'hollow forces' era had its impact on the raid in the unexpectedly high helicopter failure rate. The Commission also said that the chances for success would have been improved if more backup helicopters had been provided. Helicopter pilots' lack of access to weather information and unfamiliarity with Navy RH-53Ds was also seen as a contributing factor.

The Commission identified the lack of intelligence asserts and resources as a weakness that undercut the planning process. Weakness in intelligence was a burden during both planning and execution. 1979 was not a good year for any element of US national security capability, and especially not intelligence. Failures in Southeast Asia had led to years of widespread outside scrutiny of the intelligence community. US intelligence capabilities were either cut back or disrupted. After the hostage crisis opened, the US found that HUMINT capabilities, with their need for skilled operators and reliable contacts and sources, were almost impossible to improvise. The presence of an interagency intelligence task force to support Vaught's *ad hoc* JTF would have removed some of the burden of piecing together intelligence that was encountered by the JTF. [69]

Command, control and communications were among the twenty-three failings noted by the Holloway report. These were perpetuated from the NCA to the level of the raiders at Desert One. While the available connectivity that linked the Pentagon with Desert One was excellent, the system of which it was a part proved deficient. At the operator level, the lack of secure communications between the different elements of the force while penetrating Iran suggested that, had the raid continued, there would have been other critical co-ordination problems with the raiding force.

In the final analysis, the Commission approved of the overall plan and found that the weakness lay in the execution. 'The operation was feasible and probably represented the best chance of success at the time the raid was launched.'[70]

One thing that was not lacking was courage. From the enlisted personnel in the raiding force to the senior officers who planned the mission, each was willing to go through with a risky plan to rescue fellow Americans. The Holloway Commission agreed: 'We are apprehensive that the critical tone of our discussion could be misinterpreted as an indictment of the able and brave men who planned and executed this operation. We encountered not a shred of evidence of culpable neglect or incompetence,' the report said. Everyone, from the highest level on down, did their job and did it well. And it all still failed.

Vaught was emphatic that the paucity of intelligence had been critical to the ultimate failure of the mission[71] – 'Intelligence from all sources was inadequate from the start and never became responsive.' Intelligence short-falls included the surprise of encountering the *haboob*, even though this was a common weather condition in that part of Iran and could have been avoided.

Beckwith attributed the failure to Murphy's Law and the *ad hoc* force. 'We went out and found bits and pieces, people and equipment, brought them together occasionally, and then asked them to perform a highly complex mission,' he said. 'The parts all performed, but they didn't necessarily per-form as a team.' His recommendations were reflected in the 1980s series of reforms.

Kyle rejected the Holloway Commission's conclusions, emphasizing the chair's lack of SOF experience and unwillingness to blame the blue-water Navy for not having more and better helicopters and aircrew available on the *Nimitz* for the mission. He largely blamed Seiffert and the helicopter pilots for not climbing out of the *haboob*, for not using their radios to keep the formation intact and for the three helicopter aborts. He argued that the task force never had fewer than seven flyable helicopters. But he recognized the weaknesses of the force's organization and training. 'Ours was a tenuous amalgamation of forces held together by an intense common desire to succeed, but we were slow coming together as a team,' Kyle wrote.[72]

Seiffert praised Beckwith and Kyle but defended his own actions and those of the helicopter pilots. He defended his decision to ground the critical sixth helicopter with the failed hydraulic system. He refused to second-guess the two helicopter crews who had aborted earlier. Seiffert and Kyle differ on whether Bluebeard 5 was justified in its actions (Seiffert approving) and whether the helicopter force had well-thought-out abort criteria (Seiffert says they did).

LESSONS

The need to accommodate 1980 interservice politics, extreme operational secrecy and the distance between the Washington-based planning staff and the forces that would be committed to the mission contributed to the eventual disaster. In most successful special operations, operators need to be involved in the planning. Too wide a gap between those planning an operation and those carrying it out leads to the impossible being asked or critical alternatives being ignored.

The complexity of the raid's plan – mandating that every one of the disparate multi-service elements had to work together and work correctly at each step in the operation – helped to ensure that bad luck, mechanical failures and disregard of the military principles of simplicity (of plan) and unity (of command) would catch up with Operation Eagle Claw at Desert One. Its planners knew – but the few people cleared to review it did not – that it violated a number of the key tenets of such special operations.

The planners were unable to achieve simplicity. All the events in the long and complex series of steps had to work for the plan to proceed. While the plan was robust enough to prevent a single-point failure – an Iranian stumbling across the raiders in one of the post-Desert One hides or equipment going down – there was minimal room for error and little flexibility to change the complex plan. This reflected the highly compartmentalized operational security arrangements, which reduced the flexibility and knowledge of the raiders about the overall mission. Repeatedly, the planners made decisions that would minimize risk: to use only eight RH-53Ds, to have the helicopters penetrate in radio silence at extremely low altitude despite the limitations in Iranian air defence, to cut off the weather forecasters from the raiders and to forgo a full rehearsal. Yet together, all these risk-averse decisions did not lead to security. Rather, they contributed to the ultimate failure of the mission.

The raid was not organized to maximize independent capability and provide redundancy. There was also a great deal of interdependence between the different elements of the raiding force. It wasn't bad luck but rather the 'friction' Clausewitz had written about 150 years before that wrecked everything and turned the whole episode into a symbol of American impotence and failure.

The raid's command and control arrangements embodied its origins as an *ad hoc* organization. Luck is often synonymous with preparation. One area where preparation was lacking was in command and control. The chain of command, however qualified its members, was unclear and dysfunctional. The principle of unity of command was often violated. This was seen in the delay in appointing a deputy until April and the lack of a mission commander who would be with the raid throughout its execution. At Desert

One, there were separate site, ground force, fixed-wing air and helicopter commanders. No one had unquestionable authority. Kyle and Beckwith's advice to abort was accepted by Vaught and Washington, but Kyle's empowerment to provide this was not clear to the other senior officers on the scene.

The improvised nature of the force and the compartmentalized nature of its training were also identified as contributing to failure. However high the quality of the individual components of the raid, the force that was committed to action could in no way be called a fully trained organization. Even the individual component rehearsals had not yielded satisfactory results. The absence of joint training and rehearsal led directly to the final disaster.

The shadow of Entebbe – the successful Israeli hostage-liberation mission in Uganda in 1976 – had been key in the decision-making that led up to the Iran raid.[73] Yet the much more difficult objective, the more sophisticated opponent – the US had to consider not only Iran's defences, but Soviet sensors as well – and the greater number of steps where things could fail were among the many factors that distinguished the two situations. The importance of maintaining a liberation-mission capability, however, was underlined by the Entebbe example. That the Israelis could liberate their citizens held by Third World tyrants and the US could not – or, had the raid not been ordered, would not – was a powerful perception that transcended the difficulties and differences that distinguished the two situations.

Even though the administration had avoided micro-managing the tactical decisions of the raid, political influence was still a major contributor to ultimate failure, above and beyond those identified by the Holloway Commission. Carter came slowly and reluctantly to a military option. Yet by not keeping involved in the process of planning and preparing for the raid, he was unaware of its limitations until the last minute, both those imposed by the nature of the mission and forces and those stemming from political restrictions placed on the execution and the services involvement. While Carter had made a conscious decision not to follow the White House tactical interference exhibited in past operations, he remained unaware that decisions – or lack of them – at the political level had still shaped the plan and its execution. This political influence did not stop even with the disaster at Desert One, for the White House went on to deny permission for an air strike against the abandoned helicopters at Desert One.

The Iran raid and its results underline both the high-risk nature inherent in liberation missions and the cost of failure. The disaster at Desert One was instrumental in leading to the reform of the US armed forces in general and US special operations in particular.

In the immediate aftermath of the Iran Raid, the Joint Special Operations Command (JSOC) was established on 15 December, 1980, located at Fort Bragg, NC. JSOC is a joint headquarters designed to study special operations requirements and techniques; ensure interoperability and equipment standardization; plan and conduct joint special operations exercises and training; and develop joint special operations tactics. It has remained a critical element of US SOF since its inception.

The Holloway report was to be critical in mobilizing support for US defence reforms in the years to come, including the legislation that would lead to the establishment of SOCOM, the increased power of the Chairman of the Joint Chiefs of Staff and the increased emphasis on joint operations. These would have to wait for some years – and the lessons of later crises such as Lebanon and Grenada – but defence reform received a powerful impetus from the bitter disappointment felt by all America after the failure of the Iran raid.

CHAPTER 7
GRENADA · 25-26 October 1983

*A commander . . . has to make a vital decision on
incomplete information in a matter of seconds, and
afterwards the experts can sit down at leisure, with all
the facts before them, and argue about what he might,
could or should have done.*

Field Marshal Sir William Slim, *Unofficial History*.

Operation Urgent Fury – the US operations on the Caribbean island of
Grenada launched on 25 October 1983 and concluded over the following
ten days – was a military intervention to overturn a pro-Communist government that had overthrown the previous, also pro-Communist, regime in
a bloody *coup*. Special operations forces were an integral part of the operations and were responsible for most of the ground fighting.

Despite the bitter lessons of the *Mayaguez* incident and the Iran hostage
raid, the national command authority still needed to order US special operations forces into action to save or seize people. Liberation and seizure
missions were a key part of Urgent Fury. The perceived threat of a hostage
situation involving US citizens on the island was one of the prime motivating factors behind the intervention. The island country's governor-general,
who represented the legitimate authority, also had to be kept alive. During
the course of the operation, a raid was mounted to capture the opposition
leadership, including the would-be military strongman of Grenada.

Grenada was significant both as part of the history of the Cold War and
of US special operations forces, which were still recovering from the stigma

of the failure in the Iran hostage raid. While Operation Urgent Fury was a victory, many of the special operations on Grenada reflected the hastily improvised and inadequately planned nature of the overall operation – especially the command and control arrangements – and the limitations of available intelligence. In war, even the simplest things are difficult. So it was with the liberation and seizure missions on Grenada. Fortunately, limited resistance led to what the Pentagon terms a 'permissive environment', where the US was able to succeed despite failures likely to lead to defeat by more capable or motivated enemies. Grenada was a step on the long road to building this capability.

THE COLD WAR COMES TO GRENADA

Since taking power on Grenada in a bloodless *coup* in 1979, the New Jewel movement had established a People's Revolutionary Government (PRG). Headed by Prime Minister Maurice Bishop, Grenada soon established close ties with Cuba and the Soviet Union. The indigenous military forces of the eastern Caribbean had been minimal, but Grenada now built up a large military establishment under Cuban supervision. Armouries were filled with imported old but still lethal Communist-bloc weapons.

By 1983, in addition to an extensive Cuban diplomatic and intelligence presence on the island, a large international airport was being built by Cuban labour. While nominally intended for the tourist trade, the US regarded the armed paramilitary Cuban construction force with suspicion. The US was concerned that, once the airport was completed, Cuban MiG fighters based there could present a regional threat.

Elsewhere on Grenada, in addition to the usual tourists and expatriates that could be found on any Caribbean island, there was a concentration of US citizens in the form of the faculty and students of an 'offshore' medical school. The vulnerability of the 600-plus US citizens and other foreign nationals on the island became critical, with memories of the Iran hostage crisis still fresh in every mind.

A power struggle within the Grenadian government resulted in the arrest, on 19 October 1983, of Maurice Bishop and a number of his cabinet officials and top aides. They were subsequently executed by the Cuban-trained Grenada People's Revolutionary Army (PRA), on the orders of a radical new political group known as the 'Revolutionary Military Council'.

Deputy Prime Minister Bernard Coard and General Hudson Austin quickly moved to assume control.

Such killing was alien to eastern Caribbean politics, which while sometimes chaotic had never before been lethal. This action shocked other countries in the region into asking for US military intervention. The situation on Grenada was viewed through the prism of the Cold War. The Cuban presence and Soviet interest had made the island an issue in Washington. For the US, indirect concern now escalated to fear of a hostage crisis and the imminent arrival by aircraft of the same Cuban troops that had been used in combat throughout Africa since the 1970s. The nearest US ambassador, Milan Bish on Barbados, cabled Washington: 'There appears to be imminent danger to US citizens resident on Grenada.'[1]

Failure to prevent a hostage crisis or a Cuban military intervention would have been potentially costly to President Ronald Reagan. His election had been seen – certainly by his administration – as a repudiation of Carter's perceived weakness in the face of events such as the Iran hostage crisis. President Reagan authorized the US military to intervene on Grenada. A number of potential intervention scenarios were considered, one of which was to launch a noncombatant evacuation operation (NEO) to rescue the American students. The State Department was originally planning for such an action when the Department of Defense took over. Washington's planning shifted from an evacuation to a full-scale intervention following an urgent request from Barbados's Prime Minister Tom Adams, on behalf of the Organization of Eastern Caribbean States, for military action to restore the legitimate government on Grenada. The US defence attaché in Barbados reported that the guards at Richmond Hill Prison on Grenada had received orders to kill all prisoners in the event of an invasion. The DIA had unconfirmed reports of the execution of British subjects and foreign businessmen.[2]

PLANNING IN HASTE

The planning for intervention went into high gear on 20 October, building on the planning for an evacuation begun in the previous days. The US Navy wanted a single-service operation, planned by the Commander-in-Chief Atlantic (CINCLANT) in Norfolk, Virginia, and his Atlantic Command (USLANTCOM) staff. CINCLANT himself, Adm. Wesley McDonald, at first anticipated little trouble from a 'third-rate, lightly armed and poorly trained adversary'. CINCLANT, having turned around the Lebanon-bound USS *Independence* carrier battle group and a Marine amphibious ready group (ARG) with the 22nd Marine Amphibious Unit (MAU) (including a detachment from SEAL Team 4) on board, thought these would be adequate forces. VADM Joseph Metcalf, Commander Second Fleet on board the USS *Guam*, was in overall command of what was soon designated Joint Task Force (JTF) 120. In addition to the carrier battle group and the ARG and its embarked MAU, JTF 120 would also be placed in command of forces from other services.

The operation grew in size during the early stages of planning, the USLANTCOM planners at Norfolk initially recommending an all-Navy/ Marine Corps option until they received, late on 20 October, top-down instructions to plan for the use of a large joint task force. Unaware of OPLAN 2360, a pre-existing contingency plan for missions on small Caribbean islands such as Grenada, USLANTCOM decided to improvise the operational planning without utilizing any plans developed by other commands (including US Caribbean Command at Key West, Florida, which had exercised joint operations on Caribbean islands twice before in 1983).

Part of the reason for this change of plan reflected presidential direction. In the words of Robert Kimmitt, on the NSC staff at the time: 'Ronald Reagan told [Chairman of the Joint Chiefs of Staff GEN] Jack Vessey, "Let's go in, and whatever the number of forces you're planning to use, double them; let's do it quickly and get out of there."'[3] The Crisis Preplanning Group, bringing together the Defense and State Departments, was also convened to provide high-level planning for the operation.

CJCS Jack Vessey was put in *de facto* command of the operation but, as events were to prove, he was to have a limited capability for making decisions or providing direction once the operation opened. Meeting with McDonald at his headquarters in Norfolk on 20 October, Vessey announced that the intervention would be a multi-service operation. As in previous operations, the 'rice bowl' concerns of the services – and now, for the first time, the special operations forces – had to be reflected in planning. The disparate members of the US armed forces – including the special operations community – were all anxious to demonstrate what they could be capable of. USLANTCOM put aside CINCLANT's original idea for a Navy-only operation.

At a cabinet-level meeting of the NSC's Special Situations Group (SSG) on

20 October, Secretary of Defense Caspar Weinberger and CJCS GEN Vessey agreed that evacuation of Americans without the military acting to secure the entire island would be extremely difficult. They also drew attention to the lack of intelligence on the situation available in Washington, Norfolk and Fort Bragg.[4]

The ultimate form of Operation Urgent Fury was strongly shaped by the Joint Special Operations Command (JSOC) – a joint headquarters set up at Fort Bragg, NC, on 15 December 1980 to implement Holloway Commission recommendations, with administrative rather than command responsibilities.

BG Richard Scholtes, the JSOC commander, recommended that his forces exclusively should carry out the operation. At first, JSOC's approach was a mirror-image of CINCLANT's original plan. JSOC wanted an all-special-operations-force action without naval intervention, relying on the low-end intelligence estimates of 250 Cubans and 300 Grenadians willing to fight against the US. The intelligence community had been studying the armed forces on Grenada for years – but not other issues such as the location of US medical students – and had concluded that there was only a limited military threat present on the island.[5]

JSOC's initial approach proved to be no more feasible than CINCLANT's. Political realities as well as operational ones stemming from the worsening situation in Grenada mandated a multi-service plan with demands for inclusion similar to those imposed on the Iran raid. However, as with the Iran raid, OPSEC concerns limited the numbers of personnel that could be used to plan and organize the operation. Planning would be carried out by the Joint Chiefs of Staff with USLANTCOM participation. The units that would be participating received the call ordering them to prepare for deployment on 21 October.

The Joint Chiefs of Staff had worked out an effective compromise – Vessey had CINCLANT change its original plan to include the Army and special operations roles. However, none of the services or forces involved included the others in its planning. In most cases, they were not aware that others were being alerted to participate. As late as two days before D-Day, on 23 October, special operations forces, the 82nd Airborne and the Marines were all planning independently to seize the same objectives.[6]

What emerged as Operation Urgent Fury was a large operation with all services participating, but with special operations missions proceeding independently. The plan, hastily pulled together in Washington and Norfolk, was for a joint operation taking in a broad spectrum of units and capabilities.

Planning at all levels was hamstrung by a lack of intelligence. The lack of suitable maps of Grenada was to prove a critical handicap throughout the operation. Despite years of interest in the island by the US intelligence community, no one had prepared a tactical map.

At an SSG meeting on 22 October, Weinberger and Vessey again stressed the lack of intelligence and, rather than the CINCLANT's original preferred all-Navy and Marines option, urged the use of SOF (especially SEALs) with pre-landing reconnaissance and the use of high-altitude air reconnaissance. SIGINT assets also had to be devoted to Grenada. This was approved, and by later that day the reconnaissance aeroplanes were overflying the island. However, getting the SEALs on the ground before the other SOF were deployed would prove to be problematic.[7] Vice President George Bush, chairing the meeting, said that a quick move was imperative but that 'it had to be right'. All present knew what he meant: not another Desert One.[8]

With the Army role increasing, the commander of the 24th Infantry (Mechanized) Division, MG 'Stormin' Norman Schwarzkopf, was added to Metcalf's JTF 120 headquarters even though his division would not be taking part in the operation – first as an advisor, eventually as a deputy. Yet the Navy, through USLANTCOM, insisted that Schwarzkopf's staff be limited to two majors and restricted his ability to communicate with ground forces ashore, citing as the reason the limited number of army-compatible radios on the flagship. Until he arrived, there were only a few junior Army officers at USLANTCOM participating in the planning of the operation. Schwarzkopf was suspicious of SOF and considered that their use could be counterproductive unless thoroughly integrated with the overall operational plan.

Scholtes, while not intended to be an operational commander, was put in charge of Joint Task Force (JTF) 123, responsible for all ground special operations forces (except those involving the MAU) and directly subordinated to Metcalf. This did not include the US Air Force's AC-130s and C-130/C-141 transports, which were directly under JTF 120. Many of the most egregious problems with the command relations were straightened out at the last minute, but some persisted.

The island was operationally split in half. The Marines covered the less populated northern half of the island – including the smaller Pearl's Airport; JTF 123's special operations forces – led by the US Army's two Ranger battalions – covered the south, including the partially completed airport and the medical school. The unfinished airport at Point Salines was to be the target of a direct-action forced-entry operation by US Army Rangers. The Rangers were tasked with first securing the Point Salines Airport and then the True Blue campus of the medical school, where the students – potential hostages – were assumed to be located.

The initial plan was for the Rangers to land on the unfinished runway aboard C-130 transports. The Rangers would move out, clear up any scattered resistance and then secure the airport so that a brigade from the 82nd Airborne in C-141 transports could land and relieve them. Only then would the Rangers send a company to the True Blue campus to rescue the American students and secure the PRA camp at Calivigny. A multinational force drawn from Caribbean nations would provide a follow-on echelon.

The other SOF elements – US Army Delta Force and US Navy SEALs from Teams 4 and 6 – would carry out other missions. Securing the safety of Grenada's Governor-General Sir Paul Scoon was a crucial element of the operation. In the absence of a constitutional prime minister (he had been executed by the PRA), Scoon was the sole legitimate governing authority. His safety was key if the US invasion was to be seen as a legitimate response to a request by Grenada – even *ex post facto* – to save the island from emerging revolutionary terror. SEALs, rappelling from helicopters under cover of darkness next to Government House, would rescue the governor-general. They would secure the governor-general and his wife and evacuate them in the same helicopters. If the primary extraction plan proved unfeasible, the SEALs would protect the governor-general inside the building and await the arrival of friendly troops.

Other SOF missions included seizing PRA leaders and liberating prisoners held at Fort Rupert and Richmond Hill Prison. This mission was originally tasked to SEAL Team 6, but was re-assigned to the US Army Delta Force at the last minute, which meant that Delta had little time to plan. There was also no time to consider whether these objectives – large walled compounds with garrisons – were appropriate targets for Delta's preferred tactics of using small teams to quickly secure buildings and free prisoners. Other SEAL teams would assault Radio Grenada and insert an Air Force Combat Control

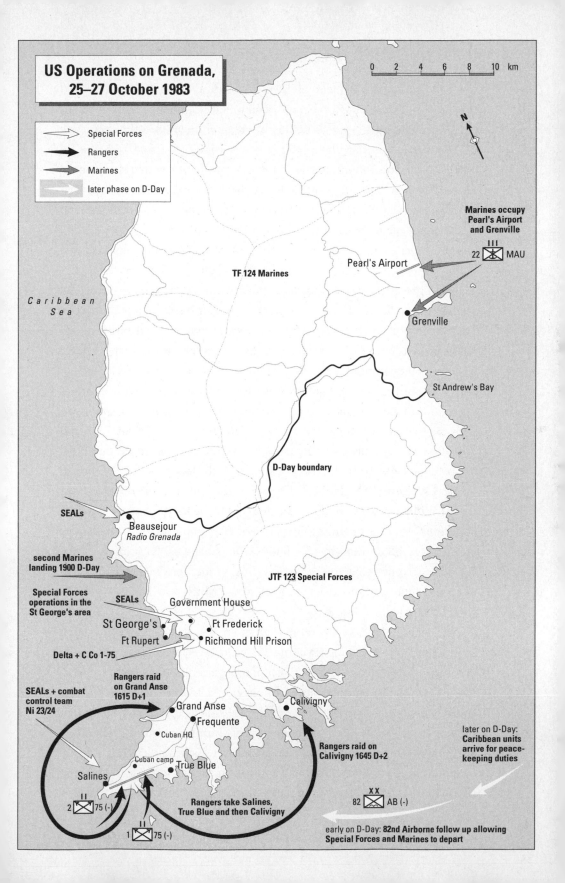

US Operations on Grenada, 25–27 October 1983

0 2 4 6 8 10 km

N

Special Forces
Rangers
Marines
later phase on D-Day

Caribbean Sea

Marines occupy Pearl's Airport and Grenville

Pearl's Airport

22 ☒ MAU

Grenville

TF 124 Marines

St Andrew's Bay

D-Day boundary

SEALs

Beausejour
Radio Grenada

second Marines landing 1900 D-Day

JTF 123 Special Forces

Special Forces operations in the St George's area

SEALs

Government House

St George's

Ft Frederick

Ft Rupert

Richmond Hill Prison

Delta + C Co 1-75

Rangers raid on Grand Anse 1615 D+1

SEALs + combat control team Ni 23/24

Grand Anse

Frequente

Caligny

• Cuban HQ

Cuban camp

True Blue

Salines

Rangers raid on Caligny 1645 D+2

later on D-Day: Caribbean units arrive for peace-keeping duties

2 ☒ 75 (-)

1 ☒ 75 (-)

Rangers take Salines, True Blue and then Caligny

82 ☒ AB (-)

early on D-Day: 82nd Airborne follow up allowing Special Forces and Marines to depart

Team at Port Salines Airfield to direct the landing of the Rangers. The US Army's 7th Special Forces Group, which had planned and trained for Caribbean contingencies, was neither alerted nor involved in the operation.

The SOF would have helicopter support from Task Force 160, the US Army's special operations aviation unit – formed to prevent a recurrence of the problems with finding suitable helicopter crews experienced in the Iran hostage raid. (One of the unit's household deities is a hangar-sized photograph of the wreckage at Desert One with the redundant caption 'never again'.) Based at Fort Campbell, Kentucky, the 160th had already demonstrated proficiency in a wide range of low-altitude and all-weather operations.

Lack of intelligence continued to hinder planning. There were no tactical maps of Grenada, which was particularly rough for special operations forces. They had to carry out both strategic reconnaissance and direct-action missions on a compressed timeline without rehearsals, proper maps or other customary preparations. The US did not have HUMINT assets on Grenada to keep track of the evolving political situation and provide needed information. US national technical means, aimed primarily at the Soviet threat, were slow to re-task and reprioritize, although high-flying SR-71s soon provided air-reconnaissance photographs. As a result, the forces committed to Operation Urgent Fury lacked precise data on the location of the American medical students (the planners did not realize that they were spread out over two campuses and multiple locations) and Sir Paul Scoon, and on the intentions of the new regime towards them. In the absence of contradictory information, US decision-makers and planners alike fell back on the widespread assumption that guided the planning – that there would be no resistance and that the Cubans would not fight – which was based largely on wishful thinking.

The decision to go for Operation Urgent Fury was made by the President on 23 October. A National Security Decision Directive was signed in the evening. In the previous hours, Washington's attention had been on Lebanon, where the US Marines at Beirut airport had been subject to a terror suicide bombing attack that left 241 dead. While the planning for Urgent Fury as a full-scale joint operation incorporating rescue and liberation missions was already underway, the events in Lebanon made the necessity of asserting US military capability even more significant. Meanwhile, on Grenada, the revolutionary regime was frantically appealing to Havana,

Moscow, anyone who would listen, to save it from its impending demise.

The late decision to go made it impossible for SOF to plan effectively, request additional intelligence or consider alternatives. At the troop level, many only found out that this was not a practice deployment when the unit arms rooms were unlocked and the troopers invited to take whatever they wanted with them on the aeroplanes (ensuring that they were heavily overloaded).

Task Force 160 was only alerted for the Grenada mission on 23 October, although planning had been going on throughout the previous week. Their AH/MH-6 and MH-60 helicopters were loaded on to C-5 transport aircraft at Fort Campbell, Kentucky, on 24 October and unloaded at Grantley Adams International Airport on Barbados only forty-five minutes before their scheduled take-off times for the original H-Hour of 0200 on 25 October. There was difficulty in assembling the helicopters: their ammunition had been offloaded at the other end of the airport. Grenada would be the first combat use of the H-60 helicopter design, which featured superior survivability and lift capability over its predecessor, the Vietnam-era UH-1 'Huey'.

This and other SOF setbacks led to H-Hour being moved back to 0600, reducing the chance for surprise and use of darkness. With US forces now pouring into nearby Barbados and the telephones into and out of Grenada still working, the chances for surprise were effectively zero.

THE SEALS AT PORT SALINES

The inability of US special operations forces to carry out strategic reconnaissance tasks contributed to making Grenada an intelligence black hole. On the night of 23 October, Navy SEAL Team 6 was launched on a strategic reconnaissance mission to Point Salines, with a secondary mission of placing marker beacons for the Rangers. Twelve SEALs and four USAF Combat Controllers static-line parachuted from two MC-130E Combat Talon aircraft at 150 m. Three Zodiac F470 rubber boats followed them.[9]

The results were disastrous. One boat sank. Four SEALs – overloaded with extra ammunition and equipment for multiple missions – tangled in their parachutes and drowned. After a search for the missing SEALs, the remaining two boat teams headed for the beach. En route, they spotted what appeared to be a hostile patrol boat. Cutting back the Zodiacs' petrol-powered outboard motors to reduce noise resulted in the boats being swamped and left drifting. The SEALs were forced to abort the mission and be picked up by the US Navy frigate *Clifton Sprague*.

Following Scholtes' recommendations to VADM Metcalf, the next night – just hours before the scheduled airdrop – the SEALs attempted to repeat the mission. As the Zodiacs reached the beach, the surf swamped them. The SEALs lost most of their equipment and were again forced to abandon the mission and return to the same frigate. Scholtes was so concerned about the lack of strategic reconnaissance for the incoming Rangers that he urged that D-Day be delayed by twenty-four hours. Metcalf, afraid that a hostage situation could develop, was only willing to postpone H-Hour on 25 October from 0200 to 0400, and then to 0500 local time. This decision would deny the cover of darkness for the special operations missions that had also been timed to start at H-Hour.

THE RANGERS AT POINT SALINES

The Rangers had concentrated their troops at Grantley Adams International Airport on Barbados when they received the signal to go against Point Salines Airport and then on to secure the True Blue campus; they had previously been planning to seize the entire island. The Rangers would have to undertake their liberation mission in daylight without recent intelligence on the airport or the presence of marker beacons. As a result of the SEALs' inability to insert either a CCT or navigational beacons, a Ranger pathfinder team, airdropped in darkness at 0330 from Lima 56, a 105 mm-armed AC-130H gunship belonging to the 16th Special Operations Squadron and flown by Maj. Michael Couvillon, preceded the insertion of the rest of the Rangers into Port Salines. The pathfinders also encountered troubles, with two being killed when their parachutes malfunctioned. The remaining two, reconnoitring the runway, found it blocked with obstacles. Lima 56's sensors confirmed their report and the information was relayed back to Barbados, location of JTF 123 forward TOC. Lima 56 then entered a holding pattern offshore, using its sensors to watch for troop movements around the airport.

LTC Wesley Taylor, commanding the 1-75th Rangers, had planned to follow up the pathfinders with an air landing of one company of Rangers from two MC-130Es on the runway at 0500 – A Company of the 1-75th, plus a runway-clearing detachment. He was counting on these aircraft being able to follow the beacons being put in place by the SEALs and their attached CCT. With the runway secured by the lead company, the remainder of his battalion, followed by LTC Ralph Hagler's 2-75th battalion, would fly in on ten C-130s and land at 0530, secure the airport and move out to evacuate the students, using gun jeeps flown in on the C-130s. The number of Rangers put into the operation was limited by a shortage of night-trained aircrew on the MC-130Es and C-130s.

The plan started to fall apart hours before the pathfinders were to jump. The C-130s did not have communications equipment for informing the Rangers in-flight of any changes to the plan, lacking hatch antennae that could be linked to the Army's command radios. Finally, at about 0400, a long-delayed message to Taylor from the DIA – passed via the Air Force – informed the Rangers that the Cubans had 23 mm anti-aircraft guns (AAA) and 12.7 mm heavy machine guns defending the airport and that the runways had been blocked by construction equipment. This information, gleaned from SR-71 aircraft reconnaissance photographs, came at the last minute and was confirmed by the pathfinders. The Rangers were also told at this time that the SEALs and the CCT had been unable to emplace the beacons.

At 0400, Taylor made the decision to change the plans. An air landing would not work. He gave the order for all the aircraft in the formation to rig for a parachute drop while in-flight. Some of the aircraft in the formation did not get Taylor's order due to the lack of hatch antennae. The message had to be relayed via the flight deck of each aircraft.

The Rangers did not receive the order to re-rig until twenty minutes before they were to jump. The aircraft had to drop out of formation and circle until the Rangers were ready. Inside the transports, adrenalin-fuelled controlled chaos reigned as the jumpmasters tried to form up sticks for jumping.

SFC Terry Allen described the scene: 'All the Rangers began helping each other rig as quickly as possible to include conducting equipment checks since the jumpmasters did not have the time. Some Rangers did not have the opportunity to re-rig their rucksacks for the jump, so they took their Claymores and M60 machine-gun ammo and stuffed it down the front of their jungle fatigue jackets.'[10]

The Rangers then requested permission for a mass parachute assault – a contingency previously planned – but the Air Force would not approve it due to concerns about aircraft vulnerability. The drop would instead use a dispersed C-130 formation. LTC Taylor made the decision to reduce the jump altitude to 150 m from the standard 240 m, hoping to fly under the fire of the AAA.

At 0445, the lead MC-130E – supposed to use its radar to act as a path-finder for the formation – experienced problems with its INS. This aircraft, intended to land first, was carrying part of A Company and the runway-clearing team. The sequence of C-130s in the formation had to be adjusted in-flight, causing over a half-hour delay.

LTC Taylor's MC-130E, flown by Lt. Col. James L. Hobson Jr., went into the lead. Over the radio from Barbados, Scholtes pushed H-Hour back to 0530. The planned night-time air landing had now become an opposed daylight airdrop.

It was the traditional way to go to war – with things screwed up. As the stretched-out formation of MC/C-130s approached the DZ, it became appar-ent that the special operations forces had not succeeded in placing the marker beacons or providing any intelligence on the condition of the runway. The MC-130E Combat Talon's terrain-following radar confirmed the DIA report – Taylor had not received the confirming pathfinders' report that the runway was blocked with construction equipment, hastily put in place by the Cubans as obstacles.

As Hobson flew the final approach to the DZ at an altitude of 150 m, a searchlight suddenly illuminated the aircraft. First out over the narrow DZ at 0531 were Taylor, a platoon of B Company Rangers from the 1-75th and the battalion Tactical Operations Centre (TOC).

They soon drew fire from Grenadian AAA: a Czech-built quad 12.7 mm HMG on a ridge north of the airport terminal and a battery of 23 mm ZU-23s at the barracks at Frequente, also north of the airport. The Cubans, waiting for orders, squeezed their first triggers at 0534. Fortunately, the fire – Grenadian and Cuban – was sporadic and poorly aimed. Hobson turned his MC-130E and dived out of the line of fire, pulling up fewer than 30 m above the sea.

These events were enough to deter the aircraft following Taylor from approaching the DZ. To Lt. Col. Bobby Mitchell, flying the other MC-130E, the brilliant display of tracers looked like the Fourth of July fireworks at the Washington Monument.[11] The two aircraft pulled away from the DZ and decided to orbit out of range of the AAA until two AC-130s could suppress the defences. This left Taylor and the Rangers from the first plane the only US forces on the ground.

The Rangers on the ground came under immediate fire from the Cuban

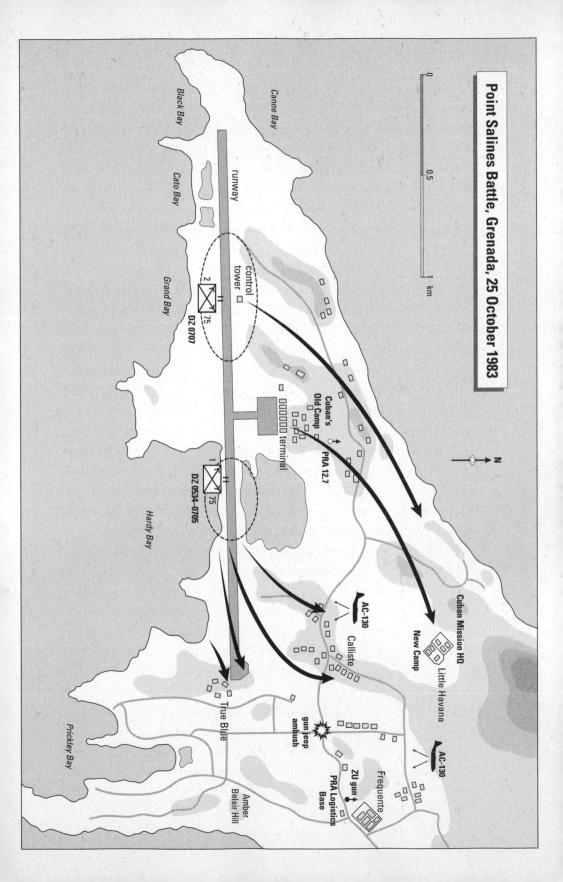

Point Salines Battle, Grenada, 25 October 1983

0   0.5   1 km

N

Black Bay

Canoe Bay

Cato Bay

runway

Grand Bay

2 ⊠ II 75

control tower

DZ 0707

terminal

Cuban's Old Camp

PRA 12.7

1 ⊠ II 75

DZ 0534-0705

Hardy Bay

AC-130

Calliste

Cuban Mission HQ

New Camp

Little Havana

Prickley Bay

True Blue

gun jeep ambush

ZU gun

AC-130

Frequente

PRA Logistics Base

Amber Belair Hill

construction workers. They were part of a paramilitary force deployed to Grenada and armed with infantry weapons, but they had received no tactical training and, until the day before, had not been organized into subunits. In spite of this, the strength of their resistance proved a tactical surprise. Unknown to the Rangers, an experienced Cuban officer, Colonel Pedro Tortolo Comas, a combat veteran in Africa and a Frunze Staff College graduate, had arrived by aircraft the day before to direct the defence of southern Grenada, and he had only had a few hours to improvise a defence strategy. He had been sent in place of the battalions of the Cuban Army that the Grenadians had requested. The Cubans' orders were not to fire unless attacked, which delayed their initial resistance against the Rangers. Cuban forces were consequently unable to deliver a counterattack in the opening minutes of the Ranger drop when only a single planeload held the ground.

Taylor, the battalion TOC and a platoon of B Company were alone at Port Salines. They set up a position south of the runway, but Taylor was not content to wait on the defensive for reinforcements. The Rangers, under intense if inaccurate fire, formed up and attacked. Hot-wiring a bulldozer that had been parked to block the runway, some of the Rangers used it to clear away obstacles under fire while two AC-130Hs – Maj. Clement Twiford's Lima 58 had joined Lima 56 – provided fire support. The Ranger's air liaison officer, Maj. James E. Roper, was soon directing the AC-130Hs to provide supporting fire to prevent a counterattack. Two destroyers were present offshore but did not provide naval gunfire support for fear of fratricide.

At 0552 – almost twenty-five minutes late arriving at the DZ – Taylor received his first reinforcements. Bobby Mitchell's MC-130E (which had been in the lead originally) circled back and dropped part of A Company of the 1-75th. He was greeted with a repeat fireworks performance from the enemy AAA. On the ground, Maj. Roper saw eight automatic weapons open fire at the incoming MC-130 and called the AC-130s in against them. The Rangers on the ground joined in. Taylor then halted his attack until he could get more reinforcements.

These arrived at 0634 aboard Maj. Michael Beach's C-130, which was making its second approach. The rest of A Company dropped, (minus seven men of the gun jeep crews), following their commander CPT John P. Abizaid ('The Mad Arab' to his Rangers). Inside the aeroplanes, Rangers climbed over piles of hastily discarded gear to jump over the tiny DZ.

On the ground, the Rangers were now thoroughly intermixed, but officers and NCOs quickly assembled small groups and moved out, attacking enemy positions north of the runway. Other Rangers resumed clearing the runway under fire, removing more oil drums and construction equipment placed as obstacles by the Cubans.

Taylor commented, 'The fighting was at least as intense as any of the fights I was in in Vietnam. And I was two years over there . . . In not one case or in not one instance was there any indication that these guys hadn't been there before. And by that I mean there was no hesitation to get in and close with the enemy. In fact, in many cases it was quite the contrary. Leaders had to work doubly hard to hold the Rangers back. And it was that ferocity that we try and build into these guys that led to their success.'[12]

The remainder of the 1-75th arrived at 0705, as the circling aircraft and those that had stood off from the AAA came in. Over one and a half hours elapsed from the first drop of 1-75th Rangers until the last unit was on the ground. This situation was far from the ideal of having massive numbers available early on to take advantage of the element of surprise and to out-number the enemy.

Rangers from the 1-75th who were not under effective fire continued to clear the runway of blocking trucks and obstacles. The 1-75th now occ-upied the east end of the runway.

At 0707, the 2-75th Rangers dropped at the Port Salines Airport DZ over a much shorter period of time. They had waited for several hours in their orbiting aircraft. While encountering less resistance, the jump was not without hazards. One Ranger broke his leg. Another Ranger's static line hung up as he jumped, dragging him against the tail of the plane before alert jumpmasters hauled him back aboard. (It later took him many months to get his combat jump credit, awarded for the jump, not the landing.) The 2-75th assembled at the western end of the runway. By 0710 the airdrop had been completed.

At around 0730, the Rangers were in a position to start their liberation mission. A Company of the 1-75th had re-formed at the eastern end of the runway. They were ordered to move on the True Blue campus to prevent US medical students being taken hostage. While two platoons engaged Cuban positions on the high ground north of the runway, number two platoon of A Company of the 1-75th moved along the beach to the True Blue campus.

More Rangers began to move out of the airport, minus the gun jeeps still on board circling C-130s. The first and third platoons of A Company of the 1-75th moved north of the runway towards the high ground overlooking it and, north of that, to Calliste, a Cuban housing area known as 'Little Havana'. They ran into heavy fire, which killed a Ranger. CPT Abizaid commandeered one of the bulldozers being used to clear obstacles. Raising the blade to provide cover for the operator, the bulldozer attacked with Rangers in close support. The attack took the high ground; a Czech-built quadruple 12.7 mm machine gun was abandoned by its crew. The A Company attack secured the middle part of the runway and the terminal area.

B Company of the 1-75th moved north, taking the control tower and fuel storage area and was able to seize part of the high ground near the Cuban headquarters at Frequente. They were soon supported by two Marine AH-1T attack helicopters. The 2-75th cleared the area west of the airfield as well as the area north of their drop zone. Cuban resistance increased. Rangers turned a captured 12.7 mm AAA gun on two mortars.

By 0750, the second platoon of A Company of the 1-75th had pushed to the True Blue campus, encountering only light opposition. The 138 students and their dependents had not been taken hostage. There was only a small contingent of guards present who fled after a brief skirmish near the gate to the school. The Rangers commenced evacuating students at 1000. During the evacuation, at about 1030, the Rangers learned that there were many more American students at the main Grand Anse campus, a few miles to the north. Previously, US intelligence – displaying its minimal preparation – had believed that all the students were at the True Blue campus. With the help of a student amateur ham radio operator and other students, they learned of enemy guards in the area. The Rangers thought that they could bring the students out. A new rescue mission was required: the evacuation of Grand Anse. But it would take until the next day for it to be organized, in part because the lack of maps made planning the operation, even against light opposition, difficult.

At 0739, the first C-130 landed on the western half of the runway – A Company was still fighting over at the eastern end. By 1000, with the Rangers having secured the high ground around the airport, the C-130s, which had gone to Barbados to refuel, now returned. They were joined by an additional ten C-130s flown in from the US.

The C-130s landed and unloaded the equipment not dropped, including the M151 gun jeeps, communications equipment and motorcycles. Two of the A Company gun jeeps, sent to reinforce the Rangers at True Blue but lacking maps, got lost and drove into a Grenadian ambush, killing four Rangers.

Arriving in the C-130s from the States were elements of TF 160. They established an operating base for their MII/UII-60 and ΛH/MH-6A helicopters near the western end of the runway.[13]

The C-130s were followed by the first airlift of the 82nd Airborne Division. The commanding general, MG Edward Trobaugh, arrived on one of the first transports. He was surprised at the unexpected resistance, the dearth of intelligence and the lack of success so far by the SOF of JTF 123. He called back to Fort Bragg: 'Keep sending battalions until I tell you to stop.'[14] Starting at 1100 and running through the next day, two brigades of paratroopers including artillery were eventually deployed to Grenada. They were joined by the first contingent of the multilateral peacekeeping force from Caribbean nations. The Rangers, not having been informed that these foreign troops would be arriving, thought at first that they were hostile forces. Ranger fire discipline alone averted a fratricide incident.

While the students were being evacuated, the Rangers at the airport were consolidating their position. Following a truce and the evacuation of wounded with the Cubans, the Ranger commander called for the Cubans to surrender, and 80 to 100 did so at about 1430. Over 250 Cubans surrendered by the time the airport was secure, although scattered resistance and sniper fire would continue for another four to five hours. Others surrendered later on D-Day, with the last resistance surrendering on D+1, after a brief fight, to the 82nd Airborne.

Following the engagement with the Cubans, the Rangers came under fire from a house on top of a prominent hill 1,000 m east of the runway. No AC-130 gunship – the special operations air support of choice – was available. Navy A-7 attack planes from the carrier *Independence* offshore finally destroyed the house. Several duds landed near the Rangers.

The Grenadians launched their largest counterattack at about 1530 towards A Company of the 1-75th at the western end of the airport. Three BTR-60PBs of the Motorized Rifle Company, the élite troops of the People's Revolutionary Army, moved towards the 2nd platoon's firing positions. Under fire from small arms, LAWs and a 90 mm recoilless rifle, two of the

BTRs collided and were disabled. The third retreated, then was hit in the rear and was finally destroyed by an AC-130H – Lima 57 – which had arrived on station to provide close air support. The repulse of the counterattack secured the Rangers' position around Port Salines Airport and True Blue campus at a cost of five dead and six wounded.

Late in the evening, the 82nd Airborne Division's 3rd Brigade began to move out from the airport. The original plan called for the 82nd to make a rapid sweep of the southern half of the island once they arrived at the airfield secured by the Rangers, but the heavier than expected resistance and the lack of intelligence had delayed this. The 82nd mopped up, with operations around the airport ending with the surrender of 'Little Havana' on D+1, starting at 0700 and finished by the afternoon.

THE MARINES ON D-DAY

One thing of which the Rangers had been unaware throughout the day was the progress of the Marines, a result of the non-compatibility of radio frequencies and procedures. The Marines had also carried out their mission, but without loss. The 22nd Marine Amphibious Unit (MAU) – built around the 2-8th Marines – landed and occupied the smaller Pearl's Airport before clearing the north sector of the island.

The Marine landing was, like the Ranger attacks, preceded by special reconnaissance. It was carried out by SEALs from the MAU and a platoon of the Fleet Marine Force Reconnaissance battalion that had been attached to the 22nd MAU and had trained with them pre-deployment. In this case, the 'Force Recon' had been successful, sending back the signal that the marines would have to rely on helicopters as the beach was not suitable for amphibious tractors.

The Marine landing – timed to coincide with the Rangers' airdrop – was unopposed and their ground forces advanced throughout D-Day to occupy the northern half of the island. The Marines, having gone through a lengthy training process before their deployment, were able to carry out their missions with minimal friction. They had, however, the advantage of working only with the forces that they had trained and rehearsed with before deployment, i.e. other Marines and naval aircraft.

SOF D-DAY MISSIONS

The remainder of the JTF 123 D-Day SOF missions – beyond the Rangers' forcible entry at Port Salines and subsequent advance to secure the students – were aimed at several targets inland from Grenada's capital, the town of St George's. One of these targets was the transmitter of Radio Free Grenada at Beausejour, which was to be seized and held for US use. The other three SOF missions were all liberation or seizure missions, aimed at ensuring the safety of Sir Paul Scoon at Government House and liberating political prisoners from Richmond Hill Prison. Fort Rupert (formerly Fort George) in downtown St George's was also thought likely to contain prisoners or PRA leaders.

All these objectives were located close to each other – although the steep hills and dense vegetation of inland Grenada limited quick movement except by helicopter. All were targeted by teams from the US's best-trained SOF – Delta Force and SEALs – to be inserted by nine MH-60A helicopters flown by TF 160. Yet despite the US ability to deploy overwhelming force, these missions demonstrated why all liberation and seizure missions are inherently high risk.

THE SEALS AT GOVERNMENT HOUSE

The most politically valuable of the SOF missions was that to save the governor-general. Sir Paul Scoon and his wife were being held under house arrest by General Hudson Austin's PRA forces in Government House near St George's. In addition to guards, Government House was defended by – unnoticed by US planners – 23 mm AAA gun emplacements in the woods next to the tennis court, and another close to the late Prime Minister Bishop's nearby residence. The mission had been assigned to Navy SEAL Team 6, hostage-rescue specialists, as it fitted closely the situations for which they had trained.

As a consequence of the shifting H-Hour, it was bright daylight when twenty-two men from SEAL Team 6 under LT John Koenig – reinforced by three US diplomats – arrived in two TF 160 MH-60A helicopters at 0615. As the helicopter crews tried to identify Government House at low altitude – the Victorian mansion was hidden under dense trees – they came under fire from the concealed 23 mm guns and small arms from inside the house.

The lead helicopter was hit, wounding the pilot and one SEAL. Despite this, the MH-60As made it to the objective. However, the terrain was unexpectedly steep and tree-covered – another surprise resulting from the poor available intelligence. The SEALs performed a fast-rope insertion, one element on the tennis court and the other on the Government House lawn. The second helicopter was forced to get out of the line of fire before four of the SEALs on board could fast-rope down. The diplomats and the primary SEAL radio, damaged by fire, were left on board.

The SEALs were able to form up and move out. They met no resistance – the PRA guards had fled under the cover of the 23 mm fire – and Government House was secured in fifteen minutes. After identifying the governor-general and his wife from photographs, the SEALs ushered them and their ten personal staff out of the line of fire and then set up firing positions with interlocking fields of fire. A SEAL sniper took position at the upstairs windows. The rest of the team quickly went to work preparing Government House for defence.

They did not have long to organize themselves before they were interrupted by a PRA counterattack launched from nearby Fort Frederick: a BTR-60PB armoured personnel carrier leading two groups of light infantry. The PRA attempted to assault through the eastern gates but were repulsed by the SEALs, even though they carried no M72 66 mm LAW rockets to counter enemy armoured vehicles.

The sniper, using a G3 SG-1 rifle, was able to shoot down many of the enemy who looked as if they were moving out to assault the house. He reportedly dropped twenty-one men during the siege. While he returned fire, the rest of the team remained concealed, conserving ammunition against a renewed assault. The PRA, even with an APC, had no stomach for an attack and settled in for a long standoff instead.

According to the plan, by now the SEALs should have been relieved by Rangers moving overland from Port Salines Airport, but the Rangers were still heavily engaged there with the Cubans. The SEALs then tried to call for supporting fire from the command staff on the USS *Guam*. Unable to get through on the tactical net via their secondary radio, LT Bill Davis used a Government House telephone to place a call to the Rangers at Port Salines Airport – though legend has it that the call was made back to Fort Bragg, NC. The SEALs asked the Rangers to contact the USS *Guam* and request fire support.

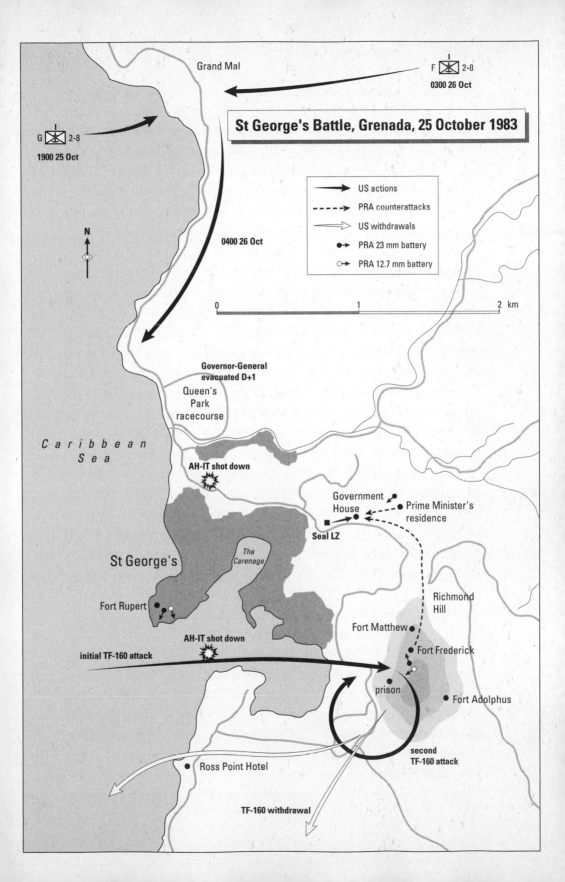

Grand Mal

F ⊠ 2-8
0300 26 Oct

G ⊠ 2-8
1900 25 Oct

St George's Battle, Grenada, 25 October 1983

0400 26 Oct

→ US actions
⇢ PRA counterattacks
⇨ US withdrawals
●▸ PRA 23 mm battery
○▸ PRA 12.7 mm battery

0   1   2   km

N

Governor-General
evacuated D+1

Queen's
Park
racecourse

*C a r i b b e a n
S e a*

AH-IT shot down

Government
House

Prime Minister's
residence

Seal LZ

St George's

*The
Carenage*

Fort Rupert

Richmond
Hill

AH-IT shot down

Fort Matthew

Fort Frederick

initial TF-160 attack

prison

Fort Adolphus

second
TF-160 attack

Ross Point Hotel

TF-160 withdrawal

The Navy had been monitoring the situation at Government House and had heard the SEALs being inserted under heavy fire. Metcalf, on the *Guam*, was aware that the Rangers were not in a position to reinforce the SEALs at Government House. The Marines, now committed to securing the northern half of the island, were not within striking distance either. Metcalf considered the situation 'very serious' and ordered air support for the SEALs.[15]

An AC-130H – Maj. Michael Couvillon's Lima 56 – arrived on the scene, diverted from the Point Salines battle. The SEALs made contact with the AC-130H and were able to direct its fire. Lima 56 put 20 mm and 40 mm fire into a wooded area northeast of the residence. The AC-130H remained on station until, short of ammunition, it had to depart on a frantic search for resupply in Barbados and Puerto Rico.

In the early afternoon, two USMC AH-1T Cobra attack helicopters arrived in response to the call to provide fire support. They were targeted against Fort Frederick, thought to be the command post for the revolutionary troops outside Government House. They were not informed about the unsuppressed AAA gun positions that had shot up the MH-60As earlier that day. The first AH-1T, piloted by Marine Cpt. Tim Howard, was hit by a 23 mm gun after five attacks on Fort Frederick. The AH-1T was crippled and crash-landed in a soccer field. Cpt. Howard was badly wounded. He was dragged from the burning AH-1T by his co-pilot, Cpt. Jeb Seagle. While Cpt. Seagle was signaling the other AH-1T for medevac, he was cut down by enemy fire. The second AH-1T was hit while giving covering fire for the Marine CH-46 medevac helicopter rescuing Cpt. Howard. It crashed into nearby St George's harbour, killing both aircrew. Fort Frederick remained operational.

Following the helicopter shootdowns, a second Grenadian assault was launched. Within moments, it ground to a halt as an AC-130 gunship – Col. David Sims' Lima 57 – arrived at 1505. The AC-130 quickly dispatched the BTR-60PB and scattered the PRA troops. The attackers retreated and had to content themselves with sporadic fire. Lima 57 was then called off to attack a BTR-60PB retreating from the defeated counterattack near the airport. It soon returned to discourage any renewal of the assault on Government House, firing its 20 mm cannon into Grenadian positions a few hundred meters away from the residence.

At 1535, an air strike – more A-7s from the USS *Independence* – destroyed the 23 mm emplacements that had shot down the AH-1Ts and hit Fort Frederick again. This led to a collateral-damage incident as one aircraft struck instead nearby Fort Matthew, which had been converted to the island's mental hospital, killing twenty-one civilians. PRA light AAA and a command post had been located at Fort Matthew, some 150 m downhill from Fort Frederick.

The enemy withdrew away from Government House, retreating and contenting themselves with sporadic fire for the rest of D-Day.

The SEALs were almost out of ammunition by the end of D-Day. However, after an uneventful night, Marines of the 22nd MAU led by their tank platoon – there had been a second landing at Grand Mal on the evening of D-Day – relieved them at 0715 on D+1. Scoon, his wife and nine of their staff were all safely evacuated to the LZ at St George's Queen's Park racetrack and then by helicopter to the USS *Guam*.

On board the *Guam*, Scoon contacted US and Caribbean heads of state before returning to a temporary seat of government set up at Port Salines Airport. There he signed his official request for US military intervention (backdated to 24 October). The document was carried by Brigadier Rudyard Lewis of the Barbados Defence Force, who was commanding the Caribbean forces on Grenada.

In addition to the helicopter losses, the only US ground casualty in the siege of Government House was one wounded SEAL. While the concern of US planners that Scoon was at risk from the revolutionary government that had killed other leading political figures on Grenada has not been confirmed by evidence in hindsight, the SEALs' raid on Government House remains an example of a special operations liberation mission success.

DELTA FORCE AT RICHMOND HILL PRISON AND FORT RUPERT

While poor intelligence affected the Rangers and the SEALs, it came close to causing disaster for Delta Force. With their training in hostage rescue, they were targeted against Fort Rupert in the built-up area of Grenada's only large town, St George's, which was thought to contain the hostile leadership of General Austin and the Revolutionary Council, and Richmond Hill Prison, which contained illegally imprisoned civil servants and others, possibly some American citizens who were thought to be at risk of execution. The intelligence available was so limited that no one knew who these prisoners were or where they were being held. Richmond Hill Prison, marked even on the poor maps available to JTF 123, seemed the obvious place. The assignment reflected the ever-present 'rice bowl' concerns. Delta could not be left out of the JTF 123 missions when the Rangers and SEALs had been given missions close to what they had trained for.[16]

The plan was for sixty Delta troopers of B Squadron, reinforced by elements of C Company 1-75th Rangers, to be tasked with liberation and seizure missions on D-Day. In command was COL Sherman Williford, Beckwith's successor as commander of Delta Force and the highest ranking SOF officer to go in at H-Hour. However, he lacked a command helicopter and his control was effectively limited to the sixty-man force. Striking at H-Hour, simultaneously with the Rangers' air landing and the SEALs' arrival at Government House, the plan was for the Delta troops to be lifted from their forward base on Barbados by six US TF 160 MH-60As to seize Richmond Hill Prison, followed by Fort Rupert.

The mission was limited by the absence of rehearsals or co-ordination and the shortage of intelligence on the objectives and who was to be liberated or seized. The prison was built on a hill with steep cliffs covered by dense foliage on three sides. The prison walls were six m high and topped with barbed wire, and watchtowers covered the area. There was no adequate LZ. Delta had no accurate maps of the prison compound or intelligence on the prison's defences. According to MAJ David Grange, B Squadron commander, 'The mission was not very clear, nor were the rules of engagement. We were not sure who we were supposed to rescue from the prison.'[17]

Overlooking the prison, on higher ground 300 m away, was Fort Frederick, with a company of PRA troops and two Czech-built quadruple 12.7 mm anti-aircraft guns. The TF 160 helicopter crews did not know about the AAA at Fort Frederick. There were no suppressive attacks planned against Fort Frederick.

Delta had initially planned on assaulting the Richmond Hill Prison compound in the pre-dawn darkness. The raiders would land outside the wall, Son Tay style, on MH-60As. They would then break in and overwhelm the defenders. When doubts were raised about the LZs, this plan was changed so that Delta troopers would use fast-rope techniques to lower themselves into the prison compound, surprise the defenders and overwhelm them. The lack of maps proved critical and the LZs had to be selected by Delta and TF 160 operators on Barbados using hastily provided SR-71 air-reconnaissance photographs, without the benefit of photo interpretation.

The mission was originally planned to be even larger, with one Delta Force Squadron lifted in MH-60As from Barbados taking out the prison. Delta's A Squadron was to be flown into Port Salines Airport on board C-141s along with TF 160 AH/MH-6A 'Little Birds'. They would then quickly assemble the helicopters and attack Fort Rupert (in the capital of St George's on the coast). But the realization that the US would have to fight for Port Salines led to the plan for ferrying in the 'Little Birds' to be dropped. The force coming from Barbados in MH-60As was now re-tasked at the last moment to raid both objectives, hitting the prison first.

Delays in H-Hour and problems with assembling the MH-60A helicopters – unloaded from C-5 transports in Barbados – pushed the raid into daylight, after the planned H-Hour for the Rangers. This ensured that the defenders would be alert. What should have been a stealthy operation became a frontal assault against an alerted defence. Takeoff from Grantley Adams International Airport on Barbados was delayed until 0530.

The MH-60As approached the prison at 0615, flying at low altitude in daylight against alerted defences. There was no chance of surprise and no diversions or suppressive fire power were available to compensate for it. They came under fire from the two Fort Frederick anti-aircraft gun positions, undetected pre-mission. Pressing on, the MH-60As were caught in crossfire from small arms and machine guns from Fort Frederick and Richmond Hill Prison. With tracers arcing towards the MH-60As, it was impossible for Delta to insert using fast-rope techniques from hovering helicopters. No fixed-wing air support had been tasked for this mission, and the AC-130s were already engaged at Port Salines. Navy aircraft from the carrier USS *Independence* had not yet been cleared to hit targets on the southern half of the island. Without support to call on, the Delta troops had to rely on their return fire from the helicopters' 7.62 mm machine guns and the raiders' M16s and CAR-15 carbines. Almost all of the machine guns jammed from sustained firing.

At least two attempts were made to bring the MH-60s in to insert the Delta troopers. The LZs proved unsuitable for landing – reflecting the lack of intelligence, especially maps – and the fire was too heavy to fast-rope from a hover. All the MH-60A helicopters were hit repeatedly; had they been Hueys, none would have survived, Grange thought.[18]

One MH-60A was badly damaged. Escorted by its wingman, it staggered towards Port Salines Airport but, passing within range of a PRA unit at Frequente, it was shot up further and forced to crash-land on Amber Belair Hill, killing the pilot, CPT Keith Lucas. A Grenadian patrol from the Frequente barracks was sent out to capture the survivors – the remainder of the crew and Rangers from C Company 1-75th who had been aboard – but they were engaged by an AC-130 that was summoned from the fighting around Port Salines Airport to cover the crash site. At 0630, a Navy SH-3 search and rescue helicopter that had been standing by offshore landed next to the downed helicopter to pick up the wounded.

David Grange recalled, 'I had seventeen wounded in my force of forty-four.'[19] Some MH-60As landed at Port Salines Airport. They would be picked up by a C-141 on D+1. Two MH-60As landed on the destroyer *Moosbrugger* for quick medical treatment for the wounded. In the air, other Delta and TF 160 wounded were delayed in getting treatment as the USS *Guam* denied Army MH-60As permission to land. VADM Metcalf soon rescinded this order. Once on board the *Guam*, the MH-60As could not be refuelled until the Army made arrangements to repay the Navy. This incident received wide publicity as an example of poor inter-service co-operation.

The JTF 123 offensive against high-value targets around St George's was called off. C Company of the 1-75th Rangers, which had been attached to JTF 123 to support Delta and other activities, was returned to the control of its battalion at the airport at 1600 on D-Day.

Following the SOF repulse, at 0945 AC-130H Lima 56 attacked Fort Rupert, firing twenty-five 105 mm rounds. Later in the day, air strikes from the carrier *Independence* were called in on Fort Rupert and Fort Frederick.

Fort Rupert and Fort Frederick would be taken by the Marines on the afternoon of the next day. By that time, the Grenadian revolutionary leadership had fled. The guards had also fled from Richmond Hill Prison. On D+2, several US journalists walked in and liberated the prison, then called in nearby Marines. The prisoners turned out to include many of the previous leaders of the island and local journalists.

THE SEALS AT RADIO GRENADA
The other D-Day JTF 123 mission fared no better. An element from SEAL Team 6 was tasked with securing Radio Free Grenada at Beausejour. The

SEALs were to capture and hold the radio station for use by an Army Psychological Operations unit, deploying from Fort Bragg.[20]

The SEALs were inserted at dawn by an MH-60 helicopter and seized the station without resistance after they had overwhelmed the small guard force. PRA forces soon counterattacked with BTR-60PB APCs. Without antitank weapons or air support, the SEALs were forced to try (unsuccessfully) to destroy the transmitter. The SEALs managed to evade and escape to the ocean. Swimming out to sea, they were picked up by the destroyer USS *Caron*. Naval gunfire and air strikes were then used – both unsuccessfully – in an attempt to silence the transmitter

RANGERS RAID AT GRAND ANSE

The improvised command structure hindered follow-up operations. Metcalf declined to appoint a ground force commander for Army, Marines and SOF, even though large numbers of all three forces were now ashore. Following Schwarzkopf's recommendations, he did give orders for the 82nd Airborne to assume command of the two Ranger battalions as of 1900 on D-Day. The 2-75th Rangers only got word of this at 2230, the 1-75th at 0630 the next morning.[21] MG Trobaugh, at the 82nd Airborne's forward TOC at Port Salines Airport, had only limited and intermittent radio contact with Metcalf even though he could see the *Guam* offshore.

While the fact that the medical students at the True Blue campus had not been held hostage reduced the urgency, there was still fear that General Hudson Austin, now a fugitive, or remnants of the PRA and Cuban forces might seize the Americans at Grand Anse campus. Fortunately, the medical students at Grand Anse campus were able to keep the US forces at Port Salines Airport appraised of the situation by telephone. The students were instructed to be ready for a rescue mission.

There was also danger to the medical students from collateral damage. The staff on the *Guam* had identified the campus as hostile and a potential target for fixed-wing aircraft. The State Department representative on the JTF 123 staff was able to get it removed from the target list.[22]

Rangers and paratroopers advanced overland towards Grand Anse from True Blue. About a mile north, they encountered Cuban resistance at Frequente. With Grand Anse apparently also heavily defended by Cubans, concerns that using supporting fire power would endanger the medical students led the ground forces to request assistance from VADM Metcalf on the *Guam*.

A heliborne rescue operation using Marine CH-46s from the *Guam* to lift Rangers from Port Salines – a distance of under two miles – was quickly planned. It was not without problems. At first, the Marines refused to lift the Rangers when given the orders. This reflected the unclear chain of command – the Marines did not know who had authority in the improvised organization – and the Marines' desire that troops from the MEU, who had trained with the CH-46 crews before embarking, be used instead. But the Marines were already committed to a mission ashore. A direct order from MG Schwarzkopf on the *Guam* was required to get the operation into motion.[23] The initial refusal of the Marines to lift the Rangers was another of the Grenada anecdotes that would have a long life.

Student phone and radio messages reported some sixty enemy troops and three machine guns, mainly Grenadian, dug in south of the Grand Anse campus. A battle or a hostage situation remained a possibility. The Rangers would fly to the objective in three waves, each composed of three CH-46s carrying a fifty-man team drawn from a company of the 2-75th Rangers.

An air strike from the *Independence*'s A-7s, artillery fire from the 82nd Airborne and mortar shells from forward battalions of the 82nd would prepare the LZ. Gunfire support would come from AC-130s, ships off the coast and the Marines' two surviving attack helicopters. Suppressive fire would continue until twenty seconds before the Rangers would land.

Planning was hastily carried out at Port Salines Airport and on the *Guam*. With radio communications limited, MG Trobaugh and the commanding officer of the 2-75th, LTC Ralph J. Hagler Jr., flew out to the *Guam*. Following the conference, the CH-46s flew from the *Guam* and linked up with the Rangers. The planning continued at Port Salines, using HUMINT provided by school officials from the True Blue campus.

The first wave, A Company, would secure the LZ. They would be followed by B Company, which would cordon off the campus. C Company would then arrive, move out and clear the campus, locate the students and evacuate them in four CH-53Ds from the *Guam* that would be in a holding pattern offshore.

The raid took off from Port Salines at 1545 after the students had been warned to get under cover and be ready for immediate evacuation. Hagler

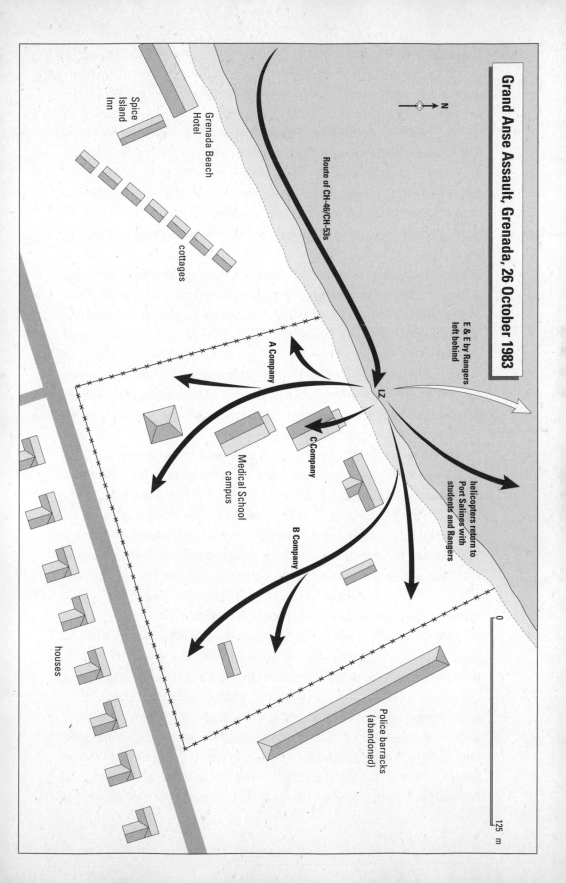

Grand Anse Assault, Grenada, 26 October 1983

N

Route of CH-46/CH-53s

E & E by Rangers
left behind

LZ

helicopters return to
Port Salines with
students and Rangers

A Company

C Company

B Company

Medical School
campus

Police barracks
(abandoned)

Grenada Beach
Hotel

Spice
Island
Inn

cottages

houses

0   125 m

led the operation from a UH-1H command helicopter. During lift-off, the helicopter formations carrying A and B Companies became intermixed. In the air, Hagler was informed that more students were arriving at the objective. The force circled for an additional fifteen minutes.

At 1605, the preparatory fire suppressed potential resistance near the LZ. A-7s strafed an abandoned police barracks east of the campus. An AC-130 destroyed buildings outside the campus.

The first wave of three CH-46s missed the designated beach in front of the campus and landed on another stretch of beach some 500 m short of the campus. There was light small arms fire, most of the defenders having dispersed under the preparatory attacks. The second wave came down closer to the campus, but still short. While A and B Companies were organizing their defensive positions, C Company landed at the objective near the campus buildings.

The only serious damage to the CH-46s came from overhanging trees. One CH-46 hit a tree on landing and was abandoned in the surf, without casualties. A Navy SH-3 helicopter on CSAR duties came in and picked up the crew. An AC-130 shot up the wreck.

The orbiting CH-53Ds were brought in to remove the students. By this time, more of the enemy force had rallied and were firing on the helicopters. The Rangers returned fire, supported by an A-7 attack. Then the CH-46s returned and, covered by fire from their on-board .50-calibre machine guns, extracted the Rangers, completing the entire operation in twenty-six minutes. The students were finally evacuated some thirty-three hours after the initial US landings. Returning to Port Salines Airport as the 1-505th Airborne was arriving, their commanding officer, LTC George Crocker, saw the Rangers' 'troopers offloading and whooping for joy at their success'.[24]

After leaving the beach, the raiders realized that eleven Rangers who had been deployed as a flank guard had been left behind. By radio, these men were told to move towards positions held by the 82nd Airborne. The Ranger force – not on the same radio net as the 82nd – were not sure they could safely enter those lines without risking fratricide. With fire from the AC-130 and the 82nd Airborne's artillery dissuading the remaining enemy from interfering with their withdrawal, the Rangers decided to use one of the inflatable rafts from the shot-up CH-46 to reach ships offshore. However, the raft had been damaged during the crash. The Rangers bailed frantically, but soon had to swim alongside their damaged raft. Battling surf and tides, they were spotted by the Navy. The destroyer USS *Caron* picked them all up at 2300.

FOLLOW-ON ACTIONS

One of the Rangers' initial D-Day objectives, Calivigny barracks, 5 km from the airfield, had not been secured. An order from the JCS – bypassing intermediate levels of command – was given for a direct assault. On 27 October, the 2-75th reinforced by C Company of the 1-75th mounted a full-scale air assault. The Rangers were lifted in on 16 UH-60s following massive fire power from 105 mm howitzers of the 82nd Airborne Division, AC-130s, A-7s and naval gunfire. Three helicopters collided over the LZ with heavy losses. The barracks were empty.

The population – despite several collateral-damage incidents – was highly appreciative and helped in the rounding up of PRA fugitives. It would take a total of ten days before the 82nd Airborne, Marines and the composite force from other Caribbean nations completely secured the island. Further students and foreign nationals who had not been evacuated were brought by helicopter to Port Salines Airport and then taken off the island.

SEIZURE MISSION FOR HUDSON AUSTIN

There was concern over the delay in seizing the hostile leadership, but there were no further seizure missions after D-Day. Coard was arrested trying to flee the island on 29 October. There was concern that General Hudson Austin, the minister of defence, head of the Revolutionary Military Council and would-be strongman, was still at large. He had walked out of PRA HQ at Fort Frederick on D-Day and, along with a small group from the regime's leadership, was looking for a boat to escape Grenada.

On 27 October, the 82nd Airborne received fresh HUMINT on Austin's location. An East German, Gerhard Jonas, reported Austin's hiding place in an empty bungalow by a dock on Grenada's rugged Westerhall Peninsula. The terrain around the hiding place, the German reported, made it inaccessible overland, and there was nowhere to land a helicopter. It could only be reached by boat. Trobaugh authorized an improvised covert amphibious seizure raid using a small local boat, the *Windfall*. Under the command of LCDR Peter Tomlin of the Barbados Coast Guard, the boat was to appear to be arriving to pick up Austin. When it came to the dock, one of Trobaugh's aides and three other paratroopers concealed below would hurl non-lethal flash-bang grenades, storm ashore and capture Austin. However, a sudden rain squall, bad weather and the tides that had proven so deadly to the SEALs days before thwarted the paratroopers and sailors.

Metcalf now turned the seizure mission over to JTF 123. The Westerhall Peninsula was to be an SOF area of responsibility. To avoid fratricide incidents, the 82nd would not operate there. However, many of the SOF assets had already been withdrawn or were still out of action following their losses earlier in the operation, and consequently on 28–29 October, US SOF were unable to find the elusive general. On 30 October, at a meeting at Trobaugh's command post, an impatient Metcalf gave the tasking to COL Steven Scott's 3rd Brigade of the 82nd Airborne.

Scott ordered the 2-505th Parachute Infantry to seal the neck of the Westerhall Peninsula that afternoon. They then moved in to sweep the area, with Scott in a command helicopter overhead. He requested a naval blockade and support from AC-130s to prevent any attempted escape.

That afternoon, a platoon from C Company of the 2-505th, accompanied by the informant Jonas, surrounded the bungalow where Austin and other members of the revolutionary leadership were reportedly cornered. Jonas invited Austin to come out with his hands up. After a lengthy argument, that was what he did. He was soon evacuated via helicopter to the *Guam*.

Other searches for fugitives continued. A minor diplomatic incident ensued when US forces searching for fugitives surrounded the Soviet embassy compound on 2 November.

GRENADA LESSONS

The Grenada mission had implications far beyond the liberation of the island itself. Politically, Grenada proved to be a success in the US. The gratitude of the returning medical students made President Reagan's political opponents reluctant to confront him on the issue. The 'rally round the flag' effect of the operation and the desire to avoid at any cost the national trauma of another hostage crisis – even though this, in hindsight, appeared unlikely – proved a powerful boost for the administration.

Despite its small scale and the serious problems in execution, it demonstrated that the US was willing to use force to reverse Communist successes in the Third World, which would no longer be quietly accepted or considered irreversible. In the Caribbean basin, countries including Nicaragua and Surinam stressed their distance from the Soviet Union and Cuba, wanting to avoid invasion. As with the Falklands War the year before, Grenada demonstrated that the West was not impotent. A sign of superpower resolution, the successful Grenada mission sent the exact opposite message from the resignation of Secretary of State Cyrus Vance after Desert One, which had seemed to indicate that the use of armed force – in the form of special operations – to resolve hostage situations was illegitimate except in response to threats of imminent execution. Grenada showed that anything that looked likely to lead to such a situation would be countered by the full resources that the US had available, including military options where this was feasible. For the US, Grenada was also key in overcoming the 'Vietnam syndrome' and demonstrating that US force would be used when necessary to defend key national interests. In the words of Robert Kimmitt, 'I think Grenada is really where the corner was turned.'[25]

Grenada was politically successful. As a military operation –particularly as a special operation – it was only saved from disaster by the relatively light resistance encountered. MG Schwarzkopf, on the *Guam*, saw 'total chaos and confusion' dominating the operations on D-Day.[26] He saw the SOF as being part of the problem, operating independently rather than being integrated with the overall operation at H-Hour. The SOF on Grenada included too many disparate forces assigned in haste to carry out too many different missions. All of the special operations were compromised. None of them had the element of surprise or even the cover of darkness. There was no attempt made at concealment or deception.

All SOF were operating with minimal co-ordination, little co-operation and inadequate IPB. They had been sent on missions as part of a hasty USLANTCOM plan that was drawn up in ignorance of JTF 123 (and SOF in general) capabilities and limitations. The availability of supporting fire power and forces – AC-130s, ships offshore, the MAU – avoided disaster in some cases. It could not prevent other tragic failures, such as the deaths of special operators trying to carry out advance reconnaissance and plant beacons at Port Salines Airport. The failure of IPB was also identified by the Army and Navy as being key to the problems encountered on Grenada. The post-operation Army Staff Study concluded that 'intelligence support and flow during

planning and employment was late, inaccurate, incomplete and uncoordinated'. The Navy study reached similar conclusions.[27]

The planning process was highly deficient, both by the SOF themselves
(as represented by JTF 123) and in the integration of SOF into the larger
Operation Urgent Fury. USLANTCOM had thought that the available intelligence justified their anticipation that Urgent Fury would be a cakewalk. Not
only did they (and the intelligence community) underestimate the initial
Cuban and Grenadian resistance, they vastly underestimated the friction
that a hastily improvised joint operation involving SOF would generate. There
was no agreement on how it was deficient. Each of the different services and
commands (including the JSOC, representing SOF) studied the problem and
came to the conclusion that Grenada would have gone better had they been
allowed to control the planning and execute the operation their way. Congress was less than impressed by this lack of a consensus view for the direction of change, which set the stage for Congress to take the lead in defence
reform in the next few years.

Fortunately, the enemy were unable or unwilling to exploit these limitations, or to take hostages or kill prisoners, which would have defeated the liberation missions. While the political impact of Grenada may have been an
overall success, it is difficult to disagree with USAF Lt. Col. Jerry Thigpen:
'Many of the same problems (command and control, joint operations, participation by all services) that had been identified during Desert One resur-
faced again.'[28] Fortunately, due to the permissive threat environment, the US
was able to declare a politically and diplomatically important victory. The US
military had fulfilled Vice President Bush's charge not to re-create Desert
One because the friction was less and the enemy weaker.

Hasty planning for the operation, including the improvised special
operation staffs reporting to commanders and staffs unfamiliar with SOF,
resulted in high casualties being incurred across the full range of special
operations missions and an inability to utilize fully SOF's unique capabilities.
The lack of a dedicated full-time special operations staff – there was obviously no time to pull together the mission-specific planning of previous raids
such as Son Tay – was critical. This would be addressed later in the 1980s.
The lack of rehearsal and thorough planning was apparent in the problems
encountered by all the SOF on D-Day. Intense operational security concerns
had meant that the many different units that had to be co-ordinated on

D-Day could not all be 'read in' on the operation in time. The SOF were unaware of each other's missions and of the missions of other US forces.

Poor communications and poor fire-support co-ordination had the potential for being lethal to SOF when they were being used as an integral part of a larger joint operation. SOF were not involved directly in any of the several fratricide and collateral-damage incidents on Grenada, but the US weakness in this area shaped the operations. The story of the SEALs at Government House making a credit-card call to Fort Bragg to arrange fire support was a powerful incentive for reform.

The forces involved had – with the notable exception of the units of the Marine 22nd MAU – insufficient mission-specific training. The Rangers, though suffering from a lack of rehearsal, were good infantry. They were able to adapt quickly, first to an airdrop rather than an air landing, then improvising the student liberation mission at Grand Anse campus. The different services all took part, but there was little joint operation. SEALs, Delta, Rangers, Marines and the 82nd Airborne all fought well but each had planned and fought their own battle. In addition to the mistakes made by the men on the scene, mistakes were made by more distant headquarters. This led to the decision to send the Rangers against the empty Calivigny barracks, a raid marred by a tragic midair collision.

Unity of effort was lacking. It was not limited to the Marines' initial refusal to carry Rangers on the mission to secure the students at Grand Anse and the reluctance to allow Army helicopters to land and refuel on Navy warships. The problems inherent in integrating liberation and seizure missions with joint operations even in a relatively permissive environment proved to be considerable. The SEALs' raid on Government House – intended to be a surprise, stealthy rescue operation – ended up becoming a lengthy siege. The story of having to use a phone to reach air support soon became widely known. The poor general level of inter-service co-ordination, the lack of intelligence and the many logistics problems did not lead to disaster only because of the limited capability of the opposing forces.

The liberation and seizure missions on Grenada suffered from poor intelligence. The IPB vacuum was comparable to Koh Tang. Had there been adequate IPB before the invasion, many of the setbacks encountered by SOF could have been avoided. The intelligence had led to the assumption that there would be minimal resistance, which proved unfounded. At Richmond

Hill Prison and Government House, helicopter insertion without the element of surprise met with intense opposition. In these actions, lightly armed SOF had to struggle to prevail against less proficient but more numerous opposing forces. In these cases, conventional forces, air and ground, were required to carry out the mission as part of the general mopping-up on Grenada starting on D+1. The lack of suitable maps made effective planning difficult and contributed to battlefield setbacks and friendly-fire incidents that cost lives.

'Hostage' is still a loaded term for US decision-makers. No one can permit US citizens to be held hostage and not appear ineffectual (or politically doomed). On Grenada, 599 Americans and eighty foreign nationals were evacuated. Fortunately, there was no concerted attempt to seize or hold hostages even after the US forces had started to land, even though the enemy had many such opportunities due to US inability to locate and secure the students in the critical opening hours of D-Day.

The permissive threat environment removed the need to operate at a high tempo and to secure high-value objectives simultaneously before the enemy could respond. The US was unable to locate, let alone secure, all the medical students on the island in the opening minutes of the operation. It had no idea where the medical students were any more than it knew the location of the enemy leadership or political prisoners. Even had the SOF known these things, they had no way of inserting forces at all these objectives at H-Hour.

It was obvious in Grenada that many of the problems encountered at Desert One and publicized by the Holloway Commission report were still unresolved. The high-level disharmony, problems with command and control and inter-service co-operation and the misuse of special operations forces were all exhibited on Grenada. The difficulties experienced in the execution of Operation Urgent Fury motivated defence reform. Problems with integrating special and joint operations led to the Goldwater–Nichols Defence Reorganization Act of 1986 and eventually to the establishment of SOCOM. These were matched by the increased resources made available for defence – including special operations – in the early 1980s. It would take a number of years for the legacy of the 'hollow forces' era that had helped produce the results at Koh Tang and Desert One to be overcome.

CHAPTER 8
PANAMA · 20 December 1989

Probably the best-conceived military operation since World War II.

GEN Edward C. Meyer, former Army Chief of Staff.

While the focus of world events was on the collapse of the Soviet empire in central and eastern Europe, the US military actions in Panama included examples of liberation and seizure missions, but also demonstrated a potential model for post-Cold War warfare, when the military operations would be about saving prisoners, preventing the taking of hostages and removing Third World dictators rather than the clash of ideologies that dominated 1945–91. The 'Panama model' would be set aside through much of the 1990s, but many of its lessons – including those for liberation and seizure missions and their relation to rebuilding post-war governance – were to be re-examined and applied in Afghanistan in 2001 and Iraq in 2003.[1]

EMERGING THREATS

In the years between Grenada and Panama, US special operations forces had not carried out any liberation or seizure missions. They had planned, trained for and rehearsed to do so: US prisoners retained after the end of the Vietnam War in Southeast Asia, US hostages held in Lebanon, terrorist leaders in Lebanon and ship and aircraft hijackers. None of these operations was carried out. In some cases, this was because those to be seized were secured through other means (the *Achille Lauro* hijackers) or those to be liberated were actually long dead (the missing prisoners in Southeast Asia, where raids into Laos were scrubbed in 1981 and 1983 due to intelligence information). What frustrated most of these prospective missions was the inability to provide timely actionable intelligence that would have made a special operations forces mission possible. But perhaps the most telling statement of the value of having a capability to carry out special operations forces liberation or seizure missions was the policy costs imposed when the US had to look to other options because the intelligence was not adequate to support launching such a mission.

In Lebanon, the US disengaged after the 1983 Beirut Airport bombing. Some twenty years later, the terrorist leaders that made that bombing possible are still walking around and have achieved a secure position in Lebanon because the US was unable to remove them. The inability of the US to liberate hostages held in Lebanon in the 1980s led to a variety of ill-advised decisions. First, in November 1984, Ronald Reagan decided to train and equip a surrogate strike team to attack terrorists pre-emptively in Lebanon. The surrogates hired others who conducted an unauthorized and unsuccessful car bombing of a senior terrorist leader in Beirut. The failed bombing caused significant collateral damage. Over eighty people were killed, heavy casualties even by Beirut standards. This led to the exposure of the surrogate programme in the media. The resulting Congressional investigation forced ultimate cancellation of the programme. Following this, in the summer of 1985, the Reagan administration decided to covertly supply guided missiles to Iran. They hoped that this would lead to the release of US hostages held by pro-Iranian terrorists in Lebanon. This approach also failed after the release of three hostages. Exposure led to a major political scandal that undercut the effectiveness of the administration. The US hostages would not all be freed until 1991.

There are many different ways for policies to fail; Desert One represented only the most spectacular. Reagan had publicly proclaimed a counter-terrorism policy of swift and effective retribution, meant to deter future terrorist acts. In Lebanon, this policy failed. If events such as the Iran raid underline the inherent high-risk nature of SOF liberation missions, then the results of the covert Lebanon anti-terrorist action and the Iran missiles-for-hostages deal underline the potential costs even if political leaders do not use SOF. There are risks in liberation missions; the US dealings over the Lebanon hostages in the 1980s shows that there are other risks imposed on policy decisions when such missions are not an option.

The use of SOF in the *Achille Lauro* hijacking showed the importance of an appropriate and tailored response to hostile activity – in this case terrorism – and the significance of the diplomatic dimension of such operations in peacetime. Following the hijacking of the Italian cruise liner *Achille Lauro* in October 1985, the Palestine Liberation Front terrorists responsible, including their leader Abu Abbas, had been allowed by the Egyptian government to leave Egypt for Tunisia on board an Egypt Air Boeing 737. The Egyptian government was reportedly not then aware that the hijackers had murdered an elderly American tourist on board the ship. US Navy F-14s from the carrier *Saratoga* intercepted the 737 in international airspace over the Mediterranean and forced it to land at the US base at Sigonella on Sicily. Once there, it was surrounded by US SOF from Delta and SEAL Team 6 under the direct command of JSOC Commander MG Carl Stiner. These forces had been forward deployed in case a liberation mission on the *Achille Lauro* had been practical. However, the interception operation had not been cleared with the Italian government. This led to a stand-off with armed Italian troops. After it was made clear that Italy would not relinquish custody of the terrorists, the US forces stood down. Although the Italians promised to try the hijackers, they were in fact allowed to leave for Yugoslavia, with Abu Abbas being tried *in absentia* after he left. He would eventually end up in US hands in Baghdad in 2003, but the incident was to have long-lasting impact in Washington. Even close NATO allies were afraid of incurring terrorist retaliation. A capability for unilateral action appeared to be an increasingly worthwhile investment.

EVOLVING SOF

Reorganization of the US military had been a major event of the second Reagan term (1985–89). Panama would be its first major test.

The Goldwater–Nichols Act of 1986 had broad-reaching impact. Its most important reform was to strengthen the authority and responsibility of the Chairman of the Joint Chiefs of Staff (CJCS), the commanders-in-chief of unified commands (CINCs, redesignated 'combatant commanders' in 2002) and the joint staffs that support them, at the expense of the services. The national command authority (NCA) now directed the CINCs through the CJCS. The CJCS was designated as the President's principal military advisor and made explicitly responsible – together with the CINCs

– for the preparation and review of contingency plans. The CINCs were given full combatant command authority over their service components.

The strengthening of joint war-fighting capabilities was seen as being hindered by the services' political strength and 'rice bowl' concerns. The services were to be taken out of the business of directing war-fighting and put into that of making ready forces and capabilities to be used in combat by the CINCs. This change was motivated by lessons from the *Mayaguez* incident, the Iran Raid, Grenada and other setbacks where command relationships were seen as having undercut the effectiveness of the fighting forces.

US Special Operations Command (SOCOM) was established by the Cohen–Nunn Amendment to the Goldwater–Nichols Act, passed in November 1986. It reflected the lessons of the Iran raid and Grenada. There had been widespread Congressional concern that special operations forces and capabilities would never receive adequate support from the individual services. After many alternative approaches were considered – some in Congress wanted to unify all special operations forces as a fifth service – the Cohen–Nunn Amendment established that while the services were still responsible for organizing and training special operations forces, they would be funded separately. SOCOM would provide the means to integrate these service-originated forces and make them available to support combatant theatre commanders as a joint capability.

SOCOM got a four-star commander-in-chief – CINCSOCOM – with sufficient stature to be heard in the bureaucratic battles on resource allocation and responsibility division in Washington. The CINCSOCOM also testifies annually before Congress, to provide a view of special operations needs and capabilities without the strong filter of service-specific interests. However, CINCSOCOM was not originally a 'supported' or 'combatant' CINC. He was a 'supporting' CINC, responsible for organizing, training and equipping the range of US SOF – Special Force, Rangers, SEALs, Air Force Special Operations (but not Marines) – to meet the requirements of the Joint Chiefs of Staff. However, when SOF were to go into action, they would not normally be under the battlefield command of CINCSOC. Rather, they would 'chop' to the operational control of a theatre CINC – CINCCENTCOM for the Gulf, for example – or directly to the Joint Chiefs of Staff for specific high-value special operations (as in the Son Tay Raid). The theatre CINCs, as America's primary war-fighters, rather than SOCOM would be responsible for deciding

how SOF would be used in action. Both the CINCs and the CJCS were authorized to form Joint Special Operations Task Force headquarters to carry out
missions.

Organizational problems had been identified as a leading cause of the
failure of earlier special operations. Now, instead of the improvised command structures familiar from Son Tay and the Iran raid, there was a full-
time highly professional SOCOM staff at MacDill AFB, Florida. In addition,
each of the US regional CINCs had under them an SOF staff, focusing on the
problems specific to their command's area. These theatre SOC (TSOC) staffs
had been largely ignored before the establishment of SOCOM. They were
now expanded, with professional staffs, under a flag officer with direct
access to the theatre CINC. Quality and quantity of manpower improved, as
a special operations career track was no longer a guarantee that an officer's
career would suffer in comparison with career tracks in other branches of
their service. The TSOCs, however, were largely kept undermanned and with
limited money for training and command post exercises until after 2001
(undercutting the capability to have a cadre of SOF familiar with each area
of operations when the war against terrorism became serious).

This arrangement was modified in 2002, allowing CINCSOCOM also to
be a combatant CINC in the war on terror in certain situations. In practice,
this system has worked well, better than the *ad hoc* arrangements that had
dominated since the end of the Second World War. However, it has led to
obvious tensions, with SOF reporting to a theatre CINC (and staff) normally
drawn from the (more numerous) combined arms forces who may not be
aware of SOF capabilities and limitations. As a general rule, CINCs and their
staff like big multi-service operations with everyone getting a chance to play
and no chance of things going wrong, followed by medals, promotions all
around and good press coverage. SOF like small low-profile operations in
which only they play and are willing to accept the risks. They could not care
less whether the story ever appears in the press. The tension between these
two approaches has been seen repeatedly since 1987.

Both Goldwater–Nichols and Cohen–Nunn encountered broad-based
opposition from the Reagan administration, the Department of Defense and
the services. The services – especially the Navy – were the most opposed. The
Navy saw in the theatre CINCs generals who would misuse their ships without understanding their capabilities and limitations. They also saw SOCOM's

centralization of SOF as making the SEALs unavailable to support the fleet in wartime (which is why the Marines kept their cherished Force Recon away from SOCOM until after 2002) and unresponsive to service concerns in peacetime.

However, the services kept the procurement dollars – except for those directly allocated to SOCOM, which received its own research and development and procurement accounts independent of service – and eventually had to recognize that these changes have brought about greater joint warfighting capability. Some of the services thought that as SOCOM had its own money, they could stick it with their less-favoured mission areas, freeing up resources for higher priorities. This approach has been seen as underlying the lack of USAF investment in the CSAR mission in the years between the two wars with Iraq.

The services had also taken steps to reflect the increased importance of special operations. In terms of training and capabilities, these service-specific changes were as important as the formation of SOCOM. The Army made its special operations forces a branch (equivalent to infantry or artillery) in 1987 and established the US Army Special Operations Command (USASOC). Also in 1987, the Navy set up a Naval Special Warfare Command (NSWC). The Air Force kept its SOCOM-committed assets under the Military Airlift Command (MAC) until 1990, when they emerged as Air Force Special Operations Command (AFSOC).

SOCOM ended up having four major component commands. These were the Joint Special Operations Command (JSOC) at Fort Bragg plus three service-specific components.

These were critical improvements for SOF. Personnel decisions are policy decisions. Following these changes, skilled SOF personnel could spend their careers in that mission area rather than dooming themselves to retire as field-grade officers unless they served in billets more favoured by service-specific promotion boards. This meant that it was easier to keep permanent – not mission-specific one-time-only – SOF headquarters up and running, and to retain skilled operators and planners.

Panama was not SOCOM's first military operation – that was Operation Earnest Will, defending maritime commerce against Iranian action in the Gulf in 1987–9 – but SOCOM had already demonstrated that the large US investment in special operations capabilities was reflected in improved operational planning. The years since Grenada had been marked by an improvement in the special operations forces that would be used for liberation and seizure missions, as well as in their command structures. The Army's Rangers had expanded to three battalions. Delta Force and the Navy SEALs had expanded their forces and refined their capabilities in response to a range of challenges, including terrorist hijackings in the Middle East, operations in Central America and keeping the Gulf open to maritime traffic. Both forces had been alerted for potential hostage-liberation situations a number of times throughout the 1980s, but were not actually called upon to carry any of them out.

This increase in capabilities was not limited to SOCOM assets. After the *Achille Lauro* incident, US Marine Corps Commandant GEN P. X. Kelley sought to make forward deployed Marine forces capable of limited hostage-rescue operations.[2] This eventually led to the training of Marine Expeditionary (formerly Amphibious) Units (MEU/MAU) to earn a special-operations-capable (SOC) designation before deploying. The MEU (SOC) is an all-arms force deployed afloat that is trained to carry out twenty-one special operations missions.[3] While not SOF, special-operations-capable MEU were to play an important role in a wide range of contingencies in the turbulent years following the end of the Cold War. Army airborne forces also trained to be able to carry out missions other than their traditional battlefield one.

PANAMA AND NORIEGA

Sir Francis Drake described Panama – as he was about to loot it – as the 'treasure house of the world'. Since then, other men-at-arms have come to Panama, some to loot, others to liberate. Operation Just Cause – the US military operations in Panama in 1989 (renamed from Blue Spoon shortly before D-Day) – was essentially about one man firmly in the looter category, namely Panamanian strongman Manuel Noriega.

The US may have originally thought Noriega was their man in Panama. He had emerged from the leadership of the Panama Defence Force (PDF) to become a particularly evil version of the Latin American *caudillo*. Known as 'pineapple face' because of his extensive facial scars, Noriega developed an intense interest in the occult, collected Hitler memorabilia and subscribed to *Soldier of Fortune* magazine. He added extensive involvement with organized crime, especially drug trafficking, to his potent personal mixture of nationalist appeal and self-aggrandizement. His widespread personal residences (with voodoo shrines), beach houses, yachts and aircraft would become military objectives in Operation Just Cause.

Despite long-standing relations with US intelligence and his show of opposition to Communists and drug-runners alike, overall US relations with Noriega deteriorated during the Reagan years. In 1985, he had ousted his own handpicked president, Nicolas Ardito Barletta, and assumed direct rule. In the words of former US Ambassador Ambler Moss, Noriega was 'driven by simple principles: power and money'.[4]

By 1987, even Washington was aware that Noriega was a danger to Panama. Then head of the PDF and *de facto* ruler, Noriega was accused by a rival, Colonel Roberto Diaz Herrera, of murdering opponents, perpetrating election fraud and making Panama a base of operations for international criminality, including narcotics traffic. This led to a breach in Noriega's relationship with Washington. The US discontinued military assistance to the PDF and called for a return to democracy. In 1987, the Senate passed a resolution urging Panama to restore a civilian government, followed by cuts in security and economic aid. The Reagan administration imposed sanctions.

Following Noriega's indictment on drug-related charges in February 1988 by two US courts, planning for US military action – started in 1987 – became a priority. Panama's nominal president, Eric Delvalle, tried to remove Noriega but lost his own job in the process. An abortive anti-Noriega *coup* attempted by the PDF in March 1988 led to purges and the appointment of pro-Noriega officers. Noriega supplemented the PDF by creating a militia of street criminals and political supporters, the eighteen Dignity Battalions ('DigBats'). Despite their name, these were not military units but rather plain-clothes, untrained groups ranging in size from about a dozen to 150 or so. Noriega used them to defeat the *coup* attempt in March 1988. Harassment of US citizens in Panama increased.

The US started planning, rehearsing and training for a military intervention. At first, this was orientated towards an SOF-only seizure mission against Noriega, with the aim of bundling him into an aeroplane to stand trial in the US. SOCOM supported this approach, but this plan was eventually put aside. Accurate intelligence as to Noriega's location was seldom available. There were fears that such an action would lead to retaliation by his supporters against the canal or US citizens.[5]

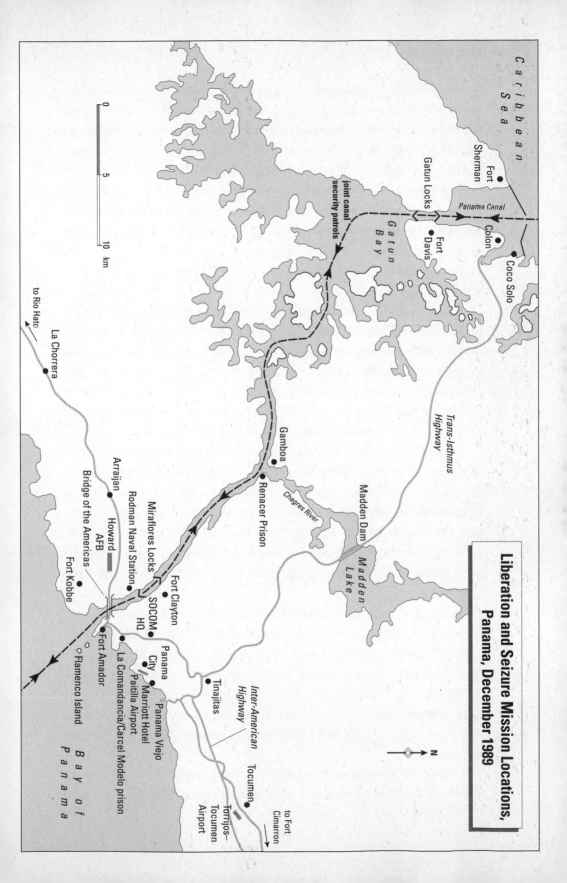

Liberation and Seizure Mission Locations, Panama, December 1989

Caribbean Sea

Fort Sherman

Gatun Locks

Colon

Coco Solo

Panama Canal

Fort Davis

Gatun Bay

joint canal security patrols

Trans-Isthmus Highway

Madden Dam

Madden Lake

Gamboa

Renacer Prison

Chagres River

to Rio Hato

La Chorrera

Arraijan

Bridge of the Americas

Howard AFB

Rodman Naval Station

Miraflores Locks

Fort Clayton

SOCOM HQ

Fort Kobbe

Fort Amador

Flamenco Island

La Comandancia/Carcel Modelo prison

Patilla Airport

Marriott Hotel

Panama Viejo

Panama City

Tinajitas

Inter-American Highway

Tocumen

Torrijos–Tocumen Airport

to Fort Cimarron

Bay of Panama

N

0
5
10
km

The planning for possible anti-Noriega action led to additional US forces being deployed to secure installations in the Canal Zone, which were all scheduled to be turned over to Panama by 2000. This in turn led to an expansion of the PDF – ostensibly for canal security, actually to secure Noriega. The PDF contained 14,000 men (at least 4,000 of whom were trained combat troops) organized into nineteen companies and six platoons armed with mortars, anti-aircraft guns, twenty-nine armoured fighting vehicles (AFVs), twelve patrol craft and twenty-eight aircraft. It had strongly fortified its headquarters in La Comandancia, in downtown Panama City, and its key bases, including Fort Amador, Rio Hato Airfield and Torrijos–Tocumen Airport.

US sanctions were not hurting Noriega, who was now dealing with Cuba, Nicaragua, Libya (which contributed $20 million in return for providing a haven for terrorist support activities) and the drug cartels. Following electoral defeat by the opposition – despite rampant voter fraud – Noriega invalidated Panamanian civil elections in May 1989. He then sent the PDF and the DigBats to brutally attack the opposition. The successful vice-presidential candidate was filmed being clubbed by a DigBat member.

Noriega was not the only potential target for a seizure mission in Panama. In September 1989, intelligence reports that Noriega ally Pablo Escobar, the Colombian drug kingpin, was in Panama led to a SOCOM seizure mission being prepared. While there was never apparently sufficient timely intelligence to launch, this incident did lead to a ruling allowing US SOF to conduct arrests of those suspected of violating US laws. There would now be no requirement for SOF to be accompanied by law-enforcement personnel on such missions.[6]

A presidential decision in July 1989 ordered military actions to deter Noriega and assert US rights under the Canal Treaty, but military action to remove Noriega remained only a contingency plan. Operation Nimrod Dancer deployed 1,900 US combat troops to Panama to protect American citizens and installations. Noriega continued to defy the Americans but he turned away from any actions that would have led to a direct confrontation. Chairman of the Joint Chiefs of Staff ADM William Crowe opposed military intervention in Panama.

Offers to drop the drug charges if Noriega stepped down were ignored. A second *coup* attempt against Noriega in October 1989 was brutally suppressed by the PDF and the DigBats before the US could put an effective response on the ground. The slowness of the US response despite advance knowledge of the *coup* was viewed with great suspicion by anti-Noriega Panamanians. After the *coup* leaders were tortured and shot, there was heavy criticism of the Bush administration for allowing US forces to stand by while Noriega increased repression. SOUTHCOM was increasingly referred to as WIMPCOM.

The senior US military leadership – including the incoming CJCS GEN Colin Powell – had to this point been invoking the 'Powell Doctrine', which opposed removing Noriega by force of arms. After October 1989, however, they largely changed their views when it seemed that escalating violence against US citizens in Panama was leading to a potential hostage situation. PDF and DigBat forces launched a systematic campaign of harassment against US dependents in Panama, culminating in the seizing and detention at gunpoint of twenty-one school buses full of children.

The US was aware that Noriega had drafted plans Genesis and Exodus for the PDF, DigBats and his *Unidad Especial de Seguridad Anti-Terror* (UESAT) anti-terrorist units to seize American hostages and move them into the interior of Panama. This would be linked to the execution of Plan Montana, calling for the PDF and DigBats to try to set up guerrilla resistance in the countryside, abandoning their garrisons.[7] Concern that Noriega might launch a pre-emptive move with the seizure of hostages or high-value assets in the Canal Zone drove US policy.

US special operations forces and intelligence assets kept Noriega under surveillance. Covert observation posts (OPs) were established. The number of US official dependants in-country – 7,000 plus some 3,000 civilian employees – was reduced. Operation Klondike Key secured and evacuated tens of thousands of Americans from Panama. Klondike Key was initiated in February and put into place, incrementally, between then and December, aiming to prevent an announcement for immediate evacuation that could trigger opportunistic hostage-taking.[8]

US PLANNING

President George H. W. Bush lost patience with the limited and gradual military response to Noriega's actions. He sacked the US commander in Panama. A new Commander-in-Chief of US Southern Command (CINCSOUTH), then headquartered in Panama, US Army GEN Maxwell Thurman, was sent down in September 1989. Thurman was more aggressive, bureaucratically and in action. It was said at the time that he was sent there so that the Panamanians would now have two military strongmen to hate. Thurman immediately went to work preparing a contingency plan for removing Noriega, using the full scope of his position's authority under the Goldwater–Nichols Act.

To enable the US to take offensive action – the headquarters set up in Panama was previously orientated towards low-level and counter-insurgency threats and training – a new operational headquarters was established in Panama, reporting directly to SOUTHCOM. Designated Joint Task Force (JTF) South, it was basically the reinforced headquarters of the US Army's XVIII Airborne Corps, specialists in rapid-reaction force projection and forcible-entry operations. The XVIII Airborne had been brought in to supersede earlier planning that had aimed mainly at deploying massive force to deter Noriega. The new approach emphasized the use of SOF to safeguard US citizens as well as the canal and to target Noriega himself. The corps commander was LTG Carl Stiner. Under Stiner, the Joint Chiefs of Staff established a Joint Special Operations Task Force (JSOTF) commanded by MG Wayne Downing. Downing had experience in both special operations and combined-arms areas and was widely respected as both a combat leader and planner. He was also aware of the political and diplomatic sensitivities that would shape SOF action in Panama.

The US operations order listed missions in order of priority, number one being the protection of US citizens, key sites and facilities. SOUTHCOM stated that the goals for this operation were 'to protect American lives, restore the democratic process, preserve the integrity of the Panama Canal treaties and apprehend Manuel Noriega'.[9] The secondary task was the capture of Noriega, the third to neutralize Noriega's capabilities for armed conflict by putting out of action the PDF, USEAT and the DigBats. Twenty-seven objectives were to be seized in the opening moves. Liberation, rescue and seizure missions were the heart of the overall military operation and were treated as being highly significant throughout the planning and execution. There were 30,000 American citizens living in Panama, 5,000 of them military dependants. SOUTHCOM set the ground rules: the operation would be considered a failure if any American military dependants were killed on a US installation in Panama or if the canal itself was destroyed or disabled.[10]

Direct action by SOF was to be an integral part of this operation, removing both the cause – Noriega, and the effect – imprisoned or threatened Americans. Making both objectives possible required pre-empting the capability of the PDF to inflict casualties to the overall operation. In the words of Stiner: 'Operation Just Cause demonstrated the utility of special operations forces as key players across the spectrum of conflict – and demonstrated the ability of special operations forces to work closely with conventional forces to speed the end of the conflict – while reducing casualties on both sides.'[11]

SPECIAL OPERATIONS IN THE JUST CAUSE PLAN

The liberation, rescue and seizure operations that were part of Operation Just Cause would be integrated, as in Grenada, with a joint-operational plan. The US had the advantage of overwhelming force, as was the case on Grenada. While victory may have been assured, the safety of prisoners and potential hostages was most certainly not. Noriega was the root cause of the conflict and his capture was seen as necessary. There was no way this could be assured simply by numbers or fire power. The operation planners put in place highly restrictive rules of engagement (RoE). Any antitank weapons or tube artillery – including the 105 mm guns of the eight AC-130s deployed to support SOF – required specific high-level authorization to open fire. The US would not be able to count on intense fire power to support its actions.

Special operations forces would be critical in Operation Just Cause. SOCOM and US Southern Command's Special Operations Command (SOUTHSOC) – CINCSOUTH's Theatre Special Operations Command (TSOC) – made SOF integration in planning and operations easier. This organization was critical to the course of the operation: special operations forces and 'conventional' forces would be under a single headquarters, working to a single operational plan, without artificial barriers to co-operation. Several command post exercises (CPXs) allowed the plans to be rehearsed and refined.

The command relationships for SOF were an improvement over those of pre-SOCOM days, though the relationship between SOCOM at MacDill AFB and SOUTHSOC in Panama was at times a difficult one. However, JTF South (the XVIII Airborne Corps) had a great deal of experience of working with special operations forces and integrating them into operational plans. Division of command was arranged between command elements sent in from SOCOM and the pre-existing Panama-based SOUTHSOC.

Under SOCOM, the long-standing practice that, for special operations, the operators should also act as planners, has been institutionalized. Normally, when a CINC receives a warning order, the staff develops a plan and passes that down to the unit(s) involved for implementation. When a special operations task force receives a warning order, it is passed to the special operations forces involved for both planning and implementation. The special operations task force and the CINC will be kept informed of the special operators' planning and, when time permits, a formal 'briefback' of the plans will be carried out. The command and control arrangements for Panama also recognized that special operators are more effective when they implement their own plans rather than those of higher headquarters.

Speed and surprise, the great strengths of successful raids, would be difficult to achieve. Although US relations with Noriega had been deteriorating for a long time, the US military presence in Panama was a long-standing one and changes in its posture or number would be evident to Noriega informers on the ground. The challenge to special operations planners and operators was, within the context of a 'standing start' with minimal surprise possible, how to free prisoners, prevent the taking of hostages and seize Noriega. Relying on the big battalions would not enable any of this to take place on a timely basis. The US staged repeated exercises and 'freedom of movement' activities, demonstrating their right to move around the Panama Canal Zone under bilateral agreements. This allowed the troops involved to become familiar with the terrain they would have to move over and allowed the US to keep up continual observation of key objectives. The long-standing US military presence in Panama allowed for clandestine positioning of special operations forces before H-Hour. US forces could carry out on-the-ground reconnaissance and surveillance of their objectives, aided by the reports of anti-Noriega Panamanians. However, Noriega ran an extensive network of informers and it had to be assumed that he would know about much of what was going on throughout Panama. The challenge was in mounting an operation to achieve multiple objectives under the noses of its targets. Throughout Panama, US liberation or seizure operations would require SOF to act in highly populated built-up areas.

THE SOF PLAN

The planners in the Joint Staff, JTF South, SOUTHCOM and SOCOM had critical H-Hour missions for the JSOTF – first, to protect American lives (and free an American prisoner); second, to get Noriega; and third, to neutralize and pre-empt resistance. JSOTF had to plan for the full range of SOF missions, which included surveillance and direct action. These missions would be an integral part of the overall Just Cause operational plan, which would include the airlift of combined-arms forces including Marines and elements of the 7th Infantry and 82nd Airborne Divisions from the continental US.

The focus of JSOTF's planning – directed by its former commander, MG Gary Luck – was downtown Panama City. This would be the mission of TF Green, under Downing. It included both special operations forces and mechanized combined-arms units (from TF Bayonet) and would operate in close co-operation with AC-130 gunships. The objectives were La Comandancia (the PDF fortress headquarters and a likely Noriega location) and the adjacent Carcel Modelo Prison, where American Kurt Muse was being held. Muse and fellow members of the Panama Rotary Club had been helping to run an anti-Noriega radio station for a year before being arrested. His captors informed him that he was a CIA agent and that they had been ordered to kill him in the event of a rescue attempt.

The immediate objective of the classic raid in downtown Panama City – codenamed Acid Gambit – was to capture Noriega, if present, and rescue Muse. The capture of La Comandancia and the prison would wait until reinforcements for TF Green arrived from TF Red forces, to be airdropped at H+45 minutes. Then, in order to secure these objectives, special forces would act in co-operation with the mechanized TF Gator, organized around the US 4-6th Infantry (Mechanized) battalion and their M113 APCs.

JSOTF committed a task force to Acid Gambit that included Delta Force elements, specialists in the tactics of hostage rescue. Delta used computerized mission-planning equipment to prepare for the Muse rescue, and blueprints of the prison were used to train the rescue force. A plywood mock-up was built in Florida for full-scale training. US officials were allowed to visit Muse in prison, providing vital eyes-on HUMINT.

TF Geen's Acid Gambit task force would have dedicated SOF air support. The 'Little Birds' would provide mobility and firepower: AH/MH-6 helicopters from the 160th Special Operations Aviation Regiment (SOAR), the

'Night Stalkers'. Built up from TF 160, which had seen action on Grenada, the US Army's SOAR had proven to be highly effective in the Gulf and Central America. AH/MH-6 helicopters from the 160th SOAR would carry Delta Force teams, riding externally. Their ability to manoeuvre between buildings and use accurately the fire power of their 7.62 mm miniguns and 2.75-inch rocket pods would be invaluable. US Air Force AC-130 gunship support would deal with PDF resistance. These gunships – also a SOCOM asset – were flown by highly proficient and professional crews that were familiar with SOF and were willing to take risks to make sure that they had precision fire power to call on. The plan for Acid Gambit was briefed all the way up to the CJCS by the JSOC commander, MG Gary Luck.

Muse was not the only prisoner that had to be rescued at H-Hour. Diego Jiminez of Miami and another American, five anti-Noriega Panamanians and a larger number of common criminals were being held at Renacer Prison on the banks of the Panama Canal, near Gamboa, about midway through the isthmus. The prison itself was surrounded on three sides by water – the Panama Canal and the Chagres River – and on the fourth by a jungle ridge.[12] The prison – a compound made up of two large concrete buildings surrounded by a barbed-wire fence – was inside a larger installation, with more buildings, fences and guard towers. Twenty to twenty-five PDF troopers had reinforced the guards. The actual prison yard was no more than 40 × 70 m. If the mission failed to succeed at H-Hour, the US prisoners were seen as potential hostages. US observation posts and exercises involving US troops provided HUMINT to guide the planning.

These prisoners were to be rescued by C Company of the 3-504th Airborne Infantry in a simultaneous air and amphibious assault supported by attack helicopters. Not a SOCOM asset but part of one of nine 'line' airborne infantry battalions in the 82nd Airborne, the company had been in Panama for scheduled jungle training when the crisis deepened. The 3-504th had received specialized urban combat training in CONUS before deploying. This early deployment provided time for reconnaissance of its intended objectives and mission rehearsal, including marrying up with the UH-1 helicopters and LCM landing craft that would lift them in days before the operation for joint rehearsal. In the event, they were unable to rehearse the amphibious operations or the attack-helicopter support component. The units involved did have an opportunity to inspect and fly over Renacer Prison and even, as part of the Sand Flea exercises, to go through a dry run of bringing the liberation force up to the prison itself (which provoked an immediate PDF response that stopped short of gunfire). 'After these operations and rehearsal we were comfortable with the actual mission,' said CPT Derek Johnson, company commander of C Company of the 3-504th.

The need to prevent a hostage situation involving vulnerable US dependants was the motivation behind Task Force Black Devil (changed from Red Devil at the last minute to avoid confusion with TF Red). Organized around the 1-508th Airborne Infantry (minus its C Company) of the Panama-based 193rd Infantry Brigade (Light), its objective was Fort Amador, where US military and Canal Commission facilities – including dependant housing – were intermixed with Panamanian facilities. The PDF 5th Rifle Company (military police) was in residence at the fort's barracks. It was believed to be a pro-Noriega outfit and had built .50-calibre machine-gun bunkers around its barracks – each camouflaged with a nativity scene!

TF Black Devil would make a two-company air assault on Fort Amador from its garrison at Fort Kobbe, also in the Canal Zone, at H-Hour. Its troopers had trained for weeks on plywood mock-ups and in its own billets. They had rehearsed potential hostage-rescue scenarios and drills for clearing areas full of noncombatants. Before H-Hour, the battalion commander, executive officer and most of the headquarters and headquarters company (HHC) were infiltrated, along with their heavy weapons, into the Fort Amador dependants' housing area. They would provide defence against a PDF attempt to take hostages.

A great deal of emphasis during the planning was placed on how to seize Noriega in the absence of assured intelligence as to his precise location.[13] It was decided that cutting off escape routes would be the first step. The largest SOF operations at H-Hour would be to secure the three main airfields in Panama: Omar Torrijos International Airport and Tocumen Airfield (respectively the civil and military sides of Panama's largest dual-use airport) and Rio Hato Airfield. The objective was to seize these so that the 82nd Airborne Division could jump or fly in for follow-on missions, to prevent PDF resistance and to block Noriega's escape by air or, ideally, capture the man himself. The international airport was a likely place where Noriega supporters could grab US hostages to try to negotiate their way out of Panama.

To carry out this mission, JSOTF organized TF Red around the three battalions of the 75th Ranger Regiment. The plan called for TF Red to perform two simultaneous parachute assaults at H-Hour – one against Torrijos Airport and the adjacent Tocumen Airfield and the other on Rio Hato Airfield.

The Torrijos–Tocumen airdrop by the 1-75th Ranger battalion (reinforced) had to seize the two airports in forty-five minutes to allow for the arrival by parachute of a brigade of the 82nd Airborne for follow-on missions. SOCOM air assets in support included an AC-130H and two AH-6s. The 1-75th's A Company was to jump in to secure the PDF facility and prevent any of the twenty PDF aeroplanes and helicopters from taking off – this was considered a likely starting point for any Noriega escape. C Company and a platoon of B Company were to secure the PDF compound, preventing the PDF's 2nd Company stationed there from interfering. The rest of B Company, reinforced with twelve armed jeeps and ten motorcycles, would clear the runways and establish blocking positions. The 3-75th's C Company would jump in and first surround and then clear the Torrijos International terminal.

TF White, the Naval SOF component of JSOTF, was deployed to Rodman Naval Station on the west side of the Panama Canal. It was under the command of Naval Special Warfare Group 2 (NSWG-2), the Atlantic Fleet Navy SOF headquarters. It was divided into four Task Units (TUs), the bulk of which were tasked to secure perhaps the most important potential 'hostage' in Panama: the canal itself.

TU Papa, the largest, was part of the SOF plan to seize Noriega. It was to use Navy SEALs to make a direct assault on Paitilla Airfield near Panama City where Noriega kept his personal jet and which was considered to be a likely H-Hour location for this prime target. The airport also contained a number of aircraft believed to be owned by drug cartels and thus possibly available for use in an escape by Noriega, who had been a gracious host to these organizations. Originally, the mission had been to put Noriega's personal jet out of action by damaging it with long-range .50-calibre rifle sniper fire if it tried to move. However, this was changed to disabling all these aircraft in their hangars. The SEAL mission was seen as key in closing the net on Noriega.

The planning for the Paitilla mission proved contentious. Options such as sniping any moving aircraft – indicating a possible Noriega escape – or

covert infiltration were rejected in favour of a direct assault. Overland infiltration was proposed but rejected because the number of vehicles required
could compromise the overall operation. Parachute and helicopter insertion
were rejected because of a lack of available SOCOM air assets and airspace
crowding control and fratricide concerns.[14] While there was concern that
the Paitilla mission was not appropriate for SEALs and should more properly
be carried out by an airdropped or heliborne Ranger or Airborne company
or an offshore Marine amphibious assault, these options were rejected due to
concerns that they would compromise operational security or further crowd
Panama's airspace at H-hour and lead to fratricide risks. The SEALs accepted
the mission and planned and rehearsed for it for weeks.[15] The SEALs were
thought more likely to be able to infiltrate the perimeter of Paitilla, while
Rangers or Marines would potentially have to fight their way in; they did not
have the SEALs' training in covert insertion.

Airfield attack has been a core special operations mission since the original
SAS was organized in 1941. The SEALs owed much of their pre-SOCOM
survival to their potential utility in this mission area against threat coastal
airfields. However, once the mission became the surgical disabling of a single
hangared aircraft rather than one involving the destruction of as many
aircraft and as much infrastructure as possible, it was much more consistent
with missions aimed at the liberation or seizure of individuals than with the
classic direct attack.

The difference between the SEALs' small-unit approach and the Army
SOF's large-unit emphasis is seen in the size of the force. Where the Army
had committed Ranger battalions to the three other major airfields in Panama,
the SEAL assault force was sixty-two men. This included forty-eight SEALs
from three sixteen-man platoons of SEAL Team 4, a seven-man SEAL
command and control element, aid men and Air Force combat controllers.
A twenty-six-man support team would deliver the SEALs. The 'rice bowl'
mentality of the high-level planners and the requirement that all services
needed to be represented, combined with the 'can-do' mentality of the operators and the unwillingness to reject difficult taskings, had the potential to
create problems that have yet to be solved by the SOF themselves in action.

Some in the Navy saw confirmed their reasons for their opposition to the
establishment of SOCOM. Not only were 'their' SEALs likely to be taken away
from the fleet-support mission, but as SOCOM's leadership and planners

were largely Army or Air Force, they would be unfamiliar with how the SEALs operated and would plan their operations using inappropriate templates. According to Army SF familiar with Paitilla, the SEALs declined to use the intelligence on the airfield developed by Panama-based forces, insisting instead on developing their own targeting.[16]

Seizing airports was only part of the special operations missions to capture Noriega. TF Black was built around the Panama-based 3-7th Special Forces Group (reinforced by A Company 1-7th SFG from Fort Bragg). TF Black's top mission was tracking down and seizing Noriega, as it was thought likely that he would be moving through their area of operations. To do this, they would keep reconnaissance watches on key routes and choke points where he might travel. To provide accurate IPB for the seizure missions against Noriega, SOUTHCOM intelligence set up a special 'Noriega Watch' cell, which included direct participation by the CIA and NSA (for COMINT). However, 'rice bowl' concerns reportedly prevented the deployment of assets from the Department of Defense Intelligence Support Activity (ISA), a HUMINT-generating organization that had evolved over the course of the 1980s, largely to provide SOF targeting.[17] Reportedly, the cell was intended to provide targeting for a Delta Force squadron that had deployed to Panama and who were on stand-by to provide a quick-reaction seizure mission if Noriega were to slip up. The cell also identified and helped to track 120 key Noriega loyalists. If Noriega was located on the ground, TF Green would have heliborne 'snatch teams', presumably made up of Delta Force specialists, ready to go. If Noriega did make it to an aircraft, terrestrial radar and E-3 AWACS aircraft would be standing by to vector AC-130s or F-16 fighters to intercept it and force it to land or shoot it down. But Noriega was a cunning and wily target. His trail went cold six hours before H-Hour.[18]

With the plans evolving, the special operations forces were able to start rehearsing their missions in installations in the US, Puerto Rico and Panama. As part of the Sand Flea exercises, US forces used their rights of access to installations in the Canal Zone under the Canal Treaty to stage dress rehearsals of the tasks they would have to perform at H-Hour. The Delta Force specialists practised the rescue of Kurt Muse in a mock-up of the Carcel Modelo Prison. The Rangers staged full-scale rehearsals at Fort Benning, Georgia, of the assault on the major airfields, which allowed for improved co-operation between Air Force and Army aviation assets. The last rehearsal of the Rio Hato Airfield assault, on 14 December, worked smoothly. The SEALs carried out a full-scale rehearsal of the Paitilla Airfield seizure at Eglin AFB, Florida, on 14 December. It was also a complete success.

THE TRIGGER

On 15 December, Noriega proclaimed himself – through the Panamanian National Assembly – supreme leader of Panama and announced that a state of war existed with the US. On 16 December, three US officers were shot at a PDF roadblock. One of them, a Marine lieutenant, was killed. A Navy lieutenant and his wife were arrested and assaulted – potentially setting the stage for the broader hostage-taking initiatives outlined in Noriega's Genesis and Exodus plans.

On the morning of 17 December, President Bush, after being informed of these events, reviewed the contingency plans. Bush asked for explicit assurances that past problems would not be repeated: the disaster of the Iran raid, or the inter-service problems of Grenada. He asked why a seizure mission aimed at Noriega – which would have fewer diplomatic and political costs – would not suffice to meet US objectives. It was explained that such an option might potentially increase the opportunity for the taking of US hostages if pro-Noriega military forces were not put out of action. His questions answered, Bush signed the order for military action.[19]

Despite the months of planning, there was now only a short time available for final refinements and troop movements before H-Hour on 20 December, set for 0100. The US preparation and the large-scale airlift into Panama would have telegraphed the coming blow even if Noriega had not run an extensive network of spies and informers. On 19 December, Kurt Muse was told by a guard that he would be executed in the event of a US invasion. In Washington, President Bush gave the order for Operation Just Cause to launch the next day. In Panama, the candidates who had been elected in the May 1989 election but prevented from taking office by Noriega were sworn in by a Panamanian judge on a US base and briefed about the impending operation. This provided, as on Grenada, the assent of the legal government for the US operations. While US SOF had lost the cover of darkness for the opening moves on Grenada, in Operation Just Cause they would make use of the additional night operations capabilities that new equipment and additional training had provided in the early 1980s defence build-up.

With US and Noriega forces starting out intermixed, surprise would be difficult to achieve, thereby greatly complicating the liberation missions. Noriega was able to elude US surveillance. In the final hours before H-Hour, the US heard Noriega's radio stations broadcasting a call for resistance, reporting that the US operations were to start at 0100. H-Hour was advanced to 0045, fearing that the element of surprise might be lost.

OPERATION ACID GAMBIT

The attack on La Comandancia and Carcel Modelo Prison began at H minus 15 minutes, at 0045 on 20 December. Four AC-130s – directed by a forward deployed US Air Force combat controller – and AH-6s opened fire on the Comandancia area. TF Gator's infantry and M113s moved to establish blocking positions to cut off the area from PDF reinforcements and prevent escape until the US could secure the area later that day.[20]

TF Green's Delta Force hostage-rescue team moved in against the prison. Sniper teams, infiltrated into firing range, cut down prison guards. Two heliborne four-man teams were inserted on to the roof of the prison by two MH-6s of the 160th SOAR. Two AH-6 attack helicopters escorted them. The AH-6s engaged and knocked out .50-calibre machine guns mounted of rooftops around the prison.

On the prison rooftop, two Delta Force troopers secured the position. The remaining six dashed to Muse's cell. With power knocked out on schedule by a Panamanian worker acting on US orders, the Delta Force troopers had to move in total darkness, relying on their night-vision goggles. Arriving at Muse's cellblock, they encountered resistance, shooting a guard and grabbing the keys.

Muse took cover in his cell when he saw a trooper in full urban fighting equipment – Kevlar helmet, fully body armour, kneepads and night-vision equipment – appear and blow open the cell lock. He recalled later, 'This apparition comes to my cell door. The guy looks like Darth Vader. He's wearing a funny-looking helmet, funny-looking goggles, funny-looking uniform, and has a funny-looking weapon [an MP5 SMG].' Putting body armour and a helmet on Muse, the trooper hustled him up past the bodies of several PDF defenders (including the one who had threatened him with execution the day before) to the roof where an MH-6 was waiting to lift him to safety. Fewer than six minutes had elapsed since it had first landed.

Capt. Greg McMillan was flying one of the AC-130s overhead. 'We got a call to support the helicopter assault on the roof while they were taking fire and covered their exfiltration. We ended up supporting the helicopter assault on the roof.'[21]

The MH-6 extracting Muse and part of the Delta team was hit by PDF automatic weapons fire from La Comandancia. The helicopter crashed in an alley north of the prison, injuring all aboard except for Muse. Crawling out of the wreckage, Muse (who had been given a 9 mm pistol), the helicopter crew and Delta personnel – one with a serious chest wound – established a defensive position around the helicopter and set out an infra-red strobe beacon to call for assistance. Fortunately, they were spotted by a 160th SOAR MH-6 and were able to contact a nearby TF Gator blocking force. Muse and the Delta team were soon evacuated by an M113 from the 4-6th Infantry. All of the wounded recovered.

PDF fire hit one of the supporting AH-6s while it was making a strafing run against rooftop PDF snipers. The AH-6 made a controlled crash-landing in the Comandancia courtyard. The two-man crew from the 160th extricated themselves from the burning helicopter, emerging in a crossfire between the PDF and the AC-130s. Through a great deal of skill and luck, the crew was able to stay under cover, uninjured, for over two hours before clambering over the back wall of La Comandancia and making their way to TF Gator, along with a captured PDF soldier.

With the Muse rescue accomplished and Noriega prevented from escaping, the next step was to secure La Comandancia. This required a day of hard fighting by TF Gator and Rangers, reinforced by other elements of TF Bayonet. By nightfall, La Comandancia had been taken and its PDF defenders captured. However, looting and fires set by PDF and DigBat fugitives in Panama City, compounded by collateral damage from the fight at La Comandancia – which had required fire support from AC-130s, AH-64s and light tanks – led to extensive damage and civilian loss of life in Panama City.

RENACER PRISON

The helicopters carrying the raiders to Renacer Prison decided against flying over the canal and instead made a more difficult but less vulnerable overland approach. CWO3 Roger Smith was flying the trail UH-1 helicopter. 'Final approach was terrain flight all the way. There were some high-tension wires that go across the bridge, there was a very low ceiling. That night we were on top of the clouds, the clouds then seemed to form on the low ground – or the fog seemed to form with the ceiling up. And Gamboa actually was socked in, for most of the trip, it looked to me like we could not get in there. But the weather did break about a mile east of Gamboa on the Chagres. It broke enough for us to come down from being on top of the clouds to get underneath the clouds. The problem at that point was that now we can't go back up through the clouds and if the clouds are too low at the bridge, we still have wires to get over. And to get over the wires and under the clouds, while flying without any lights under NVGs. That made it a little more difficult.'[22]

At H-Hour, two armed US Army OH-58C observation helicopters engaged the guard towers around the prison with machine-gun fire. A sniper in one of the OH-58Cs engaged PDF guards. They were joined by an AH-1F attack helicopter, using its 20 mm cannon against the guard quarters. Covered by the AH-1F, two UH-1 helicopters from the 1-228th Aviation Battalion landed in the cramped prison yard, each carrying a squad of paratroopers from C Company, 3-504th Airborne Infantry, reinforced with an engineer from the 82nd Airborne's 307th Engineer Battalion with a bag of prepared breaching charges for doors and walls. They were to seize and hold the prison compound until relieved by the rest of their company.

The door gunners and paratroopers opened fire from the right side at the guard positions, drawing a strong response as the helicopters landed. No one fired from the left side of the UH-1s to avoid hitting the prisoners' barracks block. The rotor downdraught scattered the low-velocity 40 mm rounds from the paratroopers' under-barrel M203 grenade launchers, something that had not come up in rehearsal. 'How we never got hit, I don't know. All we saw were tracers in front, on the side and behind us,' said CWO3 Michael Loats, flying the lead Huey. Fortunately, while there were over thirty defenders, the PDF had only a single machine gun. No one on the helicopters was hit.[23]

The US now had two squads of paratroops inside the centre of the prison and a platoon assaulting its way in from outside. They were covered by the door gunner of one of the UH-1s. CWO3 Smith said, 'There was some concern that perhaps the PDF, one or two of them, were instructed or given contingency orders that if they were under attack that they would go in and cause harm to the prisoners. Throw a couple of grenades in there or something. So if anyone ran down the hallway there toward the prisoners, then my left gun could open up, which he did. He did shoot someone there.'[24]

One squad blew open the metal door to the prisoners' barracks while the other dashed inside. The prisoners dropped to the floor and covered themselves with mattresses. Within five minutes of the helicopters landing, the prisoners were secure. Six had been wounded.

A third UH-1 landed another squad from the battalion's scout platoon north of the prison, at the Gamboa Boat Ramp, to act as a blocking force.

More US reinforcements were arriving to bolster those fighting inside the prison. At the same time, landing craft mechanized (LCM) 8508 loomed out of the dark waters of the canal and landed a platoon of paratroopers (reinforced with assault engineers and MPs to take charge of the prisoners) at a pre-surveyed landing site – designated Omaha Beach – to secure the flank and neutralize the outer ring of the prison's defences. The LCM took small arms fire from the prison's defenders during its amphibious assault. It was unable to return fire due to fratricide concerns, but there was no damage or casualties. The amphibious assault – launched two hours before H-Hour from US bases up the canal – was perfectly timed to co-ordinate with the heliborne assault.

Linking up with the platoon running up from the LCM, the paratroopers moved out to search and secure the major buildings of the compound. The paratroopers had to cut open three-metre-high chain-link fences (which somehow had not been noticed during planning), shoot open barred doors and scale the concrete walls of the prison, all under heavy fire, with the support of suppressive fire from the AH-1F and an OH-58C with an on-board sniper team.

In the headquarters building, paratroops from one squad of the heliborne force encountered CS grenades. Retreating outside to don protective masks, they then proceeded to clear the building, killing two PDF soldiers who remained to shoot it out. The other squad cleared the rest of the buildings around the inner courtyard. Thorough training and the use of night-vision goggles enabled them to identify and spare the PDF dependants hiding in the buildings.

Other paratroopers started the slow drill of searching and securing the prison compound. A second LCM arrived, bringing an 81 mm mortar platoon to set up at nearby Sturgis Point, but its illumination rounds were not required. Some guards resisted in their quarters until US AT-4 antitank weapons started blowing holes in the walls. Then they surrendered. By daylight, the prison was secured. All sixty-seven Panamanian prisoners were accounted for. They were evacuated from the area for search and inspection, with the Americans and political prisoners being liberated. C Company of the 3-504th had successfully liberated the prisoners and killed five PDF and captured twenty-two with only four paratroopers injured.

CWO3 Smith recalled, 'We started evacuating the wounded out of the prison compound at daybreak . . . got those folks to Howard [AB in the Canal Zone] and we spent at least until 1:00 or 2:00 the next day continuing to fly medevac with PDF [casualties] . . . I thought the mission probably was one of the most successful that Army Aviation has pulled off.'[25]

DEPENDANTS' HOUSING, FORT AMADOR

Fears of an impending hostage situation at Fort Amador were instrumental in advancing H-Hour. US MPs closed the main gates of the post and detained the PDF guards there at 0030, a few minutes before a PDF bus tried to run the gate and was taken under fire.

With H-Hour advanced by 15 minutes, TF Black Devil needed to open their attack by sealing off Fort Amador. Two of its scout platoons arrived by truck to seize the main gate. Meanwhile, loudspeakers broadcast the word for the Americans in dependant housing to take cover. Fort Amador itself was less than a kilometre away from the Panama City Comandancia, and the operation had to be carried out simultaneously with the TF Green operations there.

At 0100, A and B Companies of TF Black Devil's 1-508th Airborne Infantry – reinforced by two 105 mm howitzers – made a heliborne air assault landing from fourteen UH-60s (including two with female aircrew on their first US Army combat operation) on to the eighth green of the fort's golf course, behind the dependent housing area. With the element of surprise undercut by the early attack on La Comandancia, the UH-60s made their final approach through tracer fire, evading other helicopters and AC-130s involved in that action. Three AH-1F attack helicopters provided escort.

MAJ Robert Pote was executive officer of the 1-508th. 'The American civilian population was a significant problem because we had our command post in the basement of Quarters 20. Well, we had a plan to get everyone out of the quarters that directly faced the PDF barracks but that plan did not work. So the families were still in these buildings. We were damn lucky that we did not get into a massive firefight with the enemy.'[26]

The primary mission for the force – preventing PDF troops from taking hostages – was accomplished as the force moved out of the LZ. The US families were quickly warned to take cover, and some were evacuated to the post's chapel. Some dependants were put at risk by crossfire from the PDF barracks and stray rounds from the nearby fighting at La Comandancia. By 0130, the paratroopers had secured the US housing area and surrounded the PDF barracks. SGT Kent Long was a squad leader in A Company. 'Everything was really professional. They understood we didn't want to just shoot and destroy everything in sight. They just worked hard at doing only what was necessary.'[27]

The two companies linked up, having removed PDF positions threatening American dependants. This required clearing the series of PDF barracks buildings one at a time. Quarters 152 had been set aside for Noriega's personal use. It proved empty except for a voodoo shrine. A group of twelve hardcore PDF shot it out and then surrendered in the shower room of their gymnasium. An accompanying PSYOPS team started to broadcast the demand: disarm or face an assault. Snipers shot individual PDF who opened fire, but most melted away. A further lift by seven UH-60s brought in additional howitzers and vehicles. An OH-58C supporting this mission – sent to check out a ZPU-4 quadruple 14.5 mm HMG that proved to be unmanned – was hit by small arms fire and crashed into the canal.

Training and rehearsal were critical, according to MAJ Pote. 'The terrain was very familiar to us, and to be honest with you, it probably worked better in our favour than we had anticipated. The reason was we felt very confident and at home on a military installation that we had spent much time on. Most of the troops had conducted several exercises there.'

At daylight, the broadcasts were changed. Each was accompanied by an escalating display of US fire power, starting with machine guns and finishing with a 105 mm round into a building. This persuaded most of the remaining PDF garrison to surrender. Only a few snipers held out through the day as TF Black Devil assaulted the barracks and secured the remainder of Fort Amador, without US losses, by 1645 on D-Day.

TORRIJOS INTERNATIONAL AIRPORT AND TOCUMEN AIRFIELD

The Rangers' forcible-entry missions against the key airports in Panama provided the opportunity to demonstrate that everything that had gone wrong on Grenada could be done right. A four-man Air Force combat control team (CCT) went in first, inserted by 160th SOAR MH-6As, positioning navigation beacons at the ends of the runways. The attack opened at H-Hour with an AC-130H and two 160th SOAR AH-6s hitting PDF AAA positions capable of opening fire on the Rangers as they jumped. A ZPU-4 AAA piece took a direct hit from the AC-130H's 105 mm gun.

This time, all the incoming transport aircraft – launched from Hunter Army Air Field in Georgia – were linked by secure communications, including hatch-mounted radio antennae that kept them in touch with both the JSOTF on the ground and the rest of the formation in the air. A modified EC-130E ABCCC provided on-scene command and control.

The airdrop and initial assault went according to plan. At 0103, the 741 men of the 1-75th Rangers (reinforced) and C Company of the 3-75th jumped in one pass – no pathfinders were used – from seven C-141s and four C-130s. As on Grenada, the jump was made from 150 m to reduce vulnerability to ground fire. A Company secured the PDF aircraft and their ground crews. B Company established its blocking positions, a critical part of the mission as the PDF's motorized Battalion 2000 was within striking distance to deliver a counterattack. C Company of the 1-75th took the PDF 2nd Company and its compound, killing the one soldier who refused to surrender. All three companies had met scattered and sporadic resistance. A Ranger medic was killed.

Tocumen Airfield was quickly secured, but at the international terminal of Torrijos Airport, after C Company of the 3-75th Rangers surrounded the terminal complex according to plan, they unexpectedly discovered 376 civilians – many of them Americans. They were passengers from two flights that had unexpectedly arrived just before H-Hour. This limited the Rangers' use of weapons. The armed PDF outside the terminal set up the potential for a hostage situation.

Each Ranger platoon had a well-rehearsed task, entering the terminal area and moving inside the building, with opposition forces positioned outside to watch for any PDF reinforcements or attempted escape. The Rangers had been reinforced with teams from the 96th Civil Affairs Battalion, who

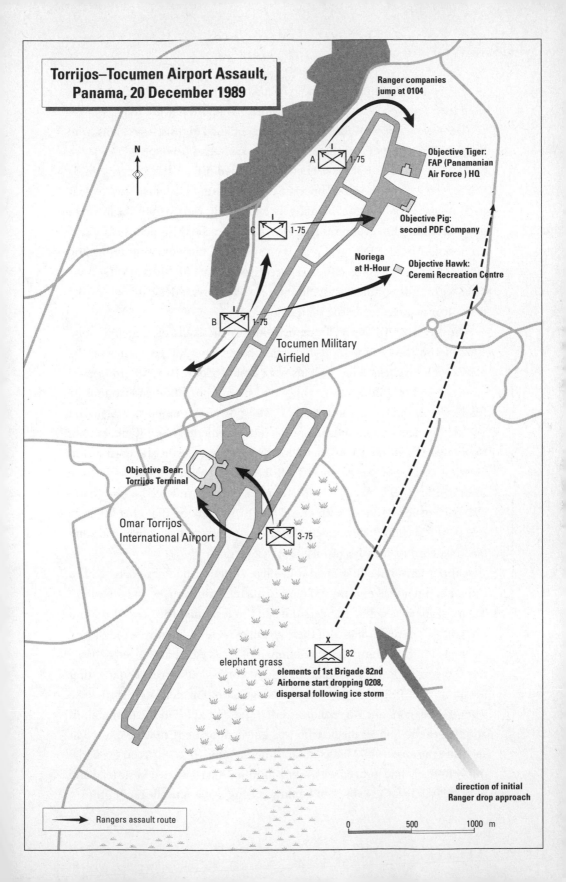

Torrijos–Tocumen Airport Assault, Panama, 20 December 1989

N

Ranger companies jump at 0104

A | 1-75

Objective Tiger:
FAP (Panamanian
Air Force) HQ

C | 1-75

Objective Pig:
second PDF Company

Noriega
at H-Hour

Objective Hawk:
Ceremi Recreation Centre

B | 1-75

Tocumen Military
Airfield

Objective Bear:
Torrijos Terminal

Omar Torrijos
International Airport

C | 3-75

X
1 | 82

elephant grass

elements of 1st Brigade 82nd
Airborne start dropping 0208,
dispersal following ice storm

direction of initial
Ranger drop approach

Rangers assault route

0   500   1000 m

organized the evacuation of the civilians, while attached PSYOPS troops used their loudspeakers, persuading armed Panamanians not to resist.

The few members of the PDF who were inclined to resist – probably from the 2nd PDF Company at the Tocumen *cuartel* – had been forced inside the terminal by the AH-6 attack. They now opened fire on the Rangers inside the terminal. The Rangers, concerned about hitting civilians, had to clear each room of the terminal building by entering it, rather than throwing in grenades. One PDF group resisted for a while on the third floor before surrendering. Another PDF group on the third floor, busy burning smuggling evidence in the customs office, also received a grenade through the door. This set off the sprinkler system and provoked surrender. The rest of the third floor was cleared in the rain, indoors.

On the second floor, PDF fugitives hid in the stalls of a men's room, standing on the commodes to hide their boots. Two Rangers entering the men's room to check it for civilians were ambushed by two PDF troopers at close range. Both Rangers were hit – one saved from fatal head wounds by his Kevlar helmet – but fought their way out of the ambush, staggering out of the men's room and calling for reinforcements. More Rangers then re-entered the men's room after throwing in grenades in standard room-clearing tactics. However, the two PDF soldiers were protected from the blast by the toilet stalls. When the Rangers entered, a fierce hand-to-hand struggle ensued. It ended with one of the PDF dead and the other knocked out of the second-floor window. He fell at the feet of a Ranger blocking position, tried to draw his pistol and was shot down.[28]

On the terminal's first floor, a hostage situation had developed with a Cuban and ten PDF fugitives holding two American females and an infant. Their escape blocked by Rangers outside the terminal, they ended up in a firefight before retreating with their hostages. After a lengthy standoff and attempted negotiations with Panamanian officials who had started to assist the Rangers, a Ranger ultimatum finally compelled surrender later that morning. The PDF's creation of a hostage situation had not delayed the Rangers' mission, and no civilians were injured or killed at the terminal. In addition to the Ranger medic who was killed, a further five were injured in securing the airport and fifteen more suffered jump injuries (as on Grenada, many Rangers had jumped with more ammunition than their basic load and were not ready for the shock of landing during a low-altitude night drop).

The airfields were secured for the 82nd Airborne to jump in as a follow-up echelon. The twenty-aircraft jump, scheduled for 0145 after the 'Rangers led the way', was delayed and spread out over a two-hour period from 0211 to 0430 by an ice storm at Pope AFB in North Carolina, the 82nd's airport of embarkation. The transports were launched one by one as they were made ready. Fortunately, the 82nd's troopers encountered no opposition on landing in Panama and they were soon formed up and dispatched on their missions. The 82nd's paratroops ended up widely spread out over the airport. A few floated down in the middle of C Company of the 3-75th Rangers as they were clearing the terminal and helped to secure the perimeter, then deployed for their D-Day missions. Transports carrying the 7th Infantry Division started to land at 0800.

The Rangers failed to capture their major objective – Noriega himself – when he presented himself in his vehicle to one of B Company's roadblocks. Noriega, knowing Just Cause was imminent, had found time for a final visit to a prostitute in the nearby Ceremi Recreation Centre on the airport grounds before becoming a fugitive. Unrecognized, Noriega was able to turn and flee, receiving only warning shots.

RIO HATO AIRFIELD

Some 100 km west of Panama City, Rio Hato Airfield was the main PDF base and also the site of Noriega's 'beach house' – a major well-fortified command post and a likely location for an alternative command post. Until HUMINT reports the day before D-Day had reported that Noriega was not there, it was to be the target of an H-Hour seizure mission by SEALs. At the last minute, it was demoted to a follow-on objective for the Rangers.

The timing of the assault did not permit the dropping of pathfinders first. The airborne assault force's main attack was to be delivered first by the 2-75th Rangers, hitting the runways and barracks. The 3-75th (minus C Company), jumping further north, guarded the flank and would clear the runway. They would then clear the PDF facilities and the 'beach house'.

Because Rio Hato was remote from population centers, the air preparation could include fighter-bombers. The USAF's F-117 Stealth fighters were to receive their baptism of fire in best 'rice bowl' planning style. JSOTF planners had wanted the two F-117s to hit the PDF barracks before the assault. This was countermanded – with the objective of minimizing PDF casualties. The aim point was changed to a field near the barracks. It was thought that the effect of the silent aircraft dropping large bombs would produce a psychological impact. As it was, the F-117s delivered their bombs on schedule – although one missed its target and impacted harmlessly near the beach.

The serious task of suppressing the Rio Hato air defences was taken over by two AH-64 and four AH-6 helicopters and one AC-130H gunship. In a three-minute air attack starting at 0100, these suppressed many of the PDF air defences. The AC-130H's cannon knocked out two ZPU-4 quadruple 14.5 mm anti-aircraft machine-gun emplacements that could have engaged the incoming Rangers. But other machine guns – fortunately no SAMs – were manned and ready. At 0103, the 2-75th in thirteen C-130s came in over the beach at 150 m into heavy machine-gun fire. Eleven aircraft were hit, with one Ranger wounded while still inside the plane. The AC-130H stayed on-station through the airdrop, firing at PDF machine guns. The suppression of enemy air defences by the helicopters and AC-130H was critical in minimizing casualties. The PDF's 6th and 7th Companies were obviously alerted and willing to resist and move on to the runways.

The Rangers' drop hit the DZ – Rio Hato's runway and taxiway – accurately, then formed up and moved out towards the PDF facilities. While the advance was cautious, there was only sporadic fire and no serious US casualties (but the low jump had injured twenty-six Rangers). SSG Richard J. Hoerner was still in his parachute when a pickup truck charged out of the darkness at him, spraying him with wild fully automatic Kalashnikov fire. Hoerner rolled out of the way at the last minute, but his parachute wrapped around the truck's drive shaft and he was dragged for 30 m before he could release the parachute, mere moments before a LAW round ended the truck's escape.[29]

The 3-75th dropped seconds after the 2-75th. Its A Company's immediate objective was the base's main gate, at the point where the Pan-American Highway entered the airfield. A heavy machine gun was knocked out in an immediate assault led by 1LT Loren Ramos, the company executive officer, while it was still firing at Rangers in their parachutes. Blocking positions were soon established on the Pan-American Highway to prevent fugitives from escaping or the arrival of PDF reinforcements. A Company ran into other PDF soldiers who gave the Rangers 'a good run for their money for

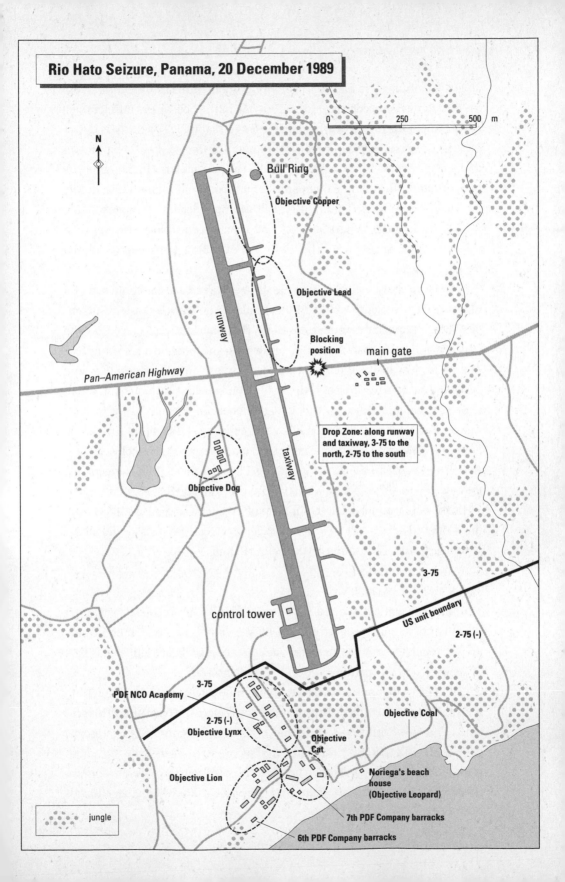

Rio Hato Seizure, Panama, 20 December 1989

N

Bull Ring

Objective Copper

Objective Lead

Blocking position

main gate

Pan–American Highway

runway

taxiway

Drop Zone: along runway and taxiway, 3-75 to the north, 2-75 to the south

Objective Dog

3-75

control tower

US unit boundary

2-75 (-)

PDF NCO Academy

3-75

2-75 (-)
Objective Lynx

Objective Cat

Objective Coal

Objective Lion

Noriega's beach house (Objective Leopard)

7th PDF Company barracks

6th PDF Company barracks

0   250   500   m

jungle

about 30 minutes', in the words of LTC Joseph Hunt, commander of the 3-75th. Rangers called in two AH-6s but one of the helicopters misidentified advancing Rangers in a nearby tree line for retreating PDF – the helicopters had not been notified that there were Rangers in the tree line – resulting in a friendly fire incident. B Company cleared the barracks and buildings of the PDF 6th and 7th Infantry Companies and secured an ammunition dump. This led to close-range fighting that left a Ranger dead. C Company of the 2-75th secured the airport facilities and then was held in reserve against counterattacks before moving out, with the AC-130H overhead, to seize the 'beach house'.

The Rangers were able, despite the stiff resistance and the confusion of a night assault, to secure some 167 PDF cadets who were looking to surrender. Rangers quickly removed obstacles that the PDF had placed on the runway and taxiways – vehicles, oil drums and other debris – and the hundreds of abandoned parachutes. Clearing the airfield of obstacles and prisoners delayed the arrival of the follow-on echelon. An hour and a half after H-Hour, Rio Hato Airfield was reopened for C-130s to fly in first, Ranger gun jeeps next and then follow-on echelons. In daylight, the airfield buildings designated objectives Lead and Copper were systematically cleaned. AH-6s were called in against remaining PDF resistance. The Rangers lost four dead – one jump casualty, two in the friendly fire incident – and eighteen were wounded. Large numbers of prisoners were taken. The beach house proved to be a 'dry hole' for all except souvenir hunters, as did all the other likely Noriega locations attacked at H-Hour.

THE SEALS AT PAITILLA

The SEALs would carry out a wide range of missions on D-Day, swimmer assaults on shipping and protection of the canal and commercial traffic among them. One of these missions, against the airfield at Paitilla, was part of the joint special operations effort to seize Noriega.

The SEALs had put a covert observation post (OP) into a house with a line of sight to the Paitilla runway in the days before the operation. This was able to provide eyes-on targeting and report any potential Noriega escape efforts. The PDF garrison was estimated at twenty to forty men, although the operation had been planned on the basis of there being only a few un-trained guards present. But more restrictive RoE than at the other airfields

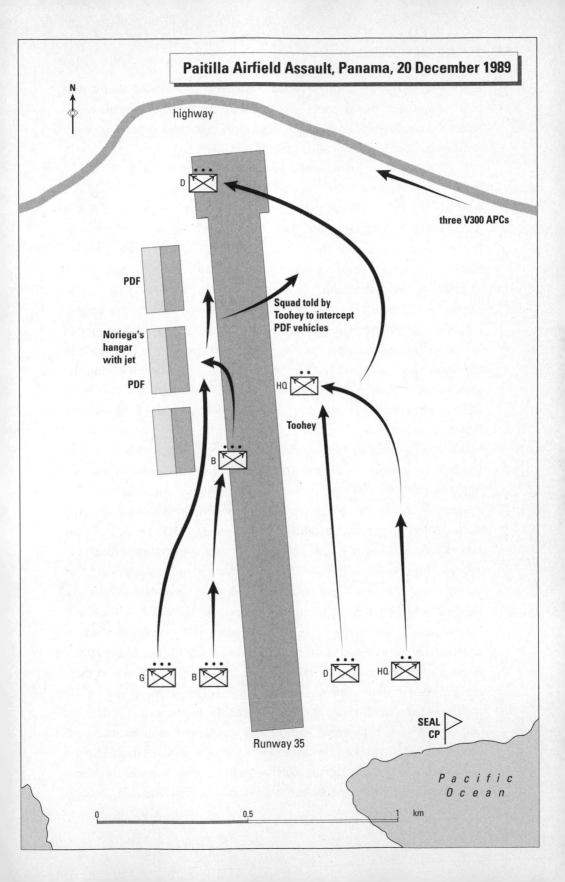

Paitilla Airfield Assault, Panama, 20 December 1989

N

highway

D

three V300 APCs

PDF

Noriega's
hangar
with jet

PDF

Squad told by
Toohey to intercept
PDF vehicles

HQ

B

Toohey

G   B   D   HQ

SEAL
CP

Runway 35

Pacific
Ocean

0   0.5   1   km

(due to its proximity to the crowded airspace over Panama) meant that SOCOM air assets would not be available to try to pre-empt possible resistance; nor could the SEALs use their standard anti-*matériel* tactic of long-range sniper fire from .50-calibre rifles.[30]

TU Papa moved out from the beach at Howard AB at 1930 on 19 December, five and a half hours before H-hour. It was carried in fifteen combat rubber raiding craft (CRRCs), led by two patrol boats, which moved across the Gulf of Panama under the cover of darkness. By 2330, the lead boats were in position off the airfield. Two SEALs swam ashore to reconnoitre the landing site and mark it with an infra-red strobe light visible through night-vision goggles.

The SEAL assault was set for the original H-Hour, 0100. The assault force was just quietly coming ashore at 0045 when they heard the sound of the attack on La Comandancia. This meant that the plan to infiltrate into concealed platoon assembly areas inside the perimeter before hitting the objective at H-Hour was not going to work. In addition, Paitilla Airfield remained brightly lit. The element of surprise was not going to be with the SEALs at Paitilla.

TU Papa formed up into its three component platoons, advancing towards the runway. One change that had been insisted on after the last rehearsal was that TU Papa's leader, CDR Thomas McGrath, and his command element should remain at the beach in radio contact with the platoons and supporting aircraft. The assault itself would be led by LCDR Patrick Toohey. These platoons were task-organized (and rehearsed) specifically for this operation. The SEALs normally worked in smaller teams, and on this occasion speed had to replace stealth in execution. The three platoons moved out towards the airfield, running up the trail from the beach and through a hole in the airfield security fence. Golf and Bravo platoons advanced up the west side of the runway, using bounding overwatch tactics to cover each rush forward. Delta platoon and the command and control element advanced the same way up the east side of the runway.

To block aircraft from landing or taking off, Delta platoon set up a hasty ambush position halfway up the runway for several minutes and then moved out to seize the control tower. Golf and Bravo platoons moved up the grass apron to the west of the north–south runway. Bravo encountered several sentries, who they disarmed, and started to drag light aircraft on to the runway. Fleeing airport employees were also encountered, and they had to be subdued and restrained. Some, apparently drug cartel security personnel, were heavily armed.

The tactical radio net provided reports of PDF vehicle and helicopter movements towards Paitilla that could have been an attempted escape. A three-APC convoy – US-made V-300 Commandos – was moving in the direction of Paitilla and a helicopter had just taken off from Colon. Both were thought consistent with a potential Noriega attempt to flee Panama. This increased the need for timely action by the SEALs. The command and control element received orders from the JTF HQ to take up ambush positions against the two potential threats. Toohey sent a team from Golf platoon towards the perimeter road, where the APCs could be ambushed if they headed towards the airfield. Moving out, they were vulnerable to PDF fire. Another team was positioned to engage an arriving helicopter.

At 0105, Golf platoon, in the lead, had advanced to the three northernmost hangars. The middle one, the PDF hangar, contained Noriega's personal jet. All three hangars were surrounded by armed PDF, alerted and well armed. The northernmost hangar had a machine gun set up in its entrance. The bright lighting put the advancing SEALs from Golf platoon at a disadvantage. The SEALs had hoped that the defenders of the hangars would surrender. The need to set up ambush positions on the road, approach the hangars, demand surrender and overawe the PDF defenders put the SEALs in a vulnerable tactical position when a vicious short-range firefight erupted.

The Golf platoon SEALs were caught in crossfire from two of the three hangars. Eight SEALs went down, five seriously wounded. Golf platoon took cover and fought on, calling for reinforcements. The lead SEAL M60 gunner in Golf platoon riddled Noriega's plane in the PDF hangar and then engaged the PDF firing from the nearby Aero Perla hangar. Bravo and Delta platoons were immediately ordered to reinforce, in effect carrying out a double envelopment of the PDF positions, led by Toohey, who had come forward accompanied by two aid men and the security element.

The firefight continued as the PDF held their ground. Bravo and Delta platoons concentrated fire on the PDF. Two more SEALs from those platoons fell.

While other SOF had benefited from AC-130H support, the SEALs were unable to make contact with the one that was in direct support of them. The gunship orbited above the airfield but – with PDF and SEALs at close range – had to hold fire.

The SEALs' own fire power prevailed against the PDF. Finally, the PDF withdrew into the darkness at about 0117. The hangars and their aircraft – including Noriega's personal jet – were damaged. Already disabled by gunfire, the jet was now hit with an AT-4 antitank rocket.

Following the firefight, the immediate priority was to secure the airfield – a task accomplished by 0145. A medevac was called in for the SEALs' wounded at 0205 – a delay caused by communications failure led to the death of at least one wounded SEAL. The SEALs now held a perimeter on the southeast side of the runway. SEAL reinforcements – a platoon that had been held in reserve at Howard AB – arrived by helicopter at around 0320. The PDF convoy and helicopter never went near Paitilla.

The AC-130H on-station over the airfield was replaced by a Georgia Air National AC-130A, which made radio contact with the SEALs. With the new gunship in support, the SEALs moved out again at dawn, conducting a reconnaissance of the hangars and dragging aeroplanes out to block the runway against any unauthorized use. The SEALs held the airfield until a Ranger company arrived by helicopter at 1400 on 21 December. SEAL casualties were four killed and eight wounded, the highest losses they had ever experienced on a mission.

CLOSING OFF ESCAPE – TU WHISKEY

With the airports targeted as primary US SOF objectives and with the AWACS ready to detect any attempt at escape by air, it appeared that the only possible escape route available to Noriega would be by sea. This led to the SEALs of TU Whiskey bring tasked with an H-Hour direct-attack mission against the 20 m armed PDF patrol boat *Presidente Porras*.[31]

The attack jumped off from Rodman Naval Station at 1900 on 19 December, with SEALs in two CRRCs from Special Boat Unit 26 cutting across the canal and hiding in a mangrove swamp near the target's anchorage at Pier 18 in Balboa harbour. Two heavily armed PBR patrol boats carrying more SEALs provided an escort and a reserve in case it became necessary for the raiders to fight their way out.

One of the CRRCs broke down, delaying the jump-off. Both swim teams had to use a single CRRC, which tried to make up for lost time by taking the SEALs closer to their target. This was difficult as Balboa harbour was brightly lit, and Panamanian harbour craft of uncertain allegiance were moving through the area. At 2330, two two-man SEAL Team 2 'swim teams' entered the water – LT Edward Coughlin and EN3 Tim Epply, ET1 Randy Beausoleil and PH2 Chris Dye – using the light-weight chest-mounted Drager pure oxygen underwater breathing apparatus that leaves no bubble trail. The CRRCs retreated back to Rodman Naval Station preparatory to picking up the exfiltrating swim teams.

Swimming 6 m under the surface, the two swim teams took half an hour, navigating by compass, to approach the patrol boat. Surfacing under Pier 18, Beausoleil and Dye found themselves in the midst of heavy fire from the shore. The PDF, alerted by the advanced H-Hour, had apparently started panic-firing wildly, including dropping grenades into the harbour. Working their way under the *Presidente Porras*, Beausoleil and Dye heard the engines start up preparatory to getting under way and attached their demolition charges to the port propeller shaft. The location had been chosen to immobilize the target while reducing the chance for casualties. Two minutes later – proceeding independently – Coughlin and Epply arrived at the target and set their demolition charges on the starboard propeller shaft. All were set to detonate at the original H-Hour of 0100.

The two swim teams withdrew to the cover of another pier. They sheltered behind the pilings against the shock of the explosions before starting the long swim back to the RV with the CRRCs on the other side of the harbour. The SEALs were supposed to have been aboard the CRRCs when the charges detonated at 0100, taking the *Presidente Porras* out of action by sending its propellers flying out of the water. This led to an increased fire power display by the alarmed PDF.

As they swam, SEAL PH2 Chris Dye later recounted: 'A freighter, making its way up the canal, forced us to dive to almost 50 feet [15 m] to avoid the suction from the propellers; that exposed us to a different kind of threat since pure oxygen can be toxic below a depth of 20 feet [6 m]. It became instantly apparent that our emphasis on the highest possible physical fitness standards was about to pay off.'[32]

The SEALs swam on to the RV accompanied by the sound of grenades detonating underwater. The CRRCs had been searching for the swim teams, now an hour overdue – their radios had malfunctioned – when they arrived. Hauling the swimmers aboard, the CRRCs retreated to join the PBRs. There was no pursuit.

TF BLACK

TF Black – charged with the mission of seizing Noriega in the Just Cause operation order (OPORD) – was heavily engaged on D-Day.[33] In addition to its reconnaissance and surveillance missions, it carried out one original direct attack mission at H-Hour to seize the Panamanian TV station. This mission was carried out at 0050 on 20 December, when a twelve-man Special Forces A Team under the command of CPT John M. Custer (reinforced with six technical experts) seized the Panamanian TV station at the broadcasting complex in the mountains northeast of Panama City. Another TF Black force then seized Radio Nacional's AM and FM stations, which had started playing a pre-recorded Noriega broadcast exhorting his followers to resist the Americans to the death (while he hid). However, a search of the target building did not turn up the FM transmitters – an intelligence lapse. The FM radio station was located later on D-Day and an SOF team was able to locate and destroy the FM antenna in the dark, silencing Noriega's radio outlets. A low-power pro-Noriega 'pirate radio' station was finally hunted down and destroyed by troops from B Company, 3-7th SFG, on 29 December.

One of TF Black's covert reconnaissance and surveillance teams spotted not Noriega, but elements of the PDF's best-armed unit, Battalion 2000, moving out from Fort Cimarron to Panama City. A heliborne quick-reaction force was ordered to block and destroy the PDF column at the Pacora River Bridge. A force of twenty-four men from A Company, 3-7th SFG, set off on the mission in three helicopters. Scheduled to take off at 1210 from Albrook AB in the Canal Zone, small arms fire erupted while the force was being loaded on the apron, forcing a hasty departure – fortunately without casualties.

At 1245 (the new H-Hour), as the helicopters approached the bridge, the crews could see six PDF vehicles approaching it. The helicopters made it to the bridge first, landing in the river valley nearby. While the PDF column was on the bridge, driving with white peacetime headlights, the SF troopers went into action, hastily moving out from the LZ. 66 mm LAWs hit the lead truck. Other troopers opened fire with M249 SAWs and M203 grenade launchers, halting the advance of the column. An Air Force combat controller with the Green Berets directed the fire of an orbiting AC-130 on to the stalled enemy column. The PDF advance on Panama City got no further. At daybreak, Special Forces reinforcements arrived to sweep the PDF's side of the river bank. Most had fled, but seventeen remained to be taken prisoner and returned to Albrook by helicopter.

TU CHARLIE AND THE ASIAN SENATOR

TU Charlie, the smallest SEAL task unit, worked closely with the larger ground forces and offshore US warships. In position at H-Hour, TU Charlie went into action with two US Navy PBR riverine boats and two Army LCMs carrying boarding parties of SEALs and soldiers, blocking all ships from entering the canal, patrolling the shipping channel near Colon and preventing the PDF from either commandeering boats to flee or trying to block the canal.

Its mission went quietly through the night. At 0930, TU Charlie received a report that a German merchant ship, the *Asian Senator*, alongside a pier in Port Colon on the Caribbean side of the canal, had been seized by some thirty PDF troops in civilian clothes. Two US Navy riverine boats and an Army LCM approached the ship. Concerned that this might be an escape attempt by Noriega or that the ship might be sunk in the channel with the intention of blocking it, their first move was to prevent the ship from putting to sea. After being fired upon, they returned fire with .50-calibre machine guns and small arms until the PDF on board fled to the pier. The SEALs, operating from CRRCs, boarded the freighter under fire from PDF on shore. They secured fourteen PDF prisoners on board and on the dock.

TU Whiskey also helped to defend the merchant ship *Emanuel B* in the canal from PDF fugitives who tried to board it on 23 December.

PARATROOPERS AT THE MARRIOTT

Heliborne US forces were able to rescue most US citizens in the few instances where Noriega forces were able to take them hostage (one US citizen had been abducted and murdered by Noriega forces, another killed at a checkpoint). The most significant of these rescue missions was a group reported to be comprised of nineteen American and 139 foreign hostages being held on the top floor of the Caesar Park Marriott Hotel in downtown Panama City.

Other guests and employees hid throughout the hotel. Armed men in civilian clothes had seized the hotel shortly after H-Hour. Some Americans were removed from the hotel and taken to unknown locations. This situation had not been foreseen. The US had also not foreseen the need to fight fires, suppress looters and restore law and order in Panama City. CJCS GEN Colin Powell told Thurman to make a liberation mission to the Marriott a priority. Powell, in turn, was responding to President Bush's concerns about a potential hostage situation. The political cost of a potential hostage incident led to high-level direction being given to the headquarters in Panama.[34]

Thurman told Powell at 1620 that Stiner would need four hours to prepare for a liberation operation. This was not satisfactory to Powell, who insisted that the hostages be freed before the end of D-Day. After quick planning at Joint Task Force headquarters, the order was received at about 1800 on the evening of D-Day by the paratroopers of the 82nd Airborne's 2-504th Parachute Infantry, whose H-Hour mission had been to air assault and neutralize the PDF and UESAT forces in and around Panama Viejo. They were informed that Delta Force and SEAL hostage-rescue specialists – indeed, all special forces – were unavailable, either committed to hunting Noriega, staging multiple quick-reaction strikes on possible locations or regrouping from H-Hour missions.

The planning for the liberation mission fell to the 2-504th's commanding officer, LTC Harry Axson, and his staff, who received a fragmentary order at 2000. They relied on reports passed over the voice radio from higher headquarters on the situation at the hotel. This was followed by in-person co-ordination with the brigade commander and staff. CPT Steve Phelps's B Company received the liberation mission from battalion at 2100. There was no formal operations order, just a verbal warning order. The company commander briefed the concept of operations at 2130. B Company and battalion headquarters were reinforced with engineers and medical assets and provided with an AC-130 overhead – with good radio links to B Company — before moving the 4 km to the hotel at 2215.

B Company encountered actual and suspected PDF ambushes and sniper fire *en route*. The AC-130 spotted a PDF ambush around a bridge on the route of advance. B Company received sniper fire, but pushed through the ambush site. The PDF had fled. Further along the route, B Company drew more sniper fire. Two paratroopers were injured and had to be evacuated in a civilian truck, which also had to fight its way through the ambush. With the aid of the AC-130, providing suppressive fire and direction from its sensors, the paratroopers advanced to the hotel. An armed truck attempted a drive-by shooting against the advancing paratroops, wounding two before being ripped apart by return fire.

SSG John Negre, a mortar section leader in B Company, was impressed by the way his unit handled the ambush – 'Good reaction . . . Awesome movement! Violence of action, speedy and casualties were taken care of' – all the while staying out of the AC-130's fire power.[35]

The AC-130 that had surprised Negre's men by opening fire unannounced had located four PDF snipers on top of a high-rise building, ready to engage the advancing paratroopers. The AC-130, after getting permission to open fire, took them out with three rounds from its 40 mm cannon.

The hostages were liberated following a firefight with the PDF outside the hotel. B Company now had to secure the hotel and the adjacent convention center. CPT Phelps wrote, 'At the Marriott, each platoon took up its assigned position and the assault began at 2240, 35 minutes after crossing the LD (local time). The front double doors were the breach point. The assault platoon, along with its first sergeant, shot open the doors and charged inside. The support platoon covered enemy avenues of approach and the building itself while the last platoon followed the first one into the buildings.' A guide from brigade headquarters used a house phone to call each room, as many hotel guests were in hiding. B Company found the hostages – twenty-nine Americans, thirty-nine from other NATO countries and fifty-five friendly Panamanians – panicked and confused and unaware they were being liberated. They were led downstairs into a secure room while the paratroopers secured the first three floors. Others came out of hiding. The paratroopers circulated a sign-in sheet and tried to ensure that none were plainclothes PDF.

CPT Phelps wrote, 'Inside the hotel, the platoons executed a standard building clearing drill. Each platoon cleared one floor at a time, with a platoon always securing the outside.' Defending the Marriott, B Company was subject to sniper fire and drive-by attacks from PDF gunmen in civilian vehicles. They were expecting to be relieved by D Company of their battalion, supported by M551 Sheridan armoured vehicles. When D Company arrived at the hotel, they were unaware that it was in US hands. A blue-on-blue firefight ensued, with B Company suffering a casualty from .50-calibre fire from the M551s before the situation could be deconflicted. Three reporters were injured and one later died.

D Company covered the evacuation of the former hostages at 1000 the following morning, although one, a Panamanian, was hit by sniper fire while leaving the Marriott. Evacuation of the hostages was delayed by many trying to take baggage with them. A UH-60 from the 1-228th Aviation Battalion landed on the roof to take off hotel guests who had fled there to escape the PDF. No hostages were harmed. Those who had been removed from the hotel were released three days later.

FOLLOW-ON OPERATIONS

The rest of Operation Just Cause proceeded largely according to plan. The H-Hour operations pre-empted resistance. Most PDF and DigBats melted away. The rapid defeat of PDF and DigBat forces engaged at H-Hour prevented any possibility of the implementation of the Genesis and Exodus plans for hostage-taking. There were also few leaders in either force who had the political will to implement such plans, knowing that this would bring a massive US response. The legitimate Panamanian government that had been elected in the 1989 elections and subsequently overruled by Noriega was put into office. The bulk of the population was opposed to Noriega. However, the DigBats and other pro-Noriega forces took the opportunity to burn and loot in downtown Panama City, Colon and other areas for several days before order could be restored (and blamed US collateral damage for the destruction and loss of life). The US plan had not included the need to quickly re-establish law and order. Most of Panama, however, remained peaceful and simply liberated itself.

This self-liberation process forced pro-Noriega officials and militiamen to flee. Most of the PDF agreed to stack their arms and turn them over to heliborne US forces after telephone negotiations (which became known as 'Ma Bell' operations). SOF were also instrumental in the follow-ups to these surrenders, working with the local population and friendly PDF members to identify Noriega weapons caches and wanted criminals who had gone into hiding. The 'Ma Bell' operations also led to the arrest of many of Noriega's lieutenants and henchmen.

An eleven-person scientific expedition team on an island off the north coast that had been seized and then abandoned by the PDF was rescued by

US Army heliborne forces on 22 December. Other reports of American hostages led to further special operations responses. SEALs assaulted the Hotel
Washington in Colon City at 0200 on 21 December in response to reports
that the PDF were holding Americans there, but this proved to be untrue.

THE GREAT NOREIGA HUNT

After D-Day, although there was no serious resistance, the mission of capturing Noriega still remained. JSOTF immediately started planning and co-
ordinating smaller raids, striking throughout Panama in search of arms
caches and Noriega lieutenants – the 120 most significant loyalists were on
a list to be picked up – throughout the rest of December. JSOTF staged over
forty operations targeted at seizing Noriega on 20–24 December.[36] SIGINT
was critical for targeting.[37] Many of the raids used fresh HUMINT developed
from anti-Noriega Panamanians. In addition, much HUMINT was developed
from the systematic debriefing of captured PDF and pro-Noriega forces by
the US military and Panamanian government; a Joint Debriefing Centre
(JDC) was established.[38] The documents captured were so extensive that it
would take years to follow the 'paper trail' to Noriega. Many of those on the
wanted list were quickly captured, but there was still no Noriega.

After the near-capture of Noriega by Rangers on D-Day, the US narrowly
missed apprehending him on several more occasions. The raids – many by
the 3-7th SFG of TF Black – were targeted on Noriega's many residences and
locations, which SOUTHCOM G-2 had identified as likely hiding places. They
found Noriega's Swiss and Grand Cayman bank account passbooks, his
Hitler memorabilia and pornography collections and evidence of his occult
practices. Multiple raids carried out over a compressed timeframe kept the
pressure on Noriega and helped to deny him hiding places. While supported
by Delta and SEAL seizure specialists, the 3-7th was selected for the main
hunt because the unit was permanently stationed in Panama. Its Green
Berets deployed to Panama on multi-year accompanied tours and knew the
country and the people. The 3-7th SFG personnel were Spanish-speaking
and could make use of intelligence gathered on-scene or brought to them by
informers.

Noriega did not seriously consider leading guerrilla resistance, even when
supporters asked him to. He ended up jettisoning all of his followers except
his bodyguard and secretary and executing a well-thought-out escape and

evasion (E&E) plan. In addition to his native cunning and a small but devoted network of followers, he had many years' experience of working with US military and intelligence. He knew how they would operate and what intelligence they would likely be receiving. He made arrangements for the transmission of misleading communications that he knew would be intercepted and decrypted and for dummy convoys to act as decoys. This allowed him to stay ahead of the hunt for four days. But because the US had closed down all means of escape – airports and ships – at H-Hour, there was no way that he could win the game by making his way to a foreign sanctuary such as Cuba.

Most of the available JSOTF assets, reinforced by Army and Marine units, were committed to the Noriega Hunt. With the airfields in US hands, the main concern was that Noriega would leave the country by sea. This put the emphasis on SEAL operations to find Noriega. SEAL TU Whiskey was used to seize and search objectives associated with Noriega: a yacht on 20 December, his yacht club at Balboa on 21 December and his island house on Culebra Island on 25 December. TU Foxtrot, on the Pacific Coast, spent 20 December on defensive missions. On 21 December, as part of the continuing hunt for Noriega, Foxtrot located and searched two of Noriega's personal yachts, the *Macho de Monde* and the *Passeportout*, capturing eighteen personnel and large quantities of arms and ammunition. TU Foxtrot searched numerous Panamanian watercraft as part of the hunt for Noriega. It had been thought that Noriega might run for a friendly embassy, and consequently the US had put cordons around those of Cuba, Nicaragua and Libya. The dragnet ended up creating diplomatic incidents, inadvertently violating foreign embassy buildings, and Washington became increasingly involved in the operations. They also wanted Noriega in hand so that they could declare victory and start the rebuilding of Panama without the fear of his return.

These raids showed how difficult it was to target Noriega, even in a situation where there was good intelligence available, for friendly Panamanians were now providing information of every possible real and imagined Noriega sighting to US forces. However, keeping him on the run prevented him from rallying resistance or ordering the taking of hostages.

At 1330 on 24 December, a Delta Force operative sought help from B Company of the 2-504th. The company was still in position near the Marriott. He said that Noriega had been seen nearby thirty minutes earlier. The Delta trooper was accompanied by an individual identified as a Noreiga bodyguard. He had deserted a few hours before, after Noriega had spent the night at a house near the Marriott.

A platoon-sized force was requested to isolate the house and, if need be, execute a forced entry. The first step was for a B Company patrol to be dispatched to the house for reconnaissance, dressed in civilian clothes left behind at the hotel by the departing hostages.

But after the patrol returned and the raid was planned, it was 1500 by the time 3 Platoon of B Company and the battalion command group was able to move out. They were accompanied by the HUMINT source. To prevent fratricide he was dressed in a US uniform – obtained by ordering one of the paratroopers remaining at the Marriott to undress. Overwatch was provided by the 2-504th's snipers on the fifteenth floor of the Marriott.

The raiders returned to the Marriott at 1630 empty-handed. The house proved to be another dry hole. Noriega had run into the nunciature half an hour before. The raid had failed because of what in retrospect turned out to be excessive time-consuming planning that precluded fast action when time was of the essence.[39]

SOF were part of the blocking for, and SEALS ended up guarding the waters around, the papal nunciature where Noriega was finally brought to bay at 1600 on 24 December. He had sought asylum there with US SOF on his trail about one hour behind him.[40]

Once Noriega was located, a large number of US forces then surrounded the nunciature, including, famously, PSYOPS loudspeakers broadcasting obnoxious loud heavy metal rock and roll music in the hope of provoking his surrender in order to achieve peace and quiet. After a ten-day stand-off, Noriega surrendered to US forces and was brought to Miami for arraignment and trial.

THE PANAMA MODEL

Panama was a demonstration of the improved capability of US joint operations and SOF forces made possible by the US defence build-up of the 1980s and the Goldwater–Nichols Act and the Cohen–Nunn Amendment. Unlike in the *Mayaguez* incident, the President could now go directly to the CJCS, rather than relying on the deliberations of the entire JCS, for military advice and action. The authority granted to the CINCs allowed GEN Thurman to prepare and run the operations while minimizing interference from others.

This included bringing in LTG Stiner and his headquarters and the JSOTF. Where there was high-level intervention – on the situation at the Marriott Hotel and during the hunt for Noriega – it was regarding liberation or seizure missions, reflecting how politically charged these missions inevitably are.

The difference between using well-established headquarters – SOCOM, the JTF based on XVIII Airborne Corps, the special forces HQ under MG Downing – and the improvised command structures that had been seen in previous raids was readily apparent. The thorough IPB and rehearsal were made possible by the lengthy crisis leading up to the decision to use military force.

The JSOTF was not able to break the services' 'rice bowls'. It did not have to. There was enough force available, and fortunately the opposition was weak enough, that the planners could allow the different SOCOM elements to carry out their 'bureaucratic preferred repertoire' effectively integrated into the larger plan. Delta Force trains to liberate hostages from buildings – that training ended up saving Kurt Muse. Rangers train to secure airfields in forced-entry missions – blocking Noriega's escape and enabling the fly-in of follow-on US forces required that the use of that skill. The SEALs train to covertly attack warships – blocking a Noriega escape by sea called on that capability.

Even at Paitilla Airfield the forces and mission were not necessarily mis-matched. Rather, Paitilla demonstrated the vulnerabilities of a force with the preferred operational approach of relying on stealth and surprise. Problems occur when these are stripped away, in this case as a result of the advance of H-Hour and prior warning being received by the enemy. This was the only example of SOF suffering from poor integration with the overall plan (whereas in Grenada only those SOF that were part of the MAU had avoided this). With airspace control and fratricide concerns ruling out an airborne or heliborne assault, the SEALs provided a viable option. That Paitilla 'wasn't a SEAL mission' has entered into accepted wisdom without necessarily being true.

While the element of surprise was not absolute due to the 'standing start' scenario and the presence of Noriega informers, the speed, shock and overwhelming force of the US attack pre-empted most resistance. The entire operation represented what the US military terms a 'dominating manoeu-vre', which more than compensated for the limited achievement of surprise. Most of the fighting was over on D-Day.

The Just Cause plan successfully targeted and defeated the enemy's limited centre of gravity. GEN Thurman identified Noriega himself as the strategic centre of gravity.[41] Getting Noriega was the focus of the operation. The US was not attacking Panama and its people or even a governmental or political movement, but rather one individual and his personal supporters. Narco-kleptocracy does not yield broad-based support, even though it is easy to rally Latin American nationalism and easier still to demonize the United States. The weakness and limited legitimacy of the Noriega regime was demonstrated by the US ability to switch to stability operations – including the Great Noriega Hunt – after the initial attack. No one was going to take to the hills for guerrilla warfare on behalf of 'pineapple face'.

The SOF direct actions in Operation Just Cause were able to accomplish their overall mission and provided a much needed element of the overall US plan. While Just Cause itself looked to many like the old days of US big-stick intervention in Latin America at a time when, in the wake of the Falklands War, democracies, however shaky, were rising in the region and *caudillos* were being discredited, it was distinguished by the use of operations to prevent hostages being taken or harmed, pre-empting resistance and – the one area where they were not an immediate success – in getting Noriega, the cause of the operation.

Operation Just Cause was, in effect, an alternative model of future war. It was, essentially, the precise planning of a special operations raid applied to an entire country. Operation Just Cause was, in effect, one large raid. The US was not looking to seize and hold Panama, but to remove a threat and then withdraw its forces. The SOF missions themselves were able to prevent hostage situations from developing – even in the middle of the fighting at the airport – that could have complicated US planning. Special operations also saved Kurt Muse and the detainees at Renacer Prison from threatened execution. They proved less successful in capturing Noriega.

The collateral damage and casualties among a friendly population, though less than critics alleged, was still painfully high. It would have been worse had the SOF not been available to deal pre-emptively with much of the potential PDF resistance, as well as preventing potential hostage situations. The JTF developed and executed a plan that successfully struck twenty-three of twenty-seven critical targets. The concern over minimizing casualties – a vital part of an operation in friendly Panama – made less sense when applied the following year to a retreating Iraqi army.

Panama was another example of the importance of intelligence to successful liberation or seizure missions. The long-standing US presence in Panama and the widespread Panamanian opposition to the Noriega regime made effective HUMINT (fused with COMINT) widely available. In many key cases – such as La Comandancia and Fort Amador – covert observation posts were able to provide 'eyes-on' intelligence right up to H-Hour. The full capabilities of US intelligence collection had been used to inform the liberation and seizure missions.

Making a broad range of intelligence sources – including national intelligence (from the big eye and the big ear) – available to the special operators rather than filtering it through 'compartmentalization' was a great advance over prior operations. One limitation was that, as Panama was in many cases the first time such intelligence had been provided, the special operators were unfamiliar with it. One tactical commander, preparing for D-Day, was briefed by a US Army TENCAP team, using national intelligence assets. However, lacking experience of training with these classified assets and consequently having no confidence in their accuracy, he did not use them. Fortunately, when there were surprises – as when the Rangers found Torrijos International Airport full of civilians vulnerable to desperate PDF – the US forces had sufficient momentum and overwhelming force to prevent their opposition from taking advantage of the situation.

The crisis and the build-up to it allowed extensive planning time for the use of SOF. The planning, while generally successful, still led the SEALs into the crossfire at Paitilla Airfield. While rehearsals were limited, they were valuable in working out the plans. The SEALs at Paitilla had several opportunities to rehearse and, had their leaders been concerned about the suitability of the plan, the plan could have been changed had they voiced their concerns. The Ranger battalions' extensive training in airfield seizure and the improvements since Grenada were evident. That the Marines who could have carried out a similar mission at Paitilla were not under SOCOM – the Marines provided no combat units to SOCOM until 2002 – was one reason why the JSOTF planners looked to the SEALs to carry out that mission. Yet non-SOCOM paratroopers and aviators carried out their well-planned and rehearsed missions at Renacer Prison and Fort Amador effectively, in addition to the hastily improvised liberation mission to the Marriott. Liberation and seizure missions cannot appropriately be said to be only the province of specialists such as Delta and SEALs, nor even exclusively of SOF.

Paitilla was not a misuse of the SEALs,[42] but it did demonstrate potential limits to the covert, small, select-team method that is the preferred approach for liberation or seizure missions carried out by Delta or SEALs. Had Paitilla been hit by a larger, less covert force, it is likely that the PDF garrison would have fled or could have surrendered without appearing ashamed or cowardly – cultural concerns that were recognized in the conduct of the 'Ma Bell' operations. Confronted with what appeared to be a single SEAL platoon, the PDF thought they might prevail in a firefight or believed that it was simply not done to give way in the face of such a numerically smaller force, however élite it might be in comparison with them. Massive numbers can deter and prevent resistance. Getting them to the objective in a timely fashion remains the problem.

Liberation and seizure operations remained integrated air–ground operations (with an amphibious component at Fort Renacer and Paitilla). The value of dedicated special operations aircrew with experience in working with SOF was again demonstrated. The 160th SOAR was vital to the SOF actions and the AC-130s delivered precision fire power.

The liberation and seizure operations demonstrated the importance of the quality of the junior officers, NCOs and the individual soldiers. The operations where individuals needed to be rescued from the PDF – such as at the airport and at Carcel Modelo and Renacer Prisons – were carried out at a decentralized level. The responsibility came down to individual soldiers for whether to engage targets that proved to be Panamanian civilians.

But the flip-side of the Panama model – that raiders can be exposed, with limited back-up potential, to bloody and intense battles in situations when even the best-trained troops will be vulnerable – was seen at Paitilla and in Somalia. The US military never embraced the Panama model. Rather, it embraced its competitor, one derived from the 1991 Gulf War air campaign and refined in the 1995 and 1999 air campaigns against the former Yugoslavia. The Panama model was to be partially revived for the operations in Afghanistan in 2001 and Iraq in 2003. In Iraq, the US military was to re-encounter, in a less permissive environment, many of the problems it had to deal with in Panama. Closer study of the Panama model would have made the military better able to cope.

CHAPTER 9 MOGADISHU, SOMALIA · 3–4 October 1993

In the Clinton administration, foreign policy was a second-level interest and its conduct was, to be charitable, often wanting.

Ambassador Jack R. Binns.

The raid in Mogadishu on 3 October 1993 was the seventh in a series of raids mounted by US special operations Task Force Ranger. It was an attempt to quickly and surgically seize members of the leadership of General Mohammed Farah Aideed's Somali militia group, which was opposing the UN forces being supported by the US. What was planned as a quick raid soon escalated into a bitter and costly two-day battle. It was the most intense fighting the US military had seen since Vietnam and it had a lasting impact. The course of events has become familiar worldwide through the Hollywood movie based on the best-selling book *Black Hawk Down*.[1]

As has usually been the case post-Cold War, the conflict in Somalia was not 'about' ideology, economics or strategy in a broader world balance, but rather about General Aideed and his faction. In a war that is essentially about an individual, raids by SOF – to liberate or to seize – become strategic operations.

WELCOME TO HELL

The US military and its SOF first came to a disintegrating Somalia in strength in Operation Eastern Exit in 1990.[2] Their mission was the evacuation of foreign civilians. In this operation, as with many of the successful US noncombatant evacuation operations (NEOs) in the 1990s, Marines were inserted at long-range by air-refuelled CH-53s while the amphibious ready group (ARG) was still approaching Mogadishu. Special operations forces – Navy SEALs and Marine Force Recon – played a key role. They went in first to mark helicopter LZs and to provide security. Marine snipers were positioned to take down anyone who looked as if they were going to interfere with the transport helicopters – escorted by armed attack helicopters – as they shuttled to and from the ships offshore. Even though shots were fired during the evacuation, in Somalia, as with most NEOs, the operation was carried out without loss. Over 3,000 civilians were evacuated.

The north and central sections of Somalia claimed to secede and managed to avoid chaos. In the south, mass starvation was prevented by UN-supported humanitarian relief. This, in turn, was often blocked by what the west termed 'warlords', former Somali government or army officials who were leading groups based on ethnic clan identification. To protect the relief supplies, the UN authorized a UN operation in Somalia (UNOSOM) in April 1992. To support it, a UN interim task force (UNITAF) was established. UNITAF sought to carry out the limited mission of securing the distribution of humanitarian aid. The senior US officials, Ambassador Robert Oakley and LTG Robert Johnson, acted to avoid a direct confrontation with Aideed while consolidating UN relief operations. This was backed up with a widespread and effective psychological operation, conducted by the US, with radio broadcasts and newspapers stressing the UN's goals and missions. Despite extensive US airlift support – Operation Provide Relief – UNITAF's limited troops on the ground were unable to assure the food supply.

By December 1992, Somalia – most notably the southern part including the capital of Mogadishu – had become what is euphemistically termed a 'failed state'. The population of Mogadishu had swelled to over a half-million with internal refugees, no longer able to grow their own food as they had in the countryside. The government had effectively collapsed, leaving a mosaic of feuding groups, largely clan-based, trying to fill the gap. Of the 'warlords', General Mohammed Farah Aideed, a Somali army officer, emerged as the main obstacle to the UN. The son of a camel-herder who had undergone professional military education in Italy and the Soviet Union, Aideed had risen to be chief of staff and ambassador to India and had been instrumental in the overthrow of Siad Barre, the previous head of state in Somalia. His support was strongest around Mogadishu, relying on the strength of his Habr

Gidr clan-based Somalia National Alliance (SNA) in the area. Aideed styled himself chief of state and was suspicious of international efforts that would undercut his claims to power. He was ruthless in his commitment to using his clan-based power to achieve the national leadership to which he believed he was legitimately entitled and of which he was being deprived by foreign intervention. He was willing to use starvation as a political tool, taking control of relief supplies and releasing them to feed his supporters and allies and starve out opponents.

A new December 1992 commitment – Operation Restore Hope – sent in US forces to allow UNOSOM to turn over its objectives to a new peacekeeping mission. In March 1993, the limited UNOSOM transitioned to the more broadly tasked UNOSOM II. Turkish LTG Cevik Bir commanded UNOSOM II. At US insistence, the on-the-scene political leadership was provided by the special representative of the UN secretary-general, retired US Navy ADM Jonathan Howe. Howe had been selected for the job by US National Security Adviser Tony Lake and had as his goal marginalizing Aideed.[3] UNOSOM II had a three-part mandate going far beyond the humanitarian security of its predecessor: disarm Somali warlords' forces, rehabilitate national political institutions and build a secure environment throughout Somalia.

While the US provided no forces directly under Bir's command, they did provide extensive logistics assistance. To support the UNOSOM II forces, the US established a Quick Reaction Force (QRF). This remained under US command, with Army MG Thomas C. Montgomery as in-country commander, US Forces Somalia (USFORSOM). He was responsible to US Central Command (CENTCOM) under Marine Gen. Joseph Hoar at MacDill AFB, Florida.

The QRF was a light infantry force built around rotational battalions from the 10th Mountain Division. It had to rely on HMMWVs and sandbagged M809 5-ton trucks for ground mobility. The QRF lacked tanks and armoured personnel carriers as well as combat engineers to deal with barriers and roadblocks in the streets of Mogadishu and on the routes humanitarian aid convoys had to travel in the countryside. MG Montgomery's request for such reinforcements for the QRF was turned down by the Clinton administration's Secretary of Defense, Les Aspin (though neither Gen. Hoar nor Chairman of the Joint Chiefs of Staff (CJCS) GEN Colin Powell put their weight behind the request) on the grounds that this would constitute escalation and would increase the US footprint in-country.

THE UN VS. AIDEED

Tension between Aideed and UNOSOM II mounted. In June 1993, it broke into open warfare. A Pakistani force trying to inspect arms caches was thought to be capturing Aideed's radio station. Radio was critical to his political base for spreading anti-Western and anti-UN propaganda and portraying him as a heroic nationalist and anti-imperialist leader. The UN force was ambushed. Some twenty-four Pakistani UNOSOM II soldiers were killed. When the QRF advanced to cover the Pakistani retreat, among the fresh graffiti on a nearby ruin were the words 'Welcome to Hell'. Fires from car tyre roadblocks covered much of the northern side of Mogadishu, reinforcing the message.

Aideed denied ordering the attack on the Pakistanis and asked for an inquiry. The UN, with strong US support, reacted with a Security Council resolution authorizing UNOSOM II to arrest and detain those responsible 'for prosecution, trial and punishment' and to use 'all necessary measures' to establish UN authority 'throughout Somalia'. This resolution, with political support from the Clinton administration, was pushed through without consultation with the US military or the Department of Defense, despite the implications of a broader conflict.

The Pentagon was obviously not driving Somalia policy, but neither did it try to stop its direction. The US backed this up by deploying SOCOM AC-130H gunships, based in Kenya, to support offensive action by UNOSOM II troops. UN Secretary-General Boutros Boutros-Ghali – seeing the Somalia situation as a key test of UN claims to the primary role in the post-Cold War international system – decided to attack Aideed's political strength. UNOSOM II went on the offensive during 12–17 June with a three-day operation, including the use of US AC-130H gunships and AH-1F attack helicopters, against much of Aideed's infrastructure: his radio station and weapons caches. The ground assault was spearheaded by the QRF – a brigade headquarters under COL Lawrence Casper – and the US 1-22nd Infantry, both from the 10th Mountain Division. Aideed escaped the multi-national force that set up a cordon and a house-to-house search for him, which utilized two Pakistani infantry battalions: 1st Punjab and 7th Frontier Force. A Moroccan battalion, part of the cordon, was ambushed. Over thirty of Aideed's armed jeeps – 'technicals' in local jargon – and many other heavy weapons were knocked out. Many weapons, but none of the targeted Somalis, were captured by the multi-national force. Within two weeks, Aideed's radio station, headquarters and main weapons cache had been taken, but not the man himself. UNOSOM II found itself conducting an urban counter-insurgency campaign. It was the first offensive action under a UN headquarters since the Korean War.

Howe – over Montgomery's objections – had leaflets offering a reward for the capture of Aideed dropped over Mogadishu. Aideed, alerted that he was a wanted man, went underground, changing location frequently. The seizure of Aideed, however, was not integrated into the overall UN – or US – plan for Somalia. It was assumed that getting him would be enough.

Aideed introduced procedures, including his own thorough OPSEC, to stay out of UN hands. He reorganized his intelligence service, purging suspected double agents and using them to plant false information about his movements. He moved often, in disguise, once or twice a night. Only a handful of aides and deputies knew his location.

Aideed demonstrated his political skills. He was able to use to his advantage collateral damage from UN fire power and from the UN returning fire at SNA snipers positioned in a hospital, rallying support on the basis of clan loyalty, Islam, nationalism, anti-imperialism and demonization of his opponents. While Aideed had no record of religious leadership, his rhetoric helped to gain him support from Islamic fundamentalists both in Somalia and worldwide, providing him with funding and a few volunteers. The Somalis demonstrated their opposition to outside forces by slaughtering and dismembering four western journalists.

With Aideed unbeaten, the UN looked to additional US capabilities. US ground forces now started playing a greater role in anti-Aideed operations. From 17 June to 11 July, the 1-22nd Infantry conducted several raids aimed at capturing Aideed or his associates. Targeting was from HUMINT provided by Somalis, but this proved inaccurate. Each mission was preceded by two to three days of preparation and rehearsal. They all concluded with the unit returning to base camp – pursued by enemy RPG or mortar attacks – without successful results.[4]

In June, Howe advised the national command authority (NCA) that a US special operations force would likely – he assessed the probability at a ninety per cent chance – quickly capture Aideed, who was not then in hiding. Howe wanted an immediate commitment of US SOF for a seizure mission, but Washington was reluctant. As a compromise, a multi-service SOF force was organized and started training at Fort Bragg and Eglin AFB for possible deployment to Mogadishu.[5]

Aideed offered to negotiate, and the AC-130Hs were returned to a US base in Italy as a sign of co-operation. However, Aideed and his allies continued to keep the military pressure on, reverting to mortar attacks. Sniping at UN forces also increased. On the streets of Mogadishu, Aideed was quick to claim the AC-130H withdrawal as a victory and the UN activities as evidence that he was the only true Somali standing up against a new imperialism. Meanwhile, the largest contributors of troops to UNOSOM II, Italy and Pakistan, were wary of escalation. They looked not to capture but rather to make a deal with Aideed, who they believed had been chastened by the June offensive.

In opposition to this view, the US – specifically the high-level foreign policy decision-makers in Washington but excluding the President – and Boutros-Ghali, wanted to ensure that Aideed was removed from Somali politics. In late June, CENTCOM directed SOCOM and SOC Control Element 520 (SOCCE), which was the operational headquarters for US special operations forces in Somalia, to develop a concept of operations for the capture of Aideed. This led to a plan devised by LTC Darrell 'Moe' Elmore, deputy commander of the 5th SFG, MAJ Dave Jesmer, commanding officer of the Mogadishu-based B Company, 1-5th SFG, and a British SAS officer. Strategic reconnaissance teams and aerial snipers in helicopters would detect Aideed when he was moving in a convoy and then call in AH-1Fs from the 10th Mountain Division and other heliborne forces to make the seizure.[6]

However, this plan was put aside in favour of a direct attack on Aideed via Operation Michigan. This had been planned without regard for the Somalia-based UN forces, but had been approved up the US chain of command to Bill Clinton himself. It opened with an attack by six US AH-1F attack helicopters firing sixteen TOW missiles at SNA headquarters on 12 July. Immediately after the helicopter attack, heliborne and road-mobile forces from the 1-22nd raided the site of the headquarters, hoping to capture any surviving personnel or at least gather intelligence. While they did not succeed in either objective, the 1-22nd was able to return to base without loss.

Aideed survived this attack, which led to the deaths of over sixty Somalis, including Habr Gidr clan elders who had been opposed to Aideed's use of the clan as a springboard for his grasp for national power. Again, Aideed used the collateral damage as evidence to show his supporters that this was an attack by Western imperialists, especially the US, on his clan, nation and religion. The impact of the attack was a powerful boost to his claims for power and in turning Somali attitudes against the foreign forces.[7]

The US forces refined their tactics for seizing Aideed. These would be integrated with the 'Eyes Over Mogadishu' day-and-night helicopter surveillance flights. The 1-22nd worked with B Company, 1-5th SFG, conducting force-protection missions in support of UNOSOM II in the Mogadishu area. The plans were a refinement of those devised in June. They included mounting a Green Beret sniper with a .50-calibre rifle in a UH-60, providing precision aerial fire power. The snipers were proficient in destroying Somali-crewed weapons and leaving their crews unharmed. The goal was, if Aideed could be located when on the move, for a sniper bullet to immobilize his vehicle while heliborne troops – supported by the AH-1Fs – came in to capture him. This mission was attempted several times in July–August, but each time, intelligence was inaccurate or higher headquarters aborted the mission.[8] In August, the 1-22nd was rotated home and replaced by the 2-14th Infantry, new to Somalia. In September, B Company, 1-5th SFG, was replaced by C Company, 3-5th SFG. Both of the most experienced US units in Mogadishu were replaced.

In the wake of these actions, it was decided that the best tool for achieving policy goals would be US special operations forces. While Gen. Hoar re-appraised the chance of success at twenty-five per cent, Secretary of Defense Aspin gave the go-ahead for deployment while asking that the larger US force have less of an on-the-ground 'footprint'. The contradictions inherent in this – like the decision itself – were not reviewed in Washington.

TF RANGER ARRIVES IN SOMALIA

On 22 August 1993, in response to attacks on US and UNOSOM II forces and installations – including a command-detonated mine that killed four US soldiers on 8 August – a Joint Special Operations Task Force (JSOTF) was ordered organized and deployed to Somalia. This was in response to UN calls for the deployment of additional US forces. Within the administration, the deployment's strongest advocate was US ambassador to the UN Madeleine Albright, backed up by Secretary of State Warren Christopher. The CJCS,

GEN Colin Powell – mindful that the commitment did not meet the criteria set out in the 'Powell Doctrine' – was reluctant to see the Somalia commitment increased without a plan for victory or an exit strategy. He found the willingness of some in the Clinton administration to send troops into action troubling. Powell realized that his opposition to Clinton administration policies was having limited effect; he would be retiring in a few months.[9]

The JSOTF was designated Task Force (TF) Ranger (after the US Army Ranger battalion that made up its main strength), but it was a 'purple' multi-service command including a squadron of Delta Force, plus forces from 160th SOAR (8 MH-60s, 4 MH-6s and 4 AH-6s), Air Force special operations forces and Navy SEALs.

TF Ranger's order of battle alone would have persuaded a less determined adversary to lie low until it was withdrawn. But TF Ranger's strength was limited to 450, on the orders of the Secretary of Defense, to reduce its 'footprint' and associated political and diplomatic visibility. It had to deploy without an extra platoon of Rangers from A Company of the 3-75th and, most importantly, without the USAF AC-130 gunships with which it had trained. Its only ground armour was provided by eight HMMWVs with extra Kevlar plates.

Joint SOF operations were greatly facilitated by the establishment of SOCOM in 1987, but service 'rice bowl' interests endured. The joint composition of TF Ranger made sure that no service was excluded. There was time for TF Ranger to undergo only limited stateside training with all its elements before deploying to the US base at Mogadishu Airport. TF Ranger was able to continue training once in Somalia, but unfortunately with only limited participation by other US or UN forces.

Reflecting the limited pre-deployment training, there was friction between the preferred operational approaches of TF Ranger's different participants. Delta is trained to work in four-man teams and preferred to insert covertly or in their 'Little Bird' helicopters (but with a support reserve within striking range). The Rangers trained to fight in battalion- or company-sized forces and preferred to insert by larger MH-60 helicopters or parachute. With different tactics and personnel (Delta's troopers are all NCOs, older and more experienced; Rangers tend to be younger and more enthusiastic) came different command styles across the forces. However, with the different forces tied together under the SOCOM structure, these divergences were much less significant than those that had emerged in the planning for the Iran raid or on Grenada.

TF Ranger's commander, Army MG William Garrison, was subordinate directly to the CINCCENT. This made the force parallel – but not subordinate – to UNFORSOM and the US-commanded QRF. While TF Ranger would co-operate with UNOSOM II, at no time was it under UN command or control. In practice neither Gen. Bir nor ADM Howe – who had been the most insistent voice for TF Ranger's deployment – nor the UN forces on the ground in Mogadishu were informed of TF Ranger missions due to operational security concerns.

A Joint Operations Centre (JOC) was established at Mogadishu Airport to fuse the multiple intelligence efforts and sensor systems searching for Aideed. The JOC would co-ordinate TF Ranger operations with those of UN and other US forces.

The force was further weakened by guidance from the NCA, relayed through Powell, that TF Ranger should reflect the minimum force required for Operation Gothic Serpent, the codename for the plan to capture Aideed. Again, Washington's goal was to reduce the visibility of the US role while keeping TF Ranger focused not on gaining victory in Mogadishu but on the specific mission of capturing Aideed. The AC-130Hs stayed in Europe.

THE INTELLIGENCE BATTLE

TF Ranger had access, through the JOC, to the full range of US intelligence capabilities and assets; despite HUMINT limitations, this included sensors that a previous generation of raiders could only dream about. National-level intelligence assets – satellites, SIGINT and cryptography – had been kept away from the troops for many of the Cold War years for fear of compromise. By 1993, US military tactical exploitation of national capabilities (TENCAP) programmes were regularly bringing their end products – suitably sanitized – to the men at the 'sharp end' with reduced time delays. This had become a standard operational procedure. Even tactical commanders had come to recognize the strengths and limitations of this intelligence support.

Above Mogadishu, even if the AC-130Hs with their night optics and experienced operators were absent, TF Ranger had support from US Navy EP-3E Orions – another national intelligence asset, with powerful communications-intercept capability and a long-range electro-optical infra-red television that could be linked down to the JOC. The JOC also received direct video feed from OH-58D Kiowa Warrior helicopters, advanced technology scouts with a mast-top multi-sensor suite and a wideband datalink.

However, overhead sensors of any type were of limited value in dealing with the overhanging roofs and crowded streets of Mogadishu. Aideed minimized the use of his command net, using Motorola commercial radios instead. The lack of working Somali electronic communications limited SIGINT. US COMINT did pick up mortar fire being adjusted in Arabic, apparently by foreign Islamic radicals who had joined Aideed's forces.[10]

The US was aware of the importance of HUMINT in Mogadishu. Over the course of 1990–93, the CIA developed a Somali HUMINT network for its own use, the Intelligence Support Activity (ISA). It was counted on to provide targeting to TF Ranger. Limiting ISA effectiveness was its reliance on agents recruited from clans other than those loyal to Aideed, which marked them as outsiders in clan strongholds. Its chief local agent was a minor warlord with a 400-man force, nominally neutral but actually anti-Aideed.[11]

The US special operations forces operating in Somalia and their associated civil affairs units had developed a HUMINT capability in the months preceding TF Ranger's arrival in Somalia. This capability was not fully developed, however, and did not end up contributing to the targeting of TF Ranger raids.[12]

Yet intelligence could only provide limited assurances of Aideed's location even in a quick-reaction situation. Aideed soon acquired the codename Elvis. Reports of Elvis sightings were treated by US intelligence with the same scepticism as their stateside equivalents. Twice, US forces claimed to have had Aideed literally in their sights, but the orders were to capture, not kill.

The ISA suffered a setback when its chief local agent lost a game of Somali roulette – the local version of Russian roulette played with a fully loaded Kalashnikov, with predictably fatal results. This happened on 25 August, the day before TF Ranger arrived in Mogadishu. The CIA tried putting in a US case officer to replace him, but this had to be abandoned in mid-September. Less-experienced Somali subordinates had to fill in to provide intelligence for TF Ranger.

THE RAIDS BEGIN

As TF Ranger was deploying, the 2-14th Infantry was launching multi-company raids (including the use of CS gas) to seize Somalis responsible for the command-detonated mine attack. Other 2-14th raids continued into September.[13]

Before the end of August, TF Ranger was in action. It carried out six raids in the Mogadishu area during September, with heliborne Delta Force seizure teams with security provided by Rangers operating in co-operation with ground raiders mounted in HMMWVs and trucks. The first raid, on 30 August, was mistakenly targeted on the Lig Ligato UN compound and captured eight local UN employees. They were caught with black market goods in a restricted area, but the negative publicity (especially in the media) and mutual distrust from the UN command generated by the incident affected later actions by TF Ranger.[14] The TF Ranger raiders used helicopters for both ingress and egress. C Company of the 2-14th stood by to support exfiltration. Co-ordination with TF Ranger was not good. CPT Lee Rysewyk of the Rangers thought their 'CO a terrible whiner, impatient and wanted to leave with Rangers still on the ground'.[15]

The initial raids were largely conducted using variations of the same tactical template, reflecting TF Ranger's training and capabilities. Due to the lack of back-up fire power, speed and surprise were stressed. Because their base at the airport was under observation by Aideed supporters, TF Ranger had to substitute speed of execution for surprise to provide security for their operations.[16] By minimizing on-the-ground exposure time to a half-hour, the template limited the forces the opposition could bring to bear against the raiders. The raiders were inserted either by ground convoy moving out from the base at the airport or by fast-rope from hovering helicopters. Due to the lack of suitable LZs near the objective, the raiders could not be picked up by helicopters in some situations if they had fast-roped down. They then relied on a quick linkup with a ground convoy and speedy egress before an effective Somali reaction could develop to compensate for their lack of surprise and mobility once landed.

The second raid, on 6 September, targeted the old Russian compound. Aideed was reportedly nearby but escaped in the darkness. The Rangers wounded two, capturing seventeen plus five weapons. Two TF Ranger personnel were slightly wounded. A platoon-sized ground reaction force (GRF) was pre-positioned nearby for support.

These raids were unsuccessful because of intelligence limitations. The third raid on 14 September captured a leader and thirty-nine well-armed men of an anti-Aideed militia group. TF Ranger used helicopters to infiltrate and exfiltrate. A GRF was pre-positioned nearby.

The fourth raid, on Radio Aideed on 17 September, proved to be a 'dry hole'. A brief firefight left one Somali killed in action and one wounded. The raiders were entirely ground-mounted. The fifth raid, on a garage, took place on 18 September. A key Aideed supporter was seen there at 0815. He was not there when the raiders fast-roped in at 0846. Most of the Aideed supporters escaped. The raiders captured eight prisoners and liberated one Somali prisoner before ground exfiltration. However, the sixth raid on 21 September – which diverted from the template in order to make use of opportunistic HUMINT – captured Osman Ato, a key Aideed financier and arms supplier. His garage had been the target of the fifth raid. He was in a moving car, being tracked by US sensors, while the helicopters were called in for a quick-reaction strike. First to engage was an MH-6 'Little Bird' from the 160th SOAR. A Delta Force sniper on board the MH-6 disabled Ato's car with three rounds through the engine block. Ato's driver was wounded. Then MH-60s brought in a Delta team to seize Ato. It was an all-Delta snatch.[17]

It became apparent that targeting Aideed's lieutenants was more feasible than looking for the elusive target himself. However, the SNA immediately struck back against a Pakistani convoy, inflicting ten casualties. Even so, the success against Ato raised US hopes and Aideed's concerns.

The raids provoked a reaction from Aideed, not limited to mass political mobilization. In addition to opposing the raids, Aideed increased sniping and mortar attacks on the airport and on UN positions and troops. A battle to open the road north of town using UN and US 10th Mountain Division forces had brought in the AH-1Fs, and yet again claims of collateral damage were used by Aideed to rally opposition.

The US was more concerned with preventing 'dry hole' raids or flying into an ambush; 35–40 raids were planned but cancelled for lack of action-able intelligence.[18] The US conducted no detailed after-action evaluations or re-evaluation of the two basic templates. While several variations from the two standard templates were used – day and night operations (three of each), with and without a ground force – it soon became apparent to Aideed and his combat veteran officers and political advisors that there was indeed a tactical template being used.[19] They started thinking about developing countermeasures. Many of them being Soviet-trained, they knew all about tactical templates and, likely, how they often, in practice, proved inadequate against wily opponents in the Horn of Africa. Their conclusion was that the best way to divide the US force and defeat the elements individually – the only way they could be defeated – was to bring down a helicopter and turn the resulting rescue into a quickly developing pitched battle in which Somali numbers rather than US mobility would prevail. The Somalis could then disperse before superior US fire power could be brought to bear.[20] Aideed and his leadership believed that a defeat of a part of the US force would lead to a withdrawal of the rest of it, as in Lebanon in 1983, and the presence of the international media would allow the effect of any US setback to be directly broadcast to the US population.

The resistance to the raids had been increasing. Aideed believed in training his men and had recently sent 250 through a facility outside Mogadishu.[21] Aideed had some truck-mounted 23 mm ZU-23 SP AAA, though these were usually kept concealed. Somalis used kites to create a barrier to night-flying helicopters. Several helicopters had to abort missions with kite string wrapped around their tail rotors. Somalis discontinued the extensive use of tracer rounds in their Kalashnikovs which gave away their position to helicopters. Somalis were reportedly able to use a modified 82 mm mortar fuse in the RPG-7's round to produce an airburst. Other airbursts were produced by aiming the grenade so that its end-of-flight self-detonation would be above the target. Fifteen RPG-7 rounds were fired at 160th SOAR helicopters during the sixth raid on 21 September. On 26 September, Courage 53, a UH-60 – a 101st Air Assault Division helicopter supporting UNFORSOM – was shot down by an RPG-7. Three Americans were killed; the two injured pilots were rescued by a patrol of UAE troops. The dead were mutilated by a Somali mob. The crash site was secured by the 2-14th Infantry after a pitched battle. Courage 53 had been conducting a high-speed low-altitude presence flight over Mogadishu. The increasing vulnerability of helicopters was becoming obvious.

Despite the mounting resistance, the decision was made in Mogadishu – under pressure from Washington for the raids to bring in results – to expand the targeting from Aideed himself to include his key lieutenants. Task Force Ranger was directed to broaden its mission set. However, TF Ranger did not ask for its withdrawn platoon, the AC-130Hs or any other reinforcements for this expanded mission. Nor were resources provided so that multiple raids could be conducted against all possible hiding places over a short time period, the tactics that had helped corner Noriega in Panama. Nor was there systematic and widespread acquisition and exploitation of HUMINT and documentary evidence by the US and local authorities to target SOF familiar with the people and territory, as in Panama. Even though the target set was broadened, TF Ranger would continue to carry out its raids one at a time with intervals of days between them.

Reflecting the increased capability of the opposition, in late September MG Garrison had predicted, 'If we go in the vicinity of the Bakara Market [where the Habr Gidr clan was strong and the population was politically mobilized, concentrated and well armed so that Aideed could quickly rally forces], there's no question that we will win the gunfight. But we might lose the war.' He stressed that TF Ranger raids had to limit their time on the ground to a half-hour.[22]

What Garrison did not know was that the war was already lost. Washington had become dissatisfied with the progress of Operation Gothic Serpent. Opposition was growing in Congress to the whole Somalia mission that the Clinton administration had embraced. Key Clinton advisors – including First Lady Hillary Clinton, then at the height of her power and influence within the administration – turned against the commitment and advocated withdrawal. In Washington, the National Security Council, meeting at the end of September, had agreed that the goal should be to seek a diplomatic solution with Aideed.

However, this decision was not communicated to Garrison. Normally, ordering raids against someone with whom you are trying to negotiate is considered counterproductive. If the National Security Council had wanted the pressure kept up on Aideed, they could have ordered that helicopter flights be continued over his territory. However, National Security Advisor Tony Lake has written: 'The policy was never to stop trying to get Aideed' but rather 'to move to more diplomatic efforts but snatch Aideed on the side'.

For MG Garrison, this was a distinction without a difference, because he was not informed of it. There was no review of the policy in Washington. Nor was Washington aware of the increasing Somali anti-helicopter action.

ORIGINS OF A RAID – 3 OCTOBER 1993

The seventh TF Ranger raid was on 3 October 1993. The objective was a house on the Hawlwadig Road where two of Aideed's subordinates – Omar Salad Elmi, Aideed's top political adviser, and Mohammed Hasan Awale, the SNA 'foreign minister' – would be meeting. Aideed might even drop by to see his friends. The objective was near the Olympic Hotel, in the Bakara Market district that Garrison had correctly identified as a centre of pro-Aideed resistance. It was some 5 km from TF Ranger's base at Mogadishu Airport. TF Ranger nicknamed the area 'The Black Sea'.

Garrison received HUMINT from a Somali agent about the meeting at around 1300. This was from a new source – an improvised CIA surveillance net – rather than those that had helped to target the previous raids. The HUMINT source marked the target for US overhead sensors by stopping his car outside and raising the bonnet.[23]

As the TF Ranger rapid-reaction (20 minutes to target) force – held in readiness for just such missions – prepared and quickly planned the operation on the basis of photographs, maps and intelligence reports, an EP-3C surveillance aircraft (with long-range Reef Point electro-optical sensors) and an OH-58D Kiowa Warrior helicopter were able to keep 'eyes on' the target via their electro-optical sensors. The rapid-reaction force was organized on the two pre-existing templates. The strong point template was to be used on buildings: Delta Force teams would enter the building and seize the prisoners, with security to be provided by a Ranger force drawn largely from B Company (reinforced) of the 3-75th Rangers, reinforced by Navy SEALs. Air Force Combat Control Teams and Pararescuemen would also participate. There would be strong command and control elements to link the force to headquarters and make available the extensive range of sensor data. The second template, the convoy, would be used to seize moving vehicles.[24]

The planning of the raid emphasized minimizing vulnerability through speed and surprise rather than superior fire power. The force would only be on the ground for an hour. There would not be time for Aideed's forces to react and concentrate. The late-afternoon timing of the raid was in part

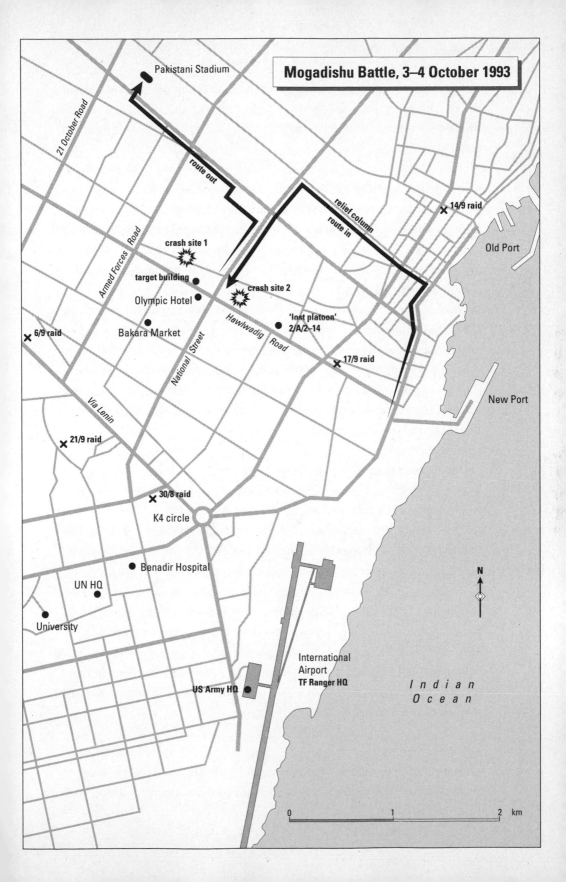

Mogadishu Battle, 3–4 October 1993

Pakistani Stadium

21 October Road

route out

relief column
route in

14/9 raid

Old Port

crash site 1

Armed Forces Road

target building

Olympic Hotel

crash site 2

'lost platoon'
2/A/2–14

6/9 raid

Bakara Market

Hawlwadig Road

National Street

17/9 raid

New Port

Via Lenin

21/9 raid

30/8 raid

K4 circle

Benadir Hospital

UN HQ

University

International
Airport
TF Ranger HQ

N

*Indian
Ocean*

US Army HQ

0   1   2   km

dictated by the widespread Somali practice, after the major midday meal of the day, of using *qat*, a mildly narcotic leaf imported from Yemen. It was thought that much of the potential opposition would be too wasted on *qat* to respond to the raid.

US Army tactical doctrine for such raids reflects the benefits of meticulous planning (and that service's predilection for such approaches). A detailed warning order, operations order, air mission briefings and extensive rehearsals following comprehensive intelligence preparation of the battlefield are called for. All potential participants – including those from forces not going on the raid – are to be involved in briefings and rehearsals. Contingency plans are developed.

However, on that day there was no time for following such a process to catch the fleeting time-critical target reported by the HUMINT. They would use the same basic template as the previous six raids. The QRF received only general last-minute notification of the impending raid. The Green Berets of C Company of the 3-5th SFG were deployed in Mogadishu but were not involved in the raid at all. They were mainly committed to keeping observation posts and sniper teams operational to contribute to the force protection mission.[25]

Garrison was aware that the previous raids had been encountering increasing resistance. As a result, on this raid, the AH-6 helicopters – two would support the raid, along with two MH-60s carrying airborne sniper teams – were authorized to use of 2.75-inch rockets for the first time. The RoE had also been changed from the first six raids. Armed Somalis could be fired upon without giving them an opportunity to surrender first.

However, the raiders would not be going in with their full capabilities. In previous raids, the raiders' large equipment loads – 31-plus kg – were found to be fatiguing in action. Heavy solider loads, it was feared, could lead to accidents when fast-roping from helicopters. Night-vision goggles and sights, canteens and the highly effective 40 mm M203 grenade launchers, mounted under the barrels of M16 rifles, were in many cases left behind. Raiders also left the back plates off their body armour.

OPENING MOVES

The raiding force was split into four elements, reflecting US Army tactical doctrine for such operations: command and control, security, support and assault. The key command and control element was the raid commander, who would command from his helicopter throughout. This was also consistent with US Army tactics. The security element was the most numerically important. These (mainly Rangers) and armed helicopters would isolate the objective area and, if required, provide suppressive fire during the withdrawal. The assault force (mainly Delta) would secure the objective, take the targeted individuals prisoner and then withdraw with them. Lacking was the support element of the raid stressed by doctrine: fire power provided by artillery, aircraft (other than the four armed helicopters supporting the Ranger security team) or ground units. The US had no artillery in Somalia. Even the 2-14th Infantry's mortars were heavily constrained by RoE.

These elements were divided between a heliborne force and a ground convoy. Fourteen helicopters from the 160th SOAR lifted out of the TF Ranger compound at Mogadishu Airport starting at 1532. The ground convoy moved out in three 5-ton trucks and nine HMMWVs three minutes later.

That the afternoon would be an unpleasant one in Bakara Market was first announced at 1540 by two AH-6s giving a final visual reconnaissance of the objective and its immediate surroundings. They were immediately followed by four MH-6s, each carrying a four-man Delta Force team. The assault element came down to surround the house that was the objective, the teams disappearing inside to carry out their speciality of close-quarters personnel seizure, using the skills honed in Fort Bragg's training facilities. To LTC Lee Van Arsdale, one of the Delta officers at the JOC, 'It all went like clockwork.' Surprised by the speed of the Delta Force attack, the entire meeting was quickly captured without a fight.[26] The raiders radioed 'Laurie', the brevity code for success, back to the JOC.

As Delta Force dashed inside and took prisoners, the MH-6s stood off to allow two MH-60s to bring in a further thirty raiders to make up the security element: a heliborne blocking force to ensure that no one escaped from or reinforced the objective. These Rangers fast-roped down and surrounded the objective, deployed by CPT Mike Steele, B Company's commanding officer. At 1545, a further four MH-60s, each carrying sixteen raiders, arrived to provide outer security. They also used fast-rope techniques to exit the hovering helicopters. The first helicopter's load of raiders – Chalk 1 – came down at the southeast road intersection, closest to the objective house.

Chalk 2 fast-roped down on the northeast intersection. Chalk 3 fast-roped in at the Hawlwadig Road southwest intersection.

The tail-end Charlie of the MH-60 flight, carrying Chalk 4, started to draw fire from the hornet's nest stirred up a few minutes before. An RPG-7 grenade burst nearby. To avoid the fire, Chalk 4's leader decided to fast-rope down a block north of his planned LZ at the northwest corner road intersection. One Ranger slipped off the rope and fell 24 m to the ground. The rest of Chalk 4 set up a perimeter and started administering first aid.

By this time the objective had been searched by Delta Force, capturing twenty-four Somalis including several senior SNA leaders. When the ground convoy led by LTC Danny McKnight – commander of the 3-75th, deputy commander of the raiders on this mission (and who had jumped into Rio Hato as executive officer of the 3-75th) – arrived at the objective at around 1553, both Delta and their security forces on the perimeter were starting to draw increasingly heavy fire. The ground convoy, which had expected the element of surprise to give them a clear route to the objective, had already had to engage several Somali ambushes. More Somalis were now obviously amassing and fire was increasing.

McKnight's first objective was to order the fallen Ranger evacuated back to base. A HMMWV used as an ambulance and two gun-armed HMMWVs as escorts moved two streets north to where Chalk 4 was now in a heavy firefight. They loaded the wounded Ranger on board and headed off at 1613.

The evacuation convoy was soon ambushed. It fought its way through, only to be ambushed again; in the words of its commander, SGT Jeff Streucher, the convoy was 'hit by fire from all directions'. A Ranger was killed – TF Ranger's first fatal casualty in Somalia – and most of the others wounded. The decision to leave off the back plates of the body armour proved to have been a costly one. Raiders hit in the back during the all-around firing of the ambushes were hit again as the exiting bullet rebounded off the inner face of their breastplates. At one time the medic tending the Ranger who had fallen from the helicopter had to hold an IV bag with one hand and fire an M16 with the other. Eventually the convoy fought its way through towards the airport base (the Ranger who fell from the helicopter was eventually to make a full recovery).

McKnight now turned to the prisoners seized by Delta and started to load them aboard his M809 5-ton trucks as the Rangers held the perimeter against increasing opposition. According to McKnight, 'Everything was going fine. We definitely achieved surprise. But when we started to load the detainees, everything changed.' Soon another three Rangers from Chalk 4 were hit. Large numbers of RPG-7 rounds were among the incoming fire. At 1558, a 5-ton truck was hit and disabled and a Ranger injured.

THE FIRST BLACK HAWK GOES DOWN

At 1620, Super 61, a 160th SOAR MH-60, was hit by an RPG-7 grenade. It had been trying to provide fire support to the Rangers on the perimeter using an airborne sniper team to disperse the crowd forming north of the objective. It crashed some three blocks away from the ground objective. The pilots were killed on impact. The two crew chiefs and three Delta Force snipers on board were badly injured.

TF Ranger had an SOP for a 'Black Hawk Down' situation. An MH-6 and an MH-60 carrying a fifteen-man combat search and rescue (CSAR) team of Delta troopers, Rangers and Air Force rescue men had been holding out of range in an orbit pattern, ready to come in if called. Both helicopters headed for the downed Black Hawk.

McKnight ordered Rangers from Chalk 1 and Chalk 2 to head for the crash site on foot. They had already moved out on their own initiative. They took several casualties – one killed and one badly wounded who died later – but kept advancing.

CWO3 Karl Meier's MH-6 was first at the crash site at 1624. It landed near to the shot-down helicopter and despite heavy fire, co-pilot CWO2 Keith Jones jumped out of the helicopter and, covered by the pilot's MP5 sub-machine-gun, recovered two wounded – a crewman and a sniper – before taking off fully loaded at 1631 to evacuate them back to the airport.

At 1628, dodging Somali bullets and clutching wounds, the Rangers from Chalks 1 and 2 arrived. They covered the take-off of the MH-6 and set up a perimeter around the shot-down helicopter, which still contained the bodies of the two pilots killed in the crash and the two remaining wounded. They had reached the downed helicopter just moments ahead of the onrushing crowds of armed Somalis.

Super 68, the MH-60 carrying the CSAR team, arrived over the crash site at 1628 and the CSAR team fast-roped down. As the last two men of the CSAR team – Air Force pararescuemen – were in midair, the MH-60 was hit

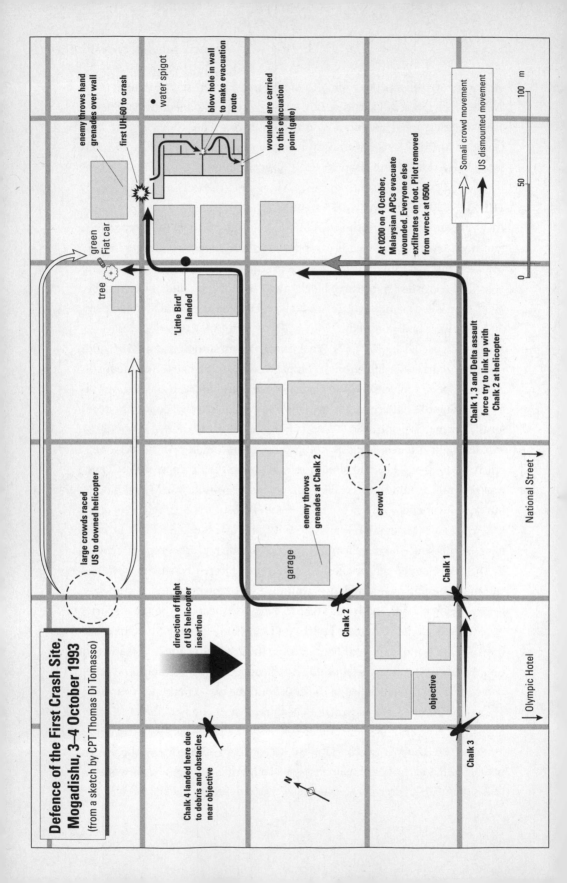

Defence of the First Crash Site, Mogadishu, 3–4 October 1993

(from a sketch by CPT Thomas Di Tomasso)

large crowds raced US to downed helicopter

direction of flight of US helicopter insertion

Chalk 4 landed here due to debris and obstacles near objective

garage

enemy throws grenades at Chalk 2

crowd

Chalk 2

Chalk 1

objective

Chalk 3

Olympic Hotel

National Street

Chalk 1, 3 and Delta assault force try to link up with Chalk 2 at helicopter

At 0200 on 4 October, Malaysian APCs evacuate wounded. Everyone else exfiltrates on foot. Pilot removed from wreck at 0500.

Somali crowd movement

US dismounted movement

100 m

50

0

enemy throws hand grenades over wall

first UH-60 to crash

water spigot

blow hole in wall to make evacuation route

wounded are carried to this evacuation point (gate)

green Fiat car

tree

'Little Bird' landed

N

by an RPG grenade. The helicopter crew fought to hold the Black Hawk steady until the two airmen were on the ground. The damaged helicopter then managed to make it back to Mogadishu Airport at 1630.

The men on the ground rushed to help Chalks 1 and 2 defending the crashed helicopter while the CSAR team's four medics went to the aid of the remaining wounded men from the crash. Somali snipers quickly hit two of the medics. The Rangers and the CSAR team expanded the perimeter around the crash site, occupying nearby buildings, and started to put down suppressive fire against the increasing numbers of attacking Somalis. Large crowds were reported moving towards the crash site.

Between attacks, they worked to free the pilots' bodies from the wreckage. Both were dead, one pinned under the weight of the crushed cockpit.

AH-6s and snipers on board MH-60s provided support that kept the position from being overrun as casualties mounted. Soon, half the force had been hit. The fire was too intense for helicopters to evacuate the wounded or evacuate the force, even if they had been willing to leave the dead pilots behind. 1LT Tom Di Tomasso, leader of Chalk 2, observed that, 'AK-47 bullets flew overhead with a loud pop, punctuated by the shriek of RPGs. As the teams fought to keep the crowds back, target identification became a problem. There were combatants mixed in the crowds of non-combatants. Women and children were screaming and running at us from all directions. Some of them had weapons and some did not. The weapons ranged from machine guns to small knives and machetes.'[27]

Back at the airport, the first reaction to the report of the helicopter crash was to pull together any possible reinforcements. These were to be launched to reinforce the crash scene, but soon word was received of a second Black Hawk down and the objective was changed. At about 1703, a scratch ground reaction force – twenty-seven personnel, mainly Rangers, including survivors of the evacuation convoy returning to the fight – with seven HMMWVs and two 5-ton trucks – had been dispatched from the airport to the (second) crash site. They were soon ambushed. By 1720 they were under heavy fire. The force tried to get around the ambush, guided by the TF Ranger command helicopter, but other routes were blocked by an earthen berm, a burning tyre obstacle and Somali fire. Without armoured vehicles they could not fight their way through, and remained pinned down at the K-4 traffic circle.

THE GROUND CONVOY MOVES ON THE FIRST CRASH SITE

Back at the initial objective, it had taken thirty minutes to secure and load the prisoners on to a sandbagged M809 5-ton truck. During this time, the ground convoy and the raiders on the perimeter were subject to increasing sniper and RPG fire. Casualties started to mount, with dead and wounded raiders being put into the ground convoy's trucks and HMMWVs.

McKnight now decided to move the ground convoy, reinforced by the Rangers' Chalk 4 – with sixty-five men, twenty-four prisoners and the dead and wounded – from the original objective to the first crash site, taking a longer route to avoid narrow streets likely to be blocked, with the objective of extracting the Rangers and the dead pilots and then heading back to base. CPT Mike Steele would lead the remaining raiders at and around the objective and would move on foot directly to the crash site to link up with the ground convoy there.

The ground convoy encountered heavy resistance. Overhead, the TF Ranger command and control MH-60 helicopter with LTC Gary Harrell of Delta Force – overall commander of the raid – on board, was also trying to direct the convoy. Even though it was netted directly to McKnight, Harrell had to monitor the other fights in which TF Ranger personnel were involved – he had vectored the CSAR element to the first crash site – and decided to let the big aeroplane with its superior optics do the driving for McKnight. The advance from the objective to the crash site went slowly, despite directions from the command helicopter and the EP-3 overhead. The latter was not directly netted in to McKnight, so its directions had a time-lag when forwarded. The EP-3 passed directions through the Joint Operations Center, leading to critical time delays. Several times, the convoy missed key turns and hit new roadblocks and ambushes. Casualties mounted on board the vehicles. At 1654, McKnight reported 'numerous casualties' back to the JOC.

At the JOC, Garrison and his staff were able to watch real-time video feed. Garrison put in a call for help to Montgomery and his QRF, asking that they be sent into action. In addition to the QRF, the remainder of its parent battalion – the 2-14th Infantry – would also be made ready to go into action. Garrison also contacted the Pakistani and Malaysian UN contingents and alerted them to the situation, asking if they could help. They had to check with their national chains of command.

McKnight had not briefed the rest of the force on the new objective. The drivers did not know where they were headed. The convoy repeatedly got lost. It circled, twice passing near the crash site but unable to link up with the raiders defending it. The EP-3 saw the Somalis emplacing barriers made of burning car tyres. Moving around them exposed the convoy to crossfire from RPG-7s at cross-streets.

The ground convoy soon became lost in the unmapped streets and ran into a Somali ambush. After losing two 5-ton trucks and an HMMWV to RPG fire and suffering numerous casualties – of the sixty-five men who started from the original objective, three were dead and forty-five, including McKnight, were wounded – the ground convoy group was forced to abort its mission of linking up with the troops at the crash site.

After forty-five minutes, McKnight's convoy ended up back at the Olympic Hotel. Casualties and damaged vehicles made further advance impossible. The vehicles were shot almost to pieces. Casualties were mounting, now including three of the twenty-four Somali prisoners. At 1715, McKnight – with most of his vehicles wrecked and more than half of his men casualties – received orders to withdraw back to the airport. Withdrawing back through the K-4 traffic circle at 1740, they linked up with the initial reaction force dispatched from the airport. The troopers from the initial reaction force provided security while they moved the ground convoy's wounded out of a disabled HMMWV (that was being pushed along by a 5-ton) on to one of their 5-tons before destroying the HMMWV. Both forces were low on ammunition and McKnight ordered the reaction force to withdraw with the ground convoy, strengthening its fire power. The ground convoy had to fight its way back to the airport, suffering more casualties, before reaching the perimeter at 1818.

While the ground convoy battle was going on – the trucks presumably attracting most of the Somali attention – the forces at the crash site were reinforced by more raiders at 1726. They fought their way on foot from the original objective in a running battle that led to more casualties, until there were about eighty raiders – eventually going up to about 100 – at the site, spread over 'The Alamo', as the troops termed the three city blocks around the wrecked helicopter. Fighting around the crash site perimeter was heavy, but there was no way that casualties could be evacuated by helicopter. Helicopters provided fire support and were able to drop in medical supplies and ammunition. The raiders informed the JOC at 1655 that they were unwilling to withdraw and leave the bodies trapped in the helicopter to be obscenely mutilated, the fate suffered by those from Courage 53. But even if they had been willing to withdraw, the increasing number of non-walking wounded made it tactically impossible for the raiders to fight their way out on foot.

THE SECOND BLACK HAWK GOES DOWN

At 1640, Super 64 – an MH-60 providing fire support to the perimeter around the crash site – was hit in its tail rotor by an RPG-7. Super 64 had replaced Super 61 when it went down, providing support near the original objective. This, in effect, set up a fresh target in a predictable flight pattern for the Somali RPG-7 gunners to try again. Although the helicopters varied their speed and altitude, the racetrack pattern made them vulnerable.

The MH-60 went down in a built-up area over 2 km from the first crash site. The two pilots and two crew chiefs on board survived the crash, all badly injured.

With the CSAR team already committed, little could be done. Other helicopters stood by to provide covering fire. At about 1717, two of three Delta Force snipers on board Super 62, MSGT Gary Gordon and SFC Randall Shugart, volunteered to fast-rope down to try to save Super 64's survivors. To the Delta snipers, trained to survey and assess a complex tactical situation, it apparently seemed that they could get on the ground, help the survivors and hold off the Somalis long enough for a rescue attempt to be made.

The first two requests to be inserted were denied over the radio, as Somali forces were amassing around the second crash site. After getting approval from the JOC, Super 62 attempted to land at the second crash site, drawing heavy fire. Instead, the two snipers were inserted 100 m to the south. They literally shot their way through to the crash site, supported by an AH-6.

At the crash site, the two snipers lifted the crew members from the wreckage of Super 64 and opened aimed fire on advancing Somalis. The wounded helicopter pilot, carried into a firing position by the snipers, also opened fire with his MP5, but had only two magazines. The AH-6 stayed in support for as long as it had ammunition, then moved in to try to lift out the wounded from the crash site. It had to be ordered back into the air when it became apparent that Somalis would reach it before the wounded helicopter crew.

At the second crash site, helicopter attacks and the snipers' accurate fire kept the Somalis at bay for as long as the ammunition lasted. At 1727, Super 62, which had stayed above the second crash site to support the snipers, was hit broadside by an RPG round. It managed to stay airborne long enough to crash-land at a UN base in the New Port area. The crew – all badly wounded – survived.

With the helicopters gone and the snipers' ammunition running out, the Somalis started to close in on the second crash site. The snipers used the helicopter crews' MP5 sub-machine-guns once their rifle ammunition was expended. SFC Shugart was fatally wounded. MSGT Gordon checked the wounded and dazed pilot, gave him Shugart's M4 carbine for self-defence and wished him good luck. Gordon defended the crash site with his pistol until he went down. Then the crash site was overrun. The crew chief's body was dragged through the streets for the benefit of video cameras, and the footage, shown worldwide, dominated the reporting of the raid. The helicopter pilot – CWO2 Michael Durant – was taken prisoner. There were no other US survivors. The snipers were awarded posthumous Medals of Honor, the first awarded since Vietnam.

THE QRF BATTLE

The QRF, under the operational command of the 2-14th's commanding officer LTC Bill David (accompanied by the two-HMMWV battalion tactical command post), was organized around reinforced C Company of the 2-14th Infantry. It was under the command of COL Casper's brigade TOC. It had been alerted at 1414, before the raid – though not told of its time or location – and therefore was standing by not at the airport but at the more distant university, where there was a UNOSOM II base. The QRF was brought to thirty-minute readiness at 1537, and at 1630 it was ordered to move to the airport. COL Casper at the TOC ordered four AH-1F and OH-58C helicopters to readiness in support.

While an advance on the second crash site may have been quicker from the university, Garrison decided to bring the QRF – mounted on nine 2.5-ton trucks and twelve HMMWVs – to the airport and reinforce it before sending it out.[28] It would be 1724 before the QRF moved up to the airport, using a longer bypass route to avoid resistance.

Arriving at the airport, David conferred with Garrison and received a quick briefing on the situation at the JOC. The QRF would be controlled by

TF Ranger. LTC Van Arsdale would go with them. The QRF was dispatched to the second crash site from the airport at 1735. Within ten minutes, it was ambushed and engaged in a firefight near National Street, 300–400 m north of the K-4 traffic circle. At 1810, the QRF was still pinned down and making slow headway. David said, 'That really surprised me because we had done extensive operations in Mogadishu and had been in a number of firefights already, but these ambushes were by far the heaviest action yet.'[29] Dismounted assaults were required to clear Somali positions.

The QRF was ordered to retreat to the airport at 1830, as the JOC was by then aware that the second crash site had been overrun. Two AH-6 helicopters were called in. The QRF managed to break contact – this took an hour of hard fighting – and withdrew towards the airport with heavy casualties. At around 1850, the AH-1Fs and OH-58Cs finally went into action to cover the withdrawal. David saw that his wounded were taken off the remaining vehicles and then reported back to Garrison. His men would be required for a new advance on the two crash sites. The delay in relief was no consolation to the men at 'The Alamo'. The JOC log entry for 2035 read: 'There is a lot of frustration over QRF/QRC not moving to assist. MG Garrison, [name deleted, probably LTC Harrell] and LTC McKnight discussing QRF plan of attack with BG Gile and QRF staff.'[30]

THE UN FORCE COMMITTED

Montgomery, realizing that further uncoordinated attempts to break through to the two crash sites were unlikely to be successful and would suffer additional casualties, ordered BG Greg Gile – from the 10th Mountain Division and temporarily in Somalia – to organize a deliberate relief attempt using UN reinforcements. A reinforced relief force consisting of a platoon with four Pakistani M48A5 tanks, two companies with twenty-eight Malaysian Condor wheeled APCs and four command APCs, and a TF Ranger force of fifty-six men and seven HMMWVs, plus US and UN trucks and HMMWVs – a total of about 100 vehicles – was organized. They would move to both crash sites and then retire with the raiders and their wounded to the Pakistani UNOSOM II base at the stadium.

Because the Pakistanis and Malaysians had not been informed of the TF Ranger operations, it had taken them five hours to get their forces ready for combat and clear the operation with their national chains of command.

These two contingents had previously had US Special Forces liaison teams attached to them, but these had been ordered to withdraw by the US earlier in 1993. The command authority was to remain unclear. The Pakistani and Malaysian forces were ready at the UN positions in the New Port area when the US component of the reinforced relief force left the TF Ranger base at the airport at 2230.

1Lt. Charles P. Ferry was executive officer of A Company of the 2-14th: 'The company commander made sure we all understood that we would not come back without all American dead and wounded.'[31]

The heavier UN forces joined up with the US forces. These included the QRF, now joined by A and B Companies of the 2-14th Infantry and any Task Force Ranger personnel still able to fight, including the survivors of the evacuation convoy, the first reaction force and McKnight's ground convoy who were now back at the airport with their surviving Somali prisoners. Other 2-14th forces soon joined them: the battalion scout and anti-armour platoons and an attached anti-armour platoon from the 1-87th Infantry. After exchanging liaison teams, the multi-national column moved off at 2330.

RAIDERS AT BAY

The UN column was ambushed soon after it left the New Port area, and by midnight had fought its way down National Street. There, at 2350, the column divided, one part, with C Company of the 2-14th, heading towards the second crash site, while the remainder, including A Company of the 2-14th, continued on to the first crash site. B Company of the 2-14th would be the reserve. The Pakistani tanks had led the column that far. Now it would be the 2-14th in Malaysian APCs. The Pakistani tanks refused to advance further. The APCs, after the 2-14th removed road blocks, reluctantly advanced.

The plan was for the 2-14th infantrymen to stay mounted for as long as possible. Once at the objective, they were to dismount to allow the wounded from TF Ranger to be loaded inside the APCs. However, neither the 2-14th light infantrymen nor the Malaysian APC crews had ever trained in these tactics. Language difficulties made co-ordination inside the APCs difficult. The lead two APCs from the force heading to the first crash site became separated and stumbled into an ambush. The APCs were knocked out by RPG-7s, killing a driver. The US troops and Malaysian APC crews were forced to take up defensive positions in nearby buildings. Helicopters – AH/MH-6s now joined by AH-1Fs – were called in to give them support. The second platoon of A Company was soon engaged with an estimated 1,500 Somalis. 'They climbed trees to shoot at us, they were inside buildings, on top of buildings, in all ways,' said SPC Ralph Scott.[32]

With most of the surviving Somali forces – depleted by losses, lack of ammunition and sheer physical exhaustion – apparently diverted to this fight, the remainder of the C Company column advanced to the second crash site at 0227. They found no Americans there, alive or dead, only the wrecked helicopter. The wreck was destroyed with thermite grenades.

The C Company column that had advanced to the second crash site now had to fight its way back. It altered its route to move towards the A Company platoon and the surviving Malaysian vehicle crews that had been in the two APCs that had become separated from the other column as they had advanced towards the first crash site. Fortunately, these troops had been able to dismount from the vehicles and set up a defensive position in nearby buildings. The mortally wounded Malaysian APC driver was recovered from his abandoned vehicle. This force then established radio contact with C Company as its forces, retiring from the second crash site, were closer than those from A Company. They held on in their defensive positions, with helicopter support, and awaited pick-up by the C Company column.[33]

The C Company column had to fight its way through. The Malaysians were reluctant to lead with their thinly armoured APCs; they had been trained to keep them back in support, their tactics modelled on the British use of Saxon wheeled APCs. C Company launched a dismounted assault, using fire-and-movement tactics. They cleared away the main blocking position and opened a path to rescue the 'lost' A Company force, then re-mounted the APCs. The C Company column then withdrew to National Street, rejoining the Pakistani tanks.

The A Company column with its Malaysian APCs had to fight its way forward to the first crash site against heavy fire. The company commander made the decision to fight through to the objective. He would not divert the advance to rescue the 'lost' men from his second platoon and the Malaysian APC crews (these would be picked up by the C Company column as it retired). Approaching the first crash site, the APCs encountered a roadblock. The Malaysians again declined to push through – an antitank mine under the obstacles could catastrophically destroy a Condor – and so A Company dismounted. This led to a large-scale firefight as A Company advanced from National Street to the vicinity of the Olympic Hotel, starting at 0036. US HMMWVs with MK-19 40 mm grenade launchers provided the infantrymen with direct support. Casualties included one dead from A Company of the 2-14th. By 0120, A Company was within 300 m of 'the Alamo' where the men of TF Ranger were holding on at the first crash site.

The perimeter around the first crash site, held by CPT Steele and ninety-nine exhausted raiders, was spread over several buildings. At 2025, they had called the JOC: 'If QRF does not get there soon, there will be more KIAs from previously received WIAs. Get the one-star to get his people moving.'[34] A resupply helicopter arrived that evening, bringing food and ammunition and evacuating some of the wounded, despite sustaining serious damage from Somali fire. Other helicopters dropped medical supplies and ammunition. The lack of night-vision equipment hindered operations.

1Lt. Di Tomasso had been forced to let his wounded lie during daylight hours: 'When darkness fell we immediately started moving the casualties into the buildings. The litter patients went first, then the walking wounded, then the dead.'[35]

Concerted attacks were made by the 'Little Bird' helicopters, which remained in support of the raiders, flying sortie after sortie, re-arming and refuelling at the airport. Many flew nine or ten sorties that day. No one was keeping count. They used running and diving fire attacks against the most threatening Somali groups. The sustained helicopter support was critical in preventing the ground force from being overrun. But even in the difficult tactical situation the helicopters still had to follow the RoE. 'Even when we knew there were bad guys, we couldn't shoot if civilians were in the way,' said CWO3 Mike Goffena.[36]

The Somalis, having suffered heavy losses in daylight, were now less able to organize sustained assaults on their defenders. Under cover of darkness, they even brought up their coveted truck-mounted 23 mm guns to hammer at the perimeter.

The relief column arrived at the first crash site at around 0200 on 4 October. Under RPG and small arms fire throughout the night, the combined relief force secured the perimeter around the crash site and worked to free the pilot's body. The surviving members of TF Ranger consolidated their defensive position, taking with them over twenty wounded and four dead.

WITHDRAWAL

A Company held the perimeter with support from AH-1Fs. By this time, A Company was starting to run low on ammunition. This was a signal for Somali fire to increase. The casualties – including the body of the pilot of the first helicopter – were loaded aboard the Malaysian APCs, which were soon retreating at high speed towards the Pakistani stadium by 0530. The remainder of the force moved out on foot by 0542, supporting the APCs. The Somalis, seeing the preparations for a withdrawal, increased their fire, throwing in last reserves. The SP 23 mm AAA went into action near the Olympic Hotel. One was knocked out by AH-1Fs.

The retreat, which has entered SOF history as the 'Mogadishu Mile', was met with small arms and RPG fire. Several Rangers were hit and loaded into the APCs. Helicopters were called in to rake cross streets with fire as the force passed. The APCs, taking fire, accelerated and lost contact with the raiders on foot who were supposed to provide mutual support. They charged through the fire, heading straight for the Pakistani base at the stadium. LTC David ordered all movement halted until the Rangers were picked up, but the Malaysians did not get the word.

Ranger Spec4 Melvin DeJesus was one of 'forty Rangers running beside the APCs. All of a sudden, the APCs took off, leaving us with no cover. We were alone in the streets.' Stranded without APC support, the raiders ran on, firing as they went.[37] APC support was requested from the JOC at 0605.

The EP-3 and helicopter video showed Garrison at the JOC that the column was in danger of disintegration. While a number of the APCs continued to head for the stadium at high speed, he was able to pass new orders. Some of A Company dismounted and launched a counterattack to link up with the running TF Ranger rearguard before it could be surrounded. The rearguard was now made up of intermixed TF Ranger and A Company personnel. Helicopter support was called in for the rearguard, including AH-1F attack helicopters of the 2-25th Aviation.

1Lt. Ferry recalled: 'As soon as the company began to move, heavy small arms and RPG fire erupted on all sides. Squads and platoons bounded by fire and movement, laying down heavy suppressive fire while elements sprinted across alleys. Several Somali gunmen were shot and killed at almost point-blank range by the lead element. The Somalis seemed to know we were making a break for it and were giving us all they could.'[38]

ABOVE 4 November 1979: CPL Steve Kirtley, US Marine guard at the Tehran embassy, surrenders to Iranian Revolutionary Guards starting the hostage crisis. *USMC*

25 April 1980: the burnt-out wreck of the EC-130 abandoned at Desert One. *Department of Defense*

OPPOSITE TOP Somalia: US troops digging in at sunset. US forces preferred to operate by night in Somalia due to their superior night-vision optics and training. *Department of Defense*

LEFT US Marine Force Recon operating from a CRRC boat. SEALs used these boats extensively at H-Hour in Operation Just Cause. *Department of Defense*

ABOVE An MC-130 demonstrates its flares, used for self-defence against heat-seeking missiles. MC-130 crews, themselves SOF, take great risks to support SOF on the ground. *Department of Defense*

SOF (USAF parajumpers) fast-rope from a US Air Force MH-53 Pave Low special operations helicopter. *Department of Defense*

ABOVE Since 11 September 2001, US SOF have been increasingly committed to the counter-terrorist mission. Here a US Marine Force Recon team exercises with the Coast Guard in Exercise Northern Edge, 2002. *Department of Defense*

A USAF MH-53 Pave Low refuels from an MC-130P tanker. This capability was key in the Son Tay and Koh Tang raids and in many CSAR operations. *USAF*

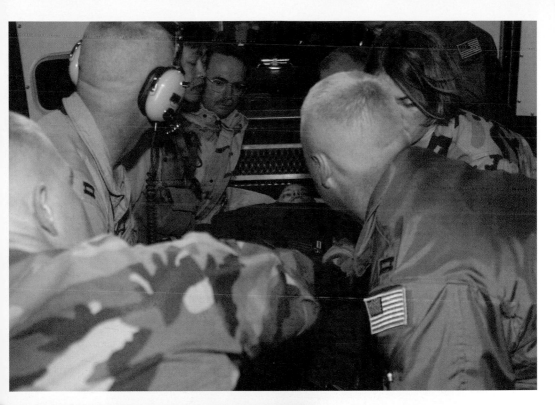

OPPOSITE TOP 22 July 2003: a 101st Air Assault Division TOW anti-tank guided missile launcher on top of a HMMWV light truck during the raid that killed Saddam Hussein's sons. *Department of Defense*

LEFT SOF operations in Afghanistan were carried out by integrated coalition forces. British and Australian officers join their US counterparts to brief Donald Rumsfeld at Bagram AB. *Department of Defense*

ABOVE Iraq, 2003: US Army PFC Jessica Lynch, back in US hands, becomes the first US PoW rescued by a successful raid since 1945. The raid encountered minimal opposition and demonstrated an effective quick-reaction planning capability. *Department of Defense*

TOP 22 July 2003: the house
where the Hussein brothers were
killed. The raid in Mosul turned
into a pitched but one-sided
battle. A TOW is in flight (next to
the utility pole), heading towards
the objective house. *Department
of Defense*

LEFT The objective house in
Mosul, showing the blast effect
around the windows from TOWs
fired inside. *Department of Defense*

BELOW Objective Rhino,
Afghanistan, 2001 – shown after
the airfield had become a US
forward operating base. The
guard tower (Objective Cobalt)
displays the damage received
during the raid of 19 October.
Department of Defense

On National Street, the column linked up again, supported by the Pakistani tanks. Some of the Rangers continued on foot. Others were picked up by US HMMWVs and trucks. By 0620, LTC David reported that all personnel were loaded and movement could continue. The retreat ended at 0630 as they moved through the perimeter of the Pakistani stadium UN position. The wounded were swiftly medevaced by helicopter to hospitals. AH-1Fs destroyed the wrecks of the two Malaysian APCs lost the night before.

Back at the airport, TF Ranger watched, on their CNN feed, video taken by a Somali journalist of the mob dragging the body of a crewman from the second lost helicopter through the streets. These powerful images, out of all that had gone on in Mogadishu over the past two days, were the first to shape the impression of events. It was a demonstration of how the realities of the twenty-four-hour news cycle and the power of instantaneous communications could affect even military operations.

This concluded what was intended to be a 'surgical' direct action and ended up as the most intense US military ground battle since the height of the Vietnam War. TF Ranger and the QRF suffered eighteen killed, one taken prisoner and eighty-three wounded. The Malaysians in the relief force suffered one killed and several wounded. The Pakistanis suffered no serious casualties, reflecting the invulnerability of main battle tanks in Mogadishu.

Somali casualties were estimated to be 200–1,000 of Aideed's fighting men dead, two to three times as many wounded and an indeterminate number of civilians. TF Ranger estimated enemy losses as 364 killed in action, 754 wounded. Even hardened Somalis such as Abu Cali, a medical worker at a Mogadishu hospital, was horrified: 'I thought all Mogadishu had died.'[39] In addition, twenty-four Aideed supporters – including some of the key lieutenants who were the original target – were captured.

When it was determined that CWO2 Durant, the surviving pilot from the second shot-down helicopter, was alive and being held by Aideed's forces, there was widespread sentiment in TF Ranger for an immediate liberation mission. But in the aftermath of the battle there was no way that US HUMINT could locate him. While loudspeaker-equipped helicopters overflew Mogadishu to reassure Durant that they would get him out, there was never sufficient intelligence to target a liberation mission. There was no alternative but to leave him in the hands of the enemy. Durant was eventually released after negotiations with Aideed.

AFTERMATH

Aideed called a unilateral cease-fire on 9 October; he had lost many of his fighting men. Meeting with US representatives soon afterwards – including LTG Anthony Zinni – Aideed appeared visibly shaken and wanted to avoid another battle. What both the UN and Washington had seen as the major impediment to the success of UNOSOM II – Aideed's power – had been crippled, even if his authority and popularity with his clan remained strong. This might have provided the opportunity for UNOSOM II to compel Aideed to agree to a cease-fire on its own terms by threatening further offensive operations. Garrison and Howe pressed their US and UN superiors respectively to take the initiative against a weakened Aideed.

Instead, it was the US political will – in Washington, not Mogadishu – that failed. Disturbed by the television images, the Clinton administration considered the battle a failure. Clinton demanded of his advisers the day after the raid: 'How could this happen?' This demonstrated how disengaged he had been from the decision-making process. In the absence of a coherent US policy in Somalia, the level of US casualties was considered unacceptable in the White House.

The lack of a coherent US policy was also evident in administration explanations to Congress. Congress, too, saw the action as a failure and would not support continuing US policy in Somalia. The decisions of the White House and Congress rather than the results of the raid ended up sending a message. To terrorists worldwide, Somalia, like Lebanon in 1982–3, was not seen as the US simply ending a costly multilateral mission that had outlived its original motivation and had limited political support at home. Rather, it appeared once again that the United States was a giant with a glass jaw. Kill a few Americans and the rest will run away. The US had proven casualty-averse. Yet, it appeared that had the administration or, in the absence of strong leadership from that direction, major Congressional leaders, chosen to galvanize and rally public opinion, such an effort would have received public support.[40]

Despite the policy collapse in Washington, the raid was itself a success. TF Ranger had won its battle, albeit at high cost. It appeared that the raid of 3 October had indeed succeeded. It had seized Aideed's subordinates – they had been captured and had survived the battle of the ground convoy – an action which had led to an unplanned decisive battle. The decision to disengage from Somalia – made on 4 October before there could be any assessment of what the fighting had really meant for the situation on the ground – ensured that this victory had little meaning. This result, in the words of SSgt. Dan Schilling, an Air Force CCT member who had fought with the raiders through the battle, 'turned what was a hard-fought, brutal victory into a defeat.'[41]

As a result, instead of following up on the fighting of 3–4 October, the US deployed additional forces to Somalia in a show of force. Tanks, AC-130s, a carrier task force and marines were all deployed. US policy was to negotiate for the return of the captured helicopter pilot from the second crash site, to bring in reinforcements with instructions to avoid conflict and to set a deadline – 1 March 1994 – for getting out. The UN would have to make its own deal. All the prisoners captured in Operation Gothic Serpent were released in January 1994.

With the US withdrawal, southern Somalia continued in anarchy. Aideed eventually died in bed in 1995. He was succeeded in his leadership role by his son, Hussein Aideed, who had served as an NCO in the US Marine Corps, including during Operation Eastern Exit. He remains a leader of the Habr Gidr.

The end result was an unhappy one. The US military identified the lack of US AFVs to extricate the special operations force as a key contributor to the events in Mogadishu. Indeed, this led to the sacking of Secretary of Defense Les Aspin, who had refused to approve their deployment. Washington had to have a scapegoat and it was not going to be the astute CJCS, GEN Colin Powell, who had invoked the 'Powell Doctrine' to advise against the commitment in the first place. The tensions over Mogadishu contributed to the bad relations between the Clinton administration and the military leadership. In the 1996 presidential election, Senator Robert Dole, challenging Clinton, would (unsuccessfully) try to make Mogadishu a campaign issue.

SOMALIA AFTERMATH

The raids of TF Ranger were intended to be limited operations aimed at a few named individuals that the US and the UN equated with the cause of conflict in Somalia. The Somali response to them was anything but limited. While the US may have considered the operations in Somalia to be 'other than war' and any combat operations 'limited' – hence the refusal to send tanks to

Mogadishu to support TF Ranger – this perception was not shared by their Somali enemies. To them, this was a conflict requiring the mobilization of every available weapon and person and to be waged until victory.

The raiders began 3 October 1993 by targeting Aideed – a legitimate mission to seize a hostile combatant. They ended up fighting an intense battle of attrition against a large number of Somalis. How a raid aimed at one target ended up fighting something quite different is a critical issue for liberation and seizure operations.

Americans love to personalize conflicts, even when they represent forces and movements much too complex and impossible to embody in a single individual. Characterizing Aideed as the centre of gravity – as Noriega was in Panama – seemed obvious at the time and led directly to the dispatch of TF Ranger. But with the advantage of hindsight, the centre of gravity was not an individual but rather the Habr Gidr clan and the SNA, coupled with their role in the brutal but effective system of armed *realpolitik* that emerged in southern Somalia after the collapse of the state. It was certainly easier to identify this man with the threat to US policy goals in Somalia than the less concrete realities of an underdeveloped and deeply divided country plunged into the status of a failed state.

The Somali response had been extensive and determined. Later accounts would ascribe it to fanaticism, bravery and the use of narcotics, or a combination of all three. Many of the individual Somalis involved had seen service either in the Somali Army in its conflict with Ethiopia in the 1970s or in the more recent civil wars. A few had fought as volunteers against the Soviets in Afghanistan (although the nationalistic Aideed did not support Islamic radicalism, he was happy to use it to gather support). They were armed, experienced and politically mobilized. The small Somali leadership cadre included trained (and competent) military officers. They were among crowds of armed men of their own blood on their own territory, resentful of the US presence. They did not need to wait for orders. They were able to take advantage of missteps by their opponents.

Aideed did not personally call out all the Somalis who engaged the raiders on 3–4 October, though he certainly helped to mobilize them. Rather, it was the nature of Somali politics and society that pushed them into the firing line when they saw others falling to the raiders' relentless fire power. The US saw what happened as an example of Third World ingratitude and intractability, revealing the Bakara Market to be but an outgrowth of Conrad's 'heart of darkness'.

In reality, what had happened on the Somali side was the same as what had happened in many places in the 1990s: a skilled, charismatic leader who had already risen to prominence under the old regime – Aideed – used long-standing clan, ethnic and religious ties to build a base of power and then used nationalism to rally mass support. With UNOSOM II having moved away from the more nuanced operational approach (and the skilful use of psychological operations) that had characterized UNOSOM I to an offensive military stance, it aided Aideed's stature and ability to rally support. Collateral damage from earlier US actions had been effectively used by Aideed to persuade the population that the foreigners were threatening the whole population, not simply him and the rest of the leadership. As a result of Aideed's political consolidation in his urban heartland, when the raiders appeared on 3 October, many Somalis responded with what they saw as the only rational response: 'You have come from a long way away for reasons I do not understand to interfere with me and my kind. I am going to make you sorry you did that.'

Fortunately for TF Ranger, their enemies – regardless of how many trained infantrymen and leaders leavened the game amateurs – were still a people in arms rather than effective infantry units and subunits. There were leaders with the training to direct fire-and-movement manoeuvres in co-ordination with those supporting weapons, to close with and destroy the enemy (which remains the infantry's business today, as it has ever been), but they were not necessarily in the right place or recognized as being in charge by the fighting men. There were few supporting weapons, regardless of how many Kalashnikovs and RPG-7s were in action that day.

The Somali tactics have been characterized as 'swarming'. Independent groups, with knowledge of the terrain and the enemy location, were not acting in response to the orders of a chain of command. Each group sought out weak spots in the US forces on the ground. However, there was no way for the Somalis to concentrate these swarming groups or organize an assault that could have overrun US positions. Since a 'swarming' force operates automatically, in response to a situation, orders do not have to be communicated. It also meant that no one – including Aideed – could have given the order to disengage and prevent a decisive battle or concentrate to wipe out one US group. The lack of a command structure reduced the effectiveness of US SIGINT in being able to determine enemy actions.[42]

The savagery of the fighting also provides a reminder that the 'barbarization of warfare' that took place in the twentieth century is unlikely to be absent even in 'other than war' situations. The Somalis demonstrated their willingness to slaughter those who fell into their hands – even noncombatant journalists – and drag and dismember their bodies. Such actions were not simple pathology, but had political impact. Film footage of US bodies being dragged from the second crash site was critical in changing the political support for the mission in Mogadishu.

LESSONS FOR SPECIAL OPERATIONS

The political and leadership issues were so profound that the hard tactical realities of the raid tended to be overlooked – at least until they appeared in a best-selling book and a Hollywood movie. The special operations response tended to focus – deservedly – on the withdrawal of the AC-130s and the failure to provide AFVs for the QRF. Yet special operations direct action cannot be restricted to missions where they can receive support from heavy forces if required. The record of the fighting shows a number of deficiencies that could have proven fatal against more capable opponents. The raid itself shared many factors with other raids that had run into trouble. It had been forced to remain too long at the objective. It had to be relieved by heavier combined-arms forces – and was fortunate that these were (belatedly) available. The level and capability of resistance had been underestimated. While the SOF in Mogadishu were much better organized, trained and equipped than those that went into Grenada, they suffered from many of the same limitations in carrying out their mission. The largely negative media treatment experienced by TF Ranger raised expectations while increasing pressure for results.[43]

The improvised and divided command structure in Mogadishu contributed to the raid turning into many separate and dispersed battles of attrition. The US won them all (except for the heroic last stand at the second crash site), but the division of forces and the lack of a concentrated reserve proved costly. The divisions between TF Ranger and the QRF were reflected in the latter force's more remote starting location, the delay in calling for them and vectoring them where they were most needed. The company of

Green Berets deployed in Mogadishu was only called in to treat the wounded. The Pakistanis and Malaysians were not available when the situation was most desperate. They and the US forces were unfamiliar with each other's tactics, limitations and the constraints imposed by their chains of command.

TF Ranger had been configured to operate independently. It was apparent that this was not feasible by 3 October, but the organizational scheme was not changed. As in earlier raids, problems with organization, compounded by lack of rehearsal (TF Ranger had had one with the QRF but none with the Pakistanis and Malaysians) were reflected in the results on the battlefield. Had the QRF been under TF Ranger and had the Special Forces liaison teams been present with the allied forces (and had the US paid the diplomatic price of asking for their support for TF Ranger before the need arose), the results of 3 October might have been different.

The events in Mogadishu never approached the stereotypical Vietnam situation where a US platoon leader in a firefight could often look up and see battalion, brigade and division command helicopters stacked up like airliners over La Guardia Airport, each one intent on issuing orders to the ground combat. The stateside command structure, at SOCOM, the Pentagon and the White House, had refrained from direct involvement in the battle. This allowed President Clinton to express his shock after the fact that such an operation had been mounted without his express approval. This contributed to the increasing political tension between the Clinton administration and the military leadership.

Although Washington did not intervene in the battle itself, there was a strong top-down component influencing how the raid was to turn into a pitched battle. There were no AC-130 gunships to support the raiders. The AC-130 has provided accurate fire-power support for US special operations forces for a generation. The AC-130s that had been in Somalia in previous months had been withdrawn by the Chairman of the Joint Chiefs of Staff to reflect the guidance for a 'minimum footprint'.

At the same time, the decision was taken to deny Garrison's request for tanks and IFVs to reinforce the QRF. The special forces liaison teams that had been attached to the Pakistani and Malaysian forces under UNOSOM I were withdrawn because no one thought these units and their AFVs would be required to support TF Ranger.

Despite TF Ranger's (curtailed) pre-deployment training and the six previous raids, this was their first real battle. As a result, even these élite troops exhibited many of the flaws seen in any unit plunged from garrison into combat. The transition from the garrison mentality – especially that of the US military of the 1990s – to one that is focused on winning under fire proved to be a difficult one, physically and mentally. It had not been carried out in Mogadishu by 3 October 1993. As the raid became a battle of attrition, even well-trained tactical commanders became indecisive, waiting for orders that never came because they were subject to multiple levels of command, theoretically all netted in to them by reliable communications and, presumably, better informed than the men on the scene because they had access to greater intelligence and battlefield awareness pictures. Orders were left unchanged regardless of the fluid nature of the situation. Despite the high level of training of the personnel involved, too often those who should have been leading ended up having to do the jobs of more junior personnel. That this should be the case even when all levels of command were significantly better trained and had the opportunities for better mission planning than in previous conflicts suggests that this problem will not be easily addressed.

The raiders and the other US forces alike fought with great bravery, but those who planned and organized the raid failed to act with sufficient tactical flexibility. The failure to pull together a second CSAR team from assets already on the ground or at the airport when the second helicopter went down meant that it was left to two courageous snipers to secure the site. They greatly deserved their posthumous Medals of Honor, but their job should have been given to a CSAR-tasked helicopter force. Quick-reaction CSAR capabilities, to extract shot-down crews before they can be killed or captured, are vital for heliborne raids. The raiders' leadership failed to have an organized reserve to extract a downed helicopter – or any other contingency during the raiders' withdrawal – or a plan to deal with losing more than one helicopter.

Liberation and seizure operations tend to be inherently joint air–ground operations. This was not reflected in the limited air assets available to the raiders or in the use of those assets that were available. The original plan – templated in haste to respond to fresh HUMINT – did not take into account the increasingly effective anti-helicopter tactics that the Somalis had demonstrated in previous weeks. The raid's planners left the MH-60s as RPG targets, orbiting the area in familiar patterns for forty minutes after the initial insertion. Even after the first Black Hawk went down, TF 160's aircrew kept their MH-60s in close support of the raiders on the ground, displaying great courage but, in the end, proving counter-productive as more helicopters went down and leading directly to the tragic last stand at the second crash site.

The reason the plan kept the MH-60s, armed only with sniper teams, in the area for such a length of time was the absence of proper air support for the troops on the ground. The 2-25th Aviation's AH-1F Cobra attack helicopters (and their associated OH-58C scout helicopters), though fully capable of daylight operations, were not used to support the raiders until the UN force was assembled. This was a major limitation. Had they been available to support the AH/MH-6 'Little Birds' of the 160th SOAR earlier in the day, it could have reduced the pressure on the Rangers.

The Somalis were indeed surprised by this particular raid. However, the advantages gained by surprise – a critical element in any raid – were negated by adherence to a template. The enemy knew how the raiders operated and their response, once the initial surprise wore off, was able to take advantage of this. The fall from the fast-ropes and then the first shootdown meant that the raiders could not withdraw from danger while they still had the benefit of surprise. The raids staged by TF Ranger had been against one objective at a time, with an interval of several days for the Somalis to recover between each one. There were not the repeated, relentless, near-simultaneous raids on multiple objectives that had been seen in the hunt for Noriega in Panama. TF Ranger lacked both the resources and intelligence support for such actions.

There is seldom enough training or rehearsal time. The QRF had only exercised one linkup with TF Ranger before being called on in deadly earnest. It is possible that with better integration, planning (especially regarding routes of advance) and rehearsal that the QRF might have fought its way to the second crash site before it was overrun. As it was, although the second crash site was fewer than 5 km from Mogadishu Airport, it might as well have been on the dark side of the moon.

TF Ranger's equipment prevented the unit from coming apart and disintegrating under relentless Somali fire power. The ability of the armoured HMMWVs to absorb hit after hit and keep moving, the troops' body armour, the widespread provision of medical supplies and knowledge all contributed to keeping alive men who in an earlier conflict would certainly have been lost.

TF Ranger's supporting weaponry was short on both precision and fire power. The helicopters had to rely on 7.62 mm machine guns and 7 cm rockets. The only precision weapons among the ground raiders were sniper rifles. Far from being able to use technology to make possible 'precision engagement', TF Ranger, returning fire, was in no position to discriminate between those Somalis with obvious weapons and those without. Any view of the nature of future war that does not take Mogadishu into account provides poor guidance indeed. Laser sights with 'death dots' or helicopters with more accurate Hellfire missiles could have inflicted heavier loss on the enemy with less collateral damage.

The raiders could not make up for the lack of precision with fire power. They had no indirect-fire weapons. LAW and AT-4 antitank weapons, left behind by the raiders, could have countered Somali RPG-7s. TF Ranger's use on vehicles of MK-19 40 mm automatic grenade launchers – an excellent suppressive weapon – was limited. The need for armour protection for gunners on HMMWVs had been identified in Panama but had not been implemented.

Garrison told a Congressional inquiry, 'I was totally satisfied with the intelligence effort – never saw anything better from the intelligence community.'[44] Even with all the strengths US intelligence had at Mogadishu, for a raid to turn into a battle of attrition unexpectedly must constitute intelligence failure. The weakness in HUMINT was more than the failure to develop networks that could locate and target Aideed. It reflected that there was no available equivalent to the Spanish-speaking Panama-based Green Berets who had used their language skills and local knowledge to chase down Noriega with the full support of the new government.

Gen. Hoar, the CINCCENT, identified a 'real problem with HUMINT. The people who provided information lacked credibility . . . The possibility of getting predictive intelligence on Aideed was poor, it was. But we did everything favourable to produce the intelligence.' The HUMINT weakness was partially responsible for TF Ranger's low operational tempo. It carried out a few large raids against high-value targets at lengthy intervals. This is less effective than many raids against the target's base of support, both cutting away the target's support infrastructure and also offering the opportunity to generate intelligence. TF Ranger did not have either the targeting information or, more importantly, the numbers, to be able to hit all possible Aideed locations in a compressed timeframe.

The communications links, which had worked perfectly in Panama, experienced a number of key lapses. Most importantly, the EP-3's key sensors were not directly available to McKnight and the ground force advancing from the original objective to the first crash site.

While press reports of the fighting placed great emphasis on TF Ranger's unwillingness to leave behind US personnel killed in the helicopter shootdowns, this actually had little direct impact on the action. There was no time at which the forces at the first crash site could have withdrawn prior to the arrival of the large relief column, even had they been willing to abandon the trapped bodies of the pilots. The commitment to 'leave no man behind' was admirable, but it was no bravado.

What saved TF Ranger from disaster and allowed it to turn a raid into a hard-won, potentially decisive victory – which was then cast away due to the inability of the US political leadership to build on it – was the quality of the troops. Despite the problems with their tactics, the lack of resources and limitations with their training – all of which were seen repeatedly under fire – they redeemed failures in the raid's planning and command. They were resolved to 'leave no man behind' and won a major victory in doing so.

THE MOGADISHU LEGACY

Since Mogadishu, at a tactical level, SOF have sought to address the problems seen in action through stressing what they term their four fundamentals: marksmanship, physical fitness, battle drills and medical training. The new marksmanship training includes the split-second target-acquisition skills required in an urban environment, including distinguishing non-combatants. The importance of medical treatment capability in keeping a unit able to fight was demonstrated in Mogadishu and such skills cannot be limited to the relatively few medics in the TO&E. It was underlined that the US cannot rely on evacuation to treat casualties. As a result, SOCOM has put an increased emphasis on medical treatment facilities and teams that can be inserted along with raiders for on-the-spot treatment. These innovations were first seen in action in Afghanistan in 2001–2.[45]

300 LEAVE NO MAN BEHIND

Somalia ensured that the 1991 Gulf War model would remain the US example for future conflicts, but modified with an emphasis on what was soon termed 'force protection'. Marine Lt. Gen. Bernard Trainor (rtd.) looked at the influences from the 1990s on US defence policy: 'The Gulf War reaffirmed the Pentagon's orientation towards classic warfare where enemies meet on a common battlefield. But there is no enemy on the horizon likely to fight that kind of war against the all-powerful US military . . . Intellectually the military recognizes this likelihood but culturally it is still wedded to its traditional concept of warfare represented by its victory in the Gulf.'[46]

The legacy of Somalia remains – despite the terrorist attacks of 11 September 2001 – in the form of political sensitivity to any level of casualties, in the hunger for an 'exit strategy' to precede any US military action and in the increasing political involvement of the military leadership. The multiple layers and parallel structures of command that undercut TF Ranger had reportedly been recreated in Afghanistan by late 2003, with similar negative impacts on SOF capture missions. This legacy effectively intersected with the lessons of Mogadishu – training for fighting in Third World conurbations and training for appropriate levels of combat at the unit level (even if high-level direction remained weak) in the streets of Baghdad in the summer of 2003.

CHAPTER 10 AFGHANISTAN: KANDAHAR AND OBJECTIVE RHINO · 19 October 2001

Too often we elevate safety of decision over decisiveness.
We may admire Jackson but we imitate McClellan.

LTC Ralph Peters, US Army (rtd).

US SOF were heavily committed to all their many missions throughout the 1990s. They were an integral part of many relief and peacekeeping operations (most notably in northern Iraq, Haiti, Bosnia and Kosovo). Non-combatant evacuation operations (NEOs) were frequently required, especially in the more turbulent areas of Africa. SOF provided training to armed forces worldwide, including nations that a few years before had been part of the Soviet Union.

SOF AFTER THE COLD WAR

US SOF structure was spared major cutbacks in the post-Cold War reduction in force that took place in the 1990s. In one three-year period alone, funding was reduced by six per cent but operations increased by over fifty-one per cent.[1] In 1991–4, SOCOM forces were dispatched to over 140 countries to accomplish 1,300 missions. But the reduction of the overall force structure meant that there was a smaller pool of trained personnel for SOF to draw on and fewer resources available. This led to a shortage of funds and a high operational tempo that made retention of skilled personnel difficult. But with support from SOCOM and Congress as well as an increased realization by Washington of their versatility and effectiveness, SOF were far from returning to the 'hollow forces' post-Vietnam era.

The threats changed, too. US SOF doctrine, tactics and training concentrated on the asymmetrical threat that had been emerging even before the end of the Soviet Union. SOF have advantages as a weapon to counter these threats. They can precisely target and defeat small-scale adversaries without the need for large-scale military operations. The gunmen in Mogadishu and their shadowy allies – trans-national terrorists, narcotics traffickers and other challenges to peace, liberal democracy and free trade – were more likely to be the future enemy than a developed country.

Because such groups place great value on holding prisoners and hostages for prestige and bargaining, and because of the importance of individual leaders to such groups – in ways familiar from the cases of Noriega and Aideed – it might be expected that liberation and seizure missions would have received a correspondingly increased emphasis as a tool of US policy. But this was not the case. Rather, the 1990s saw a greater awareness of the potential political and diplomatic costs of liberation and seizure missions that led to a reluctance to execute them even against what appeared to be suitable targets.

Part of the reason was the shadow of Mogadishu, which hung over US special operations raids for the rest of the 1990s. Also remaining strong was the 'Powell Doctrine'. Originally expressed by then CJCS GEN Colin Powell as part of his opposition to Operation Just Cause, it stressed that military force – including SOF – should only be used when the national interest is clearly at stake, when there is public support, a clearly defined national mission and exit strategy and the ability and political will to apply overwhelming force. The 'Powell Doctrine' fuelled military opposition to the US commitments in Haiti, Bosnia and Kosovo that was eventually overcome by the Clinton administration. Overwhelming force, by definition, did not apply to a raid, especially a small, covert one. The 'Powell Doctrine' also required political leaders to put themselves on the line before ordering military action. Few would be willing to do so for a high-risk operation such as a raid.

In practice, the 'Powell Doctrine' shifted the burden of US military commitment to the politicians, while its insistence on overwhelming force undercut the importance of SOF and rapid response by less than massive forces. This contributed to the continued politicization of US military decision-making and its shift towards a 'zero-defects' risk-minimizing approach. While special operations forces were heavily committed to a range of missions throughout the 1990s, the issue of liberation or seizure missions ordered by the national command authority remained a difficult one.

The rise of the terrorist threat to the US – demonstrated by the attack on the World Trade Center in 1993, the attacks on US embassies in East Africa in 1998, the attack on the USS *Cole* in 2000 and the events of 11 September 2001 – forced a reassessment of the utility of special operations raids. This brought new emphasis to SOF operations – especially seizure missions – as part of the war on terrorism. It also brought forward an explicit attempt to reverse the culture of risk aversion that had limited the use of SOF. Yet the changes brought about after 11 September could remove neither the risks nor the limitations – of which risk aversion proved to be only one – associated with liberation and seizure missions.

SOF AFTER MOGADISHU

While not called upon to carry out liberation or seizure missions, US special operations forces were heavily committed to contingencies worldwide after Mogadishu. US Army GEN Henry Hugh Shelton, CINCSOCOM, even became CJCS. Clinton appointed him after his first choice ran afoul of newspaper reports that he had committed adultery. Hugh Shelton was not considered an intellectual by the standards of US SOF. He was professional, with excellent people skills, stolid and risk-averse. At SOCOM, he had carried out the task that the Clinton administration had imposed on the military as a whole – do more with fewer resources – without complaining or calling the press to leak information (as other generals had done in order to defeat Clinton policies). Most importantly, in terms of the politics of the Clinton administration, he eschewed adultery.

The ability of theatre SOCs to support CINCs was also demonstrated in the 1990s. Their ability to work with SOCOM headquarters back in the US to project forces for a wide range of missions was demonstrated in Bosnia in 1995. Special Operations Command Europe (SOCEUR, the EUCOM TSOC) put some of the first troops on the ground during the US commitment. In the former Yugoslavia, US Air Force combat search and rescue (CSAR) and US Marine Corps tactical recovery of aircraft and personnel (TRAP) missions rescued the three US fighter pilots shot down during the conflicts there in 1995–9.

Throughout the 1990s, NEOs, especially in sub-Saharan Africa, rescued many – American citizens and others – threatened by unrest. SOCOM forces carried out many of these operations. Others were carried out by non-SOCOM forces, especially Marine Expeditionary Units (Special Operations Capable).

In 1997, the Department of Defense formalized a new mission, personnel recovery (PR), defined as 'the sum of military, civil and political efforts to obtain the release or recovery of personnel from uncertain or hostile environments and denied areas whether they are captured, missing or isolated'. However, PR was not intended to include liberation missions to free hostages, or terrorism and counter-terrorism situations. In addition to SOCOM capabilities, a Joint Personnel Recovery Agency (JPRA) was established as executive agent for PR under US Joint Forces Command, taking over the responsibility from the Air Force. In part, this reflected the Air Force's lack of priority for investment in the CSAR mission area in the fifteen years following the establishment of SOCOM.[2] The new JPRA had a mandate to work with all the services and SOCOM on developing PR capabilities. While this new redefinition of the long-standing requirements may not have added additional capabilities, it was evidence that the US defence establishment was not ignoring the issues.

While training and retention were difficult and research and development and procurement spending was limited through the 1990s, special operations forces were able to maintain their high quality of personnel and readiness. While much-needed major items of equipment – most notably the tilt-rotor MV-22 Osprey aircraft – did not appear, innovations such as computerized mission planning and improved availability of intelligence information through enhanced computer technology contributed to mission technology.

RAIDERS OF THE 1990S

Raids tend to be high-risk operations. As a result, the US military – especially the Army – of the 1990s did not consider them tactics of choice. Thus, of the 600 training missions at the National Training Center (NTC) and the Joint Readiness Training Center (JRTC) of the US Army, there were only thirteen heliborne raids during 1989–96, the timeframe that included Panama and Somalia.[3]

The Marines, however, did not share the Army's suspicion of such raids. Each MEU (SOC) had to be assessed as proficient in raiding capability before deploying. A new manual on raiding, FMFM 7-32, was issued in 1993. The Marines saw raids as being a natural extension of their most usual deployment: small, well-trained forces with integrated helicopters and reliable communications to the NCA and CINC alike, intended for quick reaction. An MEU (SOC) is not intended to fight and win decisive or prolonged combat; thus a raid may match capabilities to the task at hand. Achieving a strong raiding capability also helped the Marines to underline their utility. The MEU (SOC) remained outside SOCOM control.

The training raids carried out at the NTC and the JRTC (and many of those practised by Marines) were tactical raids. Those at the NTC and JRTC were executed on the orders of divisional commanders and were not attempting penetrations beyond the range of supporting artillery. Despite these relatively limited objectives, they still proved to be high-risk operations. Liberation and seizure raids that are not part of an overall combined arms operation – as in Grenada or Panama – are likely higher risks still. At the NTC and JRTC, the raiders suffered twenty-five to eighty-eight per cent casualties. US Army planning guidelines are that the raiders should remain at the objective for no more than thirty minutes if the helicopter LZ is at the objective (as was successfully done at Son Tay) or 120 minutes if the LZ is at a distance from the objective. At the NTC and the JRTC in 1989–96, the average time on the objective was 270 minutes.[4] Most of the raiders – Rangers included – suffered from loss of surprise, poor IPB, ineffective fire support, poor planning and loss of command and control.[5]

SEIZURE MISSIONS THAT NEVER HAPPENED

The limitations on US liberation and seizure missions certainly did not start with Mogadishu. Risk aversion is only one reason why the US has often not used its SOF in classic liberation or seizure missions when these might have been a viable policy option. This included the 1992 commitment of Delta Force to Colombia to pursue drug kingpin Pablo Escobar.[6] While Delta Force deployed to Colombia, along with specialized intelligence assets, it was decided that the operations that would end up killing Escobar had to be carried out by the Colombian police. This reflected Colombian laws, the desire not to make him a nationalist martyr, the US executive order prohibiting assassinations and the US military's reluctance to become involved in the drug wars, as well as casualty aversion.

In the former Yugoslavia, it was threatened that US special operations forces would be used to seize individuals wanted as war criminals, first in Bosnia and later in Kosovo. This threat was never carried out. The US military did covertly track some of these individuals and seizure missions were apparently planned and rehearsed, yet none was ever carried out.[7] The reasons were 'security problems, distrust among allies, a lack of useful intelligence and disagreements among senior officials over how much to risk in the attempt'.[8]

The backing for seizure missions against war criminals came from GEN Wesley Clark, then Supreme Allied Commander Europe (SACEUR), and US Secretary of State Madeleine Albright who, as ambassador to the UN, had been one of the foremost advocates of the hunt for Aideed in Mogadishu (and who was a tireless opponent of the 'Powell Doctrine'). Opposing them were on-the-scene military commanders afraid that such missions would lead to casualties or a revival of the conflict in the former Yugoslavia. The military commanders, like Powell himself, tended to be Vietnam veterans with deep and personal links to those serving at the 'sharp end'. They had seen the body bags once and were reluctant to do so again. Most notable among these was the Commander of the Stabilization Force (SFOR), the multinational force in Bosnia, US LTG Eric Shinseki (who was to be appointed Army Chief of Staff by Clinton).

In practice, the requirement for 'actionable' intelligence leading to a seizure mission was raised so high that it was not practical to achieve it in the former Yugoslavia – especially Bosnia – even with high-level US intelligence operatives and headquarters making this a priority. The fact that many of the most wanted individuals habitually went around with a large entourage of bodyguards – weapons and ex-soldiers were both inexpensive in the postwar former Yugoslavia – meant that even a successful seizure mission was likely to result in casualties. The fact that the US was operating as part of a coalition also meant that it was possible for other members (especially the French) to leak information to prevent an operation that was not seen as being in their own interests. The US responded by putting in place a US-only operation, codenamed Green Light. It was aimed mainly at seizing the former Bosnian Serb leader and wanted war criminal Radovan Karadzic. It never led to a seizure mission.

The Clinton administration proposals for the CIA to seize individuals such as Radovan Karadzic and General Ratko Mladic through covert operations did not progress because of the lack of trained personnel, leading one former administration official to complain, 'The CIA didn't have the capability to take down a three- or four-car motorcade with bodyguards.'[9]

As a result, NATO assets, chiefly but not exclusively British, German, Dutch and even French – not those of SOCOM – handled any such actions as part of a collaborative programme codenamed Amber Star. Most of those targeted, however, were low-level war criminal suspects. While Karadzic and Mladic were never the targets of a full-scale seizure mission, there are reports that some of the lesser war criminals who 'voluntarily' turned themselves in to the war crimes tribunal at the Hague – most notably Serb 'ethnic cleanser' Blagoje Simic – were in fact brought in by SOF.

RAIDS AND AFGHANISTAN: 1998

The lack of real damage resulting from the US military operations – militarily ineffective though politically significant cruise missile strikes on Afghanistan and Sudan – that followed the 1998 terrorist attacks in Africa led to an increase in Osama bin Laden's profile and influence. Indeed, the Clinton administration emphasized that the cruise missile strikes on terrorist facilities in Afghanistan were not targeted at Al Qaida terrorist group leader bin Laden in person – they did not want to be seen as targeting a specific individual, even a terrorist leader.[10] As a result, rather than returning to low-lethality cruise missile attacks, there was an increased willingness in Washington to consider raids as an option.

President Clinton himself had proposed a raid to capture bin Laden and the terrorist leadership in Afghanistan in late 1998. He asked Shelton about options involving 'boots on the ground'. The President and the civilian political leadership was hoping that the Pentagon would be able to come back with a rapier precision strike to take out bin Laden in revenge for the embassy bombings.[11]

Shelton was dubious about the feasibility of such a raid. However, some of the planners on the Joint Staff believed that a small-footprint raid, employing stealth, would be able to use speed and surprise to successfully seize bin Laden, given accurate intelligence. Accurate intelligence was the sticking point. The US reportedly had none of its own HUMINT agents on the ground inside Afghanistan and had to rely on recruited Afghans. The NSA lost its ability to monitor bin Laden's satellite communications in 1998, apparently as a result of a media leak.[12] US intelligence relied on second-hand, fragmented and often questionable HUMINT.[13]

Shelton insisted that any such raid would have to be accompanied by a 'force protection package', especially for deployment at any intermediate ('Desert One') stop. He stressed the importance of having a CSAR capability for any lost aircraft, especially SOF-carrying helicopters.[14] The requirements for such a force protection package were reportedly not so large as to make the raid unwieldy. What ended the plan was the opposition of the CINCENT, Marine Corps Gen. Anthony Zinni. He believed that such a raid, even if successful, would hurt the US diplomatically throughout the region, especially in Pakistan (whose airspace, if not territory, was likely to be required to allow access to the raiders). Shelton, whose management style was to consult with a limited number of senior officers, did not try to overcome Zinni's objections.

Instead, Shelton reportedly returned to the White House and told the administration that such an operation would require a multi-division force and many months of planning. Shelton's response was seen by the administration's civilian leadership – with the exception of Secretary of Defense William Cohen and Director of Central Intelligence George Tenet, who supported him – as non-responsive, confirming that the military was not interested in counter-terrorism in general and seizure operations in particular. Shelton reportedly thought that the military was being asked to make up for the weakness of foreign and intelligence policies through the use of high-risk actions. Shelton was expressing a consensus view of the senior US military when he opposed putting US 'boots on the ground' for a seizure mission in Afghanistan.[15] Richard Clarke, then the National Co-ordinator for Counter-Terrorism at the NSC, said, 'the overwhelming message from the uniformed military leadership was "we don't want to do this".'[16] This message was reinforced by concerns at the CIA, expressed by Tenet.[17]

As a veteran special operator, Shelton knew the record of previous liberation and seizure missions. He also would have known, as CINCSOC and then CJCS, about other raids during training. For example, at the Joint Readiness Training Center (JRTC) at Fort Chaffee, Arkansas, during Rotation 89-5 in 1989, a Ranger battalion staged a successful three-company liberation mission on a PoW camp, with one company assaulting the compound – fast-roping from helicopters – another company serving as a blocking force, the third as task force reserve. AC-130s provided suppressive fire. Despite part of the raiding force landing on the wrong LZ, the Rangers secured the PoWs and evacuated them twenty-six minutes later. A pitched battle ensued with quick-reacting enemy reserves. It was several hours before the raiding force was extracted. The cost, however, was adjudged to be 130 casualties to the Rangers. While this specific raid reflects the limitations of even the JRTC's excellent training – the enemy knew the raid was coming and had a company-sized force positioned to counterattack – after Lebanon and Mogadishu, the bottom-line figure taken into consideration when assessing the success of the mission was likely the casualties rather than the end result.[18]

Clinton decided not to push Shelton any further on his reluctance to consider a seizure mission in Afghanistan. In the words of Clinton first-term political adviser Dick Morris: 'Having ducked the draft, Clinton never felt comfortable with the prospect of sending young men and women to face death when he had refused to risk it himself.'[19] Clinton was also reluctant to force a further operation on the military with the situation in Kosovo deteriorating, husbanding both his political capital and military assets. The decision was made in 1998 that any further attacks on bin Laden would be with cruise missiles rather than SOF. 'If we really had good intelligence, missiles could get the job done more rapidly and with less risk' was how Secretary of State Madeleine Albright summarized the new emphasis.[20] Even then, when a two-hour 'window' opened during which a cruise missile attack could have been ordered on bin Laden in the fall of 1998, Clinton reportedly would not make a decision until after the opportunity had passed.[21]

The Department of Defense was reportedly not the only US government agency looking at a mission to seize bin Laden in 1998. The Federal Bureau of Investigation (FBI) planned to seize him from his compound in Afghanistan using a fly-in raid. According to press reports, the plan was rejected by Attorney General Janet Reno as being too risky.[22] One FBI agent characterized this as 'like telling the FBI after Pearl Harbor to go to Tokyo and arrest the Emperor'.[23] But this response was inherent in the Clinton administration's approach to terrorism as a law enforcement rather than a national security problem.

PLANNING REVIVED: 2000
Clinton revived the idea of a special operation raid to seize bin Laden after his visit to Pakistan in April 2000. National Security Advisor Sandy Berger had a memorandum on the efforts to locate bin Laden returned by Clinton – 'And

he wrote back, this is not satisfactory. It was particularly related to how we find this guy. We have got to do more. And that prompted us to work with the Intelligence Community and the military on a new technique for detecting bin Laden . . . Actually it was very promising as a way of determining where he would be if we had one strand of human intelligence [reported to us].'[24]

Berger, pressed by the President, reopened the issue with Shelton. After discussions with Berger and Defense Secretary William Cohen, Shelton had a paper prepared containing 'twelve or thirteen' options for military options against bin Laden. This was considered to be aimed at 'educating' (i.e. dissuading) Berger from pushing for a seizure mission. There was no request to develop any of these options further into an executable plan.[25]

In 2000, Clinton asked Shelton about 'heliborne black ninjas' staging a raid on bin Laden's headquarters in Afghanistan. Clinton had come to believe that even if bin Laden was not seized, such a raid would have considerable deterrent and diplomatic value as a show of resolve.[26]

The scope of the envisioned raid was small, involving some forty raiders to be inserted by air-refuelled helicopters launched from US warships off Pakistan's Makran coast. Once the forces were in place, such a raid could launch given six to ten hours' advance notice of bin Laden's night-time location.

The Joint Chiefs opposed such an action. The risks associated with this type of raid and the difficulties in staging it weighed against it. Reportedly the Chiefs told the White House that a small-scale raid 'would be Desert One'. This repeated earlier objections raised by the Chiefs to using US special operations forces to seize wanted war criminals in Bosnia and Kosovo. Mogadishu had made them reluctant to commit troops without large-scale back-up, including army. To ensure that Clinton would not push for such an action, they pointed out that bin Laden and the terrorist leadership often travelled with their families. This issue had reportedly been raised by Tenet in 1998 to oppose the earlier proposed raid.[27] Clinton decided that he could not accept any collateral damage from a special operation that might harm the terrorists' dependants, as distinct from a cruise missile attack. He found this argument persuasive, using it in his first post-presidential interview to explain why he had limited military action against bin Laden to the cruise missile attacks.

Shelton remained opposed to a seizure mission, citing the lack of action-able intelligence. 'You can develop military operations until hell freezes over, but they are worthless without intelligence . . . Look at the risk associated with swooping in . . . You don't put US armed forces in another country if the President doesn't declare war.'[28] This thinking would have, in effect, ruled out many of the US liberation or seizure missions already carried out since 1945. He was also opposed to joint operations with the CIA: 'I want to make sure the military piece of the plan is under military control, and not predi-cated on the CIA's piece being successful.'[29] To the CIA, however, it appeared that, as in Bosnia, the military leadership was simply raising the standards for actionable intelligence required for an operation – including a seizure raid – to a level far beyond that which the intelligence community would ever be likely to produce, thereby avoiding the need to order such a raid.[30]

Clinton did not push against the Chiefs on this issue. He managed to prevail against their opposition on a number of issues in his second term – most notably the Bosnia and Kosovo actions – but only after lining up (reluc-tant) support from Congress. He was aware that the military could prevent a raid by leaking information about it to the press – an escalating tactic in the (often poisonous) 1990s civilian–military relations in Washington.[31]

Planning for the raid had included a covert survey of a remote airfield, codenamed Rhino, which would be set up as a base for a heliborne seizure mission by Delta/TF 160 assets flown in on transport aircraft.[32] According to one officer involved in planning, the stand-down order for the raid was a blow to those who had trained for it. 'We were ready to move. We failed to receive an execute order from the President . . . So out of concern for sixty Delta Force operators and SEALs who are ready and eager to perform the mission, we lose thousands of people at the World Trade Center.' A Delta Force veteran added, 'It makes us sick to our stomachs that we couldn't go after this guy.'[33] As for the impact of calling off the operation, 'Nothing embold-ened Al Qaida more than us not going after them,' was the judgment of Michael Rolince, former head of the FBI's international terrorism section.[34]

US SOF did have the ability to operate with small teams inside Afghan-istan at that time. A CIA document commenting on the prospects of a military seizure mission against bin Laden said that there was 'lots of desire at the [military] working level' but that there was 'reluctance at the political level'.[35]

Another proposed seizure operation aimed at an unidentified terrorist was planned by Delta Force to be a covert operation carried out by a single four-man team. By the time the plan had been reviewed – presumably by the regional CINC, SOCOM and the JCS – the scope of the operation had expanded to 900 personnel. This reflected both 'rice bowl' concerns for service and force involvement and risk aversion. One senior SOF figure began referring to the Delta/SEAL liberation and seizure capability as being as expensive and as useless as 'a Ferrari that's never taken out of the garage'.[36]

With the military reluctant to launch a raid against bin Laden, the CIA decided to put together a covert paramilitary capability that could be used to seize him. In 1998, Clinton had issued a 'finding' – a classified executive order – authorizing covert action operations against bin Laden.[37] However, the actions would not be undertaken by US forces, but rather by allied forces.[38] Under the codename GE/Senior, the CIA put together a force of some thirty Afghans, able to operate as five-man scout teams, to track down bin Laden and report his location. However, they had no access to the Al Qaida leadership[39] and were never able to provide the information in a way that would make it possible for US raiders to go into action. The eyes-on HUMINT was absent.

As a result, the leader of the Afghan group proposed to the CIA that his group be concentrated together and that they ambush bin Laden. This was rejected by the CIA. It was perceived as being too close to a political assassination. This was followed by a proposed plan for the Afghan group to seize bin Laden so that he could be turned over to US law enforcement. But as bin Laden was unlikely to 'come along quietly' and was invariably accompanied by a large number of bodyguards, this was seen as equivalent to an ambush. There was no attempt made by the CIA leadership to have such covert raids approved by the White House; it was considered unlikely that the Clinton administration would be willing to carry out such actions even against bin Laden. The CIA was aware of the risks involved with such operations; this included the risks associated with HUMINT.[40]

Predator UAVs based in Uzbekistan were used to overfly Afghanistan, starting in August 2000, to search for bin Laden and reportedly spotted him three times in the course of eleven sorties during 2000. This led to extensive discussions – not put into action – of the possibility of using an armed version of the Predator to attack bin Laden. The Predator was not tested with a missile capability until after the Clinton administration left office.[41] The Clinton administration was left with cruise missiles from submarines (when collateral-damage concerns permitted) as their only policy option. While two cruise-missile-armed submarines were kept on station in range of Afghanistan off the coast of Pakistan throughout 2000, they did not fire.[42] On one occasion when a cruise missile strike was possible, the NSC was convened and decided against such a strike because of possible collateral damage to a nearby mosque.[43]

US military officials were reluctant to mount seizure missions against terrorist leadership or to support or participate in intelligence community operations, preferring instead to concentrate on the force protection mission as being more consistent with the preferred bureaucratic approach of their institutions and the risk-averse casualty-minimization priorities of the administration.[44]

The Clinton administration failed to act to seize bin Laden. Those who were involved in the decision-making defended this decision. Sandy Berger, the National Security Advisor, said, 'We did have an aggressive surveillance enterprise continually, but at no point was there actionable intelligence which would mean knowledge not only of where he might be but where he was going to be.'[45] But many involved in the process saw that against terrorists and in the former Yugoslavia, by insisting on either highly specific target information or assurances that there would be zero collateral damage, the White House and the Pentagon ensured that they would never be asked to authorize a mission that could fail.

THE 'FERRARI IN THE GARAGE'

The political and diplomatic cost of not liberating hostages or prisoners in political terms has made the risk-averse option – forswearing such operations unless there is a threat of imminent violence (as advocated by Cyrus Vance before the Iran Raid) – of limited appeal. Yet the record of the 1990s showed senior military leaders – many of them wearing multiple stars, chests full of medals for combat bravery and Ranger tabs – carrying out implicitly the policy Vance advocated explicitly (over which he was willing to resign yet unwilling to leak to the press).

In the 1990s, a 'zero defects' culture was identified as including 'first, an extreme reluctance to countenance casualties leading to an abnormal stress on force protection; second, risk aversion; and third, a lack of initiative'.[46] A British Army officer wrote of the US forces he observed in the Balkans: 'Generations of US officers are growing up without being encouraged to exercise an autonomous authority and with little instruction in how to assess and be prepared to take risks in pursuance of a military objective. Thus, there is an erosion of the key virtue that underpins every military organization: the moral courage to take risks.'[47] Such criticism is not limited to potentially envious allies. Former Army Chief of Staff GEN Dennis Reimer identified it as a 'scourge' of contemporary forces.[48]

The heyday of 'zero defects' in the 1990s (compounded by less money, a high operational tempo and the spreading influence of political correctness) contributed to the Clinton administration's appointment of generals such as Shelton and Shinseki, who shared these views, and the sacking of those, like Clark, who did not. The Clinton administration's politicization of the flag officer selection process to an extent unseen since the administration of Abraham Lincoln had a direct operational impact.

While concern about the impact of 'zero defects' has the potential to be an *apologia* for poor planning and inadequate training, it was in the 1990s – and remains – a shadow over the ability of future national command authorities or combatant commanders to use liberation or seizure operations.

The 'zero defects' era also meshed with US political trends. It was Congress that had pushed through the reforms of the 1980s and Congress that had, since then, ensured that SOCOM would not be cut back post-Cold War by passing budgets granting SOCOM its own lines of funding. The senior military leadership resented this funding. The services were still responsible for the vast bulk of military funding. They saw SOCOM's funding as an expensive luxury while, in the 1990s, they were short of money to buy and maintain tanks, aircraft carriers and fighter planes, capabilities they saw as central to US national security, while special operations were peripheral. The CINCs appreciated SOF more, especially with their ability to conduct low-profile training, assist in vital military-to-military diplomacy and help to carry out peacekeeping and NEO operations. However, neither the senior leadership in Washington nor the CINCs necessarily understood the capabilities and limitations of SOF.

2001 – OPERATIONS IN AFGHANISTAN

There was considerable continuity in the policies executed by the Clinton administration and those implemented in the opening months of the George W. Bush administration. However, the new administration started work on a more aggressive strategy against bin Laden. According to Deputy Secretary of State Richard Armitage: 'The National Security Council . . . called for new proposals [in March 2001] on a strategy that would be more aggressive against Al Qaida . . . sharp-end things that the military was asked to do.'[49]

Initially, the Bush administration continued to look at the proposal – inherited from its predecessor – for using armed Predator UAVs against bin Laden. While it was tested with the Hellfire antitank guided missile in 2001, doubts remained as to its lethality. The use of UAV attack in place of a seizure mission had not been decided.[50]

The events of 11 September 2001 changed the equation. In the words of a former Delta Force member: 'We've entered a new phase and it's about time. For the past ten years we all felt as though our hands were tied. Now it's finally down to going after the bad guys.'[51]

Within days, the US was mobilizing for military action against bin Laden's Al Qaida movement and its Taliban allies in Afghanistan. Agreements were made with neighbouring countries, most notably Pakistan. Intelligence and special operations forces teams were soon infiltrated into Afghanistan to link up with anti-Taliban forces even before the US air campaign opened on 11 October. Pre-positioning CSAR assets to support air operations over Afghanistan was considered a necessary pre-condition to the opening of the air campaign. This required deployments to neighbouring countries.

The military's hesitations and reservations were not completely gone – the JCS and CENTCOM initially insisted that any military action in Afghanistan be carried out by combined-arms forces with a ground component of multiple divisions assembled over an extended timeframe – but they were overcome by the urgency created by the terrorist attacks on the United States. Yet while the national resolve generated by the war on terrorism and policies put in place by Donald Rumsfeld as Secretary of Defense have mitigated the 'Ferrari in the garage' use of SOF from its height in the 1990s – reportedly based on a classified study that identified risk aversion in particular as having undercut the effectiveness of US SOF missions – this issue did not begin under the Clinton administration (and neither has it ended with the passing of that administration).[52]

The US military operations in Afghanistan demonstrated the full range of special operations capabilities. Combined with the Taliban's Afghan opponents, they were able to succeed in achieving military success on the ground in Afghanistan and installing a legitimate Afghan government in the capitol of Kabul, something the Soviet Union had been unable to achieve throughout its massive military engagement in Afghanistan in 1978–92.

The conflict proved, in retrospect, to be a demonstration of the capabilities of US special operations forces (and the associated covert action intelligence assets that also deployed to Afghanistan). The quality of the officers and NCOs on the ground was such that they were able to prevent the ever-present strains of Afghan politics and divisions from disrupting the war against the Taliban and Al Qaida. To the chagrin of many in the US government and media, the officers and NCOs of US special operations forces cut the Gordian knot of Afghanistan policy that had been seen as too difficult to resolve. This was made possible by the co-operation of the intelligence assets and capabilities that were thoroughly integrated in the operations.

The US special operations forces again proved to be excellent coalition warriors. They were able to work with anti-Taliban Afghans from many different political and ethnic groups. As the war progressed, special operations forces from throughout the world joined in. Foremost among them was the SAS: British, New Zealand and Australian. Special operations forces from Canada, France, Germany, Denmark, Norway, Turkey and other countries also operated in Afghanistan.

The command and inter-service relationships that had proven a burden for US special operations in previous decades were largely avoided in Afghanistan, reflecting the motivation provided by the events of 11 September and the absence of non-US command structures – UN, NATO or coalition – that had complicated operations in Mogadishu, Bosnia and Kosovo. Because Afghanistan was in its area of responsibility (AOR), the war itself was to be run by US Central Command (CENTCOM). Most of the forces came from SOCOM, playing its intended role as the 'supporting command' to CENTCOM's 'supported command'. While the SOCOM forces were to 'chop' to CENTCOM command – acting through SOCCENT, its TSOC – when in-theatre, they retained the ability to 'reach back' to SOCOM expertise to support mission planning and intelligence. While the co-location of CENTCOM and SOCOM headquarters – both at MacDill AFB, Florida – helped, SOCOM resented CENTCOM having to consider broader geopolitical concerns. Many at SOCOM also believed that CENTCOM was too orientated towards large-scale conventional operations and meeting service 'rice bowl' concerns. This divergence did lead to tensions – especially later in the campaign once larger numbers of non-SOCOM forces were deployed – but on the whole it worked better than it had in Panama. However, before the problems were resolved, Secretary of Defense Donald Rumsfeld reportedly considered putting the SOF in the theatre directly under JCS command – the 'stovepipe' model of Son Tay and Iran – and bypassing CENTCOM and its CINC, GEN Tommy Franks.[53]

The national command authority and the Joint Chiefs of Staff were also highly involved. In the wake of 11 September, the political and diplomatic dimensions were critical. This situation mandated quick and decisive action, made possible by the existence of professional special operations staffs and planners. There was no need to improvise one-time command structures for strategic raids as in previous decades.

Services were eager to demonstrate their flexibility, even with non-SOCOM assets. The Navy carrier *Kitty Hawk* was deployed to the region without an air group to serve as a floating special operations base. US Navy SEALs constituted an important part of special operations capabilities in land-locked Afghanistan. Two Marine MEUs were able to project power 'from the sea' to seize bases in southern Afghanistan with air-refuelled helicopter lifts. It was a far cry from the inter-service co-operation problems demonstrated in Grenada and Vietnam, decades before.

PLANNING FOR RAIDS

A raid to capture bin Laden or the Taliban's leader, Mullah Omar, was planned for the opening stages of the US campaign in Afghanistan. These individuals were, much like Noriega in Panama, the centre of gravity of the enemy. Putting them out of action was a primary mission of Operation Enduring Freedom, as the military operations in Afghanistan came to be designated.

Planning for the raid started in late September 2001, as US forces were deploying to the region. The plan appears to have borrowed heavily from that of the cancelled 2000 seizure missions, which would have seized Objective

Rhino as a forward operating base for a heliborne raid on bin Laden in Kandahar or elsewhere in Afghanistan. The planning was carried out, using a wide range of imagery (mainly satellite photographs), by Delta Force at Fort Bragg, North Carolina, Ranger Regiment headquarters at Fort Benning, Georgia, and SOCOM at MacDill Air Force Base, Florida.

The raid was targeted against two objectives. One was Mullah Omar's compound in Kandahar. The other was a remote airfield built on a dry lake-bed 130 km southwest of Kandahar and several compounds of associated buildings known only by the codename Objective Rhino. It had been part of the 2000 raid planning. Once secure, Rhino would serve as an FARRP for helicopters of the 160th SOAR that would be both lifting the raiding force against Mullah Omar's compound and inserting teams of special operations forces, mainly from the 5th Special Forces Group, to covertly join up with anti-Taliban Afghan forces around Kandahar. The raid on Objective Rhino was also intended to serve as a diversion from the raid on Mullah Omar's compound.

Thus there were to be, in the words of Army GEN Tommy Franks, CINCENT, 'essentially two of them [raids] . . . [One of the raids went into] Mullah Omar's compound. Another went into . . . Rhino. The rationale behind going with a special operations force raid into . . . Rhino was that we needed to understand the capability of that airfield. We wanted to understand how that airfield was defended. So that's why that objective was taken. The objective in downtown Kandahar was, for reasons you have probably already intuited, to prove the coalition forces were in this for the long haul, that we will go anywhere we chose to go. [In] part an information operation, in part in order to prove that we will place our forces in the middle of that country and in fact in Mullah Omar's home. So I think that the operation was an absolutely outstanding success both for . . . Rhino and for Omar's compound in Downtown Kandahar. It had the desired effects.' [54]

The Rangers may have felt the need to dispel the Mogadishu shadow – one reason why, as in Korea in 1950, Army cameramen would jump with them. The public – American and Afghan alike – was also looking for the 'boots on the ground' that would be the first parachute assault since Panama in 1989.

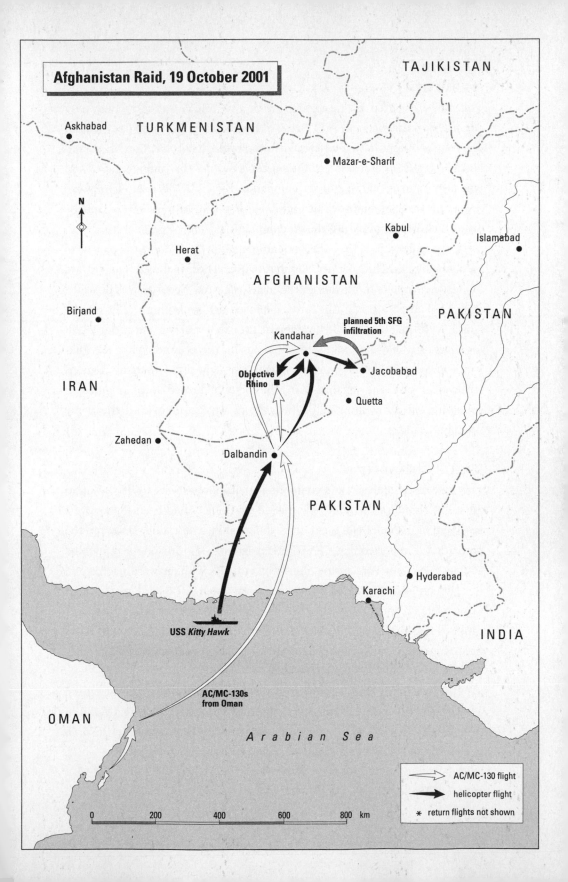

Afghanistan Raid, 19 October 2001

TAJIKISTAN

TURKMENISTAN

Askhabad

Mazar-e-Sharif

N

Kabul

Islamabad

Herat

AFGHANISTAN

PAKISTAN

Birjand

planned 5th SFG
infiltration

Kandahar

IRAN

Objective
Rhino

Jacobabad

Quetta

Zahedan

Dalbandin

PAKISTAN

Hyderabad

Karachi

USS *Kitty Hawk*

INDIA

AC/MC-130s
from Oman

OMAN

Arabian   Sea

0   200   400   600   800   km

AC/MC-130 flight

helicopter flight

* return flights not shown

PREPARATION

The raids were to be integrated with the allied air campaign over Afghanistan that opened on 11 October. The fixed-wing aircraft knocked out targets that might have interfered with the raid. The destruction of Afghan air defences was carried out in the opening days of the campaign. SOCOM was also a participant in the air campaign. By 15 October, AC-130s were operating over Afghanistan at night, joining US Army AH-64A Apache attack helicopters as part of the air campaign.

To provide support for the air campaign, SOCOM forces deployed to Jacobabad Airfield in Pakistan's Sindh province. These included Rangers and TF 160 helicopters to provide extraction if required. Security was provided at Jacobabad by a US Marine force, deployed ashore from an MEU off the coast. With their big CH-53E helicopters, they were ready to carry out TRAP missions as well as defending the US forces on the ground. While the Pakistani army guarded the outer perimeter and kept anti-American demonstrators at bay, the likelihood of the heavily armed local population squeezing off stray shots at US helicopters was so great that they only operated at night.

OBJECTIVE KANDAHAR

The raid on Mullah Omar's compound in Kandahar was to be the main effort.[55] Originally, the plan – developed by Delta – had been for a covert insertion of a small Delta team, to be followed by exfiltration. However, the plan grew – reportedly at CENTCOM insistence – to include a reinforced squadron of Delta Force using all-terrain vehicles with a covering force of a Ranger company.[56] The raid would be accompanied by US Air Force Combat Controllers. The operation as a whole would provide cover for the covert infiltration of a 5th SFG team that would work with anti-Taliban Afghans near Kandahar. Intelligence that Omar would be present was apparently limited.

Mullah Omar's compound was in a populated area near the city itself. This shaped the nature of the raid. Rather than using fixed-wing aircraft to drop bombs, SOCOM AC-130s would take out the other houses in the area before the raid. This would minimize collateral damage while hoping to force their occupants – known to be Taliban and Al Qaida leadership – to take refuge in Mullah Omar's compound, which was pointedly not targeted.

The heliborne raiding force – mainly Delta and Rangers – left the *Kitty Hawk* and staged through an unidentified Pakistani air base, presumably Dalbandin in Baluchistan province. Pathfinders were first into the LZ. The heliborne insertion – by TF 160 MH-47s – was remote from the compound to preserve the element of surprise. The helicopters then withdrew to Objective Rhino – now in US hands – to refuel and rearm.[57]

Inserted into the LZ, Delta Force used all-terrain vehicles to move out to the compound. The compound was reportedly seized with little resistance from the garrison, which mostly fled. However, as the teams cleared the buildings, it proved to be a 'dry hole'. Omar, not unexpectedly was not there.

After collecting intelligence material, Delta was preparing to withdraw when a strong force of Taliban – alerted by the fleeing garrison – staged a counterattack. The proximity to Kandahar had allowed them to gather a numerically superior force in a matter of minutes. A firefight ensued. Afghan and press sources called it intense, while a Pentagon briefing[58] described resistance as light.

AC-130s and AH-64As were available for support, inflicting heavy losses on the Taliban. Some twelve Delta troopers were wounded, one seriously. Long-range RPG-7 rounds – or, according to other reports, the raiders' own M203 40 mm grenades bouncing off objects and air-bursting – reportedly sprayed troopers with fragments. Abdur Rahman, one of the Taliban fighters involved, later claimed to a reporter that the raiders 'flew off like sparrows'.[59]

The Delta squadron used the air attacks to break contact with the enemy and egress the target area to an alternate pick-up site, rather than returning to the original LZ. Plans to infiltrate a 5th SFG team in the area that night were abandoned. Delta carried out its withdrawal successfully, without additional losses. They were able to load their vehicles back on board the helicopters. The TF 160 MH-47s were able to react and pick up both Delta and the Rangers, although not without some anxious moments. Under brown-out conditions, one MH-47 managed to take off *through* a stone and earth wall, leaving behind its nose gear. Had the wall been taller, it would have been everything Shelton and Shinseki had feared.

OBJECTIVE RHINO

Objective Rhino was, literally, not on the map. Its location, far to the south-west of Kandahar in a place remote and isolated even by Afghan standards, came about reportedly due to the desire of wealthy Arabs to fly in to enjoy hunting and falconry. The high-altitude (1,000 m) 1,950 m long dirt-surfaced runway had also reportedly been used by bin Laden, for flying out personnel and money to support terrorist efforts. The narcotics traffic in southern Afghanistan had also used the airfield. It was, as the situation in Afghanistan began to turn against bin Laden and the Taliban, an obvious place from which the leadership might attempt to flee the country. Objective Rhino was also seen as a likely place to establish the initial US conventional military presence in Afghanistan.[60]

Rhino had been kept under observation by the range of US intelligence assets – presumably satellites, aircraft, UAVs – and also through close-range reconnaissance by an eight-man SOF team, inserted to infiltrate and mark the drop zone after assessing and reporting back on the suitability for jumping and the lack of air defences. They sent back, via satellite communications, ground-level digital photographs of the installations at Rhino (a major technological improvement for raid planning). They also apparently reported back, immediately before the raid, that there were no high-value personnel at the objective. However, it was decided that the raid would go ahead, with the aim of providing a needed FARRP, gathering intelligence, providing a diversion from the Kandahar raid, providing a boost to the confidence of friendly forces and governments and putting the Taliban and Al Qaida on notice that ground forces were coming.

Insertion would be by an airdrop mounted from a base in the Gulf region not publicly identified but likely Masirah in Oman. This was also likely the site of the mock-up objective on which the raiding force rehearsed the mission.[61] The compounds around the airstrip were the ground objectives. Closest to the airstrip was objective Cobalt, a walled compound with watch-towers. MAJ Robert Whelan, S-2 of the 75th Ranger Regiment, described it as a 'frontier outpost', with a 2.5 m high wall and 9 m high towers. 'It was a self-contained compound attached to a 6,000-foot [1,820 m] runway right in the middle of Afghanistan.'[62] Objectives Tin (another compound), Iron and Copper were also to be seized.

The jump on to Rhino on the night of 19 October was carried out from four MC-130s by a 199-strong force, mainly of elements of the 3-75th Rangers with a command and control element from 75th Ranger Regiment headquarters. They were accompanied by a Delta Force team tasked with capturing any prisoners that might be in the objective's buildings and Air Force Combat Controllers to co-ordinate supporting AC-130s, control aircraft movements and to survey the airfield for its suitability for future US operations. It was to be the Rangers' preferred airfield direct-assault mission, to be followed by a withdrawal. US air strikes had already taken out the Taliban's air defence radar coverage, helping to ensure the element of surprise.

Before the Rangers arrived, the Air Force prepared the objective. The first target was Objective Tin, identified by reconnaissance as having an Al Qaida or Taliban garrison. It was hit by JDAM guided bombs dropped by a B-1B bomber. The flames from the JDAMs provided target illumination for an AC-130 to use its cannon against the enemy. Initial reports were that eleven were killed and that nine were seen to run into the darkness. AC-130s also engaged the towers and blew holes in the walls of Objective Cobalt. No targets were identified in Objective Iron, and Objective Copper could not be distinguished from the air; these were not attacked.[63]

The air attacks were followed by the insertion of a pathfinder team. While the means of their insertion has not been officially revealed, they may have jumped from an AC-130 using high-altitude low-opening (HALO) parachute techniques or were covertly positioned outside the target perimeter. They, like the in-position observation post outside the perimeter, were able to confirm back the lack of air or ground defences.

Approaching the target, four minutes out, the 3-75th's commander, LTC Joe Votel, led the Rangers in the lead MC-130 in reciting the Ranger's Creed. Special emphasis was placed on the words 'I will never leave a fallen comrade to fall into the hands of the enemy', which had acquired additional meaning since Mogadishu. As the Rangers approached the DZ, Specialist Martin Pasquez was surprised to see the MC-130 fill with dust as soon as the doors were opened, evidence of the low altitude and the fine airborne dust commonplace in Kandahar province.[64]

The Rangers jumped from 243 m. The jump itself went perfectly, with no resistance and few injuries. On the ground, the Rangers shot and killed a fleeing Taliban sentry. They quickly gathered up their parachutes (to prevent them from interfering with subsequent aircraft operations on the field) and moved out. A loudspeaker team from the 9th Psychological Operations Battalion quickly set up and broadcast demands for surrender in Pashto and Arabic.

Company A(-) and a sniper team formed up on the DZ, orientating them-selves by the fire at Objective Tin. They were the blocking force, preventing the enemy from interfering with the airfield or reinforcing Objective Cobalt. They quickly cleared Objective Iron without resistance and established their pre-planned blocking positions.[65]

Two platoons of C Company were to assault Objective Cobalt and then secure it, joining with the Delta Force team as they practised their black arts of entry and personnel seizure on the buildings. The AC-130 had not had much impact on Objective Cobalt's reinforced concrete construction, but had managed to blow a gap in the walls. The Rangers were able to carry out their well-rehearsed assault. There was no resistance. Inside, multiple locked doors and internal barriers – requiring demolition charges or being shot open – slowed the search. Clearing Objective Cobalt would take longer than planned.

The airfield and the buildings were searched for weapons. Some docu-ments were collected, few of which proved useful. A small cache of weapons and ammunition was discovered and rigged for demolition.

There was minimal resistance around Objective Rhino, but the Air Force Combat Controllers detected Taliban reaction outside the perimeter – a convoy moving towards Objective Rhino. AC-130s were called in. A further thirty enemy were believed killed.

While the plan suggests that the raiders had a good prior idea of Rhino's airfield capability, an Air Force team from the 23rd Special Tactics Squadron carried out a quick but precise survey of the airfield. It was suitable for C-130s and 'cautiously optimistic' even for C-17s. The first MC-130 to land arrived about twenty minutes after the airdrop. The MC-130 carried medical per-sonnel to treat the two injured jumpers and *matériel* to set up the FARRP. It was soon joined by other MC-130s.

Six minutes later, the helicopters of the 160th SOAR started to arrive to be refuelled. The Air Force Combat Control Team now acted as air-traffic controllers, sequencing and directing the landings and carefully controlling movement on the ground. With the FARRP operations completed and the search of the ground objectives revealing a 'dry hole', the raiders started to collapse the perimeter and withdraw to the MC-130s.[66] Clouds of fine dust raised by each aircraft created brownout conditions for up to fifteen minutes. The last MC-130 departed five hours and twenty-four minutes after the first Ranger jumped.[67]

During the raid, a Jacobabad-based MH-60 Pave Hawk helicopter crashed, killing two of the Rangers aboard and injuring three others. This helicopter had been ready to support an extraction from the raids inside Afghanistan. The crash, on the Pakistani side of the border, was reportedly caused by a brownout. The personnel and helicopter were recovered by the Marines of the 13th MEU (SOC) using CH-53Es to fly a TRAP mission on a second attempt (a previous attempt had come under fire by hostile local tribesmen).

IMPACT

The next day, the Chairman of the Joint Chiefs of Staff, Air Force Gen. Richard Myers, told a press briefing that the US had 'hoped' to capture Mullah Omar at his compound but was not surprised to find him gone. The aftermath of the raid on Mullah Omar's compound was seen in Kabul, with the hard-pressed Taliban displaying an obvious Chinook nose gear – the one sheared off by the wall – to assembled reporters and asking them to believe that the rest of the helicopter had also been shot down.

While no prisoners were taken, the raids served their usual secondary mission of making a statement as to the willingness of the US to use ground forces. Dramatic videotape of the jump was shown on US television in the days after the raid. As in 1950 (and 2003), press coverage had been among the objectives of the raid. The importance of this dimension was underlined by the raiders leaving behind posters of the American flag being hoisted over the ruins of the World Trade Center. The objectives had also included demonstrating – to enemies and friends alike – that after 11 September, US special operations forces were not going to remain impotent and were willing to close with and engage the enemy as required.

The raid became politically controversial in the US. The combination of the absence of prisoners and the presence of Army video cameras aroused media hostility, followed by leaked claims of Delta–CENTCOM divergences and the heavy fighting in Kandahar. These were swept away by the rapid victory in Afghanistan, but demonstrated the potential political risk inherent in raids. There were no further raids of this nature carried out by Rangers or Delta Force during the rest of the campaign.

The raids also served as diversions from the initial special operations helicopter insertions made the same night throughout northern Afghanistan, including in the Shomali Plain area near Kabul. The anti-Taliban Afghans saw these special operators as the evidence that the US was actually going to support them and would not limit its strike on the Taliban and Al Qaida to aircraft or to cruise missiles alone as in 1998. Thus began the military operations that were to lead to the downfall of the Taliban.

Rhino was kept under surveillance by SEALs. They were especially concerned with detecting any mines left by the Taliban to prevent use of the runway by the US. Rhino was reoccupied by a Marine heliborne assault on 25 November. It was then built up as Forward Operating Base Rhino until the Marines – joined by the 101st Airborne (Air Assault) Division flying in on C-17s and C-130s – made a heliborne advance to Kandahar, the last major Afghan city to be liberated. Mullah Omar's compound finally fell to his Afghan enemies and their US allies on 7 December 2001.

US SOF had been instrumental in the quick and decisive victory in Afghanistan. In the words of Marshall Billingslea, Deputy Assistant Secretary of Defense for Special Operations and Low-Intensity Conflict (DASD SO/LIC), 'The fight to topple the Taliban was waged on the ground by less than 500 special operation forces personnel. They mounted an unconventional warfare effort tied closely to indigenous forces and linked with United States airpower in a way that provided for a rapid and crushing defeat for the Taliban.'[68] The raids on Objective Rhino and Kandahar were peripheral to that effort.

SEIZURE OPERATIONS IN AFGHANISTAN, 2001–3

In the weeks and months after the initial raids, there were many additional raids carried out with the objective of seizing Al Qaida and Taliban personnel and equipment. Working with friendly Afghans, many of the raids used fresh HUMINT for targeting. Many raids were carried out by allied forces, one of the most successful being a full-squadron-sized operation by the British SAS.

As soon as the air bases at Bagram and Kandahar could provide jumping-off points for follow-on operations, CENTCOM set up an on-the-ground headquarters, Task Force 11, to co-ordinate US and allied special operations throughout Afghanistan.[69] The Task Force headquarters was intended to provide a quick-response capability integrating the many different SOF committed to the operations in Afghanistan, as well as providing links to the full resources of US intelligence. This aimed to address the problems with intelligence information and support being unavailable to SOF as in previous operations. This included an extensive HUMINT-generation and document-exploitation programme.

Sometimes the quick-response raids worked well. On 2 February 2002, a Predator UAV spotted Taliban Mullah Khaiullah Kahirkhwa leaving a building in Paktia province. Once the target was identified through live video feed, a quick-reaction raid, using SEALs and Danish special operations forces in a US Air Force MH-53M Pave Low helicopter, was airborne within fifteen minutes of the sighting, joining up with an escort of AH-64s. Within ninety minutes of being spotted by the UAV, the Mullah was a prisoner.

These seizure operations continued into 2003. The largest, Operation Valiant Strike, launched concurrently with the conflict in Iraq, brought in arms caches and some leaders, but not its intended objective of bin Laden and his sons.[70] While a number of these raids did manage to seize high-value prisoners, the most important targets – bin Laden and Mullah Omar – were not caught. While generally well planned and executed, a year after the operations started the major leaders of Al Qaida and the Taliban had still avoided the net. This reflects the availability of sanctuary over the Durand Line in Pakistan and the continued difficulty of carrying out such missions even with the improvements in the forces and capabilities involved.

Here, as in Panama with the Great Noriega Hunt, in Mogadishu and in Iraq in 2003, seizure missions became not a rapier thrust, but a 'battle of attrition' – removing potential hiding places – waged by SOF. The ability to hit multiple potential locations near-simultaneously and to 'roll up' the support infrastructure of a fugitive high-value target is key. The SOF suffered much fewer losses, but were more sensitive to them. Because the key target is a needle in a haystack, withholding SOF until the objective can be targeted is an ineffective strategy. Instead, the missions basically have to roll up simultaneously all locations and individuals associated with the target. Even if this does not lead to intelligence that makes possible a strike directly at the target, it reduces him to a fugitive, on the run from place to place. Without an organization to rely on, he will eventually make a mistake that will produce actionable intelligence.

By late 2002, there were criticisms that US special operations forces were concentrating on reconnaissance or searches for arms caches rather than taking the additional risks associated with raids to seize hostile leadership personnel.[71] Quick reaction had reportedly been limited by a need to submit a 'concept of operations' (less detailed than a plan or an operations order) for approval by Task Force 180, the overall US command in Afghanistan, based at Bagram Air Base. Part of the reason for this was the need to make sure that such operations were 'deconflicted' – that they were not likely to cause collateral damage by following bad intelligence and striking allied forces or friendly Afghans. The willingness of some Afghans to identify long-standing rival tribes or villages as concentrations of Taliban and consequently as suitable targets for air strikes made the US wary of uncorroborated HUMINT.

Many of TF 11's most experienced US personnel, from 5th SFG, Delta and SEALs, were sent to Iraq in late 2002. TF 11 was subsequently disbanded in mid-2003. It was replaced by TF 121, a CENTCOM-wide organization that would carry out seizure missions in Afghanistan, Iraq and throughout the CENTCOM area of responsibility. Like its predecessors, TF 121 integrates SOF and intelligence assets and, unlike them, has CIA assets as an integral part of the task force.[72]

The lessons of the CENTCOM–Special Operations friction were reflected in further refinements to the US chain of command. By late 2002, SOCOM could act as a 'supported' command, acting directly to wage the war on terror rather than organizing and providing forces for the CINCs to use as a 'supporting' command.

One of the lessons of Afghanistan has been bolstering the mission-planning capability of the TSOCs. Now the TSOCs at each CINC's headquarters will be potentially 'double-hatted', responding either to the CINC or directly to SOCOM as instructed by the national command authority. In the 1990s, the TSOCs were often short of trained personnel and resources. Since 2001 they have been considered critical in the global war on terrorism.

CHAPTER 11 IRAQ:
NASIRIYA · 2 April 2003; MOSUL · 22 July 2003;
AD DAWR · 13 December 2003

After 9/11, the gloves came off.

Cofer Black, former Director, CIA Counterterrorism Center.

This time I think the Americans are serious. Bush
is not like Clinton. I think this is the end.

Uday Hussein to Ala'a Makki, the former director
of his television station, 6 April 2003.

The war in Iraq in 2003 saw SOF take a much more significant and central place in coalition war-fighting than they had in the 1991 conflict. Several thousand SOCOM personnel were involved. US SOF were integrated with British and Australian counterparts and worked with forces from other coalition members, most notably Poland. SOF operated inside Iraq before the conflict, ranging from the borders to close to the Baghdad defences. SOF seized the key airfields in western Iraq – H3 and H4 – that in 1991 had been the base for Scud missile attacks on Israel. SOF effectively ran the northern front, working with anti-Saddam Kurds.

The 2003 SOF operations against Iraq – unlike in 1991 – included liberation and seizure operations. The liberation operations included a raid on 2 April 2003 that yielded the first US PoW freed by a raid since the nine Navy nurses at Los Banos in 1945. The seizure operations, aimed at Saddam Hussein, his sons and high-level regime leaders, encountered the same frustrations as had similar operations in Panama, Somalia and Afghanistan. But the sons were caught in a quick-reaction seizure mission in Mosul on 22 July. They were killed resisting capture by an overwhelming force. Saddam himself was seized without resistance by a raid on 13 December 2003.

OPERATION PACIFIC WIND, 1990

In the opening weeks of the 1990–91 crisis, following the Iraqi invasion of Kuwait, it appeared as if liberation missions would be a major part of any operation by US SOF working in co-operation with those of allied nations, most notably Britain. The US embassy in Kuwait City remained under virtual siege, with only a lone CIA operative acting as a courier in and out, infiltrating past the Iraqis. The British embassy was also under siege. Saddam Hussein announced his intention to use foreign nationals as 'human shields' against allied air attacks, underlining this with a bizarre television broadcast involving prisoner children.

The planning of liberation missions for both embassies and the human shields commenced at CENTCOM immediately after the invasion, co-ordinated with British liberation efforts. During the planning, intensive training and rehearsal began. A mock-up of the Kuwait City US embassy was constructed at a remote site in Eglin AFB and used by Delta and SEAL teams. Unlike the Tehran embassy, the proximity of the sea and the Saudi border alike provided opportunities for rapid infiltration and egress.

As SOF deployed to the Gulf, steps were taken to put the liberation mission into execution on short notice if it appeared that the Iraqis were about to use force against the embassy. US, British and other allied SOF soon set up contacts with the Kuwaiti resistance. US Navy SEALs carried out covert reconnaissance of possible routes to and from the sea.

The Pacific Wind plan included precision air strikes to cause an electrical power outage, suppress Iraqi defences and destroy a hotel near the US embassy that was occupied by Iraqi forces. The raiders would be inserted by helicopters which would then lift out the personnel from the US and UK embassies. Mindful of the lessons of Iran, full-scale joint rehearsals were held at a number of locations in the continental US (CONUS).

While planning and training for the liberation of the US embassy proceeded, even locating the human shields being held deeper inside Iraq was proving problematic. It was decided that three Delta troopers would be infiltrated into Kuwait and allow themselves to be rounded up in circumstances that would lead to them being identified as stay-behind civilians. They would, according to the plan, be added to the human shields. They would then use concealed transponders to provide their location.

Pacific Wind was cancelled in December 1990, with the release of the human shields and the Iraqi decision to allow the withdrawal of the US embassy personnel from Kuwait. At that time, there was also still hope that Iraq would withdraw from Kuwait in response to diplomatic pressure, and there was a reluctance in Washington to initiate military action, even for liberation missions. By this time, the embassy mission was well planned with a high degree of confidence in its success. The liberation plan for the human shields, however, still had to deal with the problem of their vulnerability to massacre by the Iraqis or to collateral damage in firefights. However, a post-war SOCOM analysis suggested that, in the light of hindsight, Pacific Wind would likely have been a success.[1]

SOF IN IRAQ, 2003

SOCOM went into the war in Iraq in 2003 with its stock higher than ever before following the victory in Afghanistan. In addition to effective joint operations, they had functioned successfully as part of a multi-national coalition. They would be called on to do so again in Iraq. In addition, SOCOM forces had been deployed worldwide as part of the war against terror, either operating directly against suspected terrorists and their infrastructure or, more commonly, training host-country military personnel in the basic elements of effective counterterrorism. However, direct-action missions – including liberation and seizure missions – remained less of a priority.

As in previous conflicts, there was tension between the special operations forces and the heavier forces. The CENTCOM–SOCOM tensions seen in Afghanistan were revisited but did not end up getting in the way of the mission as they had there. For SOF, having come from Afghanistan where they were largely running the US military operation, being considered secondary to the operations of army divisions and fighter-bombers was an area of tension. One SOF member said they felt like 'lions led by dogs'.[2] CENTSOC, CENTCOM's TSOC – under BG Gary Harrell (who as an LTC had been in the command helicopter for the decisive battle in Mogadishu) – was in a different facility from CENTCOM's main Joint Operations Center (JOC) at Doha, Qatar, and its perceived second-class status led to it being nicknamed 'The Ghetto'.

Secretary of Defense Donald Rumsfeld made a priority of opposing the Pentagon's risk-averse culture and worked to avoid repeating the policies of the 1990s that he saw as having undercut US military effectiveness. Secretary Rumsfeld's role in the Iraq conflict (as in Afghanistan) included pressing for greater reliance on and willingness to use SOF. This involved overcoming the suspicions of senior officers – in Washington and the regional combatant commands. Pressure from Washington to use SOF more effectively was reflected in CENTCOM's war plans. This led to criticism by the military that Rumsfeld and the Pentagon were micro-managing the deployment plan for the conflict. This reflected military (especially Army) mistrust of the Pentagon leadership and a belief that the Pentagon overestimated the value and effectiveness of SOF.[3] GEN Tommy Franks, the CINCENT, 'wouldn't have used special operations like he did in Iraq if Rumsfeld hadn't pushed him' according to Robert Andrews, former acting DASD SO/LIC in the Bush administration.[4] Another Washington official reported that Rumsfeld had intervened with CENTCOM to make sure that SOF were fully utilized. 'Without Rumsfeld you would not see all these things that Special Operations are doing.'[5]

Franks also developed a good relationship with Harrell and was receptive to input from him. The Army and Marine corps-level (and British) headquarters deployed to the region all had Special Operations Co-ordination Elements (SOCCE/SOCCORDs) to integrate SOF with operations in each corps area of operations. Regardless of where the pressure came from, the results contributed to the early collapse of organized Iraqi resistance and, after that, the long and difficult process of removing pro-Saddam guerrillas and groups.

THE CAPTURE OF PFC LYNCH

On the morning of 23 March 2003, five days into the conflict, it did not seem that a quick and decisive victory was in progress. Southern Iraq was proving to be infested with guerrillas – the *Fedayeen* Saddam – suicide bombers and children with handguns. The US decision to launch the conflict early – before the ground forces were assembled on the line of departure – meant that improvisation rather than detailed planning had to be relied upon.

Into the battle zone around the Iraqi city of Nasiriya came a convoy of the 507th Maintenance Company. An active army unit from Fort Bliss,

Texas, the 507th were service support troops attached to the US 3rd Infantry Division (Mechanized). Specialists in recovering and repairing weapons, the 507th were rear-echelon soldiers fresh from a stateside garrison and had been working and moving for two days with minimal rest.[6]

War remains, as Clausewitz said, the domain of friction. Vision reduced by a swirling dust storm far worse than anything seen in their desert home base, the thirty-three soldiers in the eighteen-vehicle 507th convoy were heading the wrong way. Following after the armoured spearheads, they had made a wrong turn. They were heading up a stretch of road that had acquired, the previous day, the name of 'Ambush Alley'. Elsewhere, US forces were providing strong ground and helicopter escorts for truck convoys, but there were none for the 507th. They were on their own.

The Iraqi denizens of 'Ambush Alley', by surviving the previous twenty-four hours despite the best efforts of the United States, had grasped the Darwinian lesson of soft-spot tactics. They let the armoured spearheads, with their near-invulnerable M1A1 Abrams main battle tanks covered by well-trained and armed mechanized infantry, roll past while they remained concealed. They then emerged and waited for the convoys that would be following behind to resupply and maintain the spearheads. The Iraqis positioned their weapons – including at least two T-55 tanks – and waited to see what would try to drive through 'Ambush Alley'. It proved to be the 507th's convoy. The Iraqis let the three-vehicle point detachment – led by the company commander who had got the convoy lost – drive past and waited for the main body.

SGT Shoshana Johnson, a cook, was one of the thirty-three soldiers on the six vehicles of the convoy that were in the Iraqi kill zone when they opened fire. 'We got turned around and then lost and we rolled into Nasiriya before it was secure and when we rolled in there was an ambush waiting for us.' Buses were used to block the road in front of and behind the convoy.

The lead truck was hit first. The driver pulled off the road. One soldier – no one was sure who in the swirling dust and confusion – defended the others with an M16 as they attempted to take cover, and then was hit and went down. Other trucks pulled over, trying to set up an all-around defensive perimeter against the Iraqi fire. One HMMWV, with PFC Jessica Lynch on board, was hit by an RPG round and crashed at high speed into the back of a damaged truck in the confusion of the firefight and the blowing dust. She suffered severe injuries in the crash.[7]

1SGT Robert Dowdy was in charge of the portion of the convoy caught in the kill zone. He was in a HMMWV when it was hit by an RPG, killing him. SGT James Riley, now in charge of the convoy, organized the defence while calling for help. He dismounted and tried to get the vehicles turned around and out of the kill zone. The battle lasted for fifteen minutes. Rifles and machine guns jammed in the flying dust. PFC Patrick Miller kept his M16 working; he was seen to hit up to nine Iraqis. (He was awarded a Silver Star.) In the words of SGT Riley, 'We were getting shot at from all different directions. We were like Custer. We were surrounded. We didn't have a chance.'[8]

Eleven soldiers were killed or died from their wounds. Six were captured. The remainder escaped the kill zone.

The prisoners were kicked and beaten by their Iraqi captors. Five of the live prisoners – two of them wounded – and four of the dead soldiers were soon after put on Iraqi television. Chillingly, the dead looked, from the television picture, to have been executed by single bullets to the head. At the time, it seemed to underline the unexpected friction that was threatening the success of the whole conflict.

FINDING PFC LYNCH

A liberation mission now became a priority, both for the five prisoners who had been televised, two US Army helicopter crewmen who had been shot down and captured and the sixth survivor of the 507th convoy, PFC Jessica Lynch, who had not been televised. The search continued. Marines in Nasiriya found Lynch's dog tag in the home of a Baath Party official.[9] The badly injured Lynch had been taken to an Iraqi hospital in Nasiriya.

HUMINT arrived in the form of a note written by an Iraqi woman that was passed to a US Marine near Nasiriya, saying that Lynch was still alive and giving her room number at the Saddam Hospital in that city. An American reporter near the same town was approached by an English-speaking Iraqi who provided the same information.[10]

The information went through the CIA, who confirmed it with COMINT and PoW interrogations.[11] A trusted Iraqi CIA operative used a hidden video camera to scout the hospital and its surroundings.[12]

HUMINT was also provided by Mohammed Odeh al Rehaief, an Iraqi

lawyer, who approached a Marine checkpoint and provided them with information as to Lynch's location and condition.[13] Al Rehaief claimed that he
had seen Lynch being slapped by an Iraqi security official (a claim denied by
the hospital's medical staff).[14] The medical staff claim that they shielded
their patient from Iraqi irregulars and provided her with scarce food and
medication. Al Rehaief was sent back to the hospital by the Marines, reporting back to them the number of its *Fedayeen* Saddam garrison (forty-one)
and their locations (four in front of Lynch's room) as well as approach routes.

But even the medical staff reported that Lynch was in danger from
Saddam loyalists and the Iraqi military. Dr. Harith al Houssona stalled an
Iraqi intelligence officer who ordered him to transfer her to another hospital,
where he believed she might be killed. Instead, the hospital tried to turn
Lynch over to the US military, but this action also proved highly dangerous.
On the night of 30 March, Lynch was placed in an ambulance driven by
Sabah Khazaal. She was escorted by an Iraqi officer. At an Iraqi checkpoint,
the escort officer was given a gun by an unidentified Iraqi and told to shoot
Lynch. According to Khazaal, he refused the order as contrary to Islam. The
ambulance then approached a US checkpoint. It slowed and put on its lights
but, hearing gunfire – which Khazaal assumed but did not know for certain
to be coming from the checkpoint – he turned around and returned to the
hospital.

The Iraqis decided that any attempt to turn over Lynch to US forces
would have to wait until Iraqi irregular forces had left the area. Another
ambulance driver, Abdul-Hadi Hannoon, reportedly told Lynch on 1 April
that she would be turned over the following morning. This time, she would
be transported on a donkey cart.

PLANNING THE RAID

The proposed raid soon became both a liberation and a seizure mission. The
hospital was identified as a location often associated with Saddam's cousin,
General Ali Hassan al-Majeed. The infamous 'Chemical Ali' maintained an
office there.[15]

The raid was carried out at the order of GEN Franks. The decision was
taken on the afternoon of 1 April during a video conference. Franks placed
great emphasis on maintaining operational security.[16] The White House was
given advance notice of the operations.[17]

The planning was quickly carried out at 'The Ghetto' in Doha; the units from all services were already forward deployed in Kuwait and Iraq. The plans of the hospital were quickly obtained from the foreign contractor that had constructed it.[18] In the words of Maj. Gen. Victor E. Renuart Jr., CENTCOM's director of operations, 'After some detailed planning and study, it was felt that we had not only good intelligence information and had the potential for good access, but we in fact also felt we had a feasible plan.'[19]

The units alerted for the raid received four hours' notice, which was not enough time to co-ordinate. The different unit headquarters – dispersed throughout the theatre – were given their objectives and the timeframe during which they needed to be there. The aircrew and SOF alerted for the mission were highly motivated. 'Emotions were running pretty high, especially knowing [from television footage] how they treated our POWs,' said one pilot.[20]

Rapid reaction was facilitated by the existence of a standing CENTSOC operational headquarters, Task Force 20.[21] Based on lessons learned from the operations of Task Force 11 in Afghanistan (and using many of the same personnel), it meant that there was an operational headquarters that could issue orders to SOF and also to the assets and capabilities supporting them. As in Afghanistan, close integration with intelligence was a goal of the organization. TF 20 was able to use this close integration with intelligence to rapidly package and target SOF forces against a range of potential objectives. Hunting down and neutralizing weapons of mass destruction (WMD) and their delivery systems was TF 20's primary mission. Other priority missions included direct-action, liberation and seizure missions. CENTSOC also established a Rescue Co-ordination Centre (RCC) to co-ordinate the use of SOF in personnel-recovery missions with the CENTCOM-run coalition Joint Search and Rescue Centre.

The plan that evolved fitted the parameters of a SOCOM raid. It would be executed by TF 20 using a large force, with a company of Rangers to provide security for the (primarily) SEALs and Delta Force personnel who were to make the liberation and seizure. It was an all-service operation (meeting 'rice bowl' concerns). It was close to forward Marine positions, so the raiders would have artillery support. The on-the-ground phase of the raid was to last no more than forty-five minutes.

The planners at Doha had full access to US intelligence assets, including the high-altitude Global Hawk UAV, which used a MILSTAR 5 communications satellite to pass its real-time streaming video of the objective back to the planners. This included a 'reach-back' capability to facilities in the US that could provide intelligence and planning support.[22] Communications to provide connectivity for the different elements of the raiding force and to link them to Doha would be provided by MILSTAR and Defense Satellite Communications System (DSCS) communication satellites (COMSATs).[23]

THE RAID TO NASIRIYA

Starting around 1145 on 1 April – about a half-hour before the raiding force was due to hit the hospital – Marine Task Force Tarawa launched a diversionary attack supported around Nasiriya by tanks and two AV-8B Harriers. The Marine operation was in support of but independent of the raid, which required that the two operations be deconflicted to prevent fratricide. SOCCENT was able to co-ordinate with the help of the I Marine Expeditionary Force (MEF) SOCOORD. The Marines did not have the benefits of national-level satellite imagery but had many other sources of intelligence, including UAVs and reconnaissance-pod and datalink-equipped aircraft.[24] Major Mike Tanner, Royal Marines, planned the attack. 'Within six minutes of crossing the line of departure, we had engaged the enemy and achieved the objective . . . We weren't trying to take the city but were attempting to distract them and scare the daylights out of them in order to open the way for the US special [operations] forces. It worked perfectly.'[25]

Marine AV-8Bs were put in the air to provide on-call close air support for the raiders. The AV-8Bs' pilots were tasked with monitoring the area around the hospital for Iraqi counterattacks or escapes. They were able to provide this information by streaming real-time video imagery via a datalinked Northrop Grumman Litening-2 infra-red/laser targeting pod. The AV-8Bs covered the arrival of the helicopters at the hospital, although with the limited mission-planning time available the pilots were not sure what was going on.[26]

In addition to the AV-8Bs, the raid would have the benefit of a number of airborne surveillance platforms. A US Air Force Predator UAV watched the area, providing real-time sensor feed. A US Navy EP-3E SIGINT aircraft monitored communications in case Iraqis called for reinforcements. A SOCOM AC-130 was tasked to support the raid, to provide fire support on-call.

Marine AH-1W attack helicopters and Army MH-6 'Little Birds' from the 160th SOAR would also support the raiders in addition to escorting their helicopters.

A force of SEAL Team 6 (predominating), Delta Force and Rangers from the 1-75th (to secure the area while the SEAL and Delta Force specialists carried out their search and seizure mission inside the hospital) inserted in five helicopters.[27] The Marines also provided five CH-53E helicopters and five CH-46s to insert the Army ground units participating in the raid. MH-60s configured for medical evacuation with a removable pallet including stretchers and in-flight monitoring equipment were also part of the force.

The only shooting occurred outside the hospital, from surrounding buildings, with no casualties among the rescuers. Local Iraqis and the hospital's doctors later claimed that all Iraqi military personnel and *Fedayeen* irregulars had fled the hospital area hours before the raiders arrived. The shooting was thus either from Iraqis who did not get the word to flee or a non-lethal friendly fire incident. 'The Americans were jumping over fences and running around. They could have walked into the hospital and no one would have stopped them,' was how it appeared to Hassan Hamoud, one of the hospital workers who lived nearby.[28]

The raiders searched the hospital, blowing open doors (even those reportedly unlocked) and handcuffing and holding the staff at gunpoint until the building could be secured. Some Iraqis, including the hospital's assistant manager, were taken prisoner and put aboard the helicopters (although they were released within forty-eight hours when it became apparent that they were not hostile).

PFC Lynch was hiding in her bed when the raiders arrived. One of the raiders entered her room. He called her name and received no response. Then he announced, 'Jessica Lynch, we're United States soldiers and we're here to protect you and take you home.'

'I'm an American soldier, too,' she replied. 'Please don't let anybody leave me.'[29]

A Ranger doctor was soon at her bedside, examining her and preparing her for evacuation. She was quickly strapped to a stretcher and carried outside to the waiting helicopters. She was flown immediately to a hospital, holding on to the Ranger doctor throughout the flight.

A search of the hospital for 'Chemical Ali' proved fruitless (after being thought killed in an air strike, he was later captured, post-war). The hospital had also been functioning as an Iraqi military command post, including maps, weapons and a terrain model of the area.

Prisoners were interrogated as to the locations of other Americans. One led them to the site of a mass grave behind the hospital. The Rangers used their hands – they did not carry entrenching tools – to exhume nine bodies. These were also taken aboard the helicopters. Two more bodies – later found to be Iraqis – were taken from the hospital morgue. Nine of the dead were identified as Americans, eight from the 507th battle, plus a Marine killed in ground combat the day before.

The raiding force had remained on the ground for no more than twenty-five minutes. The withdrawal was covered by the same AV-8Bs that had remained on station throughout the ground time.

The 'Success 1' signal was sent back for the liberation of PFC Lynch. 'Success 2' would have meant that 'Chemical Ali' was in the bag. A radio message advised the disparate raiding force and their support elements that things had gone well and to watch the news the next day.

IMPACT

The incident proved to be a tremendous boost for US morale, both stateside and in-theatre. As in Korea in 1950 and with Objective Rhino in 2001, favourable press coverage and its impact on friend and foe alike was a secondary objective of the mission. A night-vision camera showed Lynch being taken out of the hospital and on to the MH-60. In Washington, the President was described as being 'full of joy because of her rescue and full of pride because of her rescuers'.[30] Church bells rang in Lynch's tiny home town of Palestine, West Virginia. At the JOC in Qatar, cheering broke out, the only time it was to do so until the toppling of the massive Saddam statue in Baghdad that signalled the end of the war. Franks, characteristically, was wary of publicity and disapproved of cheering operational success.[31] He said, 'You guys act like you're surprised. Our special operations forces are the best in the world.'[32]

PFC Lynch proved to be a hero to the tastes of the American public in a war that had lacked acceptable faces to put with the names in the press reports. Young, blond, pretty, wholesome, devout, twenty years old with a goal of becoming a kindergarten teacher and coming from a working-class background (that media and political élites alike did not share), Lynch was a woman in jeopardy (a widespread contemporary popular culture plot element) who touched the gender-conscious American psyche in a way that would have been impossible for most prisoners (who tend to be professional, no longer young or pretty, male military personnel).

PFC Lynch received her proverbial fifteen minutes of fame. Her photograph appeared on news magazine covers. She was profiled in lifestyle publications and became the subject of a made-for-television movie (the American equivalent of a knighthood). She was said (by the Department of Defense at the time, though it was never confirmed) to have fought bravely with her rifle before capture (unlikely due to her wounds), to have been shot and stabbed by Iraqis (she narrowly survived the crash wounds she suffered) and to have resisted resolutely in captivity (she was too badly injured to do much and some of the soldiers escaping from the ambush misidentified PFC Miller as Lynch). While her resistance had been overestimated by the Pentagon and the media, compared to that associated with the first heroes of earlier conflicts, it appeared, in retrospect, to be positively restrained. More substantially, the Iraqi lawyer who took the risks to contact the Americans and had provided the vital HUMINT on her location was brought to the US with his family, receiving public acclaim and offers of employment (and a book contract).

The medical staff at the hospital resented the (smarter and more enterprising) lawyer getting the rewards. After providing Lynch with the medical attention that likely saved her life, all they got was to be held at gunpoint by the raiders. They told their bitter side of the story to a BBC crew eager to hear it.

While in the light of hindsight – and Iraqi sources trying to paint their actions in the most favourable way possible post war – it appears likely that had the raid not been mounted, PFC Lynch would eventually have fallen into the hands of advancing US forces, as did the other PoWs. But the potential for the use of prisoners as hostages, or that they might fall victim to the revenge-motivated violence that has remained commonplace throughout Iraq, meant that the mission was more than an exercise to raise friendly morale and damage the enemy's.[33]

FINAL LIBERATION

Searches continued for the remaining US prisoners – five from the 507th and the two pilots. The military prison at Rashid Airport on the southeast edge of Baghdad was raided by Marines on 7 April. The Marines had to defeat platoon-sized units of Iraqi paramilitary forces. The prison yielded only bloodied US uniform items.[34]

The remaining seven prisoners, after being held for twenty-two days, were abandoned by retreating Iraqi forces near Samara, north of Baghdad. They were left in a house from which they were liberated on 15 April by a patrol from the US Marines 3rd Light Armoured Reconnaissance Battalion, advancing up the highway towards Tikrit, who had been directed to the prisoners by surrendering Iraqi soldiers and local civilians encountered at a checkpoint.

The Marines, directed into a residential area, were afraid they were being led into an ambush. They were about to withdraw when they saw through a window a man in yellow pyjamas waving them towards a house.[35]

Marine LCPL Curney Russell kicked down the door of the house. A squad of Marines stormed in, ordering everyone down, then said, 'If you're an American, stand up.'[36] SGT Zachary Schneider was one of the Marines who recovered the prisoners. 'They all looked happy, they were all crying. They all had really good beards.'[37]

The prisoners reported that their treatment, rough but not brutal, had improved as it became apparent that the US was winning. By the end of their captivity, they had been handed over to the Iraqi police who were buying them food with money from their own pockets.

TRYING TO SEIZE SADDAM

Seizure missions were an integral part of the SOF role in the coalition war plan from the opening of operations. Reportedly, 100 individuals in the regime leadership were targeted.[38] After the initial strike, the national command authority specifically delegated to CENTCOM the authority to order further missions against the leadership.[39] These missions, which included CIA covert operations assets, included some in and around Baghdad as early as during the opening days of the conflict.[40]

With the recovery of the prisoners and the collapse of Iraqi organized resistance, seizure missions increased in importance. Raids were organized against many of the large number of Iraqi palaces and other areas that had been associated with the regime leadership. They were targeted by raiding parties rather than diverted ground forces, which allowed the bulk of the ground forces to maintain the advance on Baghdad and Tikrit.[41] This time, however, unlike either the Panama or 1991 Gulf War models, the US military was not going to be able to go home and declare victory.

Early on 3 April, a night-time heliborne seizure operation – using 160th SOAR MH-47s with AC-130 support – was launched against a palace on Lake Tharthar near Tikrit. It encountered only light resistance. The raiders found documents of intelligence interest, but not Saddam or any other targets.[42] BG Vincent Brooks, CENTCOM spokesman, emphasized the secondary benefits of the raid: 'This illustrates the ability of this coalition to operate anywhere against any regime target.'[43]

As coalition forces advanced on Baghdad and Tikrit, the emphasis shifted to SOF teams trying to intercept Saddam and other high-ranking officials among the 'top fifty-five' of the regime leadership as they were fleeing the country, most likely to Syria. These operations came to press attention when an Australian SAS team intercepted a convoy carrying the Russian ambassador to Baghdad.[44]

Even when the trails for Saddam and the high-level leadership had grown cold, the seizure missions continued through the spring and summer of 2003. They were not limited to SOF and were carried out by a range of coalition forces. On 14 May, the 1st Brigade, 4th Infantry (Mechanized) Division, mounted 'Operation Planet X', a large-scale ground operation. Reportedly a week in planning and making use of HUMINT, the operation involved over 500 troops (including a mechanized infantry company) with helicopter support in a five-hour ground operation against a village near Tikrit. The raid yielded one of the fifty-five 'most wanted' and several disguised Iraqi general officers among the prisoners, who had stayed in one place too long and so were vulnerable to being targeted by a large-scale raid.[45]

However, this approach to seizure missions had its downside. The large-scale searches for wanted fugitives led to riots in Iraqi towns, as in Hit on 28 May 2003 following an operation by the 3rd Armoured Cavalry Regiment. Aspects of house searches seen as interfering with the privacy of female family members were particularly resented. As in the hunt for

Noriega, raids were also mistakenly directed against embassy buildings, causing international incidents.[46]

Reports that raids were alienating the public led the US to move away from these large sweeps and instead stress more targeted seizure operations involving SOF from TF 20.[47] In Iraq, through the spring and summer of 2003, the US found itself increasingly involved in combating an insurgency through the limited application of force, a type of combat it had aimed to avoid since Vietnam. Because the US was fixed on avoiding committing its own armed forces to such conflicts, it had not spent much time or effort developing doctrine, concepts or institutions to lead to victory in insurgencies. However, it soon became apparent that seizure operations – removing the leaders of an insurgency or the regime they were trying to re-install – could potentially be valuable as part of the overall campaign.

In July, the US changed the focus of their seizure operations from focusing on high-value targets to systematically cutting away the pro-Saddam infrastructure. The operations generated further intelligence, both HUMINT and COMINT, for further targeting. MG Raymond Odierno, commanding general of the 4th Infantry Division, said, 'The people are now coming to us with information. Every time we do an operation, more people come in.' An official at CENTCOM headquarters described the process: 'You get a tip, you pull a couple of guys in, they start to talk. Then, based on that information, you do a raid, you confiscate some documents, you start building the tree. You start doing signals intercepts. And you're into the network.'[48]

The seizure operations emphasized quick-reaction raids using fresh intelligence, often HUMINT generated by Iraqis (especially those bringing news of sightings of potential targets to checkpoints) or other US forces. Reminiscent of Mogadishu in 1993, Saddam sightings became known as 'Elvis sightings' because of their frequency and unreliability.

The TF 20 assets were inserted by helicopter using fast-rope techniques, ground convoys arriving in HMMWVs, or both, timed for simultaneous arrival at the location to be raided.[49] TF 160 supports many of these raids. Their unique AH/MH-6 'Little Birds' were in evidence at the most high-value raids, inserting the seizure teams and providing direct support.

Other US forces supported these raids. Operation Ivy Serpent on 13 July was the fourth series of such raids implemented by the 4th Infantry division.[50]

In early August, the 4th Infantry Division (Mechanized) alone was putting out 300 patrols and ten raids a day in its sector around Tikrit.[51] This was a reduction from the average of eighteen raids daily being carried out by that division in July.[52] The raids were focused on both high-value targets such as Saddam and those organizing insurgent activities.

The follow-up actions at the inevitable 'dry holes' include a US Army team distributing cash to compensate for damage caused by the raiders. The presence of journalists from throughout the world – fifty-three in the 4th Infantry Division alone – helped to encourage mitigation of collateral damage.

MOSUL, 22 JULY 2003

TF 20 conducted many of the raids in conjunction with other US units, including the one resulting in the deaths of Saddam Hussein's hideous and brutal sons Uday and Quasay in the Falad district of Mosul on 22 July. Quasay was the number-two man in the regime, running the Special Republican Guard and the intelligence agencies. Uday was known for his exceptional brutality even by Saddam's standards and had helped to organize the *Fedayeen* guerrilla force.

The actionable intelligence that led to the raid came from HUMINT brought by an Iraqi volunteer source. This was not considered reliable, but US COMINT provided confirmation of a likely high-value target at the location indicated. A raid was quickly planned. While planning was in progress, the owner of the target building came to the Americans and confirmed that Uday and Quasay were indeed holed up there. The local US commanders established concealed OPs around the building, backed up by a quick-reaction force in case the targets tried to slip away. Aircraft provided high-altitude 'eyes-on' surveillance without alerting the quarry. Imagery from aircraft and ground level was sent to TF 20's headquarters at Baghdad International Airport, where it had moved from 'The Ghetto' post war. This air and ground-level imagery was used to plan the raid. Because of its potential political impact on the insurgency, planning was co-ordinated with CENTCOM and with its CINC GEN John Abizaid, who as a captain had led the Ranger assault on the high ground on Grenada.

SOF from TF 20 were deployed to Mosul. Some twelve HMMWVs, an APC and 200 soldiers from the 326th Engineer Battalion (Air Assault) and the

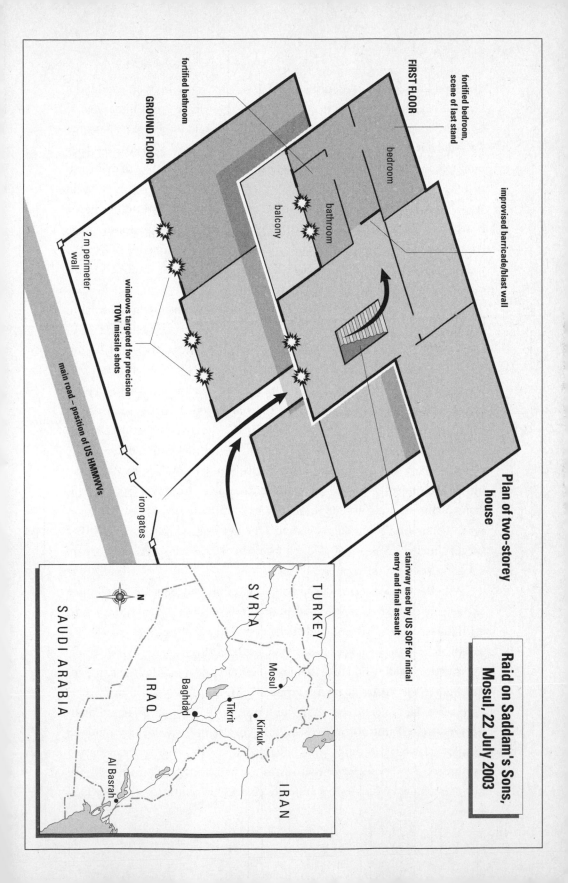

Raid on Saddam's Sons,
Mosul, 22 July 2003

Plan of two-storey
house

FIRST FLOOR

fortified bedroom,
scene of last stand

fortified bathroom

GROUND FLOOR

bedroom

bathroom

balcony

improvised barricade/blast wall

stairway used by US SOF for initial
entry and final assault

2 m perimeter
wall

windows targeted for precision
TOW missile shots

iron gates

main road – position of US HMMWVs

TURKEY

SYRIA

IRAQ

Mosul

Baghdad

Tikrit

Kirkuk

IRAN

SAUDI ARABIA

Al Basrah

N

3-502nd Infantry (Air Assault) of the 101st Air Assault Division would pro-vide the blocking and back-up force.[53] The blocking force was commanded by COL Joe Anderson, commander of the 101st's Second Brigade. The blocking force did not know the identity of the targets. 'They heard high guys but they didn't know how high,' said SGT George Granter of the 326th.[54] In the words of LTG Ricardo S. Sanchez, CENTCOM's ground-component commander in Iraq, 'The option to surround the house and wait out the individuals in the house was considered and rejected. The commanders on the ground made the decision to go ahead and execute and accomplish their mission of finding, fixing, killing or capturing.'[55] A siege situation would have made the US forces vulnerable to sniper fire from the surrounding area.

COL Anderson provided the commander's intent: 'The intent is always to ask the people to come out voluntarily.'[56] A twenty-strong Delta and SEAL team from TF 20 made the first approach to the objective at 1000 on 22 July. With the blocking force in place and weapons trained on the house, the point men literally went to the door and rang the bell. The owner (who had been a volunteer intelligence source) answered it and then, as arranged, fled with his son, who had been held as hostage for the security of the targets. The teams quickly moved in, going upstairs. They were met with a burst of fire. Three soldiers were wounded in the house and one outside in the initial burst. The raiders retreated, taking their wounded with them. (Fortunately, none of the wounds were life-threatening – the raiders' body armour was both lighter and more effective than that available in Mogadishu.)[57] The targets hurled grenades at soldiers from the 101st who were keeping up covering fire from the rooftop.

With the house surrounded, no one could slip away or get in to reinforce the defenders: Uday, Quasay, a bodyguard and Quasay's son Mustafa, armed with Kalashnikovs, were the only defenders. They kept up resistance for six hours. At first, the US made an effort to take them alive, making four attempts to enter the building and take them prisoner after demands for their surren-der were made in Arabic on a bullhorn by TF 20 psychological operations specialists. The raiders, seeking to minimize casualties and collateral dam-age, did not mount a frontal assault. Each attempt was met by renewed gunfire. The house – built with bulletproof windows – had been hastily improvised for defence, with mattresses used as sandbags. Meanwhile, the beleaguered defenders were frantically calling for reinforcements – which never arrived, for even loyal Baathists were unwilling to risk death at the hands of the covering force to rally to save the unspeakable brothers – and sending out warning calls, presumably to Saddam himself; all valuable for US COMINT.

The situation resembled that in Mogadishu: a seizure mission that, with the element of surprise gone, ended up as a battle of attrition. Except that this time there were no helicopter losses to split up the US force and no swarming reinforcements. The limited political mobilization of the opposition in Mosul in 2003 compared to that in Mogadishu in 1993 was evident.

As it became increasingly evident that the defenders were not going to be taken alive, the raiders escalated their attack after evacuating the residents from nearby houses (despite this, collateral damage included two civilian dead). COL Anderson brought up more fire power. Using AH-64 Apache attack helicopters and A-10 attack aircraft against the house was considered but rejected due to collateral damage and fratricide concerns.[58] At 1122, two OH-58D Kiowa Warrior helicopters provided precision machine-gun fire and launched ten 2.75-inch rockets. Six hit the house, starting a fire. Support weapons included .50-calibre machine guns, and MK-19 40 mm grenade launchers were brought into action.

Around noon, TF 20 tried again to move in and seize the objectives. They met with continued resistance and did not press the assault. Now HMMWV-mounted TOW wire-guided antitank missiles from the 101st were brought into action. Fired at 200 m they were guided through the windows from which the raiders had drawn fire; eleven TOWs were fired, enough to knock out a company of tanks.

At about 1320, SEALs and Delta Force made the final assault, in a situation much like those practised at the close-quarter-battle (CQB) training facilities at Fort Bragg. Two of the defenders had apparently survived the barrage of TOWs, reflecting the limited blast effects of their shaped-charge warheads. Uday barricaded himself in the toilet and resisted until the raiders forced entry with an explosive charge and killed him with aimed shots to the head. Mustafa, firing from under a bed, went the same way.

Intelligence moved in to extract any material they might have had with them. Uday made his last stand in the toilet accompanied by a briefcase full of condoms, Viagra, painkillers and cologne. Quasay had lots of cash.[59] They had – in the absence of a US capability to respond to the initial resistance with less-than-lethal force – thwarted the objective of the seizure operation by resisting to the death. MG Sanchez identified the raid as a likely turning point in the conflict against the Baathist insurgency in Iraq.

IRAQ RESULTS

Liberation and seizure missions were only a small part of the success of coalition SOF in Iraq. This included securing high-value targets (oilfields, airfields, bridges, dams); hunting for WMD, ballistic missiles and other key objectives; and working with Kurdish and anti-Saddam Iraqi forces. The lessons from Iraq have underlined the importance of SOF in the overall coalition success. Their flexibility was demonstrated in the liberation of PFC Lynch, a quick-reaction mission involving a wide range of forces. But SOF is still limited by intelligence. The seizure missions failed to bring in Saddam for many months.

The continuing operations after the fall of Baghdad and Tikrit have demonstrated the value of small footprints and precision targeting. It is better to have, whenever possible, Delta-style seizure missions than large-scale searches that evoke resentment. In late 2003, such raids – carried out by TF 121, successor to TF 20 – were said to be closing in on Saddam Hussein.[60]

SEIZING SADDAM: AD DAWR, 13 DECEMBER 2003

Saddam reportedly kept moving throughout 2003. He moved between twenty to thirty safe houses in Iraq's central 'Sunni triangle' area while a tight-knit circle of family, clan and political supporters sheltered him and carried verbal instructions to anti-coalition insurgents. In the end, Saddam trusted only the members of five families, all related to him and all sharing complicity in his regime's crimes. He travelled in disguise, by small boat, or in car boots; the threat of coalition seizure raids limited the amount of time he could spend in a single place and, therefore, his ability to support resistance.

TF 121 worked closely with intelligence – military, Grey Fox and CIA – in support of its seizure missions against the former president. Evaluating intelligence and, if actionable, planning raids within the limited timeframe imposed by Saddam's frequent moves was problematic. Apart from a single phone call intercepted at the time of the raid against his sons, there were reportedly few, if any, direct COMINT intercepts available; HUMINT became critical in the hunt for Saddam.

In September and October alone, the coalition launched eleven unsuccessful seizure raids against Saddam, now codenamed HVT-1 (High Value Target) or BL-1 (Blacklist); several times the raiders were told they had missed their quarry by hours. These frustrations led to a review of intelligence sources and procedures by a fusion cell of HVT analysts in late November. They reviewed the tasking of all the intelligence sources being used in the hunt, from national technical means and UAVs to HUMINT. Old information was revisited with the hope that new leads might turn up. As a result, a list was developed of what the cell termed 'most likely Saddam facilitators'; they identified five individuals – from the five linked families – as 'key enablers'. The goal became to get inside the closed world of the five clans that were keeping Saddam alive on a day-to-day basis. Based on the intelligence review, in late 2003 TF 121 changed its method of targeting Saddam. The raids became US-only missions, with TF 121's British and Australian SOF assigned to other targets, removing any restrictions on intelligence use that might have come from foreign security concerns.

While the high technology sources of UAVs and other sensors were re-tasked, old technology was also enlisted in the hunt. TF 121 trained tracker dogs, using scent taken from Saddam's clothing. In Tikrit, Saddam's home town and a hotbed of resistance, army intelligence analysts manually plotted out the links between Saddam's allies and relatives – who knew who – on a large chart, in a method originated by the Ohkrana, the Russian secret police, in the nineteenth century.

While TF 121 developed top-down intelligence, other US and coalition intelligence assets worked with local Iraqis and focused on HUMINT in a decentralized collection and analysis operation. The intelligence had focused on exploiting information from likely HUMINT sources: former Saddam bodyguards or members of his al-Tikriti clan. Large-scale payments to reliable informants in the Tikrit area proved successful, even though the well-publicized 25-million-dollar reward for Saddam had had little effect. MG Odierno explained, 'we brought in about five or ten members of these families and finally we got the ultimate information from one of these individuals'.[61]

A key potential source, codenamed the Fat Man, sought since the summer, was reportedly captured in a raid in Baghdad on 12 December. He had come to the attention of US intelligence as someone who was likely to have had contact with Saddam. A senior leadership figure in the Special Security Organization, Saddam's most feared inner-circle force, and a member of the five key families, he reportedly co-ordinated logistics and security for Saddam's movements. One of the five 'key enablers', he had been in US intelligence sights before, being the target of a series of unsuccessful seizure raids around Tikrit in July. However, at the time US intelligence thought only that he was linked to the local insurgents and was unaware of his ties to Saddam himself.

Then, in early December, new evidence of the Fat Man's location and of his links with Saddam came to light through intelligence analysis. Five simultaneous seizure raids were launched on Tikrit on 4 December. They were unsuccessful. The US spread its net wider, with raids on Samara (a 'dry hole' that yielded 1.9 million dollars) on 5 December and on Bayji on 7 December, until the Fat Man was finally grabbed on 12 December. To US Army 1LT Angela Santana, one of the intelligence analysts at Tikrit, this was the key break in the search: 'We had someone who was very close to Saddam talking so there was a great chance we would find him that night'.[62]

Actionable intelligence was first in hand at about 1050 on 13 December. It identified two likely Saddam locations: a house, codenamed Wolverine 1, and a farm, Wolverine 2, in the town of Ad Dawr, a Saddam loyalist stronghold some 15 km southeast of Tikrit. It was thought Saddam would be there for hours rather than minutes.

TF 121 started to plan for the raid – named Operation Red Dawn (from the 1980s movie) – preparing a force of some two dozen soldiers, including Delta troopers.[63] Whether they were already forward deployed in the Tikrit area or had to first be flown there from TF 121's base at Baghdad International Airport is uncertain. The covering force that was to block escape and reinforcement routes and stand ready to reinforce the SOF in case of strong resistance was drawn from COL Jim Hickey's 1st 'Raider' Brigade of the 4th Infantry Division, whose sector included Ad Dawr. The brigade, true to its name, had conducted some 5–600 raids since arriving in Iraq, twelve against Saddam himself and three of these in December alone. Washington was informed that a raid would be taking place. Rumsfeld was made aware of the broad outlines of the operation, but he had no reason to believe that this raid would be more productive than the many previous ones.

More intelligence was developed during the day. The original actionable intelligence came from HUMINT, reportedly from a key bodyguard or local family member with ties to Saddam (whether this was the Fat Man or not is uncertain). The objectives had been identified through multispectral surveillance; the platforms were not disclosed but probably included high-flying UAVs or aircraft that would not arouse suspicion. The surveillance detected a suspicious red-and-white taxicab in the area. Further HUMINT leads revealed the locations to be associated with one of Saddam's henchmen, vice chair of the Revolutionary Command Council, Izzat Ibrahim al-Douri, who was then still at large and thought to be playing a major role in anti-coalition resistance.

By 1630 a fairly comprehensive intelligence picture had been built up of the area to be raided and the order was given to go ahead. At 1800, some ninety minutes after receiving the order to go and seven hours after the intelligence was obtained, the 600-plus strong covering force moved out of the brigade base at Camp Raider, a former palace built on a bluff overlooking the Tigris south of Tikrit. Mounted in twenty-five M2/M3 Bradley fighting vehicles and thirty HMMWVs, the covering force was built around troops of the 1-10th Cavalry squadron, reinforced with combat engineers. M109A6 Paladin SP howitzers of the 4-42nd Field Artillery battalion and AH-64D Longbow Apache helicopters were in support. A Predator UAV was launched to provide real-time video coverage back to headquarters. The force was accompanied by a key Iraqi HUMINT source, reportedly the Fat Man himself. The many journalists with the 4th Infantry saw nothing unusual, just another raid under way.

The covering forces moved out to an assembly area at an old granary north of Ad Dawr while engineers secured the west bank of the Tigris River, several hundred metres away. The force then moved quietly into blocking positions established around the two objectives, arriving simultaneously with the heliborne raiders. TF 121 SOF, identifiable by their black uniforms, NVGs, and weapons with laser 'death dot' sights, fast-roped onto the objectives from hovering helicopters. Electricity was cut off to the area.

TF 121 SOF searched the two objectives, but once again 'dry hole' was reported back to headquarters: they were empty of any targets. The raiders' leaders conferred and talked with the HUMINT source. It was decided to move the covering force to seal off the entire area – about two square kilometres – and begin an intensive search. By December, the US forces had raided enough of Saddam's safe houses to know what they were looking for: underground tunnels or hiding places and false walls, all concealed in nondescript buildings.

Another nearby location, northwest of Wolverine 2, was suggested by the HUMINT source. Two Iraqis were seen fleeing the place as the raiders approached, apparently trying to decoy them away from the small walled-compound with a metal lean-to and a mud hut. Local Iraqis told them that an apparently harmless and apolitical local farmer, Qais Namek al-Douri, owned it. US forces had reportedly recently arrested him; it was later revealed that he was one of Saddam's former palace guards.

This information required a closer inspection. After a troop of the 1-10th Cavalry was positioned around the compound, twenty-four TF 121 troopers started their forced entry procedures. The compound appeared deserted, but undisclosed sensors – possibly ground-penetrating radar – were used in a thorough search. They disclosed a camouflaged access hatch to a 'spider hole', six to eight feet deep with enough space for someone to lie down in the bottom. Once opened, the SOF troopers considered dropping in a grenade or firing into the hole to clear it first. One had the pin out of his grenade. They held their fire when they saw the upraised hands of a bearded, bedraggled man. Saddam Hussein was found hiding in the bottom of the hole.

Saddam seemed stunned with disbelief that this was, indeed, the end. Although armed with a 9 mm Makarov pistol, he put up no resistance, saying in halting English, 'I am Saddam Hussein, the president of Iraq. I am willing to negotiate.' 'President Bush sends his regards' one of the TF 121 raiders replied. Saddam was hauled out of the hole – bumping his head – before the plastic handcuffs were slipped on. That action snapped him out of his daze and revived what was left in him of the Butcher of Baghdad: he lunged for the troopers, cursing and spitting, until he was sedated with a well-applied rifle butt (or a trooper's fist, accounts differ).

Saddam was quickly searched and hustled out of the area by helicopter to the interrogation center at Baghdad International Airport. There, the video of the oral (and head lice) examination of the dishevelled and disoriented Saddam was released to the world's media. Jerrold M. Post, founder of the CIA's Center for the Analysis of Personality and Political Behavior, wrote that 'the importance of images of a meek, humiliated Hussein giving up without a fight to his American captors cannot be overstated'.[64]

The raiders continued to search the location, finding briefcases full of Saddam's papers; $750,000 in cash; two Kalashnikovs and the taxicab. The two bodyguards who had fled the scene were captured by blocking forces; under interrogation it was found that they were the brothers of Qais Namek and that they had prepared the spider hole with their brother 'as a bomb shelter during the war'. The engineers discovered several concealed boats on the banks of the Tigris nearby. It appeared that this location had been one of several used by Saddam while on the run.

The journalists back at Camp Raider had their suspicions aroused at about 2300 when they smelled the celebratory cigars lit by the returning troops. Official confirmation that the captive was Saddam Hussein had to wait until the next day, following the results of DNA tests and positive identification by former associates. The official announcements soon followed.

Saddam's capture led to several other seizure raids in the ensuing days. The documents captured with Saddam reportedly provided targets for some of these raids, including a list of pro-Saddam Iraqis who had infiltrated the new government or were working for coalition forces. One insurgent leader was in the process of activating his E&E plan, heading out the back door of his safe house with forged papers, a briefcase full of dollars and passport in hand, when he met the coalition troops on the way in. Other coalition SOF – including the Polish Grom unit in Iraq – supported TF 121 in these follow-up actions and within a week the raids based on the intelligence captured with Saddam had netted over 200 wanted personnel.

The full impact of the seizure of Saddam Hussein will not be seen in Iraq for some time. His capture will probably remove the major constraint that hindered co-operation with the emerging post-Saddam Iraqi government: until he was seized, Iraqis could think that one day the US forces would go home and Saddam would return, and so were willing to extend at least passive support to anti-coalition forces. On the other hand, the seizure of Saddam may help remove the taint of his brutal regime from the anti-coalition forces and make Islamic and nationalist appeals to resistance more effective.

Saddam's capture was perhaps the most successful US seizure raid: no shots were fired, there were no casualties and no collateral damage. The raid itself was consistent with US Army raiding doctrine, combining the element of surprise that prevented Saddam's escape with the presence of a force (with supporting fire power on call if needed) large enough to prevail in a pitched battle should one develop. The critical element had been intelligence. Intelligence analysis had brought together the all-important HUMINT, fusing it with other sources. The presence of a key Iraqi source with the raiders, pointing out the location, shows that there remains no substitute for an on-the-ground presence, despite the availability of high technology sensor platforms.

SOF AFTER SADDAM

However, the overall success in Iraq is unlikely, by itself, to overcome the US military legacy of the 1990s: risk aversion, the 'Powell Doctrine' and an emphasis on overwhelming force. Many of the policy decisions made in conjunction with the operations in Afghanistan and Iraq have been conscious efforts to change these policies. Yet there is a limit to how much the conditions that led to the previous policies can be changed. Liberation and seizure missions will remain high-risk operations. Failures are likely to have high political costs for both government and military leaders, especially if there is no ongoing major conflict to provide the context and rationale. No one has lost their job for not ordering a raid.

The utility of liberation and seizure missions is likely to be further refined as US policies interact with the hard realities of the war on terrorism. The Clinton-era decisions by the military leadership to oppose such missions – in Afghanistan and Bosnia – without the commitment of major forces and to impose high diplomatic and political costs on the administration has not held up in hindsight. The military operations since 11 September 2001 have succeeded with smaller forces and less cost than was projected. This undercut acceptance of the military leadership's advice, even that counselling that a coalition presence in a post-war Iraq was likely to be lengthy, costly and without an obvious military solution. Here again, SOF missions – especially attempts to seize terrorist leaders – are likely to be politically significant in the future.

CHAPTER 12
LESSONS AND THE FUTURE

Systemization effected by theory does have the consequence of simplifying laws and introducing orders into categories of fact. But this is a byproduct of a more basic function: to make sense of what would otherwise be inscrutable or unmeaning empirical findings.

Abraham Kaplan, *The Conduct of Inquiry.*

Liberation and seizure missions are likely to be of continued importance to US national security, not solely the military. The preferred mode of military operations is likely to remain the measured application of precision fire power – as executed successfully across the former Yugoslavia in 1999, in Afghanistan in 2001 and in Iraq in 2003. But at times the use of armed force will be required to liberate your own people or to prevent them from being held hostage, or to enable you to lay your hands on an evildoer – tasks beyond the capability of the usual preferred means. Precision ordnance delivered from 5,500 m will not get these jobs done. The national command authority (NCA) or the CINC fighting a future conflict needs the capability to order and carry out such operations, regardless of how much US strategy may stress a preference for decisive operations and achieving liberation through regime change. The success of such missions in the future will require both investment in the forces and capabilities that will be called upon to carry them out, and detailed study of the lessons of previous operations. The need to mobilize such missions will remain despite the historical record of limited success for these great efforts and, sometimes, heavy losses in personnel and political capital. The issue is how to make the chance of successful execution higher in the future.

RAIDS: THE RISKS AND REWARDS

'Who Dares Wins' is universally recognized as the motto of Britain's Special Air Service. This is the motto most applicable to liberation and seizure operations. There is a reason why the SAS motto is not 'Who Plans Wins', despite the importance of effective planning for special operations.

Liberation and seizure operations offer a high-risk (but potentially high-payoff) capability to be used when other approaches are diplomatically, politically or militarily unfeasible. Understanding and assessing the risks of action – or inaction – are critical for the effective integration of liberation and seizure missions into the larger contexts of US national security policy or theatre war-fighting.

Liberation and seizure operations remain high-risk. In recent years, US operational capability has aimed to reduce the risks inherent in other types of missions, most notably those involving air attack. Here they are largely irreducible.

The risks range from political disaster (Iran in 1980) to the casualties encountered in Mogadishu and, notionally, those encountered during training raids at the NTC and JRTC. It has not always been US forces that have suffered the repercussions of even successful liberation and seizure missions, as illustrated by the Japanese atrocities against Filipino civilians after the Los Banos raid and the arson and looting of the *barrios* near La Comandancia by PDF fugitives and DigBats in Panama City. While there is no provable causal link between these acts – both typical of those opponents – and the US actions, it remains a potential cost that future decision-makers will have to consider. The US today is sensitive to casualties – and collateral damage to friendly or even enemy populations – to a degree seen in few other countries, ever. The readiness to accept casualties seen in the Second World War, Korea or even Vietnam would be difficult to replicate even in the current war on terrorism. In many cases, these risks will be measured against the risks to Americans being held prisoner (or who may be taken prisoner) or the risks inherent in leaving an enemy leader at large.

While the risks involved in these operations are considerable, since Los Banos the gains have been limited. American citizens snatched from imminent execution in these raids appear to have been limited to those in Los Banos and, in Panama, Kurt Muse (the two Americans in Renacer Prison in Panama might also be added to the list). American military PoWs liberated in all these missions total ten: the nine US Navy nurses at Los Banos and PFC Lynch in Iraq. Other US prisoners rescued in Korea and Iraq were already free from captivity. The number of foreign nationals liberated stands higher, including the foreign internees at Los Banos, Sir Paul Scoon on Grenada and the political prisoners in Renacer Prison. To this total may be added the allied PoWs freed in the many liberation missions other than Son Tay during the 1961–75 conflict in Southeast Asia. The crew of the *Mayaguez*, Sir Paul Scoon, the medical students on Grenada, the dependants at Fort Amador and PFC Jessica Lynch may not, in the light of hindsight, have been under the imminent threat of death or capture that motivated Washington or a CINC to stage high-risk missions to secure them. Certainly, even today, the body count of those in the hands of the Khmer Rouge, Grenadian revolutionaries or Saddam Hussein's regime was high enough to consider attempting to prevent more deaths through the use of US military action. Caution can cost lives as well as action.

Operations to seize individuals have also had limited success. Noriega, Saddam and his hideous sons were brought to bay by countrywide dragnets enabled by large-scale intelligence efforts. Aideed, Mullah Omar and bin Laden evaded seizure missions for lengthy periods. Other smaller targets that constitute the support infrastructure of these individuals – Aideed's lieutenants in Mogadishu, Taliban local leaders in Afghanistan, Baath party *apparatchiks* in Iraq – have proven easier to target and seize, especially when there is extensive HUMINT exploitation in place.

On numbers alone, there remains the bar-room logic that has been used by members of the 'conventional' forces against SOF members: we liberate (or capture) wholesale, whole countries at a time, while you do so retail, a few at a time. Campaigns stressing air-delivered precision fire power have had a low cost in terms of US lives. A raid that goes wrong has the potential for heavy casualties. The diplomatic and political costs of failed raids can be devastating, internationally and domestically. From a net assessment point of view, comparing the limited number of Americans liberated and enemy leaders captured with the human cost of the American fighting troops and friendly (or at least non-combatant) civilians killed in the actions seems a limited return for such an investment.

One of the most important decisions that can fall to the national command authority for a liberation or seizure mission is to identify the primary and secondary missions and the relative values of their accomplishment. President Ford saw the safe recovery of the *Mayaguez* crew as the primary objective of the use of military force; Secretary of State Kissinger and Vice President Rockefeller saw that concern as secondary to demonstrating US resolve. In the Iran crisis, Secretary of State Vance considered the safe return of the hostages to be the primary – indeed, the only valid – concern (along with that of establishing, demonstrating and maintaining his own bureaucratic power and that of his department against challenges from the national security advisor and the Pentagon). He resigned when the raid – which could have imperilled both of his goals – was launched. He placed no value on demonstrating US resolve or capability through military action against Iran.

The benefits gained from these operations beyond the numbers liberated or seized certainly also have to be considered. On a number of occasions, the other objectives have appeared desirable enough to justify the risks inherent in the raid even when it appeared likely that the primary mission would not be successful, as with Son Tay and Objective Rhino.

Demonstrating US resolve and capability was an explicit goal in a number of these missions: Son Tay, the *Mayaguez*, Iran and Grenada. Due to the potentially high political impact of liberation and seizure missions, they can be seen as involving the national will to an extent that few operations short of an all-out war can match. This is why failures – such as Iran – can be so politically and diplomatically costly. But when the strength of national will has been questioned, demonstrating it through a liberation or seizure mission may become the most important objective – as, in the end, it became at Son Tay.

Morale effects of raids are a legitimate concern. There is a reason why journalists or cameras were taken along on several of these raids: Sukchon–Sunchon, Objective Rhino, Nasiriya. The effect of the Son Tay raid on the morale of the remaining US PoWs and in sending a message to the North Vietnamese was also considerable.

Destroying enemy forces in battle can be another result – usually unintentional – of a liberation or seizure mission. Where the operations led to pitched battles – as at Sukchon–Sunchon in 1950 and Mogadishu in 1993 – the US forces (with allied help) emerged victorious. In the latter case, it was Washington that prevented a follow-up. But it remains the case that while these missions must include a capability for intense combat, such actions are supposed to be selective in their application of fire power, which is secondary to the overall mission.

LIBERATION AND SEIZURE OPERATIONS IN A ZERO-DEFECTS MILITARY

'Sir, we purely had bad luck,' was Charlie Beckwith's famous (exculpatory) summing-up of Desert One.[1] Of course, it was much more than that. The only reason why luck was able to do such damage at Desert One was due to flaws in organization, training, planning and execution.

Failures in planning or training should not be ascribed to bad luck. Bad luck was necessary but not sufficient to create the disaster at Desert One. Preparation is often synonymous with luck. Poor preparation contributed to bad luck at Koh Tang, in Iran and in Mogadishu. Good preparation could not compensate for the absence of prisoners at Son Tay.

However, the risk of liberation and seizure operations ending in disaster will always remain in ways that larger, more conventional operations can strive to prevent. While bad luck by itself may not be able to wreck a major combined arms theatre operation intended to produce decisive results, it surely can wreck a single raid. Machiavelli knew that the most brilliant operators – diplomatic, political or military – can still see their finest work undone by bad luck. (Generals Shelton and Shinseki likely would have agreed with him.) Machiavelli, in an earlier, simpler age, would cut the cards and accept the risks. Generals of the 1990s would walk away from the table.

LIBERATION AND SEIZURE MISSIONS AND DECISION-MAKERS

Liberating prisoners, preventing the taking of hostages or seizing enemy leaders are political actions. There is a political dimension to liberation or seizure operations that often exceeds that associated with other military operations. If things go badly, there are likely to be political repercussions. 'Hostage' remains a loaded word in US politics and administrations are likely to be willing to try almost anything in order to avoid a new hostage crisis. Political–military dynamics usually affect the highest levels of strategy and war-fighting. In liberation and seizure operations, however, the political dimension is an integral part of the operation that can have an impact down to the details of execution. Political decisions can be critical to the outcome of liberation and seizure missions. They have led to failure even when micro-management by the high-level decision-makers has been avoided.

While political decisions made before a raid have had strong repercussions on the forces involved, political micro-management of operations is rare (with the exception of the *Mayaguez* incident). Even US administrations famous for micro-management (Carter, Clinton) did not try to micro-manage the action at Desert One or Mogadishu, even though they did make decisions and set ground rules that greatly contributed to the ultimate result in both cases.

Liberation and seizure missions – or the situations that produce them – are likely to have resulted from orders issued by the national command authority. Because these operations have a potentially strategic impact and a political dimension regardless of size, decision-making authority for these operations must be centralized at the highest appropriate level. Reconciling this with the needs of time-critical targets (TCTs) is likely to provide an enduring problem. (Actions such as the raid in Mogadishu in 1993 or Nasiriya in 2003 could not have responded to quick-reaction HUMINT unless the decision to launch could be made on the spot.)

As a result of their political and diplomatic importance, commanders and planners of liberation and seizure missions must be well trained, skilled and, above all, adaptable. The President, NCA or CINC must have confidence in their abilities. It is important that the President feel comfortable with backing a commander's go or no-go decision (as Carter did at Desert One). Such confidence helped to enable the planners of the Israeli raid at Entebbe in 1976 and the SAS hostage liberation at the Iranian embassy in London in 1980. Where it is absent – as in the US military of the 1990s – such actions become less feasible. This confidence cannot automatically be assumed to flow from the quality of the professionals who are likely to plan and execute liberation and seizure missions and, critically, interact with the NCA.

With the political impact of such missions inevitable, the NCA needs to be able to trust the senior military people who will advise them on these raids, particularly on their chance for success and what assets are required for that success. This requirement may provide a continued impetus for the politicization of high-level military appointments, as was seen during the

Clinton administration. Reports that Secretary of Defense Rumsfeld, in a departure from previous US practice, insists on personally interviewing all three- and four-star officers up for new positions may illustrate one reaction to this need.[2]

Decision-makers may be likely to ask too much of an operation and are likely to receive a high degree of (unwarranted) assurance of its success from the military – even from SOF that should know better – in return. When the NCA has wanted the option of a liberation or seizure operation, they are usually shocked to find that there is a disconnect between what the NCA wants and what the military can do (usually as a result of limited investment in the military).

Politicians may have come to expect too much from SOF – witness Clinton's 2000 desire for 'black ninjas' with superhuman powers – but the military has often not been realistic in providing an assessment that does not appear to exhibit either a heedless 'can-do' attitude or an overcautious 'this requires a major theatre conflict if you do it' approach. While the special operators may have high confidence in their ability to carry out the mission, the leadership needs to understand exactly how the risks are being assessed and how things can go wrong. Similarly, assertions by the military that such an operation is likely to go wrong cannot simply be accepted at face value; the NCA must examine what the military is viewing as the major risk factors and evaluate alternatives or work-arounds.

The 'can-do' spirit has led to the NCA thinking that things were more likely to succeed than they turned out to be in reality. The 'can't-do' spirit assigns a high likelihood of disaster to options that are opposed by the senior uniformed military. In the past, the NCA has been ill-served by both the military's 'can-do' spirit (the Iran raid planning, the lack of complaints about the absence of AC-130s in Mogadishu) and their more recent 'can't-do' spirit (the reluctance to take action in Afghanistan and the former Yugoslavia in the 1990s).

That there is an active attempt by the current leadership in Washington to overcome the influence of both of these approaches to US special operations (and overall policy) was suggested by the appointment in 2003 of (previously retired) GEN Pete Schoomaker as Army Chief of Staff, a former CINCSOCOM and one of Charlie Beckwith's original officers when he formed Delta Force. In his arrival message to the Army, Schoomaker said, 'Twenty-three years ago . . . I stood in the Iranian desert on a moonlit night at a place called Desert One. I keep a photo of the carnage of that night to remind me that we should never confuse enthusiasm with capability.'

LIBERATION AND SEIZURE AND DECISIVE OPERATIONS

Armed force is usually used with a goal of achieving decisive results. A raid, whether to rescue or seize personnel, is by definition not a decisive operation. It seizes no terrain, nor does it overthrow hostile governments. Raids – including many liberation or seizure operations – can be seen as diverting resources away from the major objective. This has been at the heart of the Pentagon's suspicion of raids – and of its own raiders – that has been in evidence since the Second World War.

Some operations to liberate prisoners or seize enemy leaders – those in Grenada or Panama – were part of decisive military operations. The hostile regime was being put out of business at the same time as the SOF and raids took care of specific personnel. In Panama, Noriega was the centre of gravity and the prime US objective.

Other liberation and seizure missions took place in situations where the US was unable to defeat the enemy in the near term or, due to the fact that it was a limited conflict, such a defeat was not the US objective. The need to mount a special operation to liberate prisoners in the Philippines, North Korea or North Vietnam was great because the enemy was unlikely to be defeated before brutal treatment – if not outright massacre – killed more prisoners.

In situations where liberation and seizure missions are not part of a decisive operation, repeatability becomes a concern. In the case of the Iran raid, for example, even if it had been successful, there were enough Americans in Iran – especially journalists and intelligence operatives – that the Iranians could have replenished their stock of hostages overnight had they so wished. In addition, there remains the potential that a liberation mission may lead to the deaths of at least some of the people it was intended to free.

Liberation and seizure operations – especially those that are not part of decisive joint operations – open up US policies to setbacks far beyond the scope of the forces involved. The difficulty of mounting such raids unless a major conflict is envisioned was behind much of the opposition to them, whether from the CJCSs (Bradley in 1949 in the Angus Ward incident and

Shelton in 1998 with bin Laden) or political actors (such as Cyrus Vance during the Iran crisis). Indeed, the US Army's capstone doctrinal manual, FM 100-5 *Operations*, cautions that 'strategic guidance will constrain otherwise attractive options'. Liberation and seizure raids will inevitably remain high-risk, high-payoff operations.

The importance and indispensable nature of liberation and seizure missions are reflected in their potential costs if they do not work. These are not likely to be seen as peripheral or marginal operations, even if they are so viewed in the context of a larger conflict. The outcomes at Los Banos, Sukchon–Sunchon or Son Tay would not have affected the outcomes of wars, but a large-scale débâcle would have been costly.

The high-risk nature of liberation and seizure missions means that they can easily impose high costs, in terms of both casualties and political impact. The failure of the Iran raid helped to ensure that the Carter administration could not survive the effects of that crisis. The campaign to seize Aideed in Mogadishu did not accomplish that mission and instead led to US withdrawal.[3]

In addition to these political costs, there were physical costs associated with all these missions. However, none of these missions diverted resources that would otherwise have been used in more decisive operations. That cost, often imputed to SOF operations by the 'conventional' forces, does not appear to have been reflected in these missions. However, all the liberation and seizure missions described here – except two in Iraq – did lead to US casualties, although in a number of cases these were not fatal.

ENABLING EFFECTIVE PLANNING

The reforms that started in the 1980s, including the establishment of SOCOM, CINCSOC and the TSOCs, made planning and organizing for liberation and seizure missions more professional and likely to succeed than the improvised organizations that planned and led the Son Tay, *Mayaguez* and Iran raids.

There is no substitute for skilled planners. In special operations, operators also have to be involved in the planning. This avoids raiders being asked to do the impossible or being sent on high-risk missions by people who do not understand or who are in no danger of sharing those risks. Planning, training, organizing and executing special operations is so complex a military discipline that to be able to do it successfully requires having lots of smart people – line and staff alike – who have been properly trained and rehearsed, and who have used the results of training and rehearsals to consider how to do things better. Maintaining effective SOF commanders and staffs – and their relationship with the national command authority and CINCs that will give the orders – is not cheap or easy, but it will be required in order to keep this capability viable in the future.

A small, covert operation – conducted by a (properly supported) mission-tailored Delta Force or SEAL team making use of accurate and timely intelligence – may be able to work successfully. However, most liberation and seizure missions have turned out to be large joint operations. Some of this reflects the US military prejudice in favour of big battalions, as well as interservice 'rice bowl' issues.

But even when a raid is a stand-alone action, the actions of raiders must be integrated with those of larger forces. This could include the medical support that was put in place for the Los Banos prisoners before the raid or the actions of the carrier task forces to support the Son Tay and Iran raids. Even a small, covert Delta Force or SEAL operation will need someone to carry them to and from the objective, to take away the prisoners or to provide a blocking force.

In large joint operations, SOF may suffer if their incorporation is not central to the overall plan. This was most evident in Grenada, where the special operators were effectively on their own. In Panama, the integration of special operations with the overall plan was much better (with the exception of the SEALs at Paitilla).

IDENTIFYING THE ELEMENTS OF SUCCESS
Precision, timely, surprise action enabled by actionable intelligence is the first step towards a successful capability for liberation and seizure missions. The question for the future is how to invest to enable future provision of this capability.

The US military has identified the 'precision strike' – including those against TCTs – as one of the overarching goals to be achieved through future investments. Liberation and seizure missions have always been a form of precision strike. Their targets – the prisoners' train in 1950, the *Mayaguez* crew in 1975 – have frequently been time-critical, as well as elusive. Because they are precision missions, they are unlikely to succeed without good intelligence.

Since the enemy can negate these missions by moving (or killing) prisoners or their own leaders, surprise is also necessary. Surprise is more likely to prevail than weight of numbers, for even an outnumbered enemy force can still affect an operation's objective even if it cannot defeat the operation itself. Surprise has an importance beyond allowing a critical relative superiority at the point required for mission success. Even a greatly outnumbered enemy could still have an opportunity to kill prisoners or let a leader escape. A surprised enemy may not. The raiders need to both win the game and prevent the enemy from smashing the board.

Diversions, decoys, stealth and other means of achieving surprise have been used in many of the raids. At Los Banos and Son Tay, successful diversions limited enemy response. In the future, information-warfare techniques such as injecting false targets in battle-management systems may be used to help to mislead an enemy.

In some situations – such as Panama – dominant manoeuvre could compensate for the lack of surprise: hitting the enemy hard and fast to prevent reaction even when they knew the attack was coming. In other situations, as at Koh Tang, this was not possible, in part because of the limited size of the initial helicopter lift capability. There was no way raids such as Son Tay or Iran could have succeeded had the enemy known they were coming, no matter how effective the manoeuvre, how powerful the blow or how good the raiders.

Few military operations generate as much of what Clausewitz called friction in as short a time as a raid. Despite the use of technology and training to reduce reaction time, there is no substitute for rehearsal to remove friction. The results of the *Mayaguez* incident and especially the Iran raid were shaped by a lack of rehearsal opportunity. In some instances, such as MEU (SOC) NEO and TRAP missions, where the unit is likely to work as a self-contained whole, thorough training will work. But absent or inadequate full-scale rehearsals of an entire raid (as with the Iran raid) or part of one (as with the lack of rehearsed co-ordination between Task Force Ranger and the Quick Reaction Force in Mogadishu) still have the potential for disaster.

The quality of the raiders may lead planners and leaders to assume that they can use speed or stealth to compensate for lack of both numbers and fire power. The SEALs at Paitilla were asked to carry out a mission similar to that which, at the same time, had been assigned to entire Ranger battalions, even though the SEALs' strength and tactics made them more vulnerable to the loss of the element of surprise than the Rangers. The ground convoy in Mogadishu on 3 October 1993 was asked to break through roadblocks like a mechanized combined-arms task force. Both managed to carry out their missions, but it is likely that a heavier force would have done so with fewer casualties.

Yet there is a limit to how far heavier (and larger) can be translated into more effective. A larger force may forfeit speed and the element of surprise. A liberation or seizure operation that requires the same forces and preparation as a major theatre operation is unlikely to be effective (or be politically or diplomatically acceptable, as Clinton-era planning demonstrated). The tendency has been to omit needed backup or parts of a raiding force in order to reduce the footprint and its associated political and operational costs, and the increased chance for compromise. Yet this tendency has often led to failure when critical elements were missing: backup helicopters in Iran or AC-130s in Somalia.

One of the great tactical problems for any raid is how to prevent it from becoming a battle of attrition as the enemy brings in reinforcements, forcing the raiders to spend more time than planned in the objective area. This was avoided at Los Banos in 1945 and Iraq in 2003, with US aircraft standing by to hit any reinforcements, but it happened in Mogadishu. It has also been seen in tactical training raids carried out at the NTC and JRTC. Reserves are needed to extract the raiders or prevail in battle in such contingencies.

Psychological warfare can be an effective contributor to a successful raid. At its best, it can be used to persuade potential enemies to lower their weapons. It can also be used to remind them of the threat of prosecution – more real today than in the decades of the Cold War – for those who harm prisoners. But the effects of psychological warfare are more likely to be seen over time than at a critical moment in a raid.

Distance and time are the two critical limitations on liberation and seizure missions. There may be a way to get around 'too far'. There is no way to get around 'too late'. Lack of timely execution limited the rewards made possible by the excellent planning and organization of the Son Tay raid. Timely execution was important enough to the President in the *Mayaguez* incident and on Grenada to justify a hastily improvised operation. The time-frames involved in these missions have varied greatly. More time is better – even quick-reaction raids can benefit from additional planning time – but being able to respond within the timeframe required by the NCA or a CINC is critical.

Successful raids have been highly dependent on (time-consuming) mission-specific training, rehearsal, detailed planning and thorough IPB, benefits seldom available in missions such as CSAR. The challenge is to provide the meticulous and detailed planning that has been a prerequisite to successful raids in the past, combined with quick response.

Future liberation or seizure operations will benefit from the intersection of a number of potential changes in the US military. One is the investment in striking TCTs. During the 1991 Gulf War, TCTs – whether Scud missile launchers or Iraqi counterattacks – proved difficult for allied air power to hit, due to their emphasis on hitting preplanned targets. The 1990s saw increased investment in the form of exercises and doctrine aimed at hitting TCTs. Despite this, problems still remained in Kosovo in 1999. Improved performance against some TCTs was demonstrated in Afghanistan in 2001–2 and Iraq in 2003.

TCTs are not just missile launchers. They include shot-down aircrew as well as prisoners and enemy leaders. The raids against Noriega, bin Laden and Saddam Hussein show that the latter can be the most challenging TCTs of all. The need to act against TCTs is difficult to reconcile with need for organization, training and rehearsal and the meticulous and detailed planning and intelligence-gathering that experience has shown to be necessary for successful liberation or seizure operations. In order to be successful, the ability to use multiple types of sensors, collating and fusing their inputs for a more accurate picture, is critical; intelligence 'reach back' and reliable communications that have emerged as a result of the investment in dealing with TCTs should, where practical, also be applied to liberation or seizure operations.

The US military is increasingly stressing concepts of 'network-centric warfare' and 'information mobility' advantages for its forces. In part because of the increased flow of sensor data and the ability to use improved communications to 'reach back' for planning and intelligence support, SOF are less likely to have to operate with the hasty improvised planning of the *Mayaguez* incident or the intelligence vacuum that shaped the Sukchon–Sunchon and Koh Tang actions. Computerized mission-planning systems are valuable, but they are no substitute for experienced planners. Rather, they are tools that can reduce the work that such planners and their staffs have to perform. The use of computerized mission planning and distant 'reach back' support also means that a mission can be planned or re-planned quickly, enhancing flexibility. This appears to have been the case in the 2 April 2003 raid in Iraq. Technology offers part of the answer to reconciling the need for the required in-depth IPB and mission planning that have led to success in the past with the compressed timelines required by the nature of targets or the needs of the NCA or a CINC. In Afghanistan and Iraq, forward-deployed SOF made use of 'reach back' capabilities to enable their planning for quick-response missions. Making use of secure broadband communications and advances such as the SIPRNET, the Department of Defense secure classified Internet equivalent, specialists in planning and intelligence at SOCOM and intelligence agencies could provide needed information on a timely basis.

Modern technology and planning tools – when used by trained staffs and skilled operators – can compress the planning cycle. This has been seen in the quick-response execution of missions such as CSAR, NEO and even air strikes. Computerized mission planning is one of the key enablers for compression of the planning cycle. If updated with accurate intelligence, computerized mission planning can direct helicopters around enemy air defences, ensure that low-altitude flight paths do not intersect with power lines and that covert locations can be selected with reference to databases on population density and transportation routes. Units such as an MEU (SOC) make extensive use of such tools. This reflects their requirement to be able to launch forces within six hours of receiving a warning order.[4] The Marines train and practise these operations before an MEU (SOC) is certified as mission-ready and deployable. These tools are accompanied by improved quick-reaction planning processes. Instead of the US Army's standard fifteen-step planning process (though, in practice, the fifteen steps are frequently compressed or combined under battlefield conditions) intended to generate a detailed Operations Order, an MEU (SOC) uses a streamlined six-step order process.[5]

The importance of a rapid planning and mission co-ordination capability underlines one difference between US SOF and those of other successful practitioners such as Britain and Israel. The British and Israeli forces are relatively small. Those involved in a rapid planning situation are likely to know each other. Perhaps more importantly, those at the national command authority are also likely to know them and trust that they can rely on them. In the larger US SOF, with its associated personnel turbulence, such personal contacts are less likely to exist. In the past, personal contacts and the confidence gained during previous operations have stretched across service lines and, long before computerized mission planning systems, enabled effective quick-reaction planning of operations, as demonstrated in the Los Banos and Korea operations.

INTELLIGENCE

Even the best intelligence is insufficient for success unless it enables timely execution. Intelligence failures have contributed to many of the failures in previous liberation and seizure missions. The inability to acquire timely, accurate information about key factors – the presence of the prisoners at Son Tay, the dust cloud in Iran, the strength and armament of the Khmer Rouge on Koh Tang – has been critical in contributing to mission failures. Where intelligence proved to be lacking, the mission failed or was only redeemed by the actions of the fighting troops.

The development of sensors and expertise means that no future force will literally jump into an intelligence vacuum as the 187th did in Korea (and find an ambush the next day) or the SEALs on Grenada. Intelligence is unlikely to be kept from those having to carry out a raid, as it was at Son Tay and in the *Mayaguez* incident. Press reports of US special forces operations in Afghanistan and Iraq in 2001–3 have stressed improved SOF co-ordination with intelligence.

Effective intelligence must include not only making information available, but analysis as well. Much of the problem is with the difficulty of qualitative assessment of the enemy. Intelligence, if successful, can give you an accurate enemy order of battle and deployment. Without analysis of intelligence, it cannot tell you whether the enemy will run away at the first sight of the raiders or fight to the death while trying to slaughter any prisoners. But emerging technologies cannot provide many of the details that can determine the outcome of an operation. Analysis failure comes about when the information is available, but no one has put the pieces together, or has put them together in a misleading (often expedient) way.

The absence of effective human intelligence (HUMINT) led to the requirement for an Iran raiding force that was too large to survive helicopter mechanical failure and the 'blind' SOF insertions on Grenada. While there is no substitute for HUMINT, where it has been lacking other types of intelligence can compensate. Son Tay's meticulous planning was carried out around a lack of HUMINT. Unfortunately, HUMINT has been the area in which US intelligence has been identified as being weakest. The type of information it provides is unlikely to be duplicated by the national technical means that the US has increasingly come to rely upon in recent years. This has been compensated for in situations such as the hunts for Noriega, bin Laden and Saddam Hussein by working with the (new) host nation governments in large-scale personnel debriefing and document-exploitation efforts that have generated actionable and timely intelligence for seizure missions. But this type of HUMINT requires 'boots on the ground'; it would be difficult to achieve for the sort of seizure raids the Clinton administration considered in 1998–2000.

Other types of intelligence are also critical. SIGINT (especially COMINT) – if it can be made available in near real-time to guide the execution of an operation – is often the best indication of what the enemy knows. When North Vietnamese air defence radars and the Iranian tactical communications frequencies did not 'light up' as the raiders were ingressing, they were able to assume that the element of surprise had been maintained. COMINT is especially critical in seizure missions. It provides an opportunity to gain some idea of where a single elusive individual – a Noriega, bin Laden or Saddam Hussein – may be even if the communication itself is encrypted. This is an area where the objectives of intelligence – concerned with maintaining the value of their sources and traffic analysis – may clash with the objectives of the special operators – a successful seizure. The absence of a SIGINT capability (as in the Sukchon–Sunchon operation) or where the enemy did not rely on radar or electronic communications (Koh Tang and Mogadishu) contributed to intelligence failures. But even before fibre-optic cables and widespread computer encryption, there was a limit to what SIGINT could provide to a raid. Much of the critical information is unlikely to be transmitted by an opponent. The reported order to massacre the Los Banos internees and the one to move the US PoWs at Son Tay were not picked up, even though the US apparently had substantial intercept and decrypt capabilities in both situations.

Intelligence, surveillance and reconnaissance (ISR) support can contribute to the success of raids. In Afghanistan, US Air Force E-8C Joint Surveillance Target Attack Radar System (JSTARS) aircraft used their moving target indicator (MTI) radars to check for vehicular traffic along the ingress and egress routes of SOF helicopters. Enemy movement of reinforcements towards an LZ or objective – indications that an operation might be compromised – would also show up on the MTI. The JSTARS used its high-resolution synthetic aperture radar (SAR) capability to check out LZs before insertions. In the 2 April 2003 raid in Iraq, real-time video from AV-8Bs and UAVs was made available both to rear headquarters and also to the AC-130 supporting the raid.

Improved intelligence and IPB make raids less visible – through mission planning around radar or identifying enemy weakness – while making the enemy and their actions more visible to improved sensors and ISR capability. Future raiders are likely to have available enhanced sensor data to support their operations. The problem may be too much data, threatening to overwhelm them with information, rather than too little. The difficulty will be in making sure that information overload is avoided and that the sensors talk to those who most need the information. This means avoiding situations like the one in Mogadishu on 3 October 1993 where the aircraft and helicopters were able to provide the JOC with real-time video observation of the battle sites, but not the fighting men of Task Force Ranger or the Quick Reaction Force that needed it more.

Improved integrative technologies will reduce the navigational mistakes and command and control failures that have imperilled such missions in the past; they will prevent any more live raiders from being left behind as at Koh Tang.

Landing at the wrong LZ – as at the 'secondary school' at Son Tay – also proved to be widespread in raids attempted in training at the NTC and JRTC.[6] The ground columns in Mogadishu required helicopters to guide them. The near-universal provision of accurate GPS navigation is likely to prevent the recurrence of such problems in the future.

Much of what is ascribed to luck in military history is really only the covering up of either poor training and planning or the enemy's intelligence successes, especially HUMINT and cryptography. There is no evidence that any of these actions failed as a result of poor operational security, although the US military, with its prodigious use of the electromagnetic spectrum and tendency towards the use of mass overwhelming forces, finds it difficult to achieve operational surprise even against a relatively unsophisticated opponent. However, the cost of preventing security failures through effective operational security (OPSEC) can be high indeed, as the events of the Iran raid demonstrate. But this disaster occurred during a period when the chance for compromise, with the intelligence resources of the Soviet Union watching US activities, was much greater. This is an area where it is difficult for anyone, but especially the US armed forces, to achieve a successful balance between security and integration.

TECHNOLOGY AND EQUIPMENT

The US tends to identify capabilities with equipment. US special operations capabilities have required considerable investment in equipment (as well as training), but in return provide an unmatched capability. Today, an arsenal of specialized weapons makes US special operations forces the most lethal creatures walking on two legs. US SOCOM has its own, limited, research and development budget for producing technology to support special operations.

In the future, new technology will allow greater lethality and dispersion of raider fire power, allowing for a smaller footprint, which in turn will make raids more difficult to detect. New precision weapons will allow more effective use of fire power while minimizing collateral damage or the danger of killing the prisoners or leaders who are the objective of the raid.

Since the Second World War, most raiders have been limited to the fire power they can carry with them and use quickly. Even when air power has been available, in many of these situations it has not been possible to use it, due either to communications problems (as in Korea in 1950) or collateral-damage concerns (as at Koh Tang, Panama and Mogadishu). The most significant source of precision fire power for US raiders has been US Air Force AC-130 gunships. When their fire power has been absent – whether due to communications failures, as at Paitilla, or due to political decisions, as at Mogadishu – they have been sorely missed. Despite its potential vulnerability in light of the proliferation of man-portable surface-to-air missiles worldwide, the AC-130 is likely to continue to be a part of liberation and seizure missions in the future.

Fire power in liberation and seizure missions needs to be highly accurate. Reducing collateral damage is an obvious aim in an operation where prisoners are to be liberated or hostile leaders taken prisoner. Calling in fire power has long been a primary SOF mission. A capability for greater accuracy, as demonstrated in Afghanistan in 2001 and Iraq in 2003, has made this mission more important. Integrating this capability with liberation or seizure missions is potentially valuable. Other sources of accurate fire power are in research and development, including a laser weapon that will be capable of stopping a vehicle by burning out its engine without harming passengers.

Adapting secure communications technology to the requirements of raiders is a high-payoff area, which can include provision of remote sensor data in real-time and effective identification friend or foe (IFF) of troops on the ground to prevent fratricide. Communications breakdown – whether from equipment or user failure – was instrumental in the setbacks to the Marines at Koh Tang and during the Iran raid, and to the SEALs at Paitilla.

Communications also enable top-down micro-management, a widespread problem in the US military since the Second World War (most notably during the *Mayaguez* raid). While well-rehearsed set-piece raids such as Son Tay could be self-contained, this has not been the case for many other actions. When raids are taking place as part of larger military operations, reliable, impenetrable communications are required to integrate SOF with the other forces.

In 1950, the 187th went on the defensive at night. In Vietnam, the night was said to belong to the enemy. That conflict started the research and development in night vision. Night-vision equipment – greatly improved since Vietnam – has allowed US raiders literally to own the night. The 1980s brought about the US transformation to a true twenty-four-hour-capable military to an extent never seen before.

The same transformation may be in progress for other environments. Task Force Ranger saw the unmapped streets and alleys of Mogadishu as an unfriendly environment, to be avoided or flown over. Since then, the US military has worked on the problems of operations in Third World conurbations – including raids – and now sees them, though still not a good place to fight, as being like a jungle: a hostile environment to be sure, but one where the best-trained and toughest troops will have an advantage. This was reflected in the increased US urban warfare capabilities demonstrated in Iraq in 2003.

Effective raids have, since Korea, required effective helicopter use. Enabling this has often proved difficult, leading to the complex planning of Son Tay, the *Mayaguez* incident and the Iran raid. In each of these cases, the range and ability of CH-53-series helicopters became the critical determinant of whether the action was feasible.

The future of the US capability to carry out raids and rescues is going to be called into question as the CH-53-series helicopters reach the end of their service lives. It has long been planned to replace them with the V-22 Osprey series. Capable of high-speed long-range flight as well as vertical takeoff and landing (VTOL), the Osprey design's future is uncertain, but the same mix of capabilities is still required for rescue and raiding operations.

If it is considered important enough for strategic raids (like Iran) to be carried out effectively, SOCOM is going to need more than new helicopters or Ospreys – it will need aircraft like the Boeing ATT (Advanced Theatre Transport). This is a VTOL tailless C-130-size transport. It is currently only a 'viewgraph design' – no money has been spent on bending metal or research and development – and is likely to remain that way.

According to Randy Murphy, SOCOM deputy special programme project manager, 'SOCOM has been trying to basically run an air force and a navy on an infantry budget.'[7] SOCOM research and development spending, while effective, has so far been primarily used for adapting equipment to SOF needs (such as GPS-guided parasails for precision resupply). While no major service – and the services continue to control the bulk of research and development funding – is going to view as a priority the ATT or a comparable aircraft to enable long-range strategic raids, there may be enough overlap with future logistics-driven requirements like that for the Army's Advanced Manoeuvre Transport (AMT) Programme, which is looking towards, in the post-2020 timeframe, a heavy-lift rotorcraft capable of lifting 20 tonnes at 300 knots over a 1,000 km combat radius. Such a capability will go a long way to overcoming the limitations of the CH-53-series helicopters that have hindered raids since Son Tay.

The need to invest in major equipment in order to maintain a successful capability for liberation or seizure operations – especially at long range –

clashes with the priority to fund other investments required to create a transformation in theatre war-fighting, taking full advantage of technologies thrust forward by the microchip revolution. Complicating this is that while all US leaders know, value and appreciate having the capability to conduct liberation or seizure operations without the massive force commitments and high diplomatic costs of a decisive conflict, this does not present an incentive to invest now so that their successors in fifteen to twenty years may have an enhanced version of this capability.

LESS-LETHAL OPTIONS

Ever since Germany's GSG-9 introduced the use of British-developed 'flash-bang' stun grenades in the 1977 Mogadishu airport hijack rescue, non-lethal weapons have been part of the arsenal of raiders aiming to liberate or take prisoners. In the US, such weapons are not limited to rescue specialists such as Delta Force and SEAL Team 6. They are also now used by MEU (SOC)s, especially for NEO and crowd-control tasks. Other non-lethal weapons, including some using disabling high-power microwave technology, are currently in research and development. The high casualties suffered as collateral damage during the rescue of the theatre hostages in Moscow in 2002, however, provide a reminder that such weapons are not without their risks. Non-lethal weapons are an area where future raiders will benefit from current investment. Non-lethal weapons that can cover an area or incapacitate prisoners, high-value targets and gunmen alike at a critical point in a raid would solve many of the tactical problems encountered at the objective which currently complicate liberation and seizure missions.

The US military has also been willing to invest in less-than-maximum lethality. For all its love of big bombs and massive fire power, the US military's concern about collateral damage and the ability to achieve increased accuracy have led to greater investment in optimum rather than maximum lethality. The Air Force's newest bomb is a highly accurate 113 kg weapon, a size rejected as too small in 1941. In addition to new-technology non-lethal weapons, the US is looking at how systems such as EC-130 Compass Call jammer aircraft can be used to 'service' targets other than by destroying them.

Liberation and seizure missions are themselves less-lethal options. US prisoners and, in most cases, enemy leaders are better alive than dead. Even with the rise of precision weapons, it remains the case that 'surgical strike' is an oxymoron. If you want to get live bodies, you will still need to send live bodies – in the form of raiders – to get them. It is difficult to characterize a well-armed raider as a less-lethal system, yet a well-trained special operator with sensors and well-rehearsed procedures to engage themselves or call in supporting fire power remains the most discriminating weapons platform available. The increased availability of systems such as long-range large-calibre sniper rifles and laser sights for assault rifles have increased raiders' precision, as well as their lethality.

THE HUMAN DIMENSION

Successful special operations – including raids – require skilled personnel. At the planner/command level, this means having motivated, trained professionals who do not find their careers wilted or blocked by special operations assignment, as was often the case before the establishment of SOCOM, the US Army's Special Operations branch, and its Air Force and Navy counterparts. The US, following the re-building of US forces in the early 1980s and the reforms in the mid-1980s, has become better at training special operations personnel thoroughly and promoting those who prove most proficient at it. Initiative and creativity as much as effective planning and training are required for successful direct action. Today's SOF leaders, serving since SOCOM was established, have been able to go through service schools and joint assignments with a special operations orientation.[8] Widespread combat experience provides fertile ground for innovation.

At the operator level, the need for skilled personnel to make possible successful special operations means more than such exemplars as Delta Force, 160th SOAR and SEAL Team 6 (now NAVSPECWAR Development Group). It also includes the skills embodied in an MEU (SOC) when it has been fully trained and is ready for deployment. No amount of training or planning can take into account every possible contingency likely to be encountered during a raid or rescue. Rather, well-trained personnel have been able to avoid disaster even when things have not gone as planned.

The NCO is always the critical part of a raid, required to make sound, instant decisions in the field. This is why SOCOM stresses the maturity, age, experience and capabilities of its NCOs (another influence from the SAS). At no time have the raiders ever caused a mission to fail, even when their leaders have led them into situations such as the final evacuations from Koh

Tang in 1975 and Desert One in 1980. They have also remedied situations that could have turned into disasters, such as at Government House on Grenada.

A capability to plan, organize and execute special operations to match the capability of individuals on the ground to carry them out would be a tremendous advance. There have been many instances where planning let down the troops at the sharp end, but none where failure was due to a lack of resolve by those actually carrying out the mission. In all of these raids, at no time did the fighting troops involved fail to do all that was asked of them. The training and rehearsal of the ground combat units involved in these raids varied greatly, but none of the missions that failed did so because of the soldiers involved. Rather, the weak links have proven to be at a higher level.

Motivation and courage are not enough for a successful raid, although it is unlikely that such missions will be successful without them. But relying on motivation and courage to overcome inappropriate training, poor tactics and inadequate planning is inexcusable. Some of the missions on Grenada came disturbingly close to this model, but fortunately there were sufficiently few motivated enemy and the overall US strength was great enough to avoid disaster.

The aptness of USSOCOM's 'SOF Truths' has been demonstrated repeatedly in special operations actions from the Second World War to the present: humans are more important than hardware; quality is more important that quantity; SOF can't be mass-produced; competent SOF can't be created after an emergency occurs. Yet there is a flip side to each of these truths.

Humans are indeed more important than hardware, but it was hardware failure that doomed the Iran raid and communications failures that kept the Marines pinned down on Koh Tang. Relying on the men of TF Ranger and the QRF in unarmoured vehicles to extract the raiders in Mogadishu rather than a combined-arms force was an inappropriate reliance on humans rather than hardware.

Quality is indeed more important than quantity, but the lack of extra helicopters in the Iran raid or tanks with the QRF in Mogadishu proved decisive. Had TF Ranger been able to stage more than one raid at a time and sustain a high operational tempo, their quality might not have been undercut by a lack of quantity.

SOF cannot be mass-produced, but this raises the question that Churchill brought up with regard to them in the Second World War: what is the good of having them if they cannot be risked? They become the expensive, undriven 'Ferrari in the garage'. Congress can ensure that SOF are funded. They cannot ensure that they are effectively integrated into overall US warfighting, although that appears to be a major objective of Defense Secretary Rumsfeld.

Some of the forces that carried out raids were only created just before going into action: the 187th Airborne RCT in Korea or the Son Tay raiders, for example. The high availability of experienced personnel, especially at the leadership level, made them effective units. Where you cannot improvise a capability is in the commanders, planners and their staffs. The complexities of raids are such that they require specialists with operational experience in planning, training and organization to bring success.

THE FUTURE

The future is likely to see a continued improvement in technology balanced against a continued impetus to repeat mistakes that have caused raids either to fail or to suffer causalities in the past. Sometimes the lessons have their own costs. The determination in Mogadishu 'to leave no man behind' came from the spirit of the men themselves, but it is difficult not to see in it the – however unconscious – desire not to repeat the incident of dead bodies being left to the Iranians at Desert One or the live Marines left behind to the Khmer Rouge on Koh Tang.

The NCA or a CINC, if presented with the requirement for a liberation or seizure mission, must accept the high-risk nature of such missions and have available forces ready to carry it out even if the window of opportunity is brief. The forces need to be available and capable of planning and executing in a time-compressed situation on short notice while retaining the benefits of training, rehearsal, meticulous planning and in-depth intelligence. Reconciling these competing requirements is not impossible, but it will require extensive investment in doctrine, training, equipment and, above all, in the continued maintenance of high-quality planners, analysts and operators.

If the US strengthens its capabilities to conduct liberation and seizure missions, it will have the effect of both providing additional options to the NCA and CINCs alike and of being an example of a mission area where risk-taking – when informed by the best possible IPB and carried out by the best possible forces – is going to be the way the US military achieves success. Success in these missions is not linked to massed forces or overwhelming fire power. If the US is to win without employing these larger resources, it must invest in being able to carry out liberation and seizure operations. But developing this capability requires training, tactics and equipment and the ability for them to be enabled by effective planning and timely intelligence.

In the future, it is likely that the US will continue to invest in its extensive special operations capabilities. The need for many of them has been seen in action since the Second World War. It has been proposed that SOCOM be given primary responsibility for the military dimension of the war on terrorism, increasing its budget and responsibility accordingly.[9]

While the realities of the world situation post-11 September 2001 have not led to liberation or seizure missions re-emerging as a high-level policy or choice – notwithstanding the SOF in Afghanistan trying to seize the remaining Al Qaida and Taliban leadership and covert Delta Force and CIA teams in Iraq in the 2003 hunt for Saddam – it is likely that in the near future, both the NCA and theatre or SOCOM CINCs will have to consider the ordering and execution of liberation and seizure missions.

The bottom line is the same as Lion Gardiner's: 'policy is needful in war as well as strength.' Nowhere is the intersection of the two so pronounced as in liberation and seizure missions. While the strength of the fighting men committed to these operations – and their desire to 'leave no man behind' – never failed, the policies that sent them on the missions, organized the missions or failed to support the missions have often let them down.

Despite the tremendous strength – physical and intellectual – of the individuals involved in planning and executing these actions, even with effective support and when launched in the context of a viable overall policy – which has often not been the case – liberation and seizure missions remain high-risk operations, with the potential for high political (even if not military) costs in the event of failure. Yet there will be times when there will be no substitute for such actions. To determine when this is the case and, if so, carry out these actions successfully represents a need to combine the 'policy and strength' that has been necessary for American fighting men since Lion Gardiner first put pen to paper for their benefit in 1660.

NOTES TO THE TEXT

CHAPTER 1

1 Sources on special operations include: Arostegui, M. C., *Twilight Warriors*, New York, St. Martin's Press, 1995. Barnett, F. R., R. H. Shultz and B. H. Tovar (eds.), *Special Operations in US Strategy*, Washington, NDU Press, 1984. Brauer Jr., R. F., *A Critical Examination of the Planning Imperatives Applicable to Hostage Rescue Operations*, Carlisle Barracks, USAWC, 18 April 1984. Canby, S., E. Luttwak and D. Thomas, *A Systematic Review of 'Commando' (Special) Operations*, Potomac, C & L Associates, 1982. Darman, P., *Surprise Attack*, New York, Basic Books, 1993. Glenn, R. W., *Combat in Hell: A Consideration of Constrained Urban Warfare*, Santa Monica, RAND, 1996. Hedstrom, MAJ M. A., *Simultaneity: A Question of Time, Space, Resources and Purpose*, Ft. Leavenworth, USACGSC SAMS, 2001. Kelly, LTC P. K., 'Raids and National Command: Mutually Exclusive', *Military Review*, April 1980. Lloyd, M., *Special Forces*, London, Cassell, 1995. McKinney, Maj. M., and M. Ryan, *Chariots of the Damned*, New York, St. Martin's Press, 2002. Megill, T. A., *OOTW, Raids and Tactical Surprise*, Ft. Leavenworth, SAAMS, 14 December 1994. Mornston, MAJ H. E., *Raids at the Operational Level – to What End*, Ft. Leavenworth, USACGSC SAMS, 1992. Neillands, R., *In the Combat Zone*, New York, NYU Press, 1998. Paro, K. A., and E. G. Winters, *The Misuse of Special Operations Forces*, Monterey, USNPGS, December 1994. Perkins, C. S., *Special Operations Forces: Integral Part of the Theater Operating System*, Newport, USNWC, 8 February 1994. Putz, LTC J. L., *SOF: The Engagement Force of Choice*, Carlisle Barracks, USAWC, 12 March 2001. Rosenau, W., MR-1408-AF, *Special Operations Forces and Elusive Enemy Ground Targets*, Santa Monica, RAND, 2001. Southworth, S. A. (ed.), *Great Raids in History*, New York, Sarpedon, 1997.

2 The extensive literature of US special operations forces includes: Adams, J. A., *Future Warrior*, Carlisle Barracks, USAWC, 1 June 1996. Adams, T. K., *US Special Operations Forces in Action*, London, Frank Cass, 1998. Amato, E. J., *Street Smarts, Unconventional Warriors in Contemporary Joint Urban Operations*, Monterey, USNPGS, June 2001. Bates, C. C. and John F. Fuller, *America's Weather Warriors*, College Station, A & M Press, 1986. Brown, CPT H. S., *The Command and Control of Special Operations Forces*, Monterey, USNPGS, December 1996. Chalker, D. with K. Dockery, *One Perfect Op*, New York, Morrow, 2002. Chinnery, P. D., *Any Time, Any Place*, Annapolis, Naval Institute Press, 1994. Colburn, Maj. T., *Running on Empty*, Maxwell AFB, ACSC, March 1997. Collins, COL J. M., *Special Operations Forces: An Assessment*, Washington, NDU Press, 1994. Dockery, K., *SEALs in Action*, New York, Avon, 1992. Fisher, Dr. J. R., Dr. S. L. Sandler and Dr. R. W. Stewart, *Command History of the United States Army Special Operations Command: 1987–1992. Standing Up the MACOM*, Fort Bragg, USASOC, 1996. Flora, Lt. Col. E., *Op Art to the Rescue: Fundamentals For a Hostage Crisis*, Newport, USNWC, May 1998. Government Accounting Office, *Special Operations Forces*, GAO-NSIAD-97-85, Washington, 15 May 1997. Gustaitis, LTC P. J., *Coalition Special Operations*, Carlisle Barracks, USAWC, 1998. Haney, E. L., *Inside Delta Force*, New York, Delacorte Press, 2002. Huchthausen, P., *America's Splendid Little Wars*, New York, Viking, 2003. *Joint Military Operations Historical Collection*, Washington, OJCS, 15 July 1997. Kaputsa, LT P. E., *A*

Comparison of US Navy SEAL and US Army Special Forces, Monterey, USNPGS, June 2000. Keen, COL K., *75th Ranger Regiment*, Carlisle Barracks, USAWC, 1998. Kelly, O., *Brave Men, Dark Waters*, Novato, Presidio, 1992. Kelly, O., *From a Dark Sky*, Navato, Presidio, 1996. McDonald, Maj. R. E., *Cohesion: The Key to Special Operations Teamwork*, Maxwell AFB, AUP, 1994. McMillin, MAJ C. D., *Roles and Missions of Airborne, Ranger and Special Forces in Contingency Operations*, Ft. Leavenworth, USACGSC, 1979. Maher, J. A., *Special Operations Forces in Direct Action*, Carlisle Barracks, USAWC, 31 March 1990. Marquis, S. L., *Protecting a Precarious Value: The Fight to Revitalize US Special Operations Forces*, PhD Dissertation, Princeton University, 1995. Marquis, S. L., *Unconventional Warfare*, Washington, Brookings, 1997. Minish, T. R., *The Joint Rescue Task Force*, Newport, USNWC, 14 June 1996. Nicholson, Maj. L. D., *An Analysis of the Twenty-One Missions of the Marine Corps Expeditionary Unit (Special Operations Capable)*, Ft. Leavenworth, USACGSC, 1994. Nordberg, R. A., *High-Profile Special Operations Missions and Timing Identifying the Culminating Point of Execution*, Newport, USNWC, February 1999. Ott, MAJ P. A., *Unconventional Warfare in the Contemporary Operational Environment: Transforming Special Forces*, Ft. Leavenworth, USACGSC SAMS, 2002. Paschell, R., *LIC 2010*, London, Brassey's, 1990. Stubblefield, G. with H. Halberstadt, *Inside the US Navy SEALs*, Osceola, Motorbooks, 1985. Thompson, Maj. B., *For Valor or Value. An Examination of Personnel Recovery Operations*, Maxwell AFB, ACSC, SAAS, June 2001. USAF, Air Force Doctrine Document 35, *Special Operations*, Washington DC, 20 July 1998. US SOCOM, Annual Posture Statements, JP 3-095, *Doctrine for Joint Special Operations*, Washington, OJCS, 17 April 1998. Vandenbroucke, L. S., *Perilous Options: Special Operations as an Instrument of U.S. Foreign Policy*, New York, Oxford University Press, 1993. Walker, LT R., *Spec Fi*, Monterey, USNPGS, December 1998. Waller, D. C., *The Commandos*, New York, Simon & Schuster, 1994. White Jr., MAJ R. C., *The Airborne Force of the United States Army*, Newport, USNWC, February 1999.

3 A seminal study of liberation missions is: Bailey, Maj. M., *Prisoner of War Rescue by Air Insertion*, Ft. Leavenworth, USACGSC, 1982.

4 See generally: Malvesti, M. L., *Risk-Taking in Countering Terrorism: A Study of US Presidential Decisions to Use Special Operations and Covert Action*, PhD dissertation, Fletcher School, June 2002.

5 This concept is developed at length in McRaven, W. H., *SPEC OPS, Case Studies in Special Operations: Theory and Practice*, Novato, Presidio, 1995.

CHAPTER 2

1 Sources on the raid include: *After Action Report XIV Corps M-1 Operation*, n.d., US National Archives, RG 407, Box 4621. Headquarters Sixth Army, *Sixth Army on Luzon, Clearing Batangas and the Bicol.*, Section 2, n.d., US National Archives, RG 407, Box 2405. Headquarters, 11th Airborne Division, *After Action Report, Mike VI Operation Luzon Campaign*, 24 January 1946, US National Archives, RG 407, Box 7583. Headquarters, 11th Airborne Division, *Report on the Los Banos Operation, Luzon P.I.*, 17 March 1945, US National Archives, RG 407, Box 7585. Headquarters, 672nd Amphibious Tractor Battalion, *672nd Amphibian Tractor Battalion Unit Journal*, 23 Feb 1945, US National Archives, RG 407, Box 16652. Headquarters, 672nd Amphibious Tractor Battalion, *Historical Record of the 672nd Amphibian Tractor Battalion During the Luzon Campaign*, 30 June 1945, US National Archives, RG 407, Box 16652. *History – Luzon Campaign (Draft) – 188th Parachute Infantry Regiment – 11th Airborne Division, 31 January–31 March 1945*, pp. 12–16, US National Archives, RG 407, Box 7596. Report for Assistant Chief of Staff for Operations, 30 March 1945, US National Archives, RG 407, Box 1652. Arthur, A., *Deliverance at Los Banos*, New York, St. Martin's Press, 1985. Bailey, Maj. M. C., 'Raid at Los Banos', *Military Review*, May 1983. Burgess, H. A., *Looking Back*, Missoula, Pictorial Histories, 1993. Flanagan, E. M., *Angels at Dawn*, Novato, Presidio, 1986. Walsh Jr., LTC L. A., *Report of Airborne Operations Luzon Campaign*, 30 March 1945.

2 http://www.thedropzone.org/pacific/Ringler.html

3 Parker, CPT H. J., 'Through the Eyes of the Pilot', *Winds Aloft*, n.d., reprinted at http://groups.msn.com/G511th Airborne

4 Santos, T., 'The Provisional Recon Platoon, Spearhead of the Los Banos Raid', *Winds Aloft*, n.d.

5 Squires, M., 'The Reconnaissance Mission at Los Banos', *Winds Aloft*, reprinted at http://groups.msn.com/G511thAirborne

6 Flanagan, op. cit., p. 134.

7 Withers, B., 'The Miracle of Los Banos', *The Herald Dispatch* (Huntington WV), 20 October 2001, Internet ed.

8 Walsh, op. cit., p. 11.

9 Dougherty, CPT K., 'Rescue in the Philippines', *Soldiers*, February 1995, p. 52.

10 http://groups.msn.com/G511thAirborne

11 Dougherty, op. cit.

12 Flanagan, op. cit., p. 193.

13 Burgess, op. cit., p. 64.

14 Walsh, op. cit., p. 12. The 672nd's official accounts do not mention this incident.

CHAPTER 3

1 *Foreign Relations of the United States*, 1949, Washington, 1982, Government Printing Office, pp. 1011–23. Buhite, R. D., *Lives at Risk, Hostages and Victims in American Foreign Policy*, Wilmington, Scholarly Resources, 1995, pp. 117–35.

2 Smith, B., *The Shadow Warriors: OSS and the Origins of the CIA*, New York, Basic Books, 1983, pp. 409–10.

3 Bateman, R. L., *No Gun Ri: A Military History of the Korean War Incident*, Mechanicsburg, Stackpole, 2002, pp. 83, 98.

4 Flanagan, LTG E. M., *The Rakkasans: The Combat History of the 187th Airborne Infantry*, Novato, Presidio, 1997, pp. 147–69.

5 Pitman, P. et al., *The Battle of Sukchon-Sunchon*, Combat Studies Institute, US Army Command and General Staff College, Ft. Leavenworth, 1984, p. 19.

6 US Far East Command, General Headquarters, Operations Order Number 3, 16 October 1950, in Bailey, *Prisoner of War*, op. cit., p. 50.

7 Pitman, op. cit., p. 20.

8 'Paratroopers of the 1950s', http://www.home.hiwaay.net/~magro/abn.html

9 Sources on the battle are: 187th RCT *After-Action Report* (AAR) and War Diaries, US National Archives, RG 407, Boxes 3420–21. *187th Airborne RCT I & R Platoon Combat History 12 October 1950–9 July 1951*, Flanagan Jr., LTG E. M., papers, US Army Military History Institute, Box 8. Appleman, R. E., *South to the Naktong, North to the Yalu*, Washington, USGPO, 1992, pp. 654–63. Hockley, A. F., *A Distant Obligation*, London, HMSO, 1990, pp. 246–54. O'Neill, R., *Australia in the Korean War 1950–53, Vol. II Combat Operations*, Canberra, the Australian War Memorial, 1985, pp. 34–8.

10 674th FA (ABN) AAR 20 October 1950, in *187th RCT AAR*, op. cit.

11 'Paratroopers of the 1950s', op. cit.

12 Quoted in Chinnery, P. D., *Korean Atrocity*, Annapolis, NIP, 2000, p. 73.

13 Parsons, B., 'Aussiesome Aussies', www.rt66.com~kortent/SmallArms

14 'Paratroopers of the 1950s', op. cit.

15 The Australian Army in Korea retained the 18-inch bayonet of the Great War for their Mk III Lee Enfields for just such occasions.

16 Appleman, op. cit., p. 660.

17 Evanhoe, E., *Darkmoon*, Annapolis, Naval Institute Press, 1995. Fondacaro, MAJ S. A., *A Strategic Analysis of US Special Operations During the Korean Conflict 1950–53*, Ft. Leavenworth, USACGSC, 1988. Haas, Col. M. E., *In the Devil's Shadow*, Annapolis, Naval Institute Press, 2000.

18 Roksey, W., *Koje Island: The 1952 Korean Hostage Crisis*, The Land Warfare Papers No. 19, September 1994, Arlington VA, The Association of the US Army.

CHAPTER 4

1 Sources include: *Commander Joint Contingency Task Group Report on the Son Tay Prisoner of War Operation*, vols. I & II (hereafter referred to as JCS Report V. I or V. II), Washington, OJCS, 5 May 1976. Glasser, J. D., *The Secret Vietnam War*, Jefferson, McFarland, 1995. Haas, Col. M. E., *Apollo's Warriors: US Air Force Special Operations During the Cold War*, Maxwell AFB, AUP, 1997. McRaven, W. H., *Spec Ops*, op. cit. Sasser, C., *Raider*, New York, St. Martin's Press, 2001. Schemmer,

B. F., *The Raid*, New York, Harper & Row, 1976. Vandenbroucke, L. S., *Perilous Options*, op. cit.

Sources on other US liberation missions before and after Son Tay include: Andrade, D. and K. Conboy, *Spies & Commandos*, Lawrence, University Press of Kansas, 2002. Shultz, R. H., *The Secret War Against North Vietnam*, New York, 1999, Harper Collins.

2 Marquis, S. L., *Protecting a Precarious Value*, op. cit., p. 28.

3 Blackburn, BG D. D. (rtd), interviewed by Smith, Lt. Col. R. B., USAF, US Army Military History Institute Senior Officers Oral History Program, Project 83-9, Vol. II, pp. 371–2.

4 Blackburn, ibid.

5 Blackburn, ibid., p. 374.

6 Schemmer, op. cit., p. 80.

7 Kraljev Jr., Col. B., 'The Son Tay Raid', *Airlift Operations Review*, January 1981, pp. 28–30.

8 Quoted in Haas, op. cit., p. 319.

9 Manor, Lt. Gen. L., 'The Son Tay Raid', *Daedalus Flyer*, Winter 1995.

10 Veith, G. J., *Code Name Bright Light*, New York, Free Press, 1998, p. 266.

11 Quoted in Mitchell, MAJ J., *The Son Tay Raid – A Study in Presidential Policy*, USMC CSC, 1997, Appendix B.

12 Schemmer, op. cit., p. 177.

13 Mitchell, op. cit., p. 17.

14 Schemmer, op. cit., p. 192.

15 Quoted in Manor, op. cit.

16 ibid.

17 The events of the raid are detailed in the JCS Report V. I, pp. 46–65.

18 Waresh, J., 'A-1 Participation in the Son Tay Raid', http://www.jollygreen.org

19 Plaster, J. L., *SOG, The Secret Wars of America's Commandos in Vietnam*, New York, Simon & Schuster, 1997, pp. 84–5.

20 JCS Report, V. I, p. 161.

21 Plaster, op. cit.

22 Quoted in Henry Cunningham, 'Ex-PoWs Call Son Tay Raid A Success', *The Fayetteville Observer*, 25 November 1999.

23 Schemmer, op. cit., p. 216.

24 ibid., pp. 264–5, 297.

25 Blackburn, op. cit., p. 375.

26 ibid., pp. 377–8.

27 JCS Report, V. I, p. ii.

28 ibid., pp. 39–41, 59–61. Kraljev, op. cit., pp. 29–30.

29 Blackburn, op. cit., p. 382.

30 ibid., p. 381.

31 Veith, op. cit., pp. 352–5.

CHAPTER 5

1 Sources include: Austin, Lt. Col. R. W., Col. J. M. Johnson and D. A. Quinlan, 'Individual Heroism Overcame Awkward Command Relationships, Confusion and Bad Information Off the Cambodian Coast', *Marine Corps Gazette*, October 1977, pp. 24–34. Bates, LCDR S. E., *Command, Control, Communication and Intelligence in the* Mayaguez *Incident*, Newport, USNWC, February 1998. *BLT 2/9 Koh Tang/*Mayaguez *Historical Report*, 9 December 1975, available at Marine Corps University Archives, Quantico. Dunham, Maj. G. R. and Col. D. A. Quinlan, *US Marines in Vietnam. The Bitter End. 1973–75*, Washington, GPO, 1990. Ford, G. R., *A Time to Heal*, New York, Berkley, 1979. Guilmartin Jr., J. F., *A Very Short War: The* Mayaguez *and the Battle of Koh Tang*, College Station, Texas A & M Press, 1995. LaVelle, Gen. A. J. C., ed., *Fourteen Hours at Koh Tang*, Washington, GPO, 1975. Minutes of National Security Council Meetings 12–15 May 1975, NSC Options Paper, and Presidential Memoranda authorizing use of non-lethal gas declassified by Gerald R. Ford Library. Mueller, T. H., *Chaos Theory and the* Mayaguez *Crisis*, Carlisle Barracks, USAWC, 15 March 1980. Patrick, U. W., *The* Mayaguez *Operation*, Arlington, Center for Naval Analysis, April 1977. *Post Mortem Report, An Examination of the Intelligence Community Performance Before and During the Mayaguez Incident of May 1975*, CIA, 8 August 1975 (declassified excerpts). Rowan, R., *The Four Days of* Mayaguez, New York, Norton, 1975. US House of Representatives, Committee on Foreign Affairs, *Seizure of the* Mayaguez, 94th Cong., 1st Sess., 1975–6, Pts I–IV (Part IV was the GAO Report). US Joint Chiefs of Staff, *After Action Report, US Military Operations SS* Mayaguez, *Koh Tang Island*, Washington, OJCS, 1977 (unclassified excerpts).

2 Patrick, op. cit., p. 42.

3 NSC Meeting Minutes, 12 May 1975, 12:05 p.m. meeting, declassified version at Gerald Ford Presidential Library.

4 NSC Meeting Minutes, 13 May 1975, 10:22 p.m. meeting, declassified version at Gerald Ford Presidential Library.

5 Browning, SMSgt. G. G., *Background Paper on the* Mayaguez *Incident: An Enlisted Perspective on a USAF Security Police Tragedy*, Gunter AFB, SNCOA, 1992, p. 4.

6 ibid, p. 7.

7 NSC Meeting Minutes, 13 May 1975, 10:40 p.m. meeting, declassifed version at Gerald Ford Presidential Library.

8 Hunter, R., 'The Last Battle of Vietnam', *Vietnam Airwar*, Winter 2002, p. 25.

9 Guilmartin, op. cit., p. 56.

10 NSC Meeting Minutes, 13 May 1975, 10:40 p.m. meeting, declassified version at Gerald Ford Presidential Library.

11 Dunham and Quinlan, op. cit., p. 251. Wetterhahn, R., *The Last Battle: The* Mayaguez *Incident and the End of the Vietnam War*, New York, Carroll & Graf, 2001, pp. 62–3 on the failure to deploy 1-9th Marines.

12 Patrick, op. cit., pp. 102–3.

13 US House of Representatives, *Seizure*, GAO Report, op. cit., p. 60.

14 Patrick, op. cit., p. 89.

15 ibid., pp. 92–3.

16 NSC Meeting Minutes, 13 May 1975, 10:40 p.m. meeting. declassified version at Gerald Ford Presidential Library.

17 Kelly, O., *From a Dark Sky*, op. cit., p. 227.

18 Statement of DCI Colby quoted in NSC Meeting Minutes, 14 May 1975, 3:52 p.m. meeting, declassifed version at Gerald Ford Presidential Library.

19 Patrick, op. cit., p. 66.

20 USJCS AAR, op. cit., TAB B.

21 Wetterhahn, op. cit., p. 272.

22 Huchthausen, *Splendid Little Wars*, op. cit., p. 13.

23 Austin, Johnson and Quinlan, op. cit, p. 29.

24 Kelly, op. cit., p. 230.

25 On the left-behind Marines, see Wetterhahn, op. cit., and Hunter, R., 'Marine MIAs, Fate Unknown', *VFW Magazine*, May 2000, pp. 22–4.

26 Kelly, op. cit. p. 205.

27 Kissinger, H., *Years of Renewal*, New York, Simon & Shuster, 1999, p. 575.

28 Wetterhahn, op. cit., p. 283.

29 Butson, T. and B. Rollins, 'Phnom Penh's Version of the *Mayaguez Story*', *The New York Times*, 14 May 1975, p. 4.

30 Lamb, C. J., *Belief Systems and Decision Making in the* Mayaguez *Crisis*, University of Florida Press, 1989, pp. 31–3.

CHAPTER 6

1 The participants in the raid's memoir literature and the post-facto Holloway Commission report remain valuable sources: 'A Participant', *The Iran Hostage Rescue Attempt. A Pilot's Perspective*, Maxwell AFB, ACSC, 1982. Beckwith, C. A. and D. Knox, *Delta Force: The US Counter-Intelligence Unit and the Iran Hostage Rescue Mission*, New York, Harcourt Brace & Jovanovich, 1983. Brzezinski, Z., *Power and Principle: Memoirs of the National Security Advisor*, New York, Farrar Straus, 1983. Edson, J. R. and J. H. Kyle, *The Guts to Try: The Untold Story of the Iran Hostage Rescue Mission by the On-Scene Desert Commander*, New York, Crown, 1980. Holloway III, ADM J. L. (Chair), Rescue Mission Report, Washington, August 1980. Lenahan, R., *Crippled Eagle: A Historical Perspective of US Special Operations 1976–1996*, Charleston, Narwhal Press, 1996. Other sources include: *Department of Defense Appropriations for 1981, Hearing Before the House Appropriations Committee Subcommittee on the Department of Defense*, Part 4, H181-105, Washington, USGPO, 1981, pp. 605–75. Flora, Lt. Col. E., *Op Art*, op. cit. Gass, MAJ G. P., *Command and Control: The Achilles Heel of the Iran Hostage Rescue Mission*, Newport, USNWC, 13 February 1992. House Armed Services Committee Hearing Transcript (Lt. Gen. Gast, MG Vaught) for 6 May 1980. Kernan, LTC W. F., *The Holloway Report: Did It Reflect All the Facts and Lessons Learned?*, Carlisle Barracks, USAWC, 21 March 1987. Mis, MAJ J. M., *From Son Tay to Desert One: Lessons Unlearned,*

Newport, USNWC, 13 February 1998. Radvanyi, Maj. R. A., *Operation Eagle Claw – Lessons Learned*, Quantico, USMCCSC, 2001. Ryan, P. B., *The Iranian Rescue Mission: Why It Failed*, Annapolis, Naval Institute Press, 1985. Senate Armed Services Committee Hearing Transcripts for 2 May 1980 (Lt. Col. Kyle), 5 May 1980 (Lt. Gen. Gast, MG Vaught, COL Beckwith). Thomas, LTC C. S., *The Iranian Hostage Rescue Attempt*, Carlisle Barracks, USAWC, 23 March 1987. Washington Post Company v. Department of Defense, US District Court, District of Columbia, Civil Action No. 84-3400, documents (held at NSA/GWU). Wilson, G. C., 'Debate Rekindles on Failed Iran Raid', *The Washington Post*, 25 April 1982, pp. A1, A14.

2 The rise of US CT capability and the hostage crisis is from Martin, D. and J. Wolcott, *The Best Laid Plans*, New York, Harper Collins, 1988.

3 The author was familiar with one of the units soon after this time. It then rejoiced in the nickname 'The Jumping Junkies' and was described as '600 heavily armed drug addicts'. The unit was eventually disbanded and many personnel sent to a military prison.

4 Edson and Kyle, op. cit., p. 23.

5 On Ranger re-creation, see Hogan, D. W., *Raiders or Light Infantry? The Changing Role of US Army Rangers from Dieppe to Grenada*, Westport, Greenwood, 1992, Ch. 12.

6 Lenahan, op. cit., p. 15.

7 Follett, K., *The Wings of Eagles*, New York, William Morrow, 1983.

8 Brzezinski, Z., 'The Failed Mission', *The New York Times Magazine*, 18 April 1982, p. 28.

9 Carter, J., *Keeping Faith*, New York, Bantam, 1982, p. 507–13.

10 Ryan, op. cit., pp. 20, 85.

11 Department of Defense Appropriations for 1981 H181-105, op. cit., pp. 644, 658.

12 Turner, ADM S., *Terrorism and Democracy*, Boston, Houghton Mifflin, 1991, pp. 67–9.

13 Brzezinski, 'The Failed Mission', op. cit., p. 29.

14 Edson and Kyle, op. cit., p. 35.

15 Holloway, op. cit., p. 16.

16 Beckwith and Knox, op. cit., pp. 217–8. Edson and Kyle, op. cit., pp. 60, 88.

17 Cogan, C., 'Desert One and Its Disorders', *Journal of Military History*, January 2003, p. 211.

18 This flight is often referred to as 'Bluebird', but the original flight planning documents published in Iran show it as 'Bluebeard'.

19 Ryan, op. cit., pp. 69–84.

20 Bolger, D. P., *Americans at War 1975–1986*, Novato, Presidio, 1988, p. 126.

21 Outside review could have identified weak points. 'I'm an opera singer. I know nothing about special operations. But I can tell you that if you put the cast together for the first time on the performance night, without a complete dress rehearsal, they are inevitably going to walk into each other or the scenery and stumble over their costumes.' Ms. Leslie Matthews, communication to the author after the release of the Holloway Commission report.

22 'A Participant', op. cit., p. 56.

23 Sick, G., *All Fall Down, America's Tragic Encounter With Iran*, New York, Random House, 1985, p. 287.

24 Brzezinski, *Power*, op. cit., p. 71.

25 Edson and Kyle, op. cit., p. 33.

26 Holloway, op. cit., p. 16.

27 Brown, H. S., *The Command and Control of Special Operations Forces*, Monterey, December 1996, USNPGS, p. 20.

28 'A Participant', op. cit., p. 59.

29 Department of Defense Appropriations for 1981 H181-105, p. 665.

30 Buck, Maj. P. D., USMC, *The Iranian Hostage Rescue Attempt: A Case Study*, Quantico, USMC C & SC, 2002, p. 42.

31 Beckwith and Knox, op. cit., p. 184.

32 Turner, op. cit., p. 167.

33 Holloway, op. cit., p. 37.

34 ibid., p. 33.

35 'A Participant', op. cit., p. 14.

36 ibid., p. 19.

37 Department of Defense Appropriations for 1981 H181-105, op. cit., p. 639.

38 Edson and Kyle, op. cit., p. 165.

39 'A Participant', op. cit., pp. 11–12.

40. ibid., p. 58.

41 Turner, op. cit., p. 67.

42 Powell, J., *The Other Side of the Story*, New York, William Morrow, 1984, p. 228.

43 Edson and Kyle, op. cit., p. 216.

44 Sick, op. cit., p. 285.

45 'A Participant', op. cit., p. 33.

46 Edson and Kyle, op. cit., p. 217.

47 Buck, op. cit., p. 34.

48 'A Participant', op. cit., p. 34.

49 Edson and Kyle, op. cit., p. 279.

50 ibid, p. 274.

51 'A Participant', op. cit., p. 36.

52 Edson and Kyle, op. cit., pp. 262–3. Beckwith and Knox, op. cit., pp. 269 70.

53 Department of Defense Appropriations for 1981 H181-105, op. cit., p. 656.

54 Brzezinski, *Power*, op. cit., p. 498.

55 ibid.

56 'A Participant', op. cit., p. 37.

57 Buck, op. cit., p. 50.

58 'A Participant', op. cit., p. 48.

59 MSG Mike Vining, briefing at SOCOM 31 March 1993, quoted in Marquis, *Protecting a Precarious Value*, op. cit., p. 126.

60 'A Participant', op. cit., p. 38.

61 ibid., p. 39.

62 Edson and Kyle, op. cit., p. 303.

63 Transcripts of White House recordings made during the evacuation of Desert One, declassified excerpts forming part of Washington Post Case (NSA/GWU).

64 Department of Defense Appropriations for 1981 H181-105, op. cit., pp. 662, 668–9.

65 Vance, C., *Hard Choices: Critical Years in American Foreign Policy*, New York, Simon & Schuster, 1983, p. 408.

66 Tehran Domestic Service Persian Language Broadcast, 2 May 1980, in undated FBIS translation.

67 On Honey Badger, see Prados, J., *The President's Secret Wars*, New York, William Morrow, 1986, pp. 353–5.

68 Holloway, op. cit., p. 60.

69 ibid., p. 20.

70 ibid., p. 57.

71 Vandenbroucke, op. cit., p. 127.

72 Edson and Kyle, op. cit., pp. 322–35.

73 See generally, Houghton, D. P., *US Foreign Policy and the Iran Hostage Crisis*, Cambridge, Cambridge University Press, 2001.

CHAPTER 7

1 US House of Representatives, Armed Services Committee, *Lessons Learned as a Result of US Military Operations on Grenada*, Washington, GPO, 1984, pp. 10–11.

2 Cole, R. H., *Operation Urgent Fury Grenada*, Washington, OJCS, 1997, p. 34.

3 Alfousi, C., *Improvised Crusades. Explaining the Inconsistent Use of Military Intervention by the Bush Administration*, PhD. Dissertation, Harvard, 1999, p. 172.

4 Beck, R. J., *The Grenada Invasion*, Boulder, Westview, 1993.

5 Pirnie, MAJ B. R., *Operation URGENT FURY: The United States Army in Joint Operations*, Washington, Analysis Branch, US Army Center for Military History (declassified excerpts), 1986.

6 Additional sources on the military aspects of Grenada 1983: Adkin, M., *Operation Urgent Fury*, London, Leo Cooper, 1989, pp. 138–40. Beck, op. cit. Burrowes, R. A., *Revolution and Rescue in Grenada*, Westport, Greenwood, 1988. Center for Army Lessons Learned, Bulletin 1-88, *Light Infantry In Action*, Ft. Leavenworth, April 1988. Crocker, G. A., *Grenada Remembered*, Carlisle Barracks, USAWC, 1987. Harding, S., *Air War Grenada*, Missoula, Pictorial Histories, 1984. Loendorf, COL W. M., *Intelligence Communications. Have We Put Into Practice the Lessons Learned in Grenada?*, Carlisle Barracks, USAWC, 1991. Negrete, B. C., *Grenada*, Carlisle Barracks, USAWC, 1996. Pirnie, op. cit. *Post-Deployment Report for 22 MAU*, Camp Lejeune, USMC,11 May 1984. Senkovich, S. W., *From Port Salines to Panama City*, Ft. Leavenworth, SAAMS, 1990. US House of Representatives, Committee on Foreign Affairs, *US Military Actions in Grenada*, Washington, GPO, 1984. Zeybel, H., 'Gunships at Grenada', *National Defense*, February 1984, pp. 53–6.

7 Beck, op. cit., pp. 133–8, 146–57.

8 Pirnie, op. cit., p. 72.

9 Kelly, O., *Brave Men, Dark Waters*, op. cit, pp. 206–10.

10 Quoted in Marquis, *Protecting a Precarious Value*, op. cit., p. 166.

11 Pirnie, op. cit., p. 101.

12 ibid., p. 106.

13 ibid., p. 109.

14 Adkin, op. cit., p. 224.

15 Metcalf III, VADM J., *Decision-Making and the Grenada Rescue Mission*, n.d., briefing text, p. 11.

16 Adkin, op. cit., pp. 174–5.

17 Huchthausen, *Splendid Little Wars*, op. cit., p. 83.

18 ibid.

19 ibid.

20 Adkin, op. cit., p. 174.

21 Pirnie, op. cit., p. 126.

22 ibid, p. 140.

23 Schwarzkopf, General H. N., *It Doesn't Take a Hero*, New York, Bantam, 1992, p. 254.

24 Crocker, op. cit., p. 12.

25 Alfousi, op. cit., p. 172.

26 Schwarzkopf, op. cit., p. 250.

27 Quoted in Pirnie, op. cit., p. 192.

28 Thigpen, Lt Col. Jerry L., *AFSOC: The Air Force's Newest Command*, Carlisle Barracks, USAWC, 1991, p. 41.

CHAPTER 8

1 Operation Just Cause sources include: XVIII Airborne Corps and JTF South – Corps Historians' Personal Notes (at http://www.army.mil/cmh-pg). Akers, COL F., *The Warriors*, US Army Southern Command, n.d. Baker C., T. Donnelly and M. Roth, *Operation Just Cause*, New York, Lexington, 1991. Bloechl, MAJ T. D., *Operation Just Cause: An Application of Operational Art*, Ft. Leavenworth, USACGSC SAMS, 1993. Briggs, 1LT C. E., *Operation Just Cause*, Harrisburg, Stackpole, 1990. Cole, R. H., *Operation Just Cause Panama*, Washington, OJCS, 1995. De Mena, D., *Operation Just Cause/Promote Liberty Supplement to the US Army South Annual Command History*, HQ US Army South, Fort Clayton, 1991. Eikmeier, D. C., *The Center of Gravity Debate Resolved*, Ft. Leavenworth, SAAMS, 16 December 1998. Embrey, J. H., *Operation Just Cause*, Carlisle Barracks, USAWC, 8 April 2002. Flanagan, LTG E. M., *Battle for Panama*, Washington, Brassey's, 1993. Haight, MAJ D. B., *Operation Just Cause: Foreshadowing Example of Joint Vision 2010 Concepts In Practice*, Newport, USNWC, 13 February 1998. Helena, M. L., *The Wartime Army Lessons Learned System*, Carlisle Barracks, USAWC, 1991. Hensley, CPT C. T., *Operation Just Cause*, Ft. Benning, USAIS, 1993. Hinojosa, E. A., *Panama*, Carlisle Barracks, USAWC, 28 May 1992. Jackson, LTC J. T., *Just Cause: Some Lessons Learned*, Carlisle Barracks, USAWC, 1992. Kline, CAPT J. A., *Joint Communications in Support of JTF South During Operation Just Cause*, Ft. Leavenworth, USACGSC, 1991. McConnell, M., *Just Cause*, New York, St. Martin's Press, 1991. Powell, C. with J. E. Persico, *My American Journey*, New York, Random House, 1995. Smith, LTC D. I., *Army Aviation in Operation Just Cause*, Carlisle Barracks, USAWC, 1992. Steinke, CPT W. W., *H-Hour in Panama*, Ft. Benning, USAIS, 1993. Stephenson, B. P., *Rapid Decisive Operations*, Carlisle Barracks, USAWC, 9 April 2002. Tsouras, P. and B. W. Watson, eds., *Operation Just Cause*, Boulder, Westview, 1991. Tugman, CPT J. E., *The Seizure of Rio Hato*, Ft. Benning, USAIS, 1999. US Army, *Soldiers in Panama*, Ft. Leavenworth, Center For Army Lessons Learned, 1990. US House of Representatives, Armed Services Committee, *The Invasion of Panama: How Many Innocent Bystanders Perished?*, Washington, GPO, 7 July 1992. US SOCOM, *Command Briefing on Operation Just Cause*, n.d. US SOCOM, *15th Anniversary History*, MacDill AFB, 2002. Wassermann, M. D., *Foreign Military Intervention and Democratization. The Evidence from Panama 1960–84*, PhD dissertation, Brandeis University, February 2000.

2 Nicholson, *Analysis*, op. cit., p. 107. US Army Center For Lessons Learned, *Operation Just Cause Lessons Learned*, Bulletin 90-9, v. I–III, Ft. Leavenworth, October 1990.

3 Nicholson, op. cit.

4 Quoted in *Newsweek*, 15 February 1988, p. 34.

5 Woodward, B., *The Commanders*, New York, Simon & Schuster, 1991, pp. 89–93, 160, 170–2. Wilson, G., 'US To Add 1,300 Troops in Panama', *The Washington Post*, 2 April 1988, p. A2.

6 'US Military Given Foreign Arrest Powers', *The Washington Post*, 16 December 1989, p. A1.

7 Bloechl, op. cit., p. 23.

8 Smith, LTC D. I., op. cit., p. 4.

9 US House of Representatives Committee on Foreign Affairs, *Deployment of US Forces to Panama*, Washington, GPO, 1990, p. 1.

10 Baker, Donnelly and Roth, op. cit., p. 72.

11 Briefing, Fort Bragg, 31 March 1993, quoted in Marquis, *Protecting a Precarious Value*, op. cit, p. 337.

12 US Army, *Soldiers in Panama*, op. cit., p. 7.

13 Paro and Winters, op. cit., p. 48.

14 ibid., pp. 61–2.

15 Collins, LCDR J. W., *Blue and Purple. Optimizing the Command and Control of Forward Deployed Naval Special Warfare*, Ft. Leavenworth, USACGSC, 1997, p. 72.

16 Harris, A. J., *Presidents, Generals and Green Berets*, PhD dissertation, University of Maryland College Park, 1993, p. 323.

17 Megill, MAJ T. A., *OOTW, Raids and Tactical Surprise*, Ft. Leavenworth, SAAMS, 14 December 1995, p. 13.

18 Woodward, op. cit., p. 138, Lopez, R.,'US Army Learns Panama Lesson', *Jane's Defense Weekly*, 12 May 1990, p. 886.

19 Cole, op. cit., p. 29.

20 Muse's liberation is described in detail in Livingstone, N., 'Danger in the Air', *The Washingtonian*, June 1990.

21 Newell, J., 'Pilot Honored for Tense Rescue', *Northwest Florida Daily News*, 23 December 1999, p. A1.

22 Oral History Interview JCIT 018, US Army Center of Military History, 8 January 1990.

23 US Army, *Soldiers in Panama*, op. cit., p. 7.

24 Smith, op. cit.

25 ibid.

26 De Mena, op. cit., p. 105.

27 US Army, *Soldiers in Panama*, op. cit., p. 13.

28 The battle in the men's room has assumed epic proportions in Ranger lore. This account is based on extensive first-person Ranger accounts in the LTG Edward Flanagan papers, US Army Military Historical Institute, Carlisle Barracks.

29 Statement by SSG Richard J. Hoerner in Box 10, LTG Edward Flanagan papers, US Army Military Historical Institute, Carlisle Barracks

30 Collins, op. cit., p. 73.

31 Kelly, O., *Brave Men, Dark Waters*, op. cit., pp. 223–9. Halberstadt, H., *US Navy SEALs*, Osceola, MBI, 1992, pp. 261–7. Nadel, J. and J. R. Wright, *Special Men and Special Missions*, London, Greenhill, 1994, p. 205.

32 Statement by PH2 Dye at SOCOM briefing, 31 March 1993, quoted in Marquis, *Protecting a Precarious Value*, op. cit, p. 336.

33 TF Black activities taken from: *SOCOM Command 15-Year History*, op. cit.

34 Cole, op. cit., p. 49.

35 From the unpublished study of B Company 2-504 PIR in JUST CAUSE by CPT Steve Phelps, in the LTG Edward Flanagan Papers, box 10, US Army Military History Institute, Carlisle Barracks. This is the main source of the company's operations.

36 Trainor, B. E., 'Hundreds of Tips But Still No Noriega', *New York Times*, 23 December 1989, p. A13. Harris, D., *Shooting the Moon*, New York, Little Brown, 2003, Chapter 8.

37 Gertz, B., 'NSA Eavesdropping Was Vital in Panama', *The Washington Times*, 10 January 1990, p. A6

38 535th Military Intelligence Brigade, *The JDC Concept* (declassified excerpts), n.d., (Document at GWU/NSA).

39 From the unpublished study of B Company 2-504 PIR, op. cit.

40 Baker, Donnelly and Roth, op. cit., p. 105.

41 Trainor, op. cit.

42 Paro and Winters, op. cit., pp. 41–68.

CHAPTER 9

1 Sources include: Allard, A., *Somalia Operations: Lessons Learned*, Washington, NDU Press, 1995. Atkinson, R., 'The Night of a Thousand Casualties', *The Washington Post*, 31 January 1994, p. A1. Bowden, M., *Black Hawk Down*, New York, Grove/Atlantic, 1999. Buer, MAJ E. F., *UNITAF and UNOSOM II: A Comparative Analysis of Offensive Air Support*, Quantico, USMCCGSC, 2001. Casper, COL L., *Falcon Brigade: Combat and Command in Somalia and Haiti*, Boulder, Lynne Rienner, 2001. Clarke, W. and J. Herbst (eds.), *Learning from Somalia*, Boulder, Westview, 1997. Day, Maj. C. E., *Critical Analysis on the Defeat of Task Force Ranger*, Maxwell AFB, ACSC, 1997. DeLong, K. and S. Tuckey, *Mogadishu. Heroism and Tragedy*, Westport, Praeger, 1994. Duffield, M., *Into the Beehive – the Somali Habr Gidr Clan as Adaptive Enemy*, Ft. Leavenworth, USACGSC SAMS, March 2000. Durant, CWO4 M. J., *In the Company of Heroes*, New York, G. P. Putnam's Sons, 2003. Hackworth, D., *Hazardous Duty*, New York, Avon, 1997. Hollis, CPT M. A. B., 'Platoon Under Fire', *Infantry*, Jan–Apr 1998. Lyons, T. W., *Military Intervention in Identity Group Conflicts*, Monterey, USNPGS, December 2000. Nannini, MAJ V. J., *Decisions in Operations Other Than War. The United States Intervention in Somalia*, Ft. Leavenworth, USACGSC, 1994. Osborne, LTC D., *Failed States and the Application of National Power: A Case Study of Somalia*, Carlisle Barracks, USAWC, 2002. Powell, C. with J. E. Persico, *American Journey*, op. cit. Rysewyk, CPT L. A., *Experiences*, Ft. Benning, USAIS, 1994. Scott, G., *Operations in Somalia*, Newport, USNWC, May 1999. Smith, Col. James F., *Warlords and MOOTW: US Commanders Must Apply Operational Factors and the Principles of War*, Newport, NWC, May 2000. Stevenson, J., *Losing Mogadishu*, Annapolis, Naval Institute Press, 1995. Stewart, R. W., *The United States Army in Somalia 1992–94*, Arlington, Association of the US Army, 2002. Tolmachoff, MAJ M. A., *Is Army Aviation Doctrine Adequate for Military Operations Other Than War?*, Ft. Leavenworth, USACGSC, 2 Jun 2000.

2 Siegel, A. B., *Eastern Exit*, Alexandria, Center for Naval Analysis, 1991. Briefing by CNA, *An American Entebbe*, January 1991.

3 Durch, W., ed., 'Introduction to Anarchy, Humanitarian Intervention and "State-Building" in Somalia', *UN Peacekeeping, American Policy and the Uncivil Wars of the 1990s*, New York, St. Martin's Press, 1996, p. 341. Garcia, E., 'Where Anarchy Rules', *Soldiers*, March 1993, pp. 13–20.

4 On the 1-22, see Evans, J. R., *Task Force 1-22 Infantry from Homestead to Port-au-Prince*, Ft. Leavenworth, USACGSC, 2000, p. 44.

5 Sangvic, MAJ R. N., *Battle of Mogadishu, Anatomy of a Failure*, USACGSC, SAMA, 1998, p. 10.

6 Celeski, J. D., 'A History of SF Operations in Somalia 1992–95', *Special Warfare*, June 2002, pp. 16–28.

7 Hirsh, J. L., and R. B. Oakley, *Somalia and Operation Restore Hope*, Washington, US Institute of Peace, 1995, p. 192.

8 Casper, op. cit., p. 96.

9 Drew, E., *On the Edge*, New York, Simon & Schuster, 1994, p. 322.

10 Miniter, R., *Losing Bin Laden*, Washington, Regnart, 2003, p. 52.

11 Loeb, V., 'CIA After Action Report – Somalia 1993', *The Washington Post*, 27 February 2000, p. W06.

12 Snider, MAJ L. B,, *US Army Special Operations Forces as Providers of Human Intelligence in Humanitarian Assistance Operations*, Ft. Leavenworth, USACGSC SAMS, 1995, pp. 27–33.

13 Ferry, CPT C. P., 'Mogadishu', *Infantry*, November–December 1994, p. 38.

14 Bowden, op. cit., p. 22.

15 Rysewyk, op. cit., appendix A.

16 Lancaster, J., 'Mission Incomplete, Rangers Pack Up', *The Washington Post*, 21 October 2002, pp. A1, A26.

17 Loeb, op. cit.

18 Di Tomasso, Cpt. T., *The Battle of the Black Sea*, Ft. Benning, USAIS, 1994.

19 Atkinson, R., 'Firefight in Mogadishu', *The Washington Post*, 30 January 1994, Internet edition.

20 Huchthausen, *Splendid Little Wars*, op. cit., p, 179.

21 Rysewyk, op. cit., p. 7.

22 Atkinson, R. 'The Raid That Went Wrong', *The Washington Post*, 30 January 1994, p. A27.

23 Loeb, op. cit.

24 Di Tomasso, op. cit.

25 Celeski, op. cit.

26 *The True Story of Black Hawk Down*, History Channel television programme, produced 2002 by 44 Blue Productions in Association with Wild Eyes Production, aired 13 March 2003.

27 Di Tomasso, op. cit.

28 Hackworth, op. cit., pp. 6–10.

29 Barics, SFC E., 'We Did Right That Night', *Soldiers*, February 1994, pp. 17–20.

30 Reproduced in Rysewyk, op. cit.

31 Ferry, CPT. C. P., 'Mogadishu 1993', *Infantry*, Sept–Oct 1994, p. 26.

32 Garcia, op. cit., pp. 13–20.

33 Hollis, op cit., pp. 27–34.

34 Quoted in Rysewyk, op. cit.

35 Di Tomasso, op. cit.

36 Fedarako, K. and B. Van Voorst, 'Amid Disaster, Amazing Valor', *Time*, 28 February 1994, p. 46.

37 DeLong and Tuckey, op. cit., p. 94.

38 Ferry, 'Mogadishu 1993', op. cit., p. 30.

39 *The True Story*, op. cit.

40 Feaver, P. D. and C. Gelpi, 'A Look At Casualty Aversion', *The Washington Post*, 7 November 1991, Internet edition. Dauber, C., 'Image as Argument', *Armed Forces and Society*, Winter 2001, pp. 205–29.

41 *The True Story*, op. cit.

42 Keeler, H., 'JFCOM Continues "Swarm" Study Effort', *Defense Daily*, 14 January 2003, p. 8. Plummer, A., 'OSD Explores Swarming as an Operational Concept for Future Forces', *Inside the Pentagon*, 16 January 2003, p. 3. Trimble, S., 'Project Alpha to Launch Next Step of Emerging "Swarming" Concept', *Aerospace Daily*, 15 January 2003, p. 3.

43 Rysewyk, op. cit., p. 14.

44 Loeb, op. cit.

45 Wilson, J. R., 'The Future of Special Ops', *The Year in Defense 2003*, Tampa, Faircount, 2003, pp. 58–68, 63

46 Trainor, Lt. Gen. B., USMC (rtd.) 'The Perfect War Led America's Military Astray', *Wall Street Journal*, 2 August 2000, Internet edition.

CHAPTER 10

1 SOCOM Command 15-Year History, op. cit., p. 9.

2 Schemmer, B. F., 'No Air Force Combat Rescue Aircraft in the Gulf', *Armed Forces Journal International*, July 1991, pp. 37–8.

3 Cornstubble, MAJ B. A., *The Air Assault Raid, Mission for a New Millennium*, Ft. Leavenworth, USACGSC SAMS, 1996, pp. 15, 24.

4 ibid., p. 25.

5 ibid., p. 20.

6 Bowden, M., *Killing Pablo*, New York, Atlantic Monthly Press, 2001.

7 Newman, R. J., 'Hunting War Criminals: The First Account of Secret US Missions in Bosnia', *US News and World Report*, 6 July 1998, Internet edition.

8 ibid.

9 Waller, D., 'The CIA's Secret Army', *Time*, 3 February 2003.

10 Gertz, B., *Breakdown*, Chicago, Regnery, 2002, p. 18.

11 On the proposed 1998 raid on bin Laden: Benjamin, D. and S. Simon, *The Age of Sacred Terror*, New York, Random House, 2002, pp. 294–7. Generally: US Senate Select Committee on Intelligence and US House Permanent Select Committee on Intelligence, *Joint Inquiry Into Intelligence Community Activities Before and After the Terrorist Attacks of September 11, 2001*, S. Rept. No. 107-351, H. Rept. No. 107-792 (referred to hereafter as 9/11 Report).

12 ibid., p. 377.

13 ibid., p. 91.

14 Gellman, B., 'Clinton's War on Terror', *The Washington Post*, 19 December 2001, Internet edition.

15 9/11 Report, op. cit., p. 292.

16 ibid., p. 105.

17 Miniter, *Losing Bin Laden*, op. cit., p. 169.

18 On the JRTC 89-5 raid: Cornstubble, op. cit., p. 17.

19 Morris, D., *Off With Their Heads*, New York, Harper Collins, 2003, p. 79.

20 Albright, M., *Madam Secretary*, New York, Hyperion, 2003, p. 374.

21 Patterson, Lt. Col. R., *Dereliction of Duty*, Washington, Regnery, 2003, pp. 129–31.

22 'Plan to Capture bin Laden Called Off', UPI report, 21 May 2003.

23 9/11 Report, op. cit., p. 123.

24 ibid., p. 301.

25 ibid., pp. 305–6.

26 Woodward, B., *Bush at War*, New York, Simon & Schuster, 2002, pp. 5–7 is the source for GE/Senior options and the proposed 2000 SOCOM raid. On the proposed 2000 raid, see Benjamin and Simon, op. cit., pp. 318–23.

27 Miniter, op. cit., p. 169.

28 9/11 Report, op. cit., p. 106.

29 ibid., p. 109.

30 ibid., p. 107.

31 Benjamin and Simon, op. cit., pp. 319–20.

32 Miniter, op. cit., p. 201.

33 Bowden, M., 'US Had Capability But Lack Will to Act Against Bin Laden, Critics Say', *Philadelphia Inquirer*, 16 September 2001, Internet edition.

34 Kaplan, D. E., 'Playing Offense', *US News & World Report*, 2 June 2003, Internet edition.

35 9/11 Report, op. cit., p. 107.

36 Brant, M. and E. Thomas, 'The Education of Tommy Franks', *Newsweek*, 19 May 2003, Internet edition.

37 Gertz, op. cit., p. 13.

38 Gellman, B., 'Broad Effort Launched After '98 Attacks', *The Washington Post*, 19 December 2001, Internet edition.

39 9/11 Report, op. cit., p. 91.

40 Gertz, op. cit., p. 73.

41 'US Eyed Killing Bin Laden Before September 11 Strike', *The Washington Times*, 25 June 2003, p. 4.

42 9/11 Report, op. cit., p. 305. Elliott, M., 'They Had a Plan', *Time*, 12 August 2002, p. 28.

43 9/11 Report, op. cit., p. 282.

44 ibid., p, xvii.

45 Bowden, 'US Had Capability But . . .', op. cit.

46 Thornton, R., 'Cultural Barriers to Organizational Unlearning: the US Army, the "Zero-Defects" Culture and Operations in the Post-Cold War World', *Small Wars and Insurgencies*, Vol. 11 No. 3, Winter 2000, p. 139.

47 Eccles, Lt. Col. D., 'Risk Aversion and the Zero-Defects Culture: A Checklist for the British Armed Forces', *British Army Review*, No. 122, September 1994, p. 94.

48 Reimer, GEN D., 'Maintaining a Solid Framework While Building For the Future', *Army*, October 1995, pp. 21–6.

49 9/11 Report, op. cit., p. 104.

50 'US Eyed Killing . . .', op. cit.

51 Bowden, 'US Had Capability But . . .', op. cit.

52 'Rumsfeld Stands Tall After Iraq Victory', MSNBC Report, 20 April 2003, Internet edition.

53 Lorch, D., A. Murr and P. Wingert, 'The War of the Night', *Newsweek*, 29 October 2001, p. 22.

54 Quoted in PBS *Frontline* interview, 12 June 2002.

55 Initial details in: Hersh, S., 'Annals of National Security', *The New Yorker*, 12 November 2002, Internet edition. On the general SOF situation: Singleton, M. A., *First In, Right Choice*, Carlisle Barracks, USAWC, 9 April 2002.

56 Moore, R., *The Hunt for Bin Laden*, New York, Random House, 2003, p. 29.

57 Kiper, Dr. R., 'Into the Dark: The 3-75th Ranger Regiment', *Special Warfare*, September 2002, pp. 6–7. Gettleman, J., 'Response to Terror', *The Los Angeles Times*, 8 December 2001, p. A3.

58 RADM Stufflebeam, 5 November 2001, Pentagon news briefing.

59 'Into the Fray', *Time*, 29 October 2001, p. 26.

60 Grossman, E. M., 'Camp Rhino Offers Lessons For Expeditionary Airstrips in Sandy Areas', *Inside the Pentagon*, 9 January 2003, pp. 3–4.

61 Kiper, op. cit.

62 Sawyer, T., 'High Tech Tools and Hard, Hard Work at FOB Rhino', *Engineering News Record*, 25 February 2002, p. 20.

63 Kiper, op. cit.

64 ibid.

65 ibid.

66 Shanker, T., 'Conduct of War is Redefined by Success of Special Forces', *New York Times*, 21 January 2002, Internet edition.

67 Kiper, op. cit.

68 Wilson, J. R., 'The Future of Special Ops', in *The Year in Defense 2003*, Tampa, Faircount, 2003, p. 59.

69 Scarborough, R., 'Elite US Unit Keeps Heat on Terrorists', *The Washington Times*, 12 July 2002.

70 Rashid, A,, '1,000 Man Raid to "Trap bin Laden and Sons"', *The Daily Telegraph*, 21 March 2003, Internet edition.

71 Scarborough, R., 'Fear of Casualties Hampers Hunt For Taliban', *The Washington Times*, 9 December 2002.

72 Schmitt, E. and T. Shankar, 'Pentagon Says a Covert Force Hunts Hussein', *New York Times*, 7 November 2003, Internet edition.

CHAPTER 11

1 On Pacific Wind, see generally, Atkinson, R., *Crusade*, Boston, Houghton Mifflin, 1993, p. 141. Waller, *The Commandos*, op. cit.

2 Dao, J., 'War Plan Drew US Commandos from Shadows', *The New York Times*, 28 April 2003, Internet edition.

3 Loeb, V., 'Rumsfeld Faulted for Troop Dilution', *The Washington Post*, 30 March 2003, p. A19.

4 'Rumsfeld Stands Tall . . .', op. cit.

5 Scarborough, R., 'Special Ops Steal Show', *The Washington Times*, 7 April 2003, Internet edition.

6 The details on the 507th convoy are from the official Army report, *Attack on the 507th Maintenance Company, 23 March 2003, Al Nasiryah, Iraq*. It appeared on-line as a supplement to: Cruz, L., '507th "Fought Hard"', *El Paso Times*, 9 July 2003, Internet edition.

7 Scarborough, R., 'Crash Caused Lynch's Horrific Injuries', *The Washington Times*, 9 July 2003, Internet edition.

8 Rennie, D., 'PoWs Say Capture Was Like Custer's Last Stand', *The Daily Telegraph*, 15 April 2003, Internet edition.

9 Adler, J., 'Jessica's Liberation', MSNBC Report, 6 April 2003, Internet edition.

10 Lathen, N. and K. Sheehy, 'Saved', *The New York Post*, 2 April 2003, Internet edition.

11 Shankar, T. with J. M. Broder, 'The Rescue of Private Lynch', *The New York Times*, 3 April 2003, Internet edition.

12 Starr, B., 'An Iraqi Working for the CIA Aided Lynch Rescue', CNN.com Report, 15 April 2003.

13 Hall, M., 'Iraqi Tipster Who Helped Lynch Gets US Asylum', *USA Today*, 30 April 2003, p. 4A.

14 Baker, P., 'The Iraqi Who Saved Her', *Newsday*, 5 April 2003, pp. A5–6.

15 Adler, op. cit.

16 ibid.

17 Lindlaw, S., 'Bush Did Not Order Plan to Rescue Troop', *Seattle Post-Intelligencer*, 2 April 2003, Internet edition.

18 Schmitt, E. and T. Sklar, 'Covert Units Conduct an Invisible Campaign', *The New York Times*, 6 April 2003, Internet edition.

19 Sipress, A., 'Command Details Events Leading to Rescue of Lynch', *The Washington Post*, 6 April 2003, p. A30.

20 Wall, R., 'PoW Rescue', *Aviation Week & Space Technology*, 14 April 2003, p. 29.

21 Gellman, B., 'Covert Unit Hunted for Iraqi Arms', *The Washington Post*, 13 June 2003, p. A1.

22 Ma, J., 'Information Technology Enables Reach-Back for SEALs During War', *Inside the Navy*, 2 June 2003, p. 6.

23 Couvalt, C., 'MILSTAR Pivotal to War', *Aviation Week & Space Technology*, 28 April 2003, Internet edition.

24 Castelli, C. J., 'Marines in Iraq Lacked Access to National-Level Satellite Imagery', *Inside the Navy*, 16 June 2003, pp. 1, 4–5.

25 Smucker, P., 'Decoy Raid Opened Way for Rescuers', *The Daily Telegraph*, 3 April 2003, Internet edition.

26 Wall, op. cit.

27 Kelley, J., 'Covert Troops Fight Shadow War', *USA Today*, 7 April 2003, p. 2A

28 *War Spin*, BBC 2 television programme, 18 May 2003, 1915 BST.

29 Sipress, A., 'Command Details Events Leading to Rescue of Lynch', *The Washington Post*, 6 April 2003, p. A30.

30 Adler, op. cit.

31 Barnes, F., 'The Commander', *The Weekly Standard*, 2 June 2003, Internet edition.

32 Boyer, P. J., 'The New War Machine', *The New Yorker*, 30 June 2003, p. 68.

33 Fisher, I., 'As Hussein Faded, Prisoners Were Executed', *The New York Times*, 28 April 2003.

34 Lynch, D. J., 'Marines Find Bloodstained US Uniforms', *USA Today*, 8 April 2003, Internet edition. 'Marines Find Only Uniforms in Search for Missing Soldiers', *The Wall Street Journal*, 8 April 2003, Internet edition.

35 Baker, P., 'Rescuers Nearly Called Mission Off', *The Washington Post*, 16 April 2003, p. A1.

36 Baker, P., 'Days of Darkness With Death Outside the Door', *The Washington Post*, 14 April 2003, p. A1.

37 Filkins, D. with C. LeDuff, 'Marines Discover 7 PoWs in Town North of Baghdad', *The New York Times*, 14 April 2003, Internet edition.

38 Scarborough, 'Special Ops . . .', op. cit.

39 Lindlaw, op. cit.

40 Schmitt and Sklar, op. cit.

41 Poole, O. and M. Smith, 'SAS Join US Forces Hunting For Dictator', *The Daily Telegraph*, 11 April 2003, Internet edition.

42 Scarborough, R., 'US Seizes Saddam Airport', *The Washington Times*, 4 April 2003, Internet edition.

43 3 April 2003 press briefing, HQ CENTCOM, Qatar.

44 Forbes, M., 'SAS Gives Medical Aid as Attack on Convoy Wounds Russian Ambassador', *The Age* (Melbourne), 9 April 2003, Internet edition.

45 Rising, D., 'US Detains More than 200 In Iraq Raid, *The Washington Post*, 15 May 2003,

Internet edition. 'US Troops Seize 260 Iraqis in Dawn Raid', *The Times*, 15 May 2003, Internet edition.

46 Marshall, T., 'Riot Chases Troops Out of Iraqi Town', *Los Angeles Times*, 29 May 2003, Internet edition.

47 Gordon, M. R., 'To Mollify Iraqis, US Plans to Ease Scope of Its Raids', *The New York Times*, 7 August 2003, Internet edition.

48 Ricks, T. E., 'As US Lowered Sights, Information Poured In', *The Washington Post*, 23 July 2003, p. A1.

49 Marx, G. and E. A. Torriero, 'Secret Task Force Is Spearhead in Hunt for Hussein', *The Chicago Tribune*, 5 August 2003. Internet edition.

50 Moore, M., 'US Forces Increase Raids in Iraq', *The Washington Post*, 13 July 2003, Internet edition.

51 Sanders, E., '4th Infantry Scours Region for Hussein', *The Los Angeles Times*, 6 August 2003, Internet edition.

52 Ricks, op. cit.

53 Ratnesar, R., 'Hot on Saddam's Trail', *Time*, 3 August 2003, Internet edition.

54 Price, N. and J. Tarabay, 'Troops Didn't Know Brothers Were in Villa', *The Washington Post*, 24 July 2003, Internet edition.

55 Sanger, D. E. and E. Schmitt, 'US Defends Move to Storm House', *The New York Times*, 24 July 2003, Internet edition.

56 Price and Tarabay, op. cit.

57 Scully, M., 'New Protective Plates Cut Carrying Load, Shield Against Multiple Hits', *Inside the Army*, 11 August 2003, pp. 11–12.

58 Daniszewski, J., J. Hendren and D. Zucchino, 'Speed, Force Marked Lethal Raid', *The Los Angeles Times*, 24 July 2003, Internet edition.

59 Nordland, R. and E. Thomas, 'See How they Ran', MSNBC Report, 28 July 2003.

60 Sanger and Schmitt, op. cit.

61 Rhem, Kathleen T., 'Saddam was "Disoriented and Bewildered" When Captured', *American Forces Press Service*, 14 December 2003.

62 Fassihi, Farnaz, 'Two Novice Gumshoes

Charted the Capture of Saddam Hussein', *The Wall Street Journal*, 18 December 2003, p. A6. That press accounts in the aftermath of the Saddam seizure stressed the importance of both the analytical effort and the Fat Man, suggests that this is a cover story and that the critical information may have come from other more sensitive sources that are not being disclosed to the press.

63 Smith, Michael, 'Secret Teams Were Constantly on the Trail of "Number One"', *The Daily Telegraph*, 15 December 2003, Internet edition.

64 Post, Jerrold M., 'Rathole Under the Palace', *Los Angeles Times*, 21 December 2003, Internet edition.

CHAPTER 12

1 Beckwith and Knox, *Delta Force*, op. cit., p. 294.

2 Loeb, V. and T. E. Ricks, 'Dissension in the Ranks', *The Washington Post*, 24 April 2003, Internet edition.

3 On seizure missions, among other decapitation options in general, see: Hosmer, S. T., *Operations Against Enemy Leaders*, Santa Monica, RAND, 2001.

4 Nicholson, *Analysis*, op. cit., p. 53.

5 Cancian, Col. M. F., 'The Expanding Bureaucracy of War', *Marine Corps Gazette*, July 1999, p. 47.

6 Cornstubble, *Air Assault Raid*, op. cit., p. 25.

7 Wilson, J. R., 'The Future of Special Ops', in *The Year in Defense 2003*, Tampa, Faircount, 2003, p. 61.

8 'The Special Operations Schoolhouse', *Army*, April 1992, pp. 40–2. Bucci, Maj. S., 'Fighters vs. Thinkers', *Special Warfare*, Spring 1989, pp. 33–7.

9 Scarborough, R., 'Study Urges Wider Authority for Covert Troops', *The Washington Times*, 12 December 2002.

GLOSSARY

A-1E	Douglas A-1E Skyraider piston-engine fighter-bomber.
A-7D/E	LTV A-7D/E Corsair II attack aircraft, USAF and US Navy versions respectively of the jet attack aircraft.
AAA	Anti-aircraft artillery (automatic weapons).
AB	Air base.
ABCCC	Airborne command and control centre. Usually an EC-130E, occasionally an EC-135. A USAF airborne command post with lots of radios for talking to aeroplanes and usually none for talking to ground forces.
AC-130	Lockheed Hercules Spectre gunship. A modified four-engine turboprop transport aircraft armed with night-vision sensors, communications equipment (including radios for contacting ground forces) and multiple guns that fire from the broadside while the aircraft points its wing at the target. The AC-130A model carried 40 mm, 20 mm and 7.62 mm calibre guns; the later AC-130H/U models added a 105 mm gun. Capable of precision fire power.
ACSC	Air Command and Staff College, Maxwell AFB, Alabama.
Actionable intelligence	Intelligence of sufficient credibility, accuracy and specificity to enable implementation of a particular action. Liberation and seizure operations require detailed actionable intelligence, while other missions, such as CSAR, operate at a lower threshold.
ADM	Admiral. A highly evolved form of aquatic life.
AFB/AB	Air Force base (US)/air base.
AFV	Armoured fighting vehicle.
AGL	Above ground level.
AH-1	Bell Cobra attack helicopter used since the 1960s. The AH-1F/S/T/W versions are armed with a 20 mm Gatling gun and TOW antitank guided missiles or rockets.
AH-6A/MH-6A	Nicknamed 'Little Birds' or 'Killer Eggs': modified versions of the Hughes 500 OH-6A light observation helicopter used by the US Army in support of special operations. The MH-6A version has external seats and handholds to lift four to six Delta Force troopers. The AH-6 is armed with machine-gun or rocket pods.
ALO	Air liaison officer.

Altmark	German clandestine fleet oiler. In 1940, carrying British Merchant Navy prisoners, it was sheltering in Norwegian territorial waters when boarded by the crew of the destroyer HMS *Cossack*. The liberation of the prisoners provided a considerable morale boost.
Amtrac	Amphibious tractor. Amphibious AFV capable of carrying personnel or cargo.
ANGLICO	Air and Naval Gunfire Liaison Company (USMC/USN joint).
AOR	Area of responsibility. Geographical area for which a command is responsible.
APC	Armoured personnel carrier. A lightly armoured vehicle intended to carry troops.
AT-28	North American AT-28. Armed piston-engine 1950s-vintage trainer plane used for counterinsurgency missions in Southeast Asia.
AV-8B	US Marine Corps Harrier attack aircraft. US-built version of a British design, capable of vertical take-off and landing.
AW	Automatic weapons.
AWACS	US aircraft warning and command system. Boeing E-3 radar aircraft.
AWC	Air War College, Maxwell AFB, Alabama.
B-52	US strategic jet bomber, 1950s–present. Can deliver bombs, mines or, since the 1980s, precision-guided munitions.
Bardia	Italian fortified town in Libya, site of unsuccessful British commando raid in 1941.
BCT/BLT	Battalion combat (landing) team. A reinforced infantry battalion with combined arms attachments.
BG	Brigadier General (US Army).
Brg. Gen.	Brigadier General (USAF).
Brownout	Severely reduced visibility caused by airborne dust or sand.
BTR-60PB	Soviet-built APC armed with a turret-mounted 14.5 mm HMG.
C-17	Four-engine jet transport, in service since the 1990s.
C-47	Dakota, standard twin-piston-engine transport aircraft of the Second World War and Korea. Became a gunship in Vietnam.
C-54	Military version of the Douglas DC-4. A four-piston-engine transport aircraft of the Second World War and early Cold War era.
C-119	Nicknamed the 'Flying Boxcar', a large twin-piston-engine twin-boom transport aircraft used in Korea. Became a gunship in Vietnam.
C-130	Lockheed Hercules, a four-turboprop tactical transport aircraft able to use unimproved airfields. In service since the 1950s.
C-141	Lockheed Starlifter, four-turbofan strategic transport aircraft in service since the 1960s.
CAP	Combat air patrol comprised of fighter/ground attack aircraft.
CAS	Close air support. Aircraft used in support of ground troops in contact.
CC	Combatant commander, post-2002 designation of a commander-in-chief (CINC).
CCT	Combat control team – USAF ground force used to direct air strikes or air operations. In Vietnam and earlier, ground Army and Marine forward observers could also direct USAF close air support.

CENTCOM	US Central Command. Established in the 1980s. Responsible for the Middle East (excluding Israel and Lebanon – see EUCOM), South Asia and the Horn of Africa.
Centre of gravity	In Clausewitz's writings 'the hub of all power and movement, on which everything depends'; the decisive objective in securing the defeat of an enemy. It can be the main army in the field, a capital (less often) or a leader. Attacking the centre of gravity should be the focus of all operations.
CH-46	Boeing Vertol CH-46, nicknamed 'Frog', US Marines standard twin-rotor transport helicopter in service since 1967.
CIA	Central Intelligence Agency (US) – directly subordinate to the President and not part of the Department of Defense.
CINC	Commander-in-chief, commander of a US joint service command responsible directly to the national command authority. Redesignated 'combatant commander' in 2002.
CINCCENT	Commander-in-Chief, US Central Command.
CINCSOCOM	The Commander-in-Chief of US Special Operations Command. Also CINCSOC/USCINCSOC/USCINCSOCOM.
CJCS	Chairman of the Joint Chiefs of Staff.
Clausewitz	Karl von Clausewitz (1780–1831). Prussian staff officer in the Napoleonic Wars and major philosopher of armed conflict.
Claymore	M18 command-detonated directional fragmentation mine.
COL	Colonel (US Army).
Col.	Colonel (US Air Force or USMC).
COMINT	Communications intelligence, a subset of SIGINT.
Condor	German-built wheeled APC armed with a 7.62 mm machine gun, lightly armoured.
CONUS	Continental US.
CRRC	Combat rubber raiding craft. A heavily reinforced rubber inflatable 4.5 m Zodiac boat. Used by SEALs.
CS	Non-lethal riot control chemical agent commonly known as 'tear gas'.
CSAR	Combat search and rescue, usually carried out in enemy-controlled or -contested territory.
CWO	Chief warrant officer (US Army).
DASD	Deputy Assistant Secretary of Defense.
D-Day	Used to designate the start of a military action. Days before and after D-Day are expressed in minus/plus.
DE	Destroyer escort. Re-designated frigate in the 1970s. A small multi-mission warship normally used for anti-submarine warfare.
Delta Force	Special Forces Operational Detachment (SFOD) Delta. US Army special operations force (which officially does not exist) specializing in counter-terrorist and counter-revolutionary warfare roles. Hostage-release/prisoner-taking specialists trained in covert operations and working in small teams (but Delta itself, like 22 SAS, is a combined-arms formation). Delta recruits mainly from Special Forces. Redesignated Combat Applications Group in 2002.

DIA	Defense Intelligence Agency of the US Department of Defense.
DigBat	'Dignity Battalion', Noriega's political militia in Panama. Disbanded 1989.
DZ	Drop zone for parachute landing of personnel or supplies.
EC-121	Four-piston-engine radar plane, replaced by AWACS.
EC-130/135	Modified versions of the C-130 four-turboprop tactical or the C-135 four-turbojet transport aircraft with specialized electronics. Can be used for command and control (as an ABCCC), jamming, SIGINT or broadcasting, depending on version. The EC-130 can also function as a fuel transport using flexible bladders.
E&E	Escape and evade. If a raider misses extraction, he will generally have an E&E plan to make his way back to a pick-up point or to remain concealed until rescued.
ELINT	Electronic intelligence. Monitoring threat radars. Subset of SIGINT.
EN	Engineman (US Navy).
ET	Electronics technician (US Navy).
EUCOM	US European Command (includes Lebanon, Israel and much of Africa).
F-4	Phantom, US multi-service fighter, 1960s–90s.
F-51	Mustang, single-engine fighter used in the Second World War (as P-51) and Korea.
F-105G	'Wild Weasel' fighter-bomber used to suppress air defences, 1960s–80s.
FAC	Forward air controller. A pilot able to direct air strikes and take control of aircraft attacking a specific target. May operate in a low-and-slow or fast jet aircraft or on the ground.
FARRP	Forward aircraft refuelling and rearming point, forward helicopter field.
Fast rope	Technique for sliding down a 7.62 cm-diameter rope lowered from an object (most often a hovering helicopter) to which it is made fast. Akin to sliding down a fireman's pole, wearing protective gloves and without a harness. It is faster than rappelling (which requires attachment to the rope).
FLIR	Forward-looking infra-red. A sensor that provides a picture of any heat emissions.
FMF	Fleet Marine Force, the USMC's two corps-level headquarters at Camp Pendleton, California, and Camp Lejune, North Carolina.
Force Recon	The USMC's two FMF-level reconnaissance battalions are not under SOCOM command but are generally considered SOF.
Friction	In any military activity, this refers to uncertainties, errors, accidents, technical difficulties and the unforeseen, and to their effect on decisions, morale and actions. The term originated with Clausewitz, who called it 'the only concept that more or less corresponds to the factors that distinguish real war from war on paper' and 'the force that makes the apparently easy so difficult'.
Frunze	Main Soviet Army staff college (Moscow), equivalent of Leavenworth (US) or Camberley (UK).
GEN/Gen.	General (US Army/US Air Force and Marine Corps).
GIGN	Groupe d'Intervention Gendarmerie Nationale. French Gendarmerie hostage-rescue and anti-terrorist specialist unit.

GPS	Global positioning system satellite navigation.
Grey Fox	Recent (post-2001) codename for the Intelligence Support Activity (ISA) (pre-1995), a Department of Defense HUMINT service (post-1995) and analysis activity frequently used to support SOF.
GSG-9	Grenz Schutzen Gruppe (Border Police Group). Federal German Border Police hostage-rescue and anti-terrorist specialist unit.
H-53 series	Family of large helicopters designed and built by Sikorsky, used by USAF, Navy and Marines and by friendly and allied forces. Major versions are the CH-53 (cargo and troop carriers), the HH-53 (rescue), the MH-53 (special operations and low-altitude penetration) and the RH-53 (minesweeping). There are, however, significant differences between versions. The MH-53J Pave Low is the current USAFSOC version.
HH-3	Large (but smaller than HH-53) rescue helicopter built by Sikorsky. Nickname 'Jolly Green Giant' became generic name for all USAF CSAR helicopters.
H-Hour	Used to designate the starting time of a military action.
Hill	Hills without other names are usually designated by their height in metres.
HMG	Heavy machine gun, usually .50 calibre, 12.7 mm, 13 mm or 14.5 mm.
HMMWV	'Humvee' – the M998 series high mobility multipurpose wheeled vehicles, standard US military light truck, replacing the M151 jeep. Many are armoured to withstand Kalashnikov bullets.
HUMINT	Human intelligence. Intelligence gained by human 'assets' on the ground rather than by technical means.
INS	Inertial navigation system.
IPB	Intelligence preparation of the battlespace. A USAF/Army concept incorporating the totality of intelligence, planning and preparation required pre-operation and updated and made available during a mission.
ISA	Intelligence Support Activity (Department of Defense intelligence collection). In 1995 redesignated Defense HUMINT Service. Includes activities code-named Grey Fox.
J-3/G-3/S-3	Deputy chief of staff for operations (and the staff under him/her) at a US joint/formation/unit headquarters.
JDAM	Joint direct attack munition, guided bomb.
JOC	Joint operations centre. The operational-level version of a TOC. Able to direct multi-service operations. Handles real-time operational decision-making, with longer term planning, administrative and logistics functions handled elsewhere.
JRTC	Joint Readiness Training Center, US military training facility originally located at Fort Chaffee, Arkansas, with activities now at Fort Polk, Louisiana.
JSOC	Joint special operations command, Fort Bragg, North Carolina. Established 1980. Under SOCOM since 1987.
JTF/G	Joint task force/group.
Kalashnikovs	Soviet-designed family of infantry weapons. Most widespread are rugged, effective assault rifles such as the AK-47 and AKM/AKMS in 7.62 mm × 39 mm calibre. There are also Kalashnikov light machine guns.
Khmer Rouge	Cambodian Communist forces. While Cambodia was under their rule they killed up to two million people, one-third of the total population, in a campaign of autogenocide.

KIA	Killed in action.
L-4	Piper Cub. Two-man liaison and artillery-spotting light aeroplane, Second World War and Korea.
LAW	Light antitank weapon. M72 66 mm man-portable single-shot antitank rocket launcher.
LCM	Landing craft mechanized. A large flat-bottomed landing craft capable of delivering AFVs over a beach.
LD	Line of departure. The line or position from where an attack or movement is started. Equivalent to British start line.
LT	Lieutenant. The lowest form of commissioned life.
LZ	Landing zone for helicopter operations.
M1	Standard US service rifle of the Second World War and Korea, semi-automatic, 30.06 inch (7.62 × 63 mm) calibre.
M4	Sherman tank, standard US medium tank in the Second World War and Korea.
M4	Short carbine version of the M16, used by many SOF and support personnel. Similar to earlier CAR-15.
M14	Standard US 7.62 mm service rifle, 1950s–early 1960s. Still US Navy service rifle.
M16	Standard US 5.56 mm service rifle since mid-1960s.
M48A5	Modified version of US M48 main battle tank with 105 mm gun, laser rangefinder and diesel power pack (all lacking in earlier versions).
M60	US 7.62 mm machine gun, bipod- or tripod-mounted.
M79	US 40 mm grenade launcher, resembles a shotgun.
M113	US armoured personnel carrier, normally armed with a .50-calibre HMG.
M203	US 40 mm grenade launcher that fits under the barrel of an M16 rifle.
MAJ/Maj.	Major (US Army/US Air Force and Marine Corps).
Maj. Gen.	Major general (USAF or USMC).
Makin	Japanese fortified atoll in the central Pacific, raided by US Marines in 1942, invaded and taken 1943.
MAU	Marine amphibious unit. Redesignated MEU in the 1980s.
MC-130	Combat Talon. A USAF modified version of the C-130 transport for special operations. Unarmed, but equipped with terrain-following radar and infra-red systems for low-altitude night operations. Operated by specially trained aircrew.
MEU	Marine expeditionary unit, formerly Marine amphibious unit. An integrated air–ground force including an infantry battalion plus FMF, artillery, tanks, landing craft, amphibious tractors, engineers, attack and transport helicopters and (post-Grenada) AV-8B fighter-bombers. Includes detachments from Marine Force Reconnaissance and US Navy SEALs. Carried in several fast amphibious warfare ships.
MG	Machine gun.
MG	Major general (US Army).
MH-47	Modified special operations version of the CH-47 Chinook helicopter, used by the US Army. Capable of in-flight refuelling.

MH-60	Modified special operations version of standard UH-60 Black Hawk utility helicopter. Used by both US Army and USAF (in its MH-60G Pave Hawk CSAR version).
Minigun	Electrically powered Gatling gun, in 7.62 mm or 5.56 mm calibre.
MK-19	US (large) 40 mm grenade launcher that fits on a .50-calibre HMG mount.
MSG	Master sergeant.
NAVSPECWAR	Naval special warfare.
NCA	National Command Authority. For the US armed forces, this is the President or the Secretary of Defense or their deputies or successors.
NDU	National Defense University, Washington DC.
NEO	Noncombatant evacuation operation.
Nmi	Nautical miles.
NSA	National Security Agency, US COMINT intelligence agency.
NSA/GWU	National Security Archive of George Washington University, Washington DC.
NSC	National Security Council (at the White House).
NTC	National Training Center, Fort Irwin, California. A major US Army training facility.
NTM	National technical means. US government intelligence capabilities. Includes space-based satellites (which can use optical, infra-red, SIGINT or radar sensors) and terrestrial SIGINT capabilities.
NVG	Night-vision goggles. Passive night-vision devices allowing the user to see by any available light. Often large, heavy and uncomfortable. Early versions were monocular and lacked depth perception.
OH-58	Bell 206 Kiowa, standard US Army light observation helicopter. The OH-58D Kiowa Warrior version has a digital datalink and can transmit real-time video.
OP	Observation post.
OPSEC	Operational security.
P-3B/C (EP-3)	Lockheed P-3 Orion patrol aircraft. Designed to hunt submarines and ships, but with its excellent sensors and communications it is good for other types of mission. The EP-3 is a specialized SIGINT version, usually tasked at the national level.
P-38	Twin-piston-engine single-seat twin-boom Lockheed-designed US fighter aircraft used in the Second World War.
Pararescuemen	Also known as Parajumpers (PJs), USAF SOF intended to operate from rescue helicopters to retrieve aircrew in CSAR situations.
PBR	Patrol boat river (US Navy).
PDF	Panamanian Defence Force. Disbanded in 1989 after the fall of Noriega and replaced by a new security force.
PFC	Private first class (US Army).
PH	Pharmacist (aid man, US Navy).
Platoon	For Navy SEALs, a team with a TO&E strength of two officers and fourteen enlisted personnel. For other units, a force of twenty to sixty infantrymen led by a junior officer or senior NCO.

PoW	Prisoner of war.
'Powell Doctrine'	The views, associated with former CJCS GEN Colin Powell, that US military force should be used only when the national interest is clearly at stake, when there is public support, a clearly defined mission and the political will to apply decisive, overwhelming force.
Predator	US RQ-1 UAV. Primarily used for reconnaissance, but can be armed.
PSYOPS	Psychological operations.
Racetrack pattern	Flown by an aircraft, level flight leading to a 180-degree turn.
RCT	Regimental combat team, multi-battalion combined-arms force reinforced and configured for limited independent operations.
RESCAP	Rescue combat air patrol. Aeroplanes ordered to protect personnel on the ground – usually shot-down aircrew – and the helicopters sent to rescue them.
RF-4C	A tactical reconnaissance version of the Phantom jet fighter in service from the 1960s through the 1990s. Equipped with integral cameras and (often) infra-red sensors and ELINT capabilities.
Rice bowl	In US military use, non-meritocratic logrolling intended to promote entitlement and employment. Its UK equivalent is 'Buggins' turn'. Applies especially to the division of tasks among services or commands to ensure future allocation of resources or rewards.
RoE	Rules of engagement. Orders issued to a military force on whom or what may be shot at, and when.
ROTC	Reserve Officer's Training Corps (US, university-based). Trains under-graduates for reserve commissions.
RPG-7	Soviet-designed antitank weapon that fires an unguided rocket-propelled grenade. Widely proliferated.
RV	Rendezvous, especially after leaving the objective, where raiders will link up and count heads. 'Old SOF never die, they just RV in hell.'
SA	Small arms.
SAAS	School of Advanced Airpower Studies (USAF), Maxwell AFB, Alabama.
SAS	Special Air Service. British, Australian and New Zealand (and formerly Rhodesian) army special operations forces. Currently equivalent to US Delta Force and Special Forces. The Australian SAS also includes SEAL equivalents, which are handled in the UK by the Royal Marine Special Boat Squadron (SBS). The SAS is also capable of Ranger/Marine-type direct-attack missions.
SAMS	School of Advanced Military Studies (US Army), Fort Leavenworth, Kansas.
SATCOM	Satellite communications.
SEAL	Sea, Air, Land. US Navy special operations forces. Formed in 1962 for Vietnam from existing SOF units, including underwater demolition teams (UDTs). Post-Vietnam, tasked with supporting naval operations. Now integrated with SOCOM.
SEAL Team 6	US Navy hostage-rescue/prisoner-taking specialists, equivalent to Delta Force. Redesignated NAVSPECWAR Development Group in 2002.
SF	Special Forces. 'Green Berets', US Army Special Forces. Organized in multi-battalion groups, operating in small teams.

SFC	Sergeant first class (US Army).
SG-1	7.62 mm sniper rifle, a version of the German G3.
SGT	Sergeant (US Army).
SIGINT	Signals intelligence, gained from ELINT (radar) or COMINT (radio or telephone emissions).
SNCOA	Senior Non-Commissioned Officer Academy, USAF, Gunter AFB, Alabama.
SOAR	Special Operations Aviation Regiment (US Army). The 160th SOAR, 'The Night Stalkers', was previously known as TF 160. Consists of two battalions at Fort Campbell, Tennessee, one at Hunter Army Air Field, Georgia, and an associated battalion (1-245 Aviation) of the Oklahoma Army National Guard headquartered at Lexington, Oklahoma. Uses many types of helicopter including AH/MH-6, MH-60, MH-47 and Soviet-designed Mi-17 for low-profile operations.
SOC	Special operations capable. A designation given to USMC MEUs that have been trained in a number of special missions, including TRAP operations.
SOCCORD/ SOCCE	Special Operations Co-ordination Element. US SOF attached to a force (US or foreign) to co-ordinate US SOF actions with it.
SOCOM	US Special Operations Command; headquarters at MacDill AFB, Florida. Also USSOCOM.
SOF	Special operations forces, generic term.
SO/LIC	Special operations/low-intensity conflict.
SOP	Standard operating procedures.
SP	Self-propelled.
Squadron	The basic tactical unit of Delta Force (and the SAS). Delta Force squadrons have a baseline organization of four sixteen-man troops (each comprised of four four-man teams) plus support, headquarters personnel and communications personnel. Using cavalry terminology, it is equivalent to a company.
SR-71	Lockheed SR-71, nicknamed 'Blackbird', a very fast and high-flying USAF reconnaissance jet aircraft. Retired in the 1990s.
SSG	Staff sergeant (US Army).
SU-76	Second World War Soviet-designed self-propelled 76 mm gun on a light tank chassis, used for direct fire.
TACAN	Tactical navigation. A radio beacon for aircraft to home in on.
Team	Task-organized military force. Can be as large as a company or battalion or as small as the four-man teams that are the basic elements of Delta Force and the SAS.
TENCAP	Tactical exploitation of national capabilities. Equipment, training and procedures that ensure that troops can have access to 'national' intelligence, such as that obtained from reconnaissance satellites.
TF	Task force. Mission-organized force.
TG	Task group. US mission-organized force, smaller than a full task force (may be part of one).
TOC	Tactical operations centre. A US forward headquarters with the full range of communications links necessary for the unit to accomplish its mission.

TO&E	Table of organization and equipment. Equivalent to the UK 'war establishment' – the numbers and types of personnel, weapons and equipment held by a unit and how they are organized.
TOW	US tube-launched optical-tracked wire-guided antitank missile.
TRADOC	Training and Doctrine Command (US Army), Fort Monroe, Virginia.
TRAP	Tactical recovery of aircraft and personnel (USMC mission).
Troop	Platoon-equivalent in Delta Force, derived from SAS/cavalry terminology. Includes four four-man teams.
TSOC	Theatre special operations command. Permanent special operations staff, established to support each major US geographic CINC/Combatant Commander: Europe, Central, Pacific, South, Northern (since 2002) and US Forces Korea. Since 2002, TSOCs are 'dual hatted', supporting both their CINCs and SOCOM operations.
TU	Task unit. US mission-organized force, smaller than a task group.
Twin Otter	Canadian-built light twin-turboprop utility transport aircraft.
UAV	Unmanned air vehicle.
UII-1	US Army 'Huey' helicopter, 1960s to present.
UH-60	US Army Black Hawk helicopter, 1980s to present.
USAAF	US Army Air Forces (1941–7).
USACGSC	US Army Command and General Staff College, Fort Leavenworth, Kansas.
USAF	US Air Force (1947 to present).
USAIS	US Army Infantry School, Fort Benning, Georgia.
USAWC	US Army War College, Carlisle Barracks, Pennsylvania.
USMC	United States Marine Corps. The Marine Corps has forces that are usually considered SOF. These include MEU(SOC)s and Force Recon. However, pre-2002, only limited USMC assets were under SOCOM control.
USMCCGSC	USMC Command and General Staff College, Quantico, Virginia.
USNPGS	US Navy Post-Graduate School, Monterey, California.
'Vietnam Syndrome'	A reluctance by the US to use armed force except in overwhelming strength, with clear domestic political support, eschewing counter-revolutionary or nation-building operations, which has been characterized as guiding US policy after the end of its commitment to the Vietnam War c. 1972.
WIA	Wounded in action.
WMD	Weapons of mass destruction: nuclear, radiological, biological or chemical weapons or their components/precursors.
Zinni	Anthony Zinni. General, USMC. Clinton-appointed CINCCENT in the mid-1990s. Director of Operations for UNITAF (Unified Task Force, in Somalia), November 1992–May 1993. Assistant to the US Special Envoy for Somalia (Ambassador Robert B. Oakley) in October 1993.
ZPU-4	Soviet-designed quad 14.5 mm HMG mount, also produced in North Korea and China.

INDEX